T0305674

CONFLICT MANAGEMENT AND INTERCULTURAL COMMUNICATION

Conflict management and harmony building are two key issues of intercultural communication research and merit particular attention in the globally interconnected world. In the expanded second edition, the book explores the effective ways to manage intercultural conflict and develop intercultural harmony, and takes an interdisciplinary approach to address the two issues.

The book begins with the theoretical perspectives on conflict management and harmony building. It examines intercultural communication ethics, diversity and inclusion, conflict resolution, conflict face negotiation, and intercultural competence. It presents both Western and non-Western perspectives. The book then addresses in its second section conflict management and harmony building in specific contexts. These include communication in intergenerational relationships, multinational corporations, and virtual spaces, and covers a range of national cultures including the USA, Japan, Germany, and China.

Drawing on the current research findings, this book covers the major theoretical perspectives and provides for a wide range of discussions on intercultural conflict management. It is a crucial reference for teachers, students, researchers, and practitioners alike.

Xiaodong Dai is Associate Professor of Foreign Languages College of Shanghai Normal University, P. R. China. He currently serves as the Vice President of the China Association for Intercultural Communication (CAFIC).

Guo-Ming Chen is Emeritus Professor of Communication Studies at the University of Rhode Island, USA. He is the founding president of the Association for Chinese Communication Studies. He served as the Executive Director (2008–2014) and President of the International Association for Intercultural Communication Studies (2015–2017). Chen has published numerous books, articles, and book chapters.

'There is hardly a more timely and important subject to study than conflict, its cultural conceptions and enactment. Given the complexity of the world's stages today, there is hardly a more challenging arena in which to study conflict than through an intercultural and international lens. Here in Dai's and Chen's new edition, we have a wide range of studies that address these concerns. The international network of scholars spans a range of fields and nations and thus adds diversity in region to this type of study as well as a wide range in scholarly approaches. Readers will enjoy a breadth in views, finding conflict to be conceived, addressed, and managed in particular and multiple ways. Reading these works with an eye toward further inquiry and practice will no doubt serve as an aid to further knowledge and social betterment.'

Donal Carbaugh, *Professor Emeritus, University of Massachusetts Amherst, USA*

'This edited volume on intercultural conflict could not appear at a better time! Incorporating multidisciplinary approaches, perspectives, and contexts, the renowned contributors suggest ways to explain and diffuse enduring conflicts, predict or prevent others from erupting, and how to address or handle tensions so that constructive interconnectivity can be realized. The book brilliantly includes both established and updated thinking, Eastern and Western approaches, theoretical and applied perspectives on complex conflict landscapes, and highlights future research directions on intercultural negotiation, mediation, and harmony. As the world grapples with complex tensions within or between persons, communities, groups, or nations, this work provides scholarly hope that conflict can be meaningfully understood in more cultural contexts and managed or resolved through initiatives based on intercultural insights.'

Steve J. Kulich, *Professor, Past-President of the International Academy of Intercultural Research (IAIR) (2019–2021), Founder of the SISU Intercultural Institute (2006–) and the Journal of Intercultural Communication & Interactions Research (JICIR) (2021–, Peter Lang)*

'*Conflict Management and Intercultural Communication* treats intercultural conflict from an impressive array of theoretical and philosophical perspectives. The book also creatively explores harmony-building in vital and fascinating contexts, including virtual environments. This book is a must-have resource for anyone interested in conflict resolution across cultural landscapes.'

Alberto González, *Professor, College of Arts and Sciences, Bowling Green State University, USA*

CONFLICT MANAGEMENT AND INTERCULTURAL COMMUNICATION

The Art of Intercultural Harmony

Second edition

Edited by Xiaodong Dai and Guo-Ming Chen

Routledge
Taylor & Francis Group

LONDON AND NEW YORK

Second edition published 2023
by Routledge
4 Park Square, Milton Park, Abingdon, Oxon OX14 4RN

and by Routledge
605 Third Avenue, New York, NY 10158

Routledge is an imprint of the Taylor & Francis Group, an informa business

© 2023 selection and editorial matter, Xiaodong Dai and Guo-Ming Chen; individual chapters, the contributors

British Library Cataloguing-in-Publication Data
A catalogue record for this book is available from the British Library

Library of Congress Cataloging-in-Publication Data
Names: Dai, Xiaodong, editor. | Chen, Guo-Ming, editor.
Title: Conflict management and intercultural communication : the art of intercultural harmony / edited by Xiaodong Dai, Guo-Ming Chen.
Description: 2nd edition. | Abingdon, Oxon ; New York, NY : Routledge, 2023. | Includes bibliographical references and index.
Identifiers: LCCN 2022022285 (print) | LCCN 2022022286 (ebook) | ISBN 9781032181233 (hbk) | ISBN 9781032181219 (pbk) | ISBN 9781003252955 (ebk)
Subjects: LCSH: Conflict management. | Intercultural communication. | Multiculturalism--Social aspects.
Classification: LCC HD42 .C664 2023 (print) | LCC HD42 (ebook) | DDC 303.6/9--dc23
LC record available at https://lccn.loc.gov/2022022285
LC ebook record available at https://lccn.loc.gov/2022022286

ISBN: 978-1-032-18123-3 (hbk)
ISBN: 978-1-032-18121-9 (pbk)
ISBN: 978-1-003-25295-5 (ebk)

DOI: 10.4324/9781003252955

Typeset in Bembo
by Taylor & Francis Books

CONTENTS

ILLUSTRATIONS

Figures

Tables

CONTRIBUTORS

Benjamin J. Broome is Professor in the Hugh Downs School of Human Communication at Arizona State University. He has published numerous articles, book chapters, and encyclopedia entries.

Patrice M. Buzzanell is Distinguished University Professor in the Department of Communication at the University of South Florida and Endowed Visiting Professor for the School of Media and Design at Shanghai Jiaotong University. Fellow and past President of the International Communication Association (ICA), she is a National Communication Association (NCA) Distinguished Scholar and an NCA Carroll C. Arnold Distinguished Lecturer. She has received numerous awards for her research, teaching/mentoring, and engagement.

Guo-Ming Chen is Emeritus Professor of Communication Studies at the University of Rhode Island, U.S.A. He is the founding president of the Association for Chinese Communication Studies. He served as the Executive Director and President of the International Association for Intercultural Communication Studies. Chen has published numerous books, articles, and book chapters.

Ling Chen is a Professor Emeritus in the School of Communication, Hong Kong Baptist University. She was Editor-in-Chief of *Management Communication Quarterly* and Associate Editor of *Communication Theory*.

Xiaodong Dai is Associate Professor of Foreign Languages College of Shanghai Normal University, P. R. China. He currently serves as the Vice President of China Association for Intercultural Communication (CAFIC).

Yiheng Deng is Professor at Shanghai International Studies University, Shanghai, P. R. China. Focusing on conflict management, intercultural communication, and business communication, she has received two grants from the National Social Science Foundation of China.

Juana Du is Associate Professor and Program Head of the MA in Intercultural and International Communication on-campus program in the School of Communication and Culture at Royal Roads University, Canada. She has published numerous book chapters and peer-reviewed journal articles.

Peter Franklin is Professor at Konstanz University of Applied Sciences, Germany. He focuses on intercultural communication, competence, and management in his teaching, writing, and research. With Helen Spencer-Oatey he co-authored *Intercultural Interaction* (Palgrave Macmillan, 2009) and with Christoph Barmeyer he co-edited *Intercultural Management* (Bloomsbury, 2016). With Helen Spencer-Oatey and Domna Lazidou he co-authored *Global Fitness for Global People* (Castledown, 2022).

Yihong Gao is Professor and Director of the Research Institute of Linguistics and Applied Linguistics, School of Foreign Languages, Peking University, P. R. China. She is also the Vice President of China English Language Education Association, and served as the President of the Association of Chinese Sociolinguistics.

Beth Bonniwell Haslett is Professor Emeritus in the Department of Communication at the University of Delaware. Dr. Haslett has published four books, more than thirty articles and book chapters, and presented over sixty papers at regional, national, and international conferences.

Michael B. Hinner is Professor at the Technische Universität Bergakademie Freiberg, Germany. He is the editor of the book series Freiberger Beiträge zur Interkulturellen und Wirtschaftskommunikation (Freiberg Contributions to Intercultural and Business Communication).

Marcella Hoedl, M.A., is a management sinologist with study, work, and research experience in Japan, China, and Singapore. After working in Singapore for an international trading company, she started on an academic career-path working and teaching at the University of Passau, Germany, and later at her *alma mater* (Konstanz University of Applied Sciences), where she was responsible for cooperation with Asian universities. Marcella Hoedl also works as a freelance intercultural trainer.

Yuxin Jia is Professor of Sociolinguistics, Applied Linguistics, and Intercultural Communication at Harbin Institute of Technology, Harbin, China. He is the past President of the International Association of Intercultural Communication Studies (IAICS) and the China Association for Intercultural Communication (CAFIC).

Xue Lai Jia is Associate Professor of Intercultural Communication at the Foreign Language School of Harbin Institute of Technology (HIT), P. R. China. She has published several papers and co-authored intercultural textbooks.

Yoshiko Kameo has received her Master of Arts degree in the Department of Communicology at the University of Hawai'i at Manoa. Her research interests include the role of self-talk in intercultural conflict management.

Min-Sun Kim is a Professor at the University of Hawai'i at Mānoa. She has specialized in the area of intercultural communication and human-machine communication. She wrote *Non-Western Perspectives on Human Communication* (Sage, 2002) and co-authored, *Changing Korea: Implications for Culture and Communication* (Peter Lang, 2008) and *Hanryu: Its Influence in Asia and Beyond* (Seoul National University Press, 2011). She served as Editor of *Korean Studies*, a journal published by the Center for Korean Studies at University of Hawaii in Manoa, Chair of the Intercultural Communication Division of the International Communication Association, and President of the Korean American Communication Association.

Pamela Tremain Koch is Affiliate Professor at Seidman College of Business, Grand Valley State University, U.S.A. Her research field is cross-cultural leadership and conflict management.

Akira Miyahara is Professor of Communication Studies at Seinan Gakuin University. He has taught both in Japan and the U.S.A., and has served as President of Japan Communication Association, Japan-U.S. Communication Association (NCA affiliate) and as Vice President of Japan Health Communication Association. Miyahara has also served as Member-at-Large for East Asia for the International Communication Association. His academic interest has been in building an emic theory of "Japanese interpersonal communication as Japanese see it." He has authored communication textbooks in Japanese.

Alois Moosmueller is Professor of Intercultural Communication and Cultural Anthropology at the Ludwig-Maximilians-University Munich and an intercultural trainer and consultant. He has done extensive research on the German-Japanese and the American-Japanese Collaboration in multinational companies.

Kathryn Sorrells is a Professor in the Department of Communication Studies at California State University, Northridge (CSUN). She is author of *Intercultural Communication: Globalization and Social Justice* (3rd ed.) (Sage, 2022), and co-editor of *Globalizing Intercultural Communication: A Reader* (Sage, 2015). She has published a variety of articles and book chapters related to intercultural communication, globalization, intercultural training, and social justice. Kathryn is also the recipient of numerous national, state, and local community service awards for founding and directing the Communicating Common Ground Project.

Helen Spencer-Oatey is Emeritus Professor of Intercultural Communication at the University of Warwick, UK, and Managing Director of GlobalPeople Consulting Ltd. (GPC). Her main research interests are in intercultural interaction and intercultural relations, including in international education contexts. She has published extensively in these areas, including most recently *Intercultural Politeness* (with Kádár, Cambridge University Press, 2021) and *Global Fitness for Global People* (with Franklin and Lazidou, Castledown, 2022).

Yuko Takeshita is Professor of English and Intercultural Communication in the Department of International Communication, Toyo Eiwa University, Japan. She serves as Director of the Global Human Innovation Association. As a founding member of Asian Englishes, and former President of the Japanese Association for Asian Englishes, she has a special interest in intercultural communication between Thai and Japanese people with English as an intermediary language.

Stella Ting-Toomey is Professor of Human Communication Studies at California State University (CSU) at Fullerton. She is the 2008 recipient of the 23-campus wide CSU Wang Family Excellence Award, and the 2007–08 recipient of the CSU-Fullerton Outstanding Professor Award in recognition of superlative teaching, research, and service.

Weston T. Wiebe is an Assistant Professor, Vice President, and Chief Operating Officer at the College of the Ozarks in the U.S.A. His research interests include communication and aging, conflict management, and intergroup and intercultural relations.

Ping Yang is Associate Professor in the Department of Communication and Theatre at Millersville University, Pennsylvania. Her publications and research interests are centered around the intersection of culture, communication, and new media.

Yan Bing Zhang is a Professor in the Department of Communication Studies at the University of Kansas in the U.S.A. She studies communication, conflict management, and intergroup and intercultural relations with a particular focus on age and cultural groups. She also studies the influence of intergroup and intercultural contact on interpersonal relationships and on the reduction of intergroup prejudice and biases.

Xuan Zheng is Assistant Professor at the Institute of Linguistics and Applied Linguistics, School of Foreign Languages, Peking University, P. R. China. Her research interests include the emotional, social, and intercultural aspects of language education.

PREFACE

As one of the oldest concepts regarding human behavior, conflict management has been studied by scholars in different academic disciplines for many decades. The concept has remained significant in the contexts of both human interaction and scholarly research as human society has progressed into the 21st century. The new century, characterized by globalization accelerated by the rapid development of new technology, strongly demands a global connectivity in which intensive competition and cooperation between people from differing cultures manifests the urgent need to situate the study of conflict management in a global context.

In response to this call for the study of conflict management in a global context, the fourth biannual International Conference of Intercultural Communication, sponsored by Shanghai Normal University on December 28–29, 2014, focused on the theme of "Conflict Management and Intercultural Harmony." After the conference, 17 papers from a pool of more than 150 presentations were selected to be included in the first edition of the book. In editing this updated volume, we expand the range of discussion by inviting nine more leading intercultural scholars to join the project. The two-section structure of the first edition is kept but more issues are addressed. The authors are from different cultures and academic disciplines, and the papers deal with different aspects of conflict management from various research perspectives and in diverse cultural contexts. The diversity and richness of these papers corresponds to the need for the study of conflict management in a global society.

The publication of this scholarly manuscript would not have succeeded without support from various sources. First, we would like to express our gratitude for the authors' willingness to contribute their papers to this meaningful collection. We also greatly appreciate the College of Foreign Languages of Shanghai Normal University and the Harrington School of Communication and Media at the

University of Rhode Island for their support in the process of completing this project. Finally, our appreciation also extends to the editorial staff of Routledge, particularly Ms. Yongling Lam, for their assistance in the completion of this project.

Xiaodong Dai
Guo-Ming Chen

INTRODUCTION

Xiaodong Dai and Guo-Ming Chen

With the strengthening of global interconnectivity and interdependence, conflicts frequently arise due to tensions stemming from different cultural perceptions, disparate social preferences, or diverse value orientations. This problem has become particularly salient in recent years when people in different nations and cultures need to coordinate to combat Covid-19 but at the same time endeavor to maintain their preferred ways of life. While effective management of a conflict opens up opportunities for people to learn more about others and make a joint effort to explore better patterns of communication, mismanagement often leads to escalated hostility and damaged relationships (Ting-Toomey & Oetzel, 2001). How to manage conflicts constructively and achieve harmonious interaction is one of the main issues faced by intercultural communication scholars.

In this expanded second edition, 27 leading international scholars from diverse disciplines joined the project to explore effective ways of managing intercultural conflict and developing intercultural harmony. The volume consists of two sections. The first section includes 12 chapters which deal with the theoretical perspectives on conflict management and harmony building. It examines intercultural communication ethics, conflict resolution, conflict face negotiation, and intercultural competence. Both Western and non-Western perspectives are presented. The second section includes nine chapters which address conflict management and harmony building in cultural contexts, international business, and virtual space.

Perspectives on Intercultural Conflict Management

An intercultural conflict occurs when people have incompatible expectations, values, norms, interests, or goals in interactions (Wilmot & Hocker, 2007). A conflict may appear at the interpersonal or intergroup level and involve political, economic, or cultural factors. The complexity of the problem demands intercultural

DOI: 10.4324/9781003252955-1

communication scholars address it from different perspectives. Only through the synthesis of different perspectives can a more complete picture of intercultural conflict be presented.

In recent decades scholars have indeed approached intercultural conflict from diverse perspectives and developed useful theories and models. For example, Ting-Toomey (1988, 2005, 2017) examined conflict from the face negotiation perspective and has claimed that people in all cultures try to negotiate face in order to maintain a positive self-image in intercultural interaction. While high power distance and collectivistic cultural members tend to show more concern with other-face and mutual-face, low power distance and individualistic cultural members tend to show more concern with self-face. In managing a conflict, collectivists usually adopt avoidance, third party mediation, and integration strategies, whereas individualists tend to employ direct confrontation and domination strategies. Drawing on the social identity theory, Worchel (2005) developed a model of peaceful coexistence. He argued that it is not the group identity in itself but the perceived threat to group identity that is the root of intercultural conflicts. The recognition of others' right to exist, curiosity and interests in their cultures, and a willingness to engage in a cooperative interaction with them are the key to peaceful coexistence. Moreover, Moran, Abramson, and Moran (2014) have argued that effective intercultural conflict management is based on five steps: (1) describing the conflict in a way that is understood in both cultures; (2) examining the problem from both cultural lenses; (3) identifying the causes from both cultural perspectives; (4) solving the conflict through synergistic strategies; and (5) determining whether the solution works interculturally.

When analyzing an interpersonal or intergroup conflict, most scholars emphasized the influence of cultural values on conflict behavior and the cross-cultural comparison of conflict styles. Some scholars have examined how cultural diversity is managed in organizations, but they have tended to focus on a single level of intercultural conflict (e.g., Oetzel, Dhar, & Kirschbaum, 2007). Meanwhile, others have tackled the issue from the perspective of a specific culture. For example, Chen (2001, 2009, 2014) has developed a theory of harmony to deal with conflict from the Chinese cultural perspective. For future research, we suggest that intercultural scholars further explore the concept of intercultural conflict with an approach that considers the interactive process of conflict management and the ethics of conflict negotiation, and adopts a multilevel perspective.

Comparing different conflict styles allows people to understand the preferred way of handling an intercultural conflict, but it is only the first step toward solving the problem. In order to effectively manage an intercultural conflict, it is necessary to address the interactive process regarding how differences are reconciled or integrated, how intercultural agreements are reached, and how commonalities and consensuses are constructed. As intercultural conflict management involves individual, group, and cultural factors, focusing on one factor alone will not satisfactorily resolve the problem. Although taking the multilevel perspective is challenging for scholars, it can provide a more comprehensive understanding of the issue and help them reach an effective way of dealing with intercultural conflict (Oetzel et al., 2007).

In many cases, intercultural conflicts are difficult to resolve and take more time and energy to negotiate a solution. Even if the solution has been reached, other conflicts may emerge if one party feels that it is being treated unfairly (Worchel, 2005). Conflict negotiation ethics is therefore an integral part of the intercultural conflict management process. The ethics of intercultural conflict negotiation provides people from different cultures with mutually shared moral norms and principles that can be used to guide their mutual interaction. Moral principles such as human dignity, equality, justice, nonviolence, sincerity, tolerance, and responsibility are conducive to conflict resolution and achieve lasting outcomes (Chen, 2015; Christians, 2014; Ojelabi, 2010).

Conflict Management in Cultural Contexts

Cultural value defines what is right, equal, fair, and safe, and what is wrong, unequal, unjust, unfair, and dangerous (Marsella, 2005). It shapes the way we perceive the world and the way we respond to social reality (Chen, Ryan, & Chen, 2000). Culture is a key determinant in conflict management. Examining how a conflict is managed in diverse cultural contexts allows us to learn about a counterpart's communication behavior, so that intercultural harmony can be constructed in interaction.

Over the years, scholars have widely investigated conflict behavior in various cultural contexts. For example, Kozan and Ergin (1998) examined the differences in preference for third party help in conflict management between Americans and Turks. They found that the Turkish people are more collectivistic and prefer third party mediation in conflict management; they also found that this tendency is particularly strong in females. Siira, Rogan, and Hall (2004) compared conflict management between Americans and Finns. The authors found that Americans and Finns have a similar preference for the use of non-confrontation strategies, but Finns use more solution-oriented strategies and Americans use more controlling behaviors. Chen (2010) discussed conflict management strategy in Chinese state-owned enterprises. He pointed out that the Chinese emphasize harmony in social communication by applying accommodation, collaboration, and avoidance strategies in conflict resolution, and the elderly tend to use these strategies more frequently than the young.

A number of empirical studies in this area also focused on conflict styles and strategies by employing Hofstede's culture value orientations as their analytical framework. However, most of these studies conducted intercultural comparisons using the dimensions of individualism and collectivism and power distance rather than examining how conflicts are negotiated and resolved. For future research, we suggest that more attention be paid to: intracultural diversity; situational factors; comparative studies between non-Western cultures; and negotiation processes.

First, Hofstede's theory presents a useful framework for identifying cultural differences and the root of intercultural conflicts, but it does not consider intracultural variations. Within a nation in which co-cultural groups exist, it is necessary to take the issues of diversity into account in order to manage conflict successfully. For example, when communicating with a subordinate, Mexican Americans place less emphasis on other-face and more likely use the aggressive strategy than European Americans. However, when communicating with a superior, Mexican Americans place more emphasis on other-face and are more likely to use obliging and integrating strategies (Tata, 2000). In China, people generally are restrained when it comes to solving interpersonal conflicts, but Northerners are more emotional and aggressive than Southerners (Yu, 2013).

Second, situational factors such as ingroup/outgroup membership and conflict salience also influence intercultural conflict management (Ting-Toomey & Oetzel, 2003). For instance, Japanese are direct in expressing personal opinions when interacting with ingroups, but they are highly indirect when interacting with outgroups. Moreover, the Chinese tend to be polite when face is being maintained in a conflict situation but may become fiercely confrontational when it is lost (Chen, 2010).

Third, world cultures are interrelated, especially in this globalized society. Merely comparing Western and non-Western cultures reflects the bias of Eurocentrism (Miike, 2010). To explore the differences between non-Western cultures and between Western cultures respectively is to allow people to reach a better understanding of conflict management. For example, while Japanese and Brazilians are both collectivists, Brazilians use emotional expressions to maintain relationships and Japanese negatively view overt emotional expressions as standing in the way of relational harmony (Graham, 1985). Kozan (1989) also found that, when managing a conflict with subordinates, Turkish managers use the collaborating style more than the forcing style and that Jordanian managers use the collaborating style more than the compromising style.

Finally, conflict management is a dynamic process. The examination of intra/intercultural conflict negotiation can help one see how diverse strategies are enacted and what factors shape the process of conflict management. A variety of factors, such as relationships, power, identity, economic interest, and social justice, affect conflict negotiation and therefore need to be included in the study of intercultural conflict management. For instance, the Chinese tend to invite a high status person or a person known to both parties to be the mediator for the conflict (Han & Cai, 2015). In Chinese society, a powerful mediator can facilitate constructive interaction and help the parties in question reach an agreement. In addition, scholars need to investigate how various factors interact with one another. Analyzing the complex interplay of multiple factors is the key to grasping the true nature of a conflict and developing effective ways to resolve it. Ting-Toomey and Oetzel (2001) have identified four factors that determine the result of intercultural conflict negotiation: primary orientation, situational and relationship boundary, conflict process, and conflict competence. These interrelated factors work together to bring about productive and satisfactory outcomes, which attests to the fact that intercultural conflict management is a dynamic process.

Overview of the Book

This volume has two sections. The first section deals with the multiple perspectives on conflict management and harmony building, and the second section explores conflict management in diverse cultural and communication contexts. The first section begins with two chapters that address the ethics of conflict management and harmony building. The following ten chapters explore conflict management and harmony building from culture-general and culture-specific approaches.

In the first chapter, Benjamin J. Broome explores a viable way to bring harmony to our conflictual world. According to Broome, conflict is part of the harmonizing process, and dialogue provides an important means to manage it. By bringing individuals with different perspectives together in a safe place, different views are articulated and opportunities for mutual learning are created. Thus, the inherent tension between self and other can be productively managed. When the issues are fully examined and when all voices are heard, it becomes possible to synthesize differences and work toward the state of intercultural harmony.

In the second chapter, Yuxin Jia and Xue Lai Jia present a dialogic approach to intercultural conflict by exploring how communication ethics works in the process of conflict management. The authors argue that building up a sound dialogic ethics is central to reaching conflict resolution and intercultural harmony. While modern ethics emphasizes the self, postmodern ethics emphasizes the other. The modern perspective may lead to the dichotomy of self and other. The postmodern perspective may suffer from the problem of "all for the other," which may result in a dependent relationship between self and other. The dialogic approach is a better alternative than both the modern and postmodern approaches. It incorporates the concern for self and the concern for the other. This dialogic approach is best exemplified by Confucian *ren*, which offers a viable way to manage conflicts in a multicultural world.

In the third chapter, Patrice M. Buzzanell discusses conflict management from the organizational communication perspective. She focuses on the conflict between managerialist perspectives and diversity, equity, and inclusion (DEI) in an organizational context and conceptualizes such technical–social conflict as a wicked and complex problem that defies a rational approach. Buzzanell argues that it requires design thinking and a constitutive approach to effectively manage the conflicts that arise between traditional organizing and diversity and inclusion for equity and accountability.

In the fourth chapter, Xiaodong Dai addresses intercultural conflict management from the perspective of interculturality. According to Dai, in order to effectively manage an intercultural conflict people need to examine the interactive process of interculturality development, which is the process through which a possible means of harnessing the intercultural tension can be obtained. Interculturality not only cultivates a positive attitude toward cultural diversity, but also fosters an intercultural perspective that facilitates joint actions in intercultural conflict management.

In the fifth chapter, Beth Bonniwell Haslett proposes a new approach to conflict management. Because most scholars focus on the use of different conflict styles, how the development of common ground serves to manage intercultural conflict deserves further investigation. Haslett posits that honoring face is an important element in the process of intercultural conflict management. Those commonly shared values such as respect, trust, empathy, pluralism, openness, and equality are essential components of the universal face, which can be employed to broaden the way that conflict management is examined in future research.

In the sixth chapter, Stella Ting-Toomey reviews the evolutionary process of her conflict face-negotiation theory (FNT). FNT is based on the studies of face from Hsien Chin Hu (1944), Erving Goffman (1955), and Penelope Brown and Stephen Levinson (1987). The theory stipulates cultural, individual, and situational factors that shape conflict style in interaction. The first version of FNT emphasizes the functional link of Hall's high-context and low-context cultural schema to conflict styles. The second version focuses on how individualism and collectivism affect conflict styles. The third version further deals with individual-level factors regarding the face concern and conflict styles, and also addresses the issue of conflict competence. According to Ting-Toomey, scholars need to further examine complex situational and identity issues in the study of intercultural conflict management in order to expand the scope of FNT.

In the seventh chapter, Kathryn Sorrells presents an intercultural praxis approach to conflict management. Her intercultural praxis model consists of six key elements: inquiry, framing, positioning, dialogue, reflection, and action. Sorrells thinks that nonviolence principles can meaningfully inform conflict management. It is possible to work out effective ways to deal with intercultural conflicts in the neoliberal global context and facilitate reconciliation, harmony and "beloved community" by integrating nonviolence principles with the intercultural praxis model.

In the eighth chapter, Min-Sun Kim and Yoshiko Kameo examine how multi-cultural identity contributes to developing conflict communication competence. They argue that multicultural identity embodies individuals' psychological growth, which facilitates frame switching. Multicultural individuals can easily transcend cultural boundaries and adapt to diverse cultural perspectives in order to apply appropriate conflict management styles in organizations and interpersonal settings.

In the ninth chapter, Akira Miyahara de-Westernizes conflict management models from the Japanese perspective. Western models/theories tend to regard assertiveness as positive or effective behavior and avoiding it as negative or ineffective behavior in communication. However, in Japanese culture, avoiding, as a typical manifestation of "air reading" (ku'uki wo yomu), is not only accepted but encouraged in many situations. Miyahara cautions that although "air reading" is an effective way to avoid conflict, it has its dark side and cannot be blindly employed in social communication.

In the tenth chapter, Guo-Ming Chen approaches conflict management from the Chinese perspective. Chen argues that communication is contextually dependent, and that each culture has its own unique way of managing conflict. In light of Chinese philosophy, conflict should be treated as a holistic system which is formed by the dynamic and dialectic interaction between the two parties of yin and yang. Although each party possesses its own identity, the identity cannot be fully developed individually. When a conflict arises, the two parties should be treated as an interrelated whole, so that the conflict can be constructively managed and that unity in diversity can be attained.

In the eleventh chapter, Yiheng Deng and Pamela Tremain Koch propose a Chinese model of constructive conflict management. They combine Western theories with Chinese values and concepts to develop strategies of conflict management that can work in a cross-cultural context. The model indicates that collectivism, harmony, face, *guanxi* (relationships), and power are the central values of Chinese culture. Strategies such as constructive confrontation, open and direct discussion, seeking hard facts, resorting to off-line talk, and turning to a third party of higher authority for intervention are effective ways for the Chinese to manage conflicts.

In the twelfth chapter, Helen Spencer-Oatey takes an interdisciplinary perspective on intercultural competence and harmonious intercultural relations. She points out that while most of the intercultural competence theories fail to identify relationship management as a core component, interpersonal pragmatics can inform our understanding on intercultural competence and help improve the problem. From the perspective of interpersonal pragmatics, the evaluation of individuals' relational management competence consists of four key elements: contextually-based judgment of normalcy of behavior, judgment of behavior and agent, judgment of appropriateness of behavior and agent, and impact on interpersonal rapport. The pragmatic perspective on the evaluation process provides us with an alternative approach to intercultural competence.

The second section (Chapters 13–20) deals with conflict management in diverse cultural and communication contexts. Conflict management in China, the U.S.A., and Japan are investigated first, followed by international trade and business contexts and virtual space.

In the thirteenth chapter, Xuan Zheng and Yihong Gao investigate Chinese parent-child conflict management strategies. Based on discursive evidence, they find that among the five preferable strategies for Chinese students dealing with this type of conflict—integration, compromising, obliging, dominating, and avoiding—dominating and avoiding rank the highest. Zheng and Gao also find that the strategy of articulating is favored more by university students. The students use it to construct an independent self and equal relationship with their parents.

In the fourteenth chapter, Yan Bing Zhang and Weston T. Wiebe investigate the intergenerational conflict between older adults and younger adults in the U.S. Their research finds that there seems to be no intergenerational conflict between older and younger adults. Factors contributing to this situation include lack of interaction and interpersonal boundaries, as well as mutual respect, relational closeness, understanding of the other's perspective, attentive communication and listening, and topics of mutual interest.

In the fifteenth chapter, Yuko Takeshita discusses intercultural communication management professionals in Japan. Despite the development of globalization in Japanese society, people have few opportunities to practice intercultural communication and often encounter linguistic and cultural problems when interacting with foreigners. Intercultural communication management professionals play an important role in helping their fellow citizens manage intercultural conflict and create new business opportunities.

In the sixteenth chapter, Michael B. Hinner analyzes intercultural conflict management, in particular the pseudo-conflicts, in the context of international business.

Although English is used as a lingua franca in international business communication, misunderstandings and intercultural conflicts often occur because of differing cultural backgrounds. Hinner identifies five key factors—identity, culture, perception, self-disclosure, and trust—that shape the communication process in intercultural conflict management. The five factors help people better perceive and manage misperception and misunderstanding, which often lead to intercultural conflict in the context of international business transactions.

In the seventeenth chapter, Juana Du and Ling Chen conduct a case study on intercultural conflict management in transnational mergers and acquisitions. They find that cultural differences affect international business communication. The poor management of misunderstandings may lead to intercultural conflict. Misunderstanding and subsequent intercultural conflict can lead to failed business acquisitions. Du and Chen suggest that corporations need to engage each other in open dialogue to develop culturally appropriate strategies that will allow acquisition to proceed without issue.

In the eighteenth chapter, Marcella Hoedl and Peter Franklin shed light on the bright side of Sino-German cultural differences. According to their study, some of the cultural differences, such as Chinese relationship management and German task management, German risk and uncertainty avoidance and Chinese experimentation with diversification, German love of detail and Chinese big picture, and German pursuit of perfection and Chinese pragmatic solution-orientation, have the potential for cultural synergy.

In the nineteenth chapter, Alois Moosmueller examines intercultural conflict management in multinational corporations (MNCs). Cultural diversity is generally regarded as a valuable asset for MNCs. Three examples provided by Moosmueller demonstrate that although MNCs endeavor to cultivate a global mindset, ethnocentric attitudes and work habits still dominate daily communication in MNCs. Moosmueller indicates that cultural difference remains a challenge for MNCs. To develop the potential for innovation and improve the efficiency of company management, MNCs need to incorporate diversity into their general operating strategies.

Finally in the twentieth chapter, Ping Yang addresses the characteristics, approaches, and strategies of conflict management in virtual space from a dialectical perspective. Her study shows that online conflict management is characterized by complexity, nonverbal communication, quicker escalation, more violence, and salience of power and control; online approaches to intercultural conflict include productive vs destructive and competitive vs cooperative; frequently used online conflict strategies include domination, collaborating, compromising, and avoiding, which depend on context, topic, relationships, and desired outcomes.

Conclusion

Conflict is a complex problem that affects the whole process of intercultural communication. Scholars have studied the nature of conflict from diverse perspectives; addressed the management of conflict at both interpersonal and intergroup levels; and conducted cross-cultural comparisons on conflict styles and strategies. These studies have contributed to the understanding of the concept, but many questions still remain unanswered. Specifically, more research should focus on the interactive process of conflict negotiation and the management of conflict among non-Western cultures. The trend of globalization has increased interconnectivity and interdependence among nations and cultures. Only through an appropriate and effective management of intercultural conflict can people establish harmonious relationships in our global society.

The complexity of conflict management and resolution demands further research. This expanded new edition, as the first edition, attempts to explore theoretical issues as well as conflict management in diverse cultural and communication contexts. We hope that the chapters in this volume can further enrich the scholarly literature and provide some practical suggestions in the area of intercultural conflict management.

References

Brown, P., & Levinson, S. (1987). *Politeness: Some universals in language usage*. Cambridge, UK: Cambridge University Press.

Chen, G. M. (2001). Toward transcultural understanding: A harmony theory of Chinese communication. In V. H. Milhouse, M. K. Asante, & P. O. Nwosu (Eds.), *Transcultural realities: Interdisciplinary perspectives on cross-cultural relations* (pp. 55–70). Thousand Oaks, CA: Sage.

Chen, G. M. (2009). Chinese harmony theory. In S. Littlejohn & K. Foss (Eds.), *Encyclopedia of communication theory* (pp. 95–96). Thousand Oaks, CA: Sage.

Chen, G. M. (2014). Harmony as the foundation of Chinese communication. In M. B. Hinner (Ed.), *Chinese culture in a cross-cultural comparison* (pp. 191–209). New York, NY: Peter Lang.

Chen, G. M. (2015). Theorizing global community as cultural home in the new century. *International Journal of Intercultural Relations*, 46, 73–81.

Chen, G. M. (2010). The impact of harmony on Chinese conflict management. In G. M. Chen (Ed.), *Study on Chinese communication behavior* (pp. 16–30). Hong Kong, China: China Review Academic Publisher.

Chen, G. M., Ryan, K., & Chen, C. (2000). The determinants of conflict management among Chinese and Americans. *Intercultural Communication Studies*, 9, 163–175.

Christians, C. G. (2014). Primordial issues in communication ethics. In R. S. Fortner & P. M. Fackler (Eds.), *The handbook of global communication and media ethics* (pp. 1–19). Malden, MA: Wiley Blackwell.

Goffman, E. (1955). On face-work: An analysis of ritual elements in social interaction. *Psychiatry: Interpersonal and Biological Processes*, 18, 213–231.

Graham, J. (1985). The influence of culture on the process of business negotiations: An exploratory study. *Journal of International Business Studies*, 85, 81–96.

Han, B. & Cai, D. (2015). A cross-cultural analysis of avoidance: Behind-the-scene strategies in interpersonal conflicts. *Intercultural Communication Studies*, 24, 84–122.

Hu, H. C. (1944). The Chinese concept of "face." *American Anthropologist*, 46, 45–64.

Kozan, M. K. (1989). Cultural influences on styles of handling interpersonal conflicts: Comparisons among Jordanians, Turkish, and U.S. managers. *Human Relations*, 42, 787–799.

Kozan, M. K. & Ergin, C. (1998). Preferences for third-party help in conflict management in the United States and Turkey: An experimental study. *Journal of Cross-Cultural Psychology*, 29, 525–539.

Marsella, A. J. (2005). Culture and conflict: Understanding, negotiating, and reconciling constructions of reality. *International Journal of Intercultural Relations*, 29, 651–673.

Miike, Y. (2010). Culture as text and culture as theory: Asiacentricity and its raison d'être in intercultural communication research. In T. K. Nakayama & R. T. Halualani (Eds.), *The handbook of critical intercultural communication* (pp. 190–215). Oxford, UK: Wiley-Blackwell.

Moran, R. T., Abramson, N. R., & Moran, S. (2014). *Managing cultural differences*. New York, NY: Routledge.

Oetzel, J., Dhar, S., & Kirschbaum, K. (2007). Intercultural conflict from a multilevel perspective: Trends, possibilities, and future directions. *Journal of Intercultural Communication Research*, 36, 183–204.

Ojelabi, L. A. (2010). Values and the resolution of cross-cultural conflicts. *Global Change, Peace & Security*, 22, 53–73.

Siira, K., Rogan, R. G., & Hall, J. A. (2004). "A spoken word is an arrow shot": A comparison of Finnish and U.S. conflict management and face maintenance. *Journal of International Communication Research*, 33, 89–107.

Tata, J. (2000). Implicit theories of account-giving: Influence of culture and gender. *International Journal of Intercultural Relations*, 24, 437–454.

Ting-Toomey, S. (1988). Intercultural conflicts: A face-negotiation theory. In Y. Y. Kim & W. B. Gudykunst (Eds.), *Theories in intercultural communication* (pp. 213–235). Newbury Park, CA: Sage.

Ting-Toomey, S. (2005). The matrix of face: An updated face-negotiation theory. In W. B. Gudykunst (Ed.), *Theorizing about intercultural communication* (pp. 71–92). Thousand Oaks, CA: Sage.

Ting-Toomey, S. (2017). Conflict face-negotiation theory: Tracking its evolution journey. In X. D. Dai & G. M. Chen (Eds.), *Conflict management and intercultural communication: The art of intercultural harmony*. Abingdon, UK: Routledge.

Ting-Toomey, S. & Oetzel, J. G. (2001). *Managing intercultural conflict effectively*. Thousand Oaks, CA: Sage.

Ting-Toomey, S. & Oetzel, J. G. (2003). Cross-cultural face concerns and conflict styles: Current status and future directions. In W. B. Gudykunst (Ed.), *Cross-cultural and intercultural communication* (pp. 127–147). Thousand Oaks, CA: Sage.

Wilmot, W. & Hocker, J. (2007). *Interpersonal conflict* (7th ed.). Boston, MA: McGraw-Hill.

Worchel, S. (2005). Culture's role in conflict and conflict management: Some suggestions, many questions. *International Journal of Intercultural Relations*, 29, 739–757.

Yu, Q. Y. (2013). *Culture in rivers and mountains*. Wuhan, China: Changjiang Publishing.

Perspectives on Intercultural Conflict Management and Harmony Building

Section One

Perspectives on Intercultural
Conflict Management and
Harmony Building

1

MOVING FROM CONFLICT TO HARMONY

The Role of Dialogue in Bridging Differences

Benjamin J. Broome

It is easy to become pessimistic about the possibility of living in harmony in our increasingly diverse world. We hear daily reports in the media about suicide bombings, drone strikes, terrorist attacks, violent protests and demonstrations, gang warfare, organized crime, human trafficking, and many other forms of violence. Indeed, there is abundant evidence of violent conflicts occurring around the world. In their analysis of armed conflicts from 1946–2013, Themnér and Wallensteen (2014) report that since the end of World War II, there have been 254 armed conflicts active in 155 locations around the world. In 2013 alone, there were 33 armed conflicts occurring in 25 locations worldwide. Disturbingly, there were 15 new conflicts in the three years preceding their analysis. Many of these conflicts are civil wars, lower-level insurgencies, and other forms of conflict that can tear a country apart for decades, and sometimes permanently.[1] Although there are also many positive and uplifting stories of people working together cooperatively, and despite the study by Pinker (2011) that shows violence is lower today than during previous periods of history, the prevalence of war and other forms of violent conflict could certainly create a perception that the world is hopelessly embroiled in violent conflicts.

High-tension conflicts are costly. Some of the effects are material: human lives are lost, physical property is destroyed, essential infrastructure is damaged, public health systems no longer function properly, the education system is severely disrupted, and outside investment dries up. All of these can have devastating effects on the economy and future development of a country in conflict (Glaeser, 2009).[2] Other costs are less visible and less quantifiable but can have consequences that last for generations: loss of family members, relatives, and close friends; population displacement; constant disruption and fear for one's life and the post-trauma mental conditions that often result; injuries and disability; malnutrition leading to lower life expectancy; loss of normal childhood and adolescence for many children and young people; disrupted,

DOI: 10.4324/9781003252955-3

delayed, and often never-completed education; brain drain from the emigration of educated work force; reduced investment and tourism from abroad and the devastating effects of a breakdown in trust, manifesting itself both in individual confidence in society and divisions between groups that once lived together. And the effects go far beyond the country in which the war is taking place, affecting neighboring states and areas far away from the conflict itself, as we are seeing now with the refugee crisis in Europe.[3]

Given the overwhelming negative consequences of conflict and violence, clearly there is a need to promote greater harmony in the face of the increasing number of confrontations. Unfortunately, the quest for harmony can seem despairingly out of reach in a world filled with tensions emanating from racial, religious, and resource-based conflicts. For some, discussions of peace and harmony might seem wishful thinking or even delusional. Even for those dedicated to building peace, many questions arise when discussing harmony and conflict: What has brought about the breakdown in harmony that seems to characterize today's world? Can anything be done to counteract the disruptive forces acting against harmony? Is harmony even possible in the face of so much violence and destruction? Is there reason to believe that harmony will be achieved someday? These are all reasonable questions, but they are often guided by a view that harmony is a quiet and stable state of existence where people are in agreement about issues and everyone acts in concert within an established order. Such a view of harmony is an idealistic aim that is unachievable and even dysfunctional in a healthy society.

In this chapter, a conception of *harmony* is adopted that emphasizes difference rather than sameness, and that focuses on process rather than outcome. Drawing on both ancient Greek and Chinese approaches to harmony, the argument will be made that instead of viewing conflicts as a threat to harmony, they should be seen as an essential part of the harmonization process. Indeed, conflicts over seemingly incompatible goals can sometimes serve as the impetus for individual and social changes that need to be made in order to address the underlying causes for the conflicts. And although differences, by their very nature, will cause disagreement and discord, we are not destined to live in a violent world. An alternative to violence is *dialogue*, which has the potential to promote harmony and lead to greater peace in conflict-torn societies. This chapter will suggest ways in which dialogue can help bring about more peaceful ways of dealing with differences, contributing to a process of harmony that embraces, rather than avoids, diversity and change.

Harmony: Going beyond Agreement and Conformity

Harmony has been seen as important throughout history and across cultures; the concept of harmony is reflected in music, art, politics, religion, and other aspects of society (Xie, 2012). At first glance, harmony would seem to be a rather straightforward concept that is easy to define. In the English language, the word "harmony" is usually associated with agreement, getting along without problems, tolerating differences, avoiding conflicts, and experiencing consensus across issues of concern to society.

Even with positive connotations, the pursuit of harmony is often regarded in the West as naïve or even harmful in the face of strong differences. Perhaps because of the individualistic focus in the West, harmony is considered a somewhat weak concept. Although it is a positive value, it is not one to be placed above standing up for one's rights or defending one's position when there are conflicts. Many influential academic and activist figures, including political liberals and staunch defenders of humanities education, focus more on justice and human dignity than on finding ways to pursue harmony (see, for example, Martha Nussbaum, 2001). Harmony is often juxtaposed with the need to fight for one's rights. For Westerners, the choice is clear: you must stand up for your beliefs and be willing to fight for what you believe is rightfully yours, rather than "give in" so that the harmony will not be disturbed.

In the East, harmony is treated quite differently, particularly in places such as Thailand, Japan, Korea, and China. In these societies, harmony is viewed as one of the primary values, and it is seen as underlying much of human interaction (Chen, 2011). The group-based and hierarchically-oriented nature of many Asian societies leads people to seek harmony by avoiding outward displays of anger (Hu, Grove, & Zhuang, 2010), refraining from engaging in argument especially when it involves disagreement (Hazen & Shi, 2009), showing self-restraint, saving face, avoiding direct criticism of others, exhibiting modesty, and practicing generosity (Wei & Li, 2013). Sustained by politeness and respect, societies with a Confucian tradition will usually display a courteous attitude toward others, in an effort to build a harmonious communication climate (Chen, 2014). In general, the emphasis on harmony means that people are more disposed to engage in negotiation when differences arise, more willing to compromise, and less inclined to engage in confrontation when faced with conflicts.

In contrast to contemporary treatments of harmony in both the West and the East that tend to emphasize agreement and similarity, ancient conceptions of harmony gave importance to tension and dissimilarity. The English term *harmony* is from the ancient Greek word *a'rmonia*, which means the joining or coming together of different entities. The ancient Greek philosopher Heraclitus (6th century BCE), defined harmony as opposites in concert, believing that harmony exists when disparate forces are held in tension (Graham, 2015).[4] Using the example of the bow and lyre, Heraclitus demonstrated that tension and opposition are essential to harmony, and that unity is made possible because of opposing tensions. He used the example of night and day, which are opposites but are intimately connected and interdependent. If you lose day, you lose night as well. Heraclitus gave us the well-known insight that a person can never walk in the same river twice, as both the person and the river are constantly changing. For Heraclitus, harmonization happens through this constant change, not through seeking agreement and sameness. Everything is subject to internal tension, and harmony comes from opposing elements and movements pulling in opposite directions but finding equilibrium. Harmony is not a matter of properly orienting ourselves to preexisting structures or conditions; rather, the structure of the world is itself the result of the harmonizing process, in which different forces are integrated into dynamic unity (Li, 2008).

The emphasis on diversity and unity was also reflected in the teachings of the Chinese philosopher Confucius, who like Heraclitus lived during the 6th century BCE. For Confucius, harmony is a generative and creative process in which diverse elements are brought together to form a complex and inclusive world. To produce good music, musicians must be able to mix together very different sounds so that they complement and complete one another. Likewise, to produce a delicious dish, good cooks must be able to mingle ingredients with contrasting flavors and different tastes. With both music and food, different elements complete each other and enhance one another, coming together in a coherent and harmonious way. However, harmony is much more than simply mixing sounds and mingling flavors; rather, it requires that the various elements enrich one another by forming a relationship in which they mutually compensate for one another's shortcomings, mutually reinforce one another's strengths, and mutually advance each other's paths toward fulfillment. Even the five virtues of Confucianism—human excellence, moral rightness, ritualized propriety, wisdom, and sageliness—need to be practiced in harmony in order to achieve happiness and the prosperity of the world (Li, 2008).

As with Heraclitus, Confucius stresses the dynamic nature of tension and diversity within harmony. In the Confucian view, conflict between parties, when it is handled properly, serves as a step toward harmony. Although the Confucian way advocates self-restraint, subduing emotions in public, and indirect expressions of approval, it is at the same time built around the coexistence of difference. When facing a controversial issue, the Confucian approach calls for taking into account the whole picture, and resolving the differences through facework, social connections, and reciprocity (Wei & Li, 2013). For Confucians, harmony is dependent on a continuous process of managing opposing forces through give and take. Li (2014) uses the example of rocks and water in a river, where both have to yield in some way. Through this "negotiation" process, order is established, although this order is constantly changing.

While they have different starting points and base their thinking within different cosmologies, both Heraclitus and Confucius understood harmony as an ongoing process in a constantly changing world. For both, the goal of harmony is not to conform to a fixed underlying structure of the world; rather, structure itself is a result of the harmonizing process. And in both approaches, harmony is much more than sameness; in fact, harmony has to be achieved through difference. As Li (2014) argues, since harmony is a composite, it can only be realized by the successful integration of different elements. This need for integration makes harmony inclusive in nature, since during the harmonization process each component finds an appropriate place, and none of the components exclude or suppress one another. Even when elements are in conflict, one or more of them can change positions, or at least be stabilized within the system so that they are not disrupting it in ways that are damaging to the overall structure or to the long-term viability of the system.

Although harmony emphasizes balance and equilibrium, conflict is also part of the harmonization process. Unlike simple differences, where harmony can be achieved when contrasting elements complement one another within a larger pattern, conflict produces a level of tension that can put harmony at risk. This usually necessitates a negotiation process in which parties need to jointly explore ways to modify their positions to accommodate the other, or find creative ways to satisfy the needs of both parties. By taking an inclusive approach and using the tension between positions to engage in creative exploration, it is possible to find harmonious solutions to conflicts.

While there is no panacea, one of the important means of encouraging and nurturing harmony across difference is *dialogue*, a concept and a practice that, like harmony, is frequently misunderstood, and, despite having positive associations, is not widely seen as a powerful force in the face of conflict. But if we can move beyond a view of harmony as sameness, accord, conformity, and uniformity, and instead understand harmony as encompassing diversity and creative tension, then we will be positioned to understand how dialogue can help transform conflict into harmony. The next section will explore the nature of dialogue and will propose several ways in which it can be a key component in harmonizing the tension that is inevitable in today's conflict-filled world.

Dialogue: A Path from Conflict to Harmony[5]

The question of how to harmonize protracted conflict situations is one that has long concerned diplomats, community leaders, researchers, and anyone seeking to bridge the divide between disputing parties. Certainly there are no easy answers, and any possibility for progress will need to involve multiple levels of society and numerous approaches for moving forward. But *dialogue* can be a key piece of the strategy for both preventing societies from falling apart under pressures from seemingly insurmountable differences, and for engaging in a healing process once societies have succumbed to the ravages of violence. By bringing individuals with a variety of perspectives together in a safe space, different voices can be heard and creative ideas can be generated, providing opportunities to learn from others and expand one's perspective on the conflict and the possibilities for the future.

Contemporary understandings of dialogue are influenced significantly by the philosopher, theologian, playwright, and educator Martin Buber (1958). His seminal work *I and Thou* led to a shift in our thinking about communication, relationships, and the possibility for genuine human interaction. He distinguishes between the "I–It" encounter, in which people are treated as if they were objects to be manipulated or changed in some way, and the "I–Thou" relationship, in which people are viewed as having unique histories that shape their beliefs, attitudes, and values. An I–Thou encounter is characterized by curiosity, discovery, and learning, while an I–It encounter is centered on persuasion, positioning, and argument. In Buber's view, dialogue is a way of being with others, a way of acknowledging the complexity of other people's experiences and seeking understanding of their perspectives. Buber's views reflect the type of harmony that is described in the previous section, and communication that is characterized by I-Thou dialogue can play a critical role in the harmonization process that needs to occur in response to conflict.[6]

One of the concepts introduced by Buber, the notion of the "between," has gained traction among several scholars who study dialogue. Buber (1958) uses the "between" as a metaphor for the dialogic space that exists between persons in a relationship. This common center of discourse brings people together in conversation, allowing meaning to be co-constituted during dialogue. In this way, people create new understandings through their interaction by engaging in a process that Stewart (1983) labels "inter-pretive listening," Bohm (1996) refers to as "collective intelligence," and Broome (2009) terms "relational empathy." By giving attention to the "between," dialogue points to the *interdependence* of self and other, the *intersubjectivity* of meaning, and the *emergent* nature of understandings (J. Stewart, 1978, 1983). This type of exchange is perhaps the best way to harness the tension of conflict and use it as a springboard for transforming relationships and generating creative ideas, both of which are key to the process of harmonization in conflict situations.

On a practical level, dialogue often takes the form of structured group interaction. Individuals from opposing sides of a conflict are brought together in a safe space, usually under the guidance of a third-party, in which participants can engage in facilitated discussions. Although it usually requires great care to set up and special expertise to facilitate, structured dialogue groups can provide a setting for examining the basis for a conflict, repairing damaged relationships, and exploring steps that might be taken to address critical issues that are embedded in the conflict. Structured dialogue groups can take a variety of forms, from small informal meetings to institu-tionalized discussion groups that meet on an ongoing basis over a long period of time.[7] But the essence of any form of dialogue is to enable an exchange of views, perspec-tives, and ideas that is centered on fostering mutual respect and understanding, and creating mutually embraced pathways for joint action.

There are a number of approaches to intergroup dialogue in conflict situations. Some are highly structured and predominantly analytical (Burton, 1969; Sandole, 2001), dealing primarily with the substance of the conflict. Through intensive discus-sions over a period of several days, a third-party helps participants analyze the sources of the conflict and develop possible solutions. Other approaches are less structured and more informal efforts to ease tensions and improve relations in international conflicts. These sessions are primarily oriented toward helping participants learn about each other, developing better communication across the divide, and establishing working relationships (Doob, 1981; Volkan, 1998; Wedge, 1967). In the psychodynamic approach, an attempt is made to humanize the "enemy," build confidence, and overcome hatred, all of which helps uncover emotional issues that might otherwise affect the conflict negatively. Between the rational and psychodynamic approaches are those that focus on both relationship and substance (Azar, 1990; Fisher, 1997; Kelman, 1982). Typically, these approaches give equal emphasis to both the educational and the political aspects of the conflict; they attempt to produce changes in the attitudes and perceptions of the participants while simultaneously transferring these changes to a broader societal discussion or to the political arena.

Of course, in situations with a long history of division, making progress requires a systematic, prolonged set of dialogues committed to the transformation of conflictual relationships. Decades, or even centuries, of enmity cannot be overcome overnight, and there are many forces in the society and larger context of the conflict that can quickly undo any progress from dialogue sessions. Lederach (1997) suggests that dialogue must give emphasis to both peace *and* justice, as well as to both truth *and* mercy, in order to be effective. The goal of dialogue is the long-term transformation of a "war system" into a "peace system" that is characterized by political and economic participation, peaceful relationships, and social harmony (Lederach, 1999, 2003). The aim is to create an *infrastructure for peace* that simultaneously addresses—and involves— all the different levels of a society that have been affected by conflict: from the grass-roots level (the vast majority), to national leaders (ethnic/religious leaders, leaders of NGOs, academics/intellectuals, among others), and to the top level of political and military leadership (Lederach, 1997).

Although most intergroup dialogue approaches are not grounded specifically in the literature of harmony, their purposes are highly compatible with the conceptualization of harmony described in the previous section. With their emphasis on listening, non-polarized discourse, and the creation of new understandings, most approaches to intergroup dialogue contribute in significant ways towards the goal of bringing balance and equilibrium to difficult conflict situations. While recognizing that harmony within a particular society or within the overall global system depends on many system-level factors, dialogue can play a critical role in shaping these factors. Through dialogue, impetus for necessary changes at the societal level can be cultivated, new ideas can emerge for reaching effective agreements at the political level, increased levels of understanding can be achieved, and new relationships can be formed that will promote the cooperation that is required for changes to be implemented successfully both before and after a political settlement. All of these possible outcomes contribute immensely to the process of establishing, restoring, and maintaining harmony in conflict situations. The remainder of this section will connect dialogue to the key characteristics of harmony that were discussed earlier.

Identifying Differences

Conflict occurs at least in part because of differences in perspectives, goals, and the means to achieve desired outcomes. Often in conflict situations, groups on each side will operate according to stereotypes and misconceptions that can keep them apart and lead them to take unnecessary actions against the other party. It is important to identify and acknowledge these differences so they can be appropriately addressed by the conflicting parties. Unfortunately, conflict can further reinforce and promote bias and prejudice by preventing the type of contact that can break down misconceptions and help each party better understand the other. Over time this tends to become institutionalized, which further solidifies the boundaries between the parties in the conflict (Hewstone & Greenland, 2000).

Structured dialogue provides an important avenue for helping groups understand each other's views of the conflict, learn about each other's aspirations for the future, and identify the issues on which they hold contrasting opinions. Of course, simply bringing people together will not by itself lead to the constructive identification of differences. The contact hypothesis that Gordon Allport (1954) originally described in his book, *The Nature of Prejudice,* which was extended by Amir (1969), Cook (1978), Hewstone and Greenland (2000), and Pettigrew (2008), among others, demonstrates that intergroup contact is effective primarily in conditions of equal status, sustained interactions, cooperative interdependence, and social norms of equality. These conditions can be cultivated through dialogue, allowing groups to effectively identify the differences that divide them. Only when this happens can groups start the process of finding ways to build harmony based on these differences.

Harnessing and Transforming Tension

The differences that exist within any society are always a potential source of destructive tension. In a harmonious world, tension is the basis for a strong society, as it is for the bow and lyre that Heraclitus described in his writings. And it is the basis for a prosperous society, where a mix of perspectives, practices, and dreams allows a society to flourish with creative and innovative ideas. But the tension that arises from violent conflict has a destructive effect, driving people apart and suppressing imagination and originality. Anxiety and fear dominate, and people put up defensive walls to protect themselves. These walls constrain interaction, stem the free flow of ideas, and thwart the possibility for collaborative inquiry. Instead of diversity leading to a bold and exciting future, differences set society on a regressive path of short-sighted policy decisions and repressive measures.

Dialogue provides a way to harness potentially damaging tension and redirect it toward healthy growth. Exploring the tensions that are fueling the conflict can relieve some of the pressure, so that it no longer plays such a dominating role in the discourse. The act of sitting together and learning from one another, engaging in conversation that explores the basis for differences that exist between competing groups, can help tilt the flow of negative energy toward positive ends. As Salomon (2009) suggests, it is critical to cultivate more positive attitudes toward the other side and more positive attitudes toward peace. Bar-Tal (2009) agrees when he advocates developing "an emotional orientation of hope that reflects the desire for the positive goal of maintaining peaceful and cooperative relations with the other party" (p. 369). Dialogue can aid in creating a "positive vision based on humanistic and inclusive ideals without an inherent destructive potential. ... [with a] focus on the possibility of, and satisfactions inherent in connection to, community and peace" (Staub, 1996, p. 147).

Restoring Balance and Equilibrium

Many of the conflicts described in the introductory section are part of systems that have been characterized by disharmony for an extended period of time. They have become what Coleman (2003) terms intractable conflicts, often involving ethnic victimization, unaddressed historical grievances and traumas, economic asymmetries, unequal distribution of resources, and structural inequalities. Resulting in assault, torture, murder, and other heinous crimes, the outcome is an imbalance that shifts society further away from the possibility of harmonious relations. The grievances that residents of conflict zones accumulate leave deep scars of anger and a sense of victimhood and a will for revenge (Bar-Tal, 2009). Bringing society back to a state of equilibrium is not an easy task when there is a culture of conflict, mistrust, and suspicion, as well as a flourishing of "enemy images." The atrocities committed by parties against each other create a tendency for individuals in violent conflicts to demonize those on the other side, causing them to attribute the causes of their suffering and experiences of injustice exclusively to the other.

To restore balance and equilibrium to the system, participants must break loose from the confining emotions of fear, anger, and hatred that shackle them to memories of the horrors of violent conflict. The opportunity to engage in meaningful dialogue offers individuals and groups the possibility of moving beyond the past while still acknowledging the events that frame the conflict (Saunders, 2003). The pain from past events cannot be erased, but perhaps it can be dealt with in a healthier manner by meeting individuals from the other community as fellow human beings. Participants have an opportunity to describe to the other the harm they have suffered and the pain they have experienced because of actions by the other side. Dialogue can allow the group to validate the pain and grief of its members, create feelings of empathy for the suffering many have experienced, and offer support for everyone's constant struggle to deal with the psychological (and often physical) wounds inflicted by the conflict. Through such frank and honest exchange, participants often move to a point where they can recognize and acknowledge the responsibility of their own side in the conflict. By engaging in such dialogue, they create an awareness of shared humanity, an important building block that brings into balance the forces that were pushing people apart.

Nurturing Inclusiveness

One of the most destructive aspects of violent conflict is the inevitable formation of ethnic and sectarian factions (Montville, 1990). Humans have a deep-rooted psychological tendency, at both individual and group levels, to dichotomize by creating "enemies" and "allies." Unconscious impulses often result in former neighbors harming and killing each other simply because they belong to different national/ethnic groups (Mack, 1990). As events unfold, each side adopts a partisan, skewed, and unilateral declaration of grievances and becomes fiercely preoccupied with asserting its rights, making it blind to the need to attend to and mend interethnic relations. Giving so much attention to one's own grievances and rights simply deepens the estrangement of the communities in conflict, and there is little concrete engagement between the two sides.

Dialogue allows individuals from conflicting groups to turn toward each other, gaining an awareness of their interconnectedness, common humanity, and shared interests. Through the experience of sitting in the same room with one another, participants can come to understand each other's culture and everyday concerns, and learn about their history and personal experiences. By exchanging personal stories and engaging in mutual analysis of the conflict and its effects, the other can be legitimized and humanized. Kriesberg (2004) suggests that a regard for the other takes hold in dialogue groups, allowing for the possibility of different ways of life existing side-by-side. By listening to what the other has to say, and allowing for its authenticity, respect can slowly emerge. Mutual recognition of each other's humanity and legitimacy enables accommodation and may eventually allow participants to come to see their adversaries as worthy of respect. Such respect, and the corresponding trust that often accompanies it, develops gradually as participants slowly and carefully reveal their own hurt and pain and find a positive reception from the other. With sufficient dialogue, rivals can become legitimate partners in peace (Bar-Tal, 2009). Conflict can slowly move from the disharmony of exclusiveness to the harmonious relations made possible by inclusiveness.

Promoting Cooperation

Perhaps the key to maintaining a healthy degree of harmony is good working relationships among the disparate elements of the system. Unfortunately, one of the earliest casualties of protracted conflict is cooperation between the parties. As trust breaks down and relations deteriorate, the disputing sides quickly stop working together. On the individual level, without regular task-oriented interaction, individuals on opposite sides of a conflict no longer have a way to experience the give-and-take that comes with working on a project together. The practice in compromising that one usually gains through daily problem-solving no longer occurs, making it even more difficult to consider compromise on larger issues that divide parties. And from a very practical standpoint, the many issues that require close cooperation are left unattended, causing losses for both sides.

In the view of Morton Deutsch (1973), cooperative relations have characteristics such as effective communication, respect, fair treatment, enhancement of one another's knowledge and skill, and recognition of the legitimacy of each other's interests. Such actions, which must be based on mutual trust, have to be cultivated gradually. Through experience in ongoing intergroup dialogues, individuals gain necessary contacts with the other community, and they become progressively sensitive to the concerns of the other community. They also become aware of some of the issues that might cause misunderstanding and conflict, while learning some of the skills for dealing with it. And when groups work together in a cooperative manner, they tend to generate positive reciprocity. Through their initial steps at cooperation, they often expand their collaboration in other areas (Staub, 1996). If cooperative ventures can be conducted successfully, they can help rebuild trust, a component of reestablishing and maintaining societal harmony.

Conclusion

Violent conflict can be devastating to a society. It disrupts harmony in the strongest of ways, turning the differences on which harmony depends into tension that rips it apart. There is no magic potion for preventing violent conflict, and there are no guarantees that it can be restored. But dialogue brings hope, both for preventing a devastating breakdown of harmony during conflicts, and for reestablishing the balance and equilibrium after violent conflict. Dialogue offers the possibility of bringing diverse elements together to help build a complex and inclusive world, two key aspects of harmony.

Dialogue does not, by itself, have the capacity to restore harmony after violent conflict; however, it is a vital component of the harmonization process. Dialogue can help uncover differences that need to be addressed; it can assist in transforming tension from a negative force to a healthy energy; it can play an important role in restoring balance and equilibrium after tension reaches damaging levels; it can encourage a sense of connection and shared aims; and it can promote coordination and cooperation in working toward common goals. Significantly, these elements are interdependent, working together with one another in a supportive way. If cooperation is the desired objective, it requires diversity, reduction of tension, balance, and inclusiveness. Taken together, these outcomes and their supportive relations provide the basic components of harmony and the harmonization process.

While it has the potential to support harmony, dialogue does not necessarily happen easily or naturally. It requires participants' willingness to take risks, knowing that their perspective might be altered. Change is often threatening, even when participants are hoping for something better. Dialogue can shape participants in ways that affect their identity, and the views of one's self that are carried into the dialogue might not match the views of self that are required to change the situation. The perspectives encountered in dialogue may be radically different for each participant, and it is natural to resist and even reject such differences. Dialogue, however, is dependent on such risk-taking, without which harmony may not happen.

Dialogue is also unpredictable. Like harmony, dialogue is a nonlinear, emergent process, always shifting, remaining fluid throughout. Meanings are constantly revised and remade. Rather than smoothing over the tension that results from conflict, dialogue can create even more tension between participants. But this tension is integral to the process of dialogue just as it is to harmony. In their struggle to cope with tension, individuals in dialogue often develop creative ideas or new ways of approaching problems. This process of dealing with tension can push toward a synthesis of positions that serves the needs and interests of participants much better than any of their initial positions.

It is important to keep in mind that, as desirable as it might seem, dialogue may not always be possible. Social, economic, and symbolic conditions that are out of balance give rise to inequities, and the resulting social asymmetries alter the dynamics of dialogue. They can prevent people from coming together in the first place, and they can make it very difficult for either side to move past their preconceptions and unhealthy communication patterns that resulted from so many years of inadequately dealing with the differences that divide them. Those at the top of the power hierarchy may even believe that entering into dialogue with lower status individuals is a threat to their privilege and position. Additionally, we must remember that dialogue depends on reciprocity. Dialogue is a cyclic process, and when one side is still trapped in the vicious cycle of conflict and not ready to meet the other, dialogue is not possible.

As Li (2014) reminds us, "harmony is not always rosy and pretty" (p. 13). From a dialogic perspective, the tensions that result from conflict are a potential obstacle to productive exchange and simultaneously a key to resolving conflict. If key differences can be identified through dialogue, and the tension that drives them can be positively directed, perhaps disharmony can be brought into balance, allowing an inclusion-based cooperation to occur. The hope is that a creative breakthrough becomes possible in which the paradox of opposites is transcended by synthesis. When this synthesis occurs, tensions can be transformed into positive energy that can drive momentum toward intercultural harmony.

Endnotes

1. Fearon and Laitin (2003) report that between the end of World War II and the beginning of the 21st century more than 70 countries were involved in civil wars. These wars often lasted more than a decade, with a median length of seven years, and the death total was over 16 million. This toll has continued to rise in the last decade and has escalated in the last two to three years.

2. Although the economic effects are difficult to directly measure (see Hess, 2009), a comprehensive World Bank report on violence provides a low-end estimate of over USD 1 trillion for the overall annual cost of organized violence, not taking into account military expenditures and other direct and indirect effects of conflict and violence (Skaperdas, Soares, Willman, & Miller, 2009). Added to these sums are recovery efforts, which require large investments of time, attention, and other resources to deal with the devastation caused by conflicts and to bridge the divide that is created between people in society (F. Stewart, 2002). It is estimated that if the costs of violence could be reduced to the lowest practically attainable levels (between two and three deaths per 100,000 population), nearly USD 2 trillion in economic losses could be saved, an amount equivalent to 2.64 per cent of the global GDP in 2010.

3. Researchers estimate that 60 million people are displaced worldwide. Globally, one in every 122 humans, nearly half of them children, is now either a refugee, internally displaced, or seeking asylum (UNHCR, 2015).

4. Heraclitus was the earliest Greek philosopher to write specifically about harmony, but his contemporaries (e.g., Pythagoras) and later Greek philosophers (e.g., Plato) gave more emphasis to an ideal order, deviating from Heraclitus' conception of harmony.

5.   This section draws from Broome (2013) and from the opportunities I have had
     to work with dialogue groups in numerous settings, particularly from groups
     I've facilitated in the eastern Mediterranean island of Cyprus, a divided country
     where a dedicated group of individuals and organizations have been working
     for several decades to bring together the two communities. See Broome (2005),
     available for download at the following location: www.cy.undp.org/content/
     dam/cyprus/docs/ACT%20Publications/Building_Bridges_English.pdf
6.   In addition to Buber, there are several scholars in the West who have
     advanced the study of dialogue. Among other influential theorists is David
     Bohm (1996), whose work was applied in the "learning organization"
     concepts espoused by Senge (1990), Isaacs (1993), and Schein (1993).
     Cissna and Anderson (1998) trace the concept of dialogue through a
     multiplicity of disciplines, including anthropology, education, psychology
     and psychotherapy, sociology, management, political theory, philosophy,
     linguistics, and religion. In communication, dialogue has been studied
     from the perspective of rhetoric (Johannesen, 1971), philosophy and
     communication (J. Stewart, 1978), interpersonal communication (Baxter &
     Montgomery, 1996), performance studies (Conquergood, 1988), organiza-
     tional communication (Deetz, 1992), health communication (Geist &
     Dreyer, 1994), culture and communication (Philipsen, 1992), and conflict
     communication (Pearce & Littlejohn, 1997).
7.   Advances in communications technology open new possibilities for bringing
     people into contact and facilitating dialogue, but most dialogue groups meet
     face-to-face.

References

Allport, G. (1954). *The nature of prejudice*. Boston, MA: Beacon Press.

Amir, Y. (1969). Contact hypothesis in ethnic relations. *Psychological Bulletin*, 71(5), 319–342.

Azar, E. E. (1990). *The management of protracted social conflict. Theory and cases*. Aldershot: Dartmouth.

Bar-Tal, D. (2009). Reconciliation as a foundation of culture of peace. In J. Rivera (Ed.), *Handbook on building cultures of peace* (pp. 363–377). New York, NY: Springer.

Baxter, L. A., & Montgomery, B. M. (1996). *Relating: Dialogues and dialectics*. New York, NY: Guildford Press.

Bohm, D. (1996). *On dialogue*. London, UK: Routledge.

Broome, B. J. (2005). *Building bridges across the green line: A guide to intercultural communication in Cyprus*. Nicosia, Cyprus: United Nations Development Program.

Broome, B. J. (2009). Building relational empathy through an interactive design process. In D. J. D. Sandole, S. Byrne, I. Staroste-Sandole, & J. Senihi (Eds.), *Handbook of conflict analysis and resolution* (pp. 184–200). New York, NY: Routledge.

Broome, B. J. (2013). Building cultures of peace: The role of intergroup dialogue. In J. G. Oetzel & S. Ting-Toomey (Eds.), *Sage handbook of conflict communication: Integrating theory, research, and practice* (2nd ed., pp. 737–762). Los Angeles: Sage.

Buber, M. (1958). *I and Thou* (R. G. Smith, Trans., 2nd ed.). New York, NY: Scribner.

Burton, J. W. (1969). *Conflict and communication: The use of controlled communication in international relations.* London, UK: Macmillan.

Chen, G. M. (2011). An introduction to key concepts in understanding the Chinese: Harmony as the foundation of Chinese communication. *China Media Research,* 7(4), 1–12.

Chen, G. M. (2014). The two faces of Chinese communication. In M. K. Asante, Y. Miike, & J. Yin (Eds.), *The global intercultural communication reader* (2nd ed., pp. 273–282). New York, NY: Routledge.

Cissna, K. H., & Anderson, R. (1998). Theorizing about dialogic moment: The Buber-Rogers position and postmodern themes. *Communication Theory,* 8, 63–104.

Coleman, P. T. (2003). Characteristics of protracted, intractable conflict: Toward the development of a metaframework. *Peace and Conflict: Journal of Peace Psychology,* 9(1), 1–37.

Conquergood, D. (1988). Health theater in a Hmong refugee camp. *Journal of Performance Studies,* 32, 171–208.

Cook, S. W. (1978). Interpersonal and attitudinal outcomes in cooperating interracial groups. *Journal of Research and Development in Education,* 12, 97–113.

Deetz, S. (1992). *Democracy in an age of corporate colonization.* Albany, NY: State University of New York Press.

Deutsch, M. (1973). *The resolution of conflict: Constructive and destructive process.* New Haven, CT: Yale University Press.

Doob, L. W. (1981). *The pursuit of peace.* Westport, CT: Greenwood Press.

Fearon, J. D., & Laitin, D. D. (2003). Ethnicity, insurgency, and civil war. *The American Political Science Review,* 97(1), 75–90.

Fisher, R. J. (1997). *Interactive conflict resolution.* Syracuse, NY: Syracuse University Press.

Geist, P., & Dreyer, J. (1994). The demise of dialogue: A critique of the medial encounter. *Western Journal of Communication,* 57, 233–246.

Geneva Declaration on Armed Violence and Development. (2015). Retrieved from www.geneva declaration.org.

Glaeser, E. L. (2009). The political economy of warfare. In G. D. Hess (Ed.), *Guns and butter: The economic causes and consequences of conflict* (pp. 33–74). Cambridge, MA: MIT Press.

Graham, D. W. (2015). Heraclitus. In E. N. Zalta (Ed.), *The Stanford Encyclopedia of Philosophy* (Fall 2015 ed.). http://plato.stanford.edu/archives/fall2015/entries/heraclitus.

Hazen, M. D., & Shi, R. (2009). Argument processes, harmony and conflict in Chinese societies. *China Media Research,* 5(2), 75–88.

Hess, G. D. (2009). *Guns and butter: The economic causes and consequences of conflict.* Cambridge, MA: MIT Press.

Hewstone, M., & Greenland, K. (2000). Intergroup conflict. *International Journal of Psychology,* 35(2), 136–144.

Hu, W., Grove, C. N., & Zhuang, E. (2010). *Encountering the Chinese: A modern country, an ancient culture* (3rd ed.). Yarmouth, ME: Nicholas Brealey Publishing.

Isaacs, W. N. (1993). Taking flight: Dialogue, collective thinking, and organizational thinking. *Organizational Dynamics,* 22, 24–39.

Johannesen, R. L. (1971). The emerging concept of communication as dialogue. *Quarterly Journal of Speech,* 57, 373–382.

Kelman, H. C. (1982). Creating the conditions for Israeli-Palestinian negotiations. *Journal of Conflict Resolution,* 26(1), 39–75.

Kriesberg, L. (2004). Comparing reconciliation actions within and between countries. In Y. Bar-Siman-Tov (Ed.), *From conflict resolution to reconciliation* (pp. 81–110). Oxford, UK: Oxford University Press.

Lederach, J. P. (1997). *Building peace: Sustainable reconciliation in divided societies.* Washington, DC: United States Institute of Peace.

Lederach, J. P. (1999). *The journey toward reconciliation.* Scottdale, PA: Herald Press.

Lederach, J. P. (2003). *The little book of conflict transformation.* Intercourse, PA: Good Books.

Li, C. (2008). The ideal of harmony in ancient Chinese and Greek philosophy. *Science + Business Media,* 7, 81–98.

Li, C. (2014). *The Confucian philosophy of harmony.* New York, NY: Routledge.

Mack, J. (1990). The enemy system. In V. D. Volkan, J. V. Montville, & D. A. Julius (Eds.), *The psychodynamics of international relationships, vol. I: Concepts and theories* (pp. 83–95). Lexington, MA: Lexington Books.

Montville, J. V. (1990). The psychological roots of ethnic and sectarian terrorism. In V. D. Volkan, J. V. Montville, & D. A. Julius (Eds.), *The psychodynamics of international relationships, vol. I: Concepts and theories* (pp. 121–134). Lexington, MA: Lexington Books.

Nussbaum, M. C. (2001). *The fragility of goodness: Luck and ethics in Greek tragedy and philosophy* (Revised ed.). New York, NY: Cambridge University Press.

Pearce, W. B., & Littlejohn, S. W. (1997). *Moral conflict. When social worlds collide.* Thousand Oaks, CA: Sage.

Pettigrew, T. F. (2008). Future directions for intergroup contact theory and research. *International Journal of Intercultural Relations,* 32, 187–199.

Philipsen, G. (1992). *Speaking culturally: Explorations in social communication.* Albany, NY: State University of New York Press.

Pinker, S. (2011). *The better angels of our nature: Why violence has declined.* New York, NY: Viking.

Salomon, G. (2009). Peace education: Its nature, nurture and the challenges it faces. In J. Rivera (Ed.), *Handbook on building cultures of peace* (pp. 107–121). New York, NY: Springer.

Sandole, D. J. D. (2001). John Burton's contributions to conflict resolution theory and practice: A personal view. *International Journal of Peace Studies,* 6(1). Retrieved from: www.gmu.edu./programs/icar/ijps/vol6_1/Sandle.htm.

Saunders, H. H. (2003). Sustained dialogue in managing intractable conflict. *Negotiation Journal,* 19, 85–95.

Schein, E. H. (1993). On dialogue, culture, and organizational learning. *Organizational Dynamics,* 22(2), 40–51.

Senge, P. M. (1990). *The fifth discipline.* New York, NY: Doubleday.

Skaperdas, S., Soares, R., Willman, A., & Miller, S. C. (2009). *The costs of violence: World Bank report.* Retrieved from http://siteresources.worldbank.org/EXTSOCIALDEVELOPMENT/Resources/244362-1239390842422/6012763-1239905793229/costs_of_violence.pdf.

Staub, E. (1996). The psychological and cultural roots of group violence and the creation of caring societies and peaceful group relations. In T. Gregor (Ed.), *A natural history of peace* (pp. 129–155). Nashville, TN: Vanderbilt University Press.

Stewart, J. (1978). Foundations of dialogic communication. *Quarterly Journal of Speech,* 64, 183–201.

Stewart, J. (1983). Interpretive listening: An alternative to empathy. *Communication Education,* 32, 379–391.

Stewart, F. (2002). Root causes of violent conflict in developing countries. *British Medical Journal,* 324 (7333), 342–345.

Themnér, L., & Wallensteen, P. (2014). Armed conflicts, 1946–2013. *Journal of Peace Research,* 51(4), 541–554.

UNHCR. (2015). *World at war: UNHCR global trends – forced displacement in 2014.* Retrieved from Geneva, Switzerland: http://unhcr.org/556725e69.html.

Volkan, V. D. (1998). Ethnicity and nationalism: A psychoanalytic perspective. *Applied Psychology,* 47(1), 45–57.

Wedge, B. (1967). Psychiatry and international affairs. *Science*, 281–285.

Wei, X., & Li, Q. (2013). The Confucian value of harmony and its influence on Chinese social interaction. *Cross-Cultural Communication*, 9(1), 60–66.

Xie, M. (2012). Harmony in difference: Tension and complementarity. In M. I. Spariosu & J. R. Rüsen (Eds.), *Exploring humanity—intercultural perspectives on humanism* (pp. 181–198): Taipei, Taiwan: National Taiwan University Press.

2

A DIALOGIC APPROACH TO INTERCULTURAL CONFLICT MANAGEMENT AND HARMONIOUS RELATIONSHIPS

Dialogue, Ethics, and Culture

Yuxin Jia and Xue Lai Jia

Introduction

In the 1960s, Marshall McLuhan prophesied that, as a result of media, the world is shrinking into a global village, and now in the 21st century people in the world have become highly interrelated, interconnected, and interdependent. However, the effect of media is double-edged. On the one hand, advanced communication technologies, especially the internet, have helped to promote intercultural communication. On the other hand, they have threatened the development of human relationships. As Hoffer (2014) observed, "While the highly developed communication technology facilitates communication, miscommunication and conflicts are also facilitated" (p. xiii). Conflicts underscored by miscommunication, inappropriate behavior, and immoral attitude occur every day in the globalizing world. It is reasonable to say that the age of instant communication is also the age of instant miscommunication and conflict. However, when well managed conflicts contribute to the progress of human society. Intercultural communication scholars have developed a variety of theories and approaches to deal with the complexity of conflict management. For example, Rahim and Bonoma (1979) categorized a conflict into two basic dimensions, the concern for the self and the concern for others. Based on the two dimensions, the authors proposed five conflict management strategies, namely, integrating, obliging, dominating, avoiding, and compromising. Ting-Toomey (2005) developed the face-negotiation theory by identifying cultural, individual, and situational variables that shape an individual's face concerns and conflict strategies in social encounters. Yu and Chen (2014) addressed conflict management style in a cross-cultural organization, which focuses on the affective dimensions of cross-cultural conflict management. Moreover, Zhang and Ting-Toomey (2014) developed a multi-level social ecological framework which deals with social, cultural, historical, and ecological conflicts.

DOI: 10.4324/9781003252955-4

In our globalizing society, the more conflicts are resolved, the more they seem to result in the emergence of more conflicts. International confrontations, racial discriminations, and the fight for natural resources become common in contemporary human society. It is inevitable for people and governments to discuss possibilities for resolving these conflicts through dialogues. However, why do dialogues often fail to solve problems? The main reason is because cultural differences often prevent people from engaging others in genuine dialogue. What, then, is genuine dialogue?

It is worth noting that feminists in recent years have affirmed particular values that draw our attention to the ethical aspect of humanity. They proposed a dialogic approach, in which relationship, affection, and responsibility rather than human rights and dignity are the central concern in human interactions. This dialogic approach has emphasized the important role ethics plays in the process of intercultural interaction. In this chapter, we propose a dialogic approach that is based on the feminist dialogic ethics and that will facilitate genuine dialogue. This approach can serve as an ideal way to reach effective intercultural conflict management and establish harmonious relationships. We also argue that intercultural communication is an ethical process, in which every act is regulated by moral/ethical norms between the self and the other.

Recently, studies on intercultural ethics from communication scholars have moved beyond both the objectifying-other and the concern-for-other approaches to the level of intersubjective interaction embedded in the application of a dialogue. The dialogic approach advocates the idea of "being for both self and other." The approach further indicates that a dialogue is a dynamic and on-going process of intersubjective communication. The essence of this approach is consistent with the Confucian ethics of "the concern and responsibility for both self and other," in which all participants are interconnected, interdependent, and mutually transformed, and work together to negotiate shared meanings and explore reciprocal relationships. The approach demonstrates a promise to develop a third culture in intercultural communication (Kramsch, 1998). We believe that the dialogic approach also provides an ideal ground for the establishment of a global community, where the co-humanity can grow and the intercultural conflict can be appropriately and effectively managed.

The Modern Ethics: "Being for the Self"

The building of dialogic ethics in communication began with the reflection on and critique of the essentialist "universal" modern ethics, which is broadly characterized by the belief that "the other is not important" (Olson, 1997, p. 126), or "there is 'no other': the other is either fundamentally like me or is irrelevant" (p. 128). The ethics of modernity centers on the rights, dignity, and interests of atomistic and ego-centered individualistic self. It neglects the importance of the other, or the social and moral responsibility necessary for the value of relationship and community. The modernist universal, transcendent, and objective individualistic approach is translated into language-symbolic ethical communication and interaction underpinned by the ethics of being honest and the use of standard language which presumes "that meanings [as well as opinions, decisions, purposes, etc.] can be controlled and possessed and utterances mean what they are intended to" (Bauman, 1994, p. 217), and the claim for consensus, unity, and agreement rather than difference, diversity, particularism, and relativity in human interaction. This ethics leads to objectifying-other or the typical linear sender-to-receiver communication. It is characterized by self-domination embedded in persuading, changing, influencing, and even imposing upon others.

The essentialist universal and objective approach can also be identified with the four Gricean maxims (i.e., quantity, quality, relation, and manner), which are associated with the cooperative principle in human interaction (Grice, 1989). The four maxims are simply the application of essentialist philosophical rationality; they refer to the minimally necessary abstractions explaining the actual use of language. The rational means advocated in the Gricean maxims, which are associated with the cooperative principle, does not consider the communication behaviors of the different cultures. The Eastern high-context ambiguity or indirectness style in communication is incompatible with the Gricean maxims, as the latter do not take into consideration the Eastern negative face. The Gricean maxims also ignore human affections such as sympathy, empathy, and non-verbal behaviors that are considered by the essentialists to be embodied thus "irrational."

Postmodern Ethics: "Being for the Other"

Challenging the dichotomous "either-or" orientation is the postmodern ethics, which is constructed on the belief that the other is important in human interaction. Postmodernists advocate the ethics of care, concern, and responsibility for the other. The recognition of the importance of the other entails the notion that there is:

> a need to be attentive to that which lies beyond the margins of our identity, our concepts, our projects – that which is 'other' to me or us. Especially important here is the appreciation of how the very process of constructing, developing concepts and conceiving projects necessarily generates 'others.'
>
> *(White, 1990, p. 81)*

The postmodern ethics building began with the feminists' call for a dialogic model of communication which takes into consideration the other. The feminists emphasize humanity and the use of a language of relationship, affection, and the sense of responsibility in human interaction. As Nodding (1984) pointed out, "ethical caring, the relation in which we do meet the other morally ... [arises] ... out of natural caring – that relation in which we respond as one—caring out of love or natural inclination" (pp. 4–5). Dietz (1989) went even further to claim that the ethical care revolves more around responsibility and relationships than rights. He argued that:

> Every act should have as its ethical dimension an attempt to keep the conversation going, that is, communicative action and communication research

should have as normative aim an attempt to establish the condition for further less restrained communication.

(p. 11)

Dialogue presupposes the importance of relationship and the other. As Bhabha (1994) stated, "The other is never outside or beyond us, it emerges forcefully within the cultural discourse when we think we speak intimately and indigenously between ourselves" (p. 41). To Casmir (1997), what is required "is not merely awareness of the generation of others but the necessity to face the process or how, when and why such generations take place when we build, when we construct and when we organize" (p. 92). However, "Moderns have neglected the moral dimension, the dimension of otherness" (p. 92).

The transformation from self-enhancing to other-enhancing and from self-celebration to "the celebration of the other" (Sampson, 1993, p. 186) overcomes the objectifying-other, self-domination approach prevalent in individualism oriented Western cultures. This transformation is meritable, however, it is hardly a viable path in global society, because the recognition and practice of pluralism in it may lead to the recognition and practice of "all depends" or "dependence" rather than "interdependence" or "all for the other", which in turn causes cultural fragmentation and ethnocentrism. Cultural fragmentation refers to the lack of a common ethical standard as to what should be tolerated, respected, empathized with, and accepted. Ethnocentrism may result in the acceptance of the right of a more powerful culture that leads to cultural imposition, especially in the name of human rights.

Byram's (1989, 2008) notion of "relativize self", "value others," and "de-center" is related to the post-modern approach. The typical example for the practice is that "being for the other" ethics is the golden rule, i.e., "While being in Rome, do as Romans do." In the Chinese tradition, the practice of being modest, accommodating others, being self-effacing, and having concern for the other's face concern also falls into this category. With different emphases, they all demonstrate consideration for the other and ethical responsibility.

The Dialogic Ethics in Globalizing Society

Dialogic Interaction and the Ethics of "Being for Both Self and Other"

We propose a dialogic approach to effective conflict management and the building of a harmonious relationship in intercultural communication, which is dictated by the principle of co-humanity. This dialogic approach treats intercultural communication as a dynamic, on-going, and intersubjective process in which self and other are interrelated, interdependent, and mutually shaped, and work together to establish a harmonious relationship. The incorporation between self and other and "being for both self and other" gives meaning to the dialogic ethics proposed in this chapter. The approach challenges the essentialist ethic of "being for self", which assumes that cultural differences represent polarities by indicating a binary distinction between self and other, subject and object, local and global, east and west, human and nature, and mind and body. It also challenges the notion that communication is embedded in consensus, unity, agreement, and universality in terms of shared meanings, values, norms, behavior, and ideologies in human interaction.

Cultural meanings and symbols are not static. As Bhabha (1994) pointed out, "even the same sign can be appropriated, translated, re-historicized and read anew" (p. 41). From this perspective, self and other are expected to work together to co-create shared meanings and values. In other words, "The dialogue setting is absolutely essential" (Gibbons, 1991, p. 96). The attempt to develop a framework of the dialogic ethics is a direct response to the building of this dialogue setting from Gibbons. The framework of the dialogic ethics is based upon the following assumptions:

1. We must go beyond the ethics of "being for self" by emphasizing the ethical dimension of otherness (Casmir, 1997).
2. The development of the ethics of self-other incorporation and "concern and responsibility for both self and other" demands the ethics of "being for the other," and the realization of the assumption relies on sympathy and empathy.
3. In addition to the ethic of concern and responsibility for otherness, the framework of dialogic ethics requires the awareness of pluralism which keeps communication open in an intercultural context.
4. Keeping communication going entails of the ability to cross cultural boundaries and acknowledge differences, diversities, and cultural relativities.
5. While the dialogic approach calls for the need to appreciate, respect, and accept cultural differences, it also embraces a critical and self-reflective mind in intercultural interaction.

To summarize, the dialogic approach seeks the acknowledgment of differences, diversities, and relativities rather than consensus, agreement, conformity, and universality in global society. The new century of human society requires a global ethics that promotes genuine intercultural dialogues, and through which people can engage in an on-going negotiation to explore the intersubjective self-other and establish mutually beneficial relationships.

The Confucian Ren (仁, Humanity) as an Ideal Ground for Dialogic Ethics

The Confucian concept of ren (仁) reinterpreted and revitalized by neo-Confucians is regarded as the universal virtue under which all Chinese virtues are subsumed. This concept of ren forms the basis of the Chinese ethical system which demands unity, consistence, and coherence (Hall & Ames, 1987).

Ren (仁) means person (人) in Chinese, though with a distinct graphic form. However, it reflects one's successful status achieved through the interaction between two persons. The difference in the graphic form representing this qualitative achievement lies in the simple yet significant addition of the numeral, *two* (*er*, 二) to the pictograph person (人). The formation of the concept of *ren* by the metaphorical amplification adds three important ethical implications. First, it indicates the relatedness of self and other. That is, the self is relational. This value orientation presupposes the ethics of unity between self and other (我者与他者为一体), and the unity of self with heaven, Earth, and myriad things (天人合一) (Tu, 1998). It illustrates that self and other co-create a reciprocal and equal subject-to-subject relationship on the basis of mutual responsibility, rather than a dichotomous relationship in which the self is the center of the universe. Second, it indicates that an individual is socially expected to achieve a higher level of personhood. The achievement of the high personhood is a dynamic and on-going process, in which the self is extended to and integrated with others to attain the gradual transformation of humanity. Finally, the necessity for interaction between two persons for *ren* constitutes a ground for the development of a third culture through symbolic exchange. Only through the building of the third culture can an intercultural communication space or interculturality that facilitates open dialogues dictated by global ethics be achieved.

The Concept of *Ren* as the Embodiment of "Being for Both Self and Other"

The ethics of concern only for the self is egocentric. "Being for the other" is more desirable, but it tends to sacrifice one's own interests and rights. Hence, it is not an ideal ethical principle either. Confucius's *ren* demonstrates the embodiment of "being for both self and other" which can serve as an ideal ethical code in global society.

According to Hall and Ames (1987), in Confucian holistic humanism *ren* refers to accepting others as part of oneself, i.e., showing concern for others and making them an integral part of one's own personhood. It aims to reach the goal of mutual incorporation or togetherness between self and other. According to Hall and Ames (1987), mutual incorporation lies in Xun Zi's explication of the Confucian concept of humanity or the relationship between loving others and the self.

> The love originated by the benevolent person is a ground of mutual incorporation between the self and the other. The lowest level entails conducting oneself in such a manner as to occasion other people taking one's concerns as their own. While this is praiseworthy conduct, there is a selfishness here. The next level is for one to take the concerns of others as one's own. This is perhaps higher, but is self-effacing: one's own legitimate concerns are not served. The highest level is necessarily reflexive, incorporating in one's own person the entire field of self-other concerns.
>
> *(pp. 121–122)*

In light of Confucianism, the ideal ethics in human interaction is embedded in the responsibility and concern for others and the self. It focuses on the relationship rather than the individual right by expecting an incorporation between self and other, which shows that in Confucian holistic humanism the boundary between self and other, subject and object is blurred. As relational and communal beings, people should transcend the opposites through the extension of selves to and integration with others. In this sense, going intercultural or global is an integral part of becoming a whole person. It is the humanity that relies upon the humanity of the other, and that makes us what we are as human beings. The intercultural integration is an extension, the further development and enrichment of our cultural self, and a broader conceptualization of humanity.

Dialogic Ethics as an On-Going Self-Transformation

The dialogic ethics proposed in this chapter is embodied in the concept of *ren*, which calls for the moral transformation through ceaseless and unending self-extension to and identification with others. The ethics of "being for both self and other" entails, according to Confucius, the self-building in and through dialogic interactions. It involves a two-way transformation in the sense that the self not only influences others but also is influenced by others. As Mead (1934) indicated,

> Every individual self within the human social process of experience and behavior reflects, and is constituted by, the organized relational pattern of that process as a whole; but each individual self-structure reflects, and is constituted by, a different aspect or perspective of this relational pattern from its own unique standpoint.
>
> *(p. 201)*

> The response of the 'I' involves adaptation, but an adaptation which affects not only the self but also the social environment which helps to constitute the self; that is, it implies a view of evolution in which the individual affects the environment as well as being affected by it.
>
> *(pp. 214–215)*

This on-going self-transformation is a process of building a third culture or interculturality in which cultures and identities keep "on broadening/widening all kinds of boundaries on the one hand and on the other keeps on strengthening or firmly articulating existing boundaries" (Lie, 2003, p. 119). In this dynamic intercultural communication space, the self grows neither from the private mentality of an individual nor from its environment (Mead, 1934). In other words, the self is not something that exists first and then enters into a relationship with others. Instead, the self is regarded as an eddy in the social current and a constituent part of the current (Mead, 1934).

Mead's notion of the on-going process of self-building was further stipulated as "Each of us takes in other selves to build a self. The self in this case is thus a field of selves that results from taking in other selves and making them a part of our communal self" (Hall & Ames, 1987, pp. 118–119). A person's value is therefore measured by one's extension into and identification with other selves. That is, the value and meaning of being a person is manifest in the process of communication that constitutes a community. The quality of personhood is then a function of both the richness and diversity of contributing selves, through which the person displays the particular focus and successfully maximizes creative possibilities. Thus, the degree of one's extension and adaptation to, and integration and identification with others determines one's quality as a person (Hall & Ames, 1987). It reveals that the degree of incorporation with the other defines one's selfhood.

Finally, the key to translating this self-other incorporation ethics into practice lies in the moral principle of the dictum of "Don't do unto others what you don't want them to do unto yourself" specified by Confucius. The dictum demands the implementation of social responsibility in human interaction. As Tu (1998) quoted from Confucius, "If you want to establish yourself, you must help others to establish themselves. If you want to make yourself outstanding, you must help others to make themselves outstanding" (p. 46). Fei (2007) put it in a different way, "Better yourself, and help others to better themselves, and in so doing and only in so doing, we can better self and other together, and eventually we can do general good to the commonwealth" (p. 441). This commonwealth equates to the global community. The ethics of responsibility for both self and other as an ideal form of human relationship promotes the essence of co-humanity. It not only concerns the effective management of intercultural conflicts but also, more importantly, will decide the fate of the global community in the new century of human society.

References

Bauman, Z. (1994). Is there a postmodern sociology? *Theory, Culture, and Society*, 217, 217–237.

Bhabha, H. (1994). *The location of culture*. New York, NY: Routledge.

Birlin, I. (1990). *The cracked timber of humanity*. Princeton, NJ: Princeton University Press.

Byram, M. (1989). *Cultural studies in foreign language education*. Clevedon, UK: Multilingual Matters.

Byram, M. (2008). *From foreign language education to education for intercultural citizenship*. Clevedon, UK: Multilingual Matters.

Casmir, F. L. (Ed.). (1997). *Ethics in international and intercultural communication*. Mahwah, NJ: Lawrence Erlbaum Associates.

Dietz. M. (1989). Context is all: Feminism and theories of citizenship. In J. Conway, S. Bourque, & J. Scott (Eds.), *Learning about women: Gender, politics, & power* (pp. 1–24). Ann Arbor, MI: The University of Michigan Press.

Fei, X.-T. (2007). *On culture and cultural awareness*. Beijing, China: Qunyan Publishing House.

Gibbons, M. T. (1991). The ethic of postmodernism. *Political Theory*, 19(1), 96–102.

Grice, P. H. (1989). *Study in the way of words*. Cambridge, MA: Harvard University Press.

Guilherme, M. (2002). *Critical citizens for an intercultural world*. Clevedon, UK: Multilingual Matters.

Hall, D. L. & Ames, R. T. (1987). *Thinking through Confucius*. New York, NY: State University of New York Press.

Hoffer, B. (2014). Intercultural nonverbal communication (in)competence. In B. Hoffer *et al.* (Eds.), *Intercultural communication: East and West* (pp. 273–300). Shanghai, China: Shanghai Foreign Languages Education Press.

Jia, Y.-X. (2014). From FLT to FLE in the anthropocosmic perspective. A keynote speech delivered at international conference at Shanghai University, Shanghai, China.

Kramsch, C. (1998). *Language and culture*. Oxford, UK: Oxford University Press.

Lie, R. (2003). *Spaces of intercultural communication*. Cresskill, NJ: Hampton Press, INC.

Mead, G. H. (1934). *Mind, self, & society*. Chicago, IL: The University of Chicago Press.

Nodding, N. (1984). *Caring: A feminine approach to ethics*. Beverley, CA: University of California Press.

Olson, S. R. (1997). Encountering the other: Ethics and the role of media in international and intercultural communication. In F. L. Casmir (Ed.), *Ethics in international and intercultural communication* (pp. 123–150). Mahwah, NJ: Lawrence Erlbaum Associates.

Rahim, M. A., & Bonoma, T. V. (1979). Managing organizational conflict: A model for diagnosis and intervention. *Psychological Reports, 44*, 1323–1344.

Sampson, E. E. (1993). *Celebrating the Other: A dialogic account of human nature*. Boulder, CO: Westview Press.

Ting-Toomey, S. (2005). The matrix of face: An updated face-negotiation theory. In W. B. Gudykunst (Ed.), *Theorizing about intercultural communication* (pp. 71–92). Thousand Oaks, CA: Sage.

Tu, W.-M. (1998). The ecological turn in new Confucian humanism: Implications for China and the world. *Harvard International Review, 20*(3), 243–263.

White, S. K. (1990). Heidegger and the difficulties of postmodern ethics and politics. *Political Theory, 80*, 80–103.

Yu, T. & Chen, G. M. (2014). Intercultural sensitivity and conflict management styles in cross-cultural organizational situations. In B. Hoffer *et al.* (Eds.), *Intercultural communication: East and West* (pp. 406–422). Shanghai, China: Shanghai Foreign Languages Education Press.

Zhang, R.-F. & Ting-Toomey, S. (2014). Analyzing an intercultural conflict case study: Application of a social ecological perspective. In B. Hoffer, Y.-X. Jia, N. Honner, & L. Song (Eds.), *Intercultural communication: East and West* (pp. 381–405). Shanghai, China: Shanghai Foreign Languages Education Press.

3
CONSTITUTING INTERCULTURAL HARMONY BY DESIGN THINKING

Conflict Management in, for, and about Diversity, Equity, and Inclusion Work

Patrice M. Buzzanell

For a number of years, I've been involved in the work of diversity, equity, and inclusion (DEI) at my own and at other institutions of higher education in the United States and in Denmark. Conceptualizations of DEI vary widely but often focus on groups' or organizations' demographic compositions (diversity), on member participation and feelings of belongingness in and value to collectivities (inclusion), and on accountability for equity (Buzzanell, 2021; Klarsfeld, 2010, 2014; Roberson, 2006). Although many in the United States would profess that they believe in equality, do not differentiate in treatment of others who appear different or act dissimilarly from them, and are not biased in gendered, raced, and classed ways, research indicates that there is much evidence to the contrary (e.g., Pearce, Wald, & Ballakrishnen, 2015). These biases may include prejudices against immigrants, transsexual individuals, people having disabilities, among others, when, on the face of things, interactions appear civil and even welcoming (Muhr & Sullivan, 2013; Werbner, 2013).

Indeed, individuals who are members of underrepresented groups experience many microaggressions, defined as brief and commonplace indignities that range from being subtle and ambiguous to blatant (Sue, 2010). These acts might be neither overtly hostile nor even intentional but are products of ambivalence to difference (e.g., Fiske, 2012), with those who are subject to microaggression perceiving greater discrimination in experimental vignettes and in everyday life experiences than those without experiences in these biases and potential discriminatory behaviors (e.g., Basford, Offermann, & Behrend, 2014; Gutiérrez y Muhs, Niemann, González, & Harris, 2012). Often it is not a single act that discourages individuals' full participation in organizational and community activities but a series of seemingly small injustices that accumulate over time and that prompt individuals to leave their workplaces and express dissatisfaction (Gutiérrez y Muhs et al., 2012; Sue, Alsaidi, Awad, Glaeser, Calle, & Mendez 2021; Valian, 1998).

DOI: 10.4324/9781003252955-5

If most people in the United States profess to be unbiased and believe that they are acting with good intent toward others, then why does there continue to be overt and covert attitudes and differential treatment toward others who are different from members of privileged groups? Indeed, rational approaches toward mitigating detrimental effects and enhancing the benefits of diversity and inclusion have invested heavily in transformational scholarship and interventions. These rational approaches recommend remedies including training to explain the causes and effects of biases, to show how groups cannot innovate and achieve competitive advantage without incorporation of diversity, and to bolster commitment by showing how increased excellence and enrollments in colleges and universities cannot be achieved without recognition by faculty, staff, and administrators that the status quo no longer exists. Most of these approaches are based on the idea that increasing numbers of under-represented group members would solve the problems without changing interactions, what is valued, and organizational culture (see Buzzanell, 1995; Hearit & Buzzanell, 2016). Although these programs have had some return on investment— often because of strengthening the attitudes and behaviors of those who already subscribe to diversity and inclusion—such approaches fail to address the underlying causes and to produce and sustain intercultural harmony. In this chapter, I first discuss why I believe that (a) diversity and inclusion are wicked problems. I then provide (b) a mini case study of diversity and inclusion as a wicked problem, and conclude by describing how scholars can engage in (c) constituting inclusion and accountability toward equity through the design lens of intercultural harmony.

My goal is to walk through thinking and support for a different way of processing diversity, equity, and inclusion such that deeper and more sustainable solutions can be reached. I contend that intercultural harmony is a key lens through which DEI efforts can be achieved. Intercultural harmony work requires dialogic efforts, including constant attention and growth of mindfulness to order, balance, respect, well-being, sensitivity to and empathy with others, and obligations to self and others. Intercultural harmony work addresses DEI because these efforts do not have smooth trajectories nor are they end products. Rather, DEI is a *process* that is contested, constrained, embraced, and embodied. Even so, mindfulness and efforts to grow in harmony are insufficient. Intercultural harmony work for DEI also requires acknowledgment that difference is often enacted as a wicked problem and thus requires design thinking and a constitutive communicative approach (see Buzzanell, Eddington, Pyatovskaya, & Mestrovich Seay, in press; Eddington, Corple, Buzzanell, Zoltowski, & Brightman, 2020).

Diversity and Inclusion as Wicked Problems

As mentioned already, rational approaches constructed to broaden participation directly involve: online training, networking, participating in mandatory workshops, engaging in educational seminars, and so on. Yet, the fundamental reasons behind low diversity and inclusion remain. In a nutshell, the typical arguments and solutions remain ineffective because diversity and inclusion seem to operate as wicked problems or intractable conflicts. This means that interventions typically do not address the deep seated nature of the issues. To develop this argument, I discuss: (a) differentiating and understanding conflict in diversity and inclusion work, and (b) framing diversity and inclusion as wicked problems.

Differentiating and Understanding Conflict in Diversity and Inclusion Work

In this section, conceptualizations of diversity, inclusion, and intersectionalities are provided. For a start, diversity and inclusion are different. The forms that they take in particular contexts diverge based on socio-historical, political economic, and cultural reasons (Eddington et al., 2020; Klarsfeld, 2010, 2014). Diversity is often discussed as representation, with a focus on the numbers or proportion of different categories of people based on their social identities and membership groups. Complexities in representation arise because individuals are not easily categorized (e.g., racial and ethnic classifications in the United States). Complexities also arise as one moves from context to context where different identities matter and where policies that are designed for particular groups produce ironic consequences, including opposite results from those that were desired (Klarsfeld, 2010, 2014). In large part such outcomes happen because attention to numbers and representation in key units neglects to attend to the fundamental reasons where there might be inequality. These reasons include instances when people are treated as members of monolithic groups lacking variation and when efforts are missing or ineffective in creating infrastructures, rewards, and cultures that promote feelings of and actions associated with belongingness.

Feelings and actions aligned with belongingness create inclusion. Here, individuals who are considered different in some respect are not only invited but also sought out and encouraged to participate in formal and informal gatherings and activities. Moreover, community members take it upon themselves to insure that others know that they are valued, are not left out, and are provided with the support that they need to be successful. Inclusion means that individuals have a voice in discussions and that their points of view and shared experiences, especially when different from those with more mainstream experiences and identities, are taken seriously and considered in deliberations. Similar to the ethical stances recounted by other speakers at the 2014 International Conference of Intercultural Communication, hosted by Shanghai Normal University, inclusion works toward intercultural harmony and dialogue (e.g., Jia, 2014). Inclusion is an ongoing process that shifts as individuals learn more about themselves and others as well as the context. Inclusion is more than representation and surface understanding that everyone is a cultural being. Inclusion is the moral imperative to take into consideration diverse people's standpoints, understanding that these are politicized discussions where the meanings being constructed might differ radically from those espoused by the majority of members. Moreover inclusion is an ongoing process—not a singular problem to be solved through interventions that address only one facet of the issue. Thus, inclusion requires divergent thinking, acceptance of contradiction and ambivalence, and an understanding that issues regarding difference evolve as solutions are tested and evaluated.

Inclusion necessitates an intersectionality lens because difference is never simply one factor in life (for difference, see Allen, 2011; Mumby, 2010; Putnam, Jahn, & Baker, 2011). Coined by Crenshaw (1988, 1989/1993, 1991), the term intersectionality/ intersectionalities was developed originally to depict and parse out how different identity categories interlocked, became additive, and/or were more or less con-sequential to processes and outcomes in particular contexts. Crenshaw examined how racism and sexism affected legal cases, particularly violence, and failed to account for compound marginalizations. In all discussions of intersectionality, core com-mitments and analyses involve critique, power, praxis, embodiment, and change (Davis, 2008; Dhamoon, 2011; Holvino, 2010). Intersectionality explores women's lives, as well as men's (Wingfield, 2009) and the societal structures that mutually construct and maintain power imbalances. As Bilge (2010) puts it:

> Intersectionality reflects a transdisciplinary theory aimed at apprehending the complexity of social identities and inequalities through an *integrated approach*. It refutes the compartmentalization and hierarchization of the great axes of social differentiation through categories of gender/sex, class, race, ethnicity, disability and sexual orientation.
>
> *(p. 58)*

An intersectionality lens invites explication of simultaneous, multiple, interacting, situated identities within structures of power and privilege. It considers power struggles nested within and surfacing as primary in particular contexts. It offers possibilities for disruption of power and deconstruction of civilities that mask discriminatory behavior and structures (Bilge, 2010; Collins, 2000; Werbner, 2013).

The important lesson of intersectionality for our discussion is that individuals are both marginalized and privileged by their group membership. An intersectionality lens enables us to examine how people are both privileged and marginalized by providing nuanced and complicated ways of parsing out what has happened in specific situations. An intersectionality lens draws upon the bases of diversity as representation and inclusion as belongingness in different ways.

Although the complexities of diversity and inclusion can be understood and studied through an intersectionality lens, scholars and practitioners advocating diversity and inclusion often seem no closer to achieving their goals than others were decades ago, meaning that there are other processes to consider. From the representation or numbers standpoint, there are still few women and underrepresented group members at the top of corporations, known as the glass ceiling effect and its many variations (Buzzanell, 1995); from an inclusion standpoint, the interests, concerns, and values of marginalized groups still tend to be discounted, trivialized, or ignored unless these are recognized as having market value. A different entrée point into the conundrum of diversity and inclusion thinking and strategies is to consider these processes to be wicked problems.

Framing Diversity and Inclusion as Wicked Problems

Wicked problems are typically considered to be intractable problems the solutions and contexts of which are so deeply interdependent as to mean that efforts to solve one aspect make visible and/or give rise to other problems (see http://en. wikipedia.org/wiki/Wicked_problem; see also Conklin, 2006; Fyke & Buzzanell, 2013; Rittel & Webber, 1973). Wicked problems involve deeply embedded contradictions that encompass seemingly incompatible values. The shape of problems varies insofar as they reoccur in different forms, cannot be resolved with simple solutions, and resist change. Often, they are not understood or even envisioned as wicked until a solution has been attempted and the deep-rooted nature of problems and their political implications becomes apparent. For example wicked problems typify the intertwined grand challenges people face: poverty, climate change, food unsustainability and famine, clean water, land disputes, energy, and global population spread and life requirements. These challenges play out globally and locally (e.g., Dougherty, 2011). What would seem to be simple solutions—namely, to provide resources to underserved parts of the world—can promote short- and long-term consequences that become ironic insofar as they do not deal with even the surface problems and prove detrimental because they may change the nature of societies and cultures in unforeseen, detrimental, and irreversible ways (see Ting-Toomey, 2011).

With regard to the communicative underpinnings of wicked problems, the language used to discuss assumptions and issues must frame situations in helpful, complicated, political, and/or contradictory ways. If language is not carefully selected and used, it might exacerbate the problem. As a case in point, Fyke and Buzzanell (2013) describe ethical leadership development as wicked insofar as "dealing with ethical dilemmas by training leaders to be more ethical through particular ideological lenses can, itself, become 'wicked'" (p. 1622). They note that discussions about Enron highlight how requirements for efficiency and return on investment were perceived and practiced as oppositional to transparency and ethical conduct. As Fyke and Buzzanell (2013) found in their study of ethical leadership development in a consultancy centered on the global movement and strategy for competitive advantage called Conscious Capitalism (e.g., www.consciouscap italism.org), the microdiscourses or everyday talk and interaction undermined the macrodiscourses and espoused values of social change, ethics, equality, and conscious behavior to develop a better world:

> Specifically, the consultants and leaders simultaneously appropriate the language of capitalism (i.e., competition, free markets) while trying to subvert it in some ways through a focus on mindfulness, care, and concern. However, we argue that this subversion is necessary but insufficient for dealing with the ideological constructions that promote dominant power interests.
>
> (p. 1633)

The issue here is that a focus on solutions without understanding as fully as possible the underlying interests, values, cultural beliefs, and contradictions that produce the problem means that problems become wicked with those involved sometimes becoming increasingly discouraged as systemic considerations become apparent and magnified.

The issue here also is that many wicked problems such as issues of diversity and inclusion are, by their very nature, intractable conflicts (see Gray, Coleman, & Putnam, 2007). What might seem to pose a simple problem with a fairly easy solution becomes fixed over time. Intractable conflicts are protracted, persistent, destructive, and deeply rooted in ideological and material structures. Because they reoccur, they become so entrenched that they seem normative. Not only do wicked problems encompass the qualities of intractable conflicts but they are also manifest communicatively as phenomena where people face simultaneous demands to act in oppositional ways because there are seemingly incompatible meaning systems. For instance, one way of looking at the typical diversity and inclusion interventions is to align with the conscious or unconscious assumption that the majority of members who promote diversity and inclusion willingly forfeit the benefits of their privilege in society so that others also may reap these advantages. Similarly, organizations benefit from the primacy of work and the calling as optimal career mentality in U.S. employees' lives and thinking despite talk about and policies promoting work and personal life balance (see Buzzanell, 2012; Kirby & Buzzanell, 2014). Even when organizational members recognize the benefits of sustainable work-personal life balance and strive to incorporate work-life and work-family practices into workplaces, seemingly incompatible ethics of justice and care can manifest themselves in different ways from boss-employee conflicts to lack of policy use (Liu & Buzzanell, 2004; Kirby & Krone, 2002).

Structures and everyday discourses along with the attendant materialities are reproduced because they are deeply layered in everyday life. With regard to diversity efforts, the discourses and materialities that resist representational and inclusionary efforts produce and are produced by inequity regimes (see Acker, 2006). Rules for social practices are reproduced by and reproduce structures (called structurational divergence, see Nicotera & Clinkscales, 2010; Nicotera & Mahon, 2013; Nicotera, Mahon, & Zhao, 2010). Breaking these cycles involves changing the rules, which also means changing social practices and structures.

As one example, Wingfield and Alston (2014) illustrate how whiteness is privileged in numerous ways including how people of color reinforce the status quo through doing "racial tasks" that reinforce racial hierarchies within organizations and broader society. Using this case and others, I argue that diversity and inclusion can be considered a "wicked problem." This contention addresses the question of why diversity and inclusion are so difficult to understand and remedy despite millions of dollars, decades of different efforts on multiple levels, and being localized through massive campaigns (e.g., training sessions, networking, organizational policy and reward system changes, national and professional association mandates). Thus, I argue that diversity and inclusion are wicked problems for which the typical remedies and analyses fail to uncover and address the deep-seated contradictions and power dynamics. As a result, individuals and collectivities continue to do "more of the same" (Watzlawick, Beavin, & Jackson, 1967). Their good intentions and sufficient observable successes continue in programs but without iterative and substantive changes that could lessen the inequities underlying the need for diversity and inclusion. They believe that they have addressed the problem without realizing that the multifaceted issues require sustained transformation processes. They believe that they have addressed the manifestations that they have identified as the problem. They do not continue to ask questions and render the environment suitable for strategies and multiple design cycles (Grint, 2005).

Mini Case Study of Diversity and Inclusion as a Wicked Problem

For the purposes of this chapter, I provide a brief case study that highlights the everyday discourse or talk in interaction that constructs and supports the lack of diversity and inclusion in particular contexts. I also invoke the macrodiscourses or cultural formations, called Discourses, that sustain dominant interests by making particular interpretations seem reasonable and natural (Alvesson & Kärreman, 2011; Fairhurst & Putnam, 2014). These distinctions between discourses and Discourses make it appear as though there are only micro and macro constructions of social realities being constituted communicatively, however there are in fact many intersecting and overlapping layers to the discursive construction of realities. Moreover, Kuhn et al. (2008; see also Kisselburgh, Berkelaar Van Pelt, & Buzzanell, 2009) note that discourses and Discourses act as resources that can frame past and current events for self and others' interpretations and guide our own constructions of individuals, experiences, occupations, and institutions.

This case study is set within the context of higher education, particularly the professional and institutional environment of diversity and inclusion in the United States. Specifying this setting is important because diversity and inclusion have different meanings and strategies throughout the world and in diverse sectors (e.g., Klarsfeld, 2010, 2014). Academic institutional contexts operate within different employability, career, and reward structures such that, at least in the contemporary U.S. promotion and tenure systems, those in professorial ranks who have the most structural power hold—at least in principle if not always in practice—particular academic freedoms, autonomies, and intellectual capitals (Bailyn, 1993; Valian, 1998)—making academe both unique and representative of diversity and inclusion issues.

In U.S. academe, diversity and inclusion efforts focus on gender, race and ethnicity, nationality, religion, sexual-social orientation, amidst other differences and intracategorial differences (e.g., women and men of color; instructors holding advanced degrees who are not in tenure-track lines; status according to academic rank and in institutions listed as research intensive or through other Carnegie designations). Diversity and inclusion research indicates that there can be chilly climates for women faculty, especially women of color and those in male-dominated occupations such as engineering, but that women faculty sometimes collude with and resist their marginalizations (e.g., Buzzanell, Long, Kokini, Anderson, & Batra, 2015; Fotaki, 2013; Kossek, Dumas, Piszczek, & Allen, 2021; Maranto & Griffin, 2011; van den Brink & Benschop, 2012).

To develop this case, I use a discursive lens to provide an entrée into the wicked nature of diversity and inclusion and to specify the different aspects of problem identification including power dynamics. In doing so, I first provide some examples from data gathered by one of my research teams whose members interviewed male engineers about the inclusion of women in their professions (Arendt, Dohrman, Buzzanell, Rajan, O'Connor, Litera, & Armstrong, 2014). While espousing equality, these men simultaneously undermined these values thus indicating that diversity and inclusion are not singular problems but a series of interconnected and nested problems that are both ideological (e.g., equality set within a neocapitalistic, highly competitive system rewarding the "best") and practical (e.g., people do not see what they are saying). For example, different men in the interview set who are training to become professional engineers passed remarks on the diversity and inclusion efforts, especially the recruitment and retention of women in their fields, as follows and as reported in Arendt et al. (2014):

> usually the criteria for women is a little lower than men, to help get more women into the field.
>
> See I think, again, myself, I'm not very gender-biased. I mean there are certain things which women are better at, but I think still, I would like to be a gender neutral environment.
>
> Because, sure you can have a lot of people, but I think quality is more important that quantity. So if they're [women] not interested, maybe they shouldn't be in it [engineering] in the first place.

Without going into too much elaboration, suffice it to say that these quotes and the remainder of these men's interviews indicate that male engineering students from the United States and from around the globe believe that women have different interests, skills, and abilities from men. They see recruitment and retention efforts regarding women in engineering not only as attempts to increase the numbers or representation of women (quantity) but also as having negative consequences for the quality of engineering work and their own university's and cohort's reputation as excellent and distinctive. Their references to quality also mean that they believe that the "criteria for women" are lower for women's admission into engineering studies than for men. Because they believe that criteria are lower, they also believe that the women who enter programs are not sufficiently trained, deserving, and/or motivated to excel in engineering.

Moreover, they believe that members of particular social identity groups, such as women, who need to be recruited into particular fields, such as engineering, do not deserve to be members. Their reasoning is that they themselves did not need to be explicitly sought out and encouraged to apply to, select, and remain in engineering studies. Therefore, they are more deserving of their place within engineering than those for whom the field is perceived as a forced choice, that is, not their preference or first inclination. They perceive these women to be taking the seats—literally and figuratively—of men who deserve, desire, and appreciate the opportunity to study and practice engineering. As a result, if women are "not interested, maybe they [women] shouldn't be in it [engineering] in the first place."

Despite the verbatim quotes listed above and the accompanying analyses, these men explicitly espouse the values of equality. By noting that admissions and retention criteria should be based on merit, interest, and quality within gender-neutral environments, they do not recognize or acknowledge that their own interests in engineering have been cultivated by teachers, parents, and other socialization agents. They also disregard the training that they have received on the benefits of diversity and inclusion for engineering disciplines and for design outcomes. They most likely are unaware of the fact that women engineers in their program have met higher admissions requirements than they themselves had to meet for entrée into this College of Engineering (e.g., Holloway, 2013). They would not recognize how their own behavior might push women away from engineering.

Constituting Inclusion through the Design Lens of Intercultural Harmony

The mini case of men in engineering provides an empirical example of how individuals say and believe one thing, but expose what they value and how these values and beliefs influence everyday action in their talk and interactions. In design thinking, when explicating interests and needs, problem specifications, and other aspects of problem setting phases of diversity and inclusion work, scholars and practitioners examine not only what people say that they want to accomplish in their design processes but also what they do not say or do not perceive to be the underlying interests in their desired end state. For example, when members of rural Ghanaian villages with which my Purdue engineering design team connected, the Ghanaian members, or potential "users" of the designs, said that they wanted their village water pumps fixed (see Buzzanell, 2014). Yet the problem was not simply that the pumps needed to be fixed. There were multiple nested problems: the water was insufficient in volume for village needs; the water had not been tested for quality; the depth to which the well had been dug was not deep enough to access below-surface water repositories; the materials with which the apparatus for pumping water were made were valuable meaning that they were often stolen from surrounding villages; the daily hand pumping of water was politically charged insofar as one villager had the key to the pump and residents were regulated according to timetables for water distribution; and so on. As a result, villagers used surface water for cooking and other uses. This surface water dried up during dry seasons of the year and was in the area through which people and animals travelled to get to the other side of the standing water.

Similarly problem specification and user connections in human-centered design work for diversity and inclusion require a deep understanding of the people who are both marginalized and privileged in their particular contexts as well as the social and technical complexities that they face (Buzzanell, 2014; Zoltowski, Oakes, & Cardella, 2012; for overview, see Radcliffe & Fosmire, 2014). In the problem setting and problem solving iterations of design work, multiple and unanticipated points surface that must be unraveled and dealt with to even begin to understand how to develop alternative solutions, prototypes, and strategies (Eddington et al., 2020). During these phases, design thinking and accomplishment relies upon ambiguity, tensions between discourses and materialities, human and non-human or material agents, empathy, and ethical stances (e.g., see Barley, Leonardi, & Bailey, 2012; Buzzanell et al., in press; Zoltowski et al., 2012). In other words, to design productively for DEI efforts, a constitutive approach must be taken.

Diversity Work as Constitutive

To address the fundamental incompatibilities between what people might say, the values they espouse and believe, and the conflicts, ironies, and political dynamics in particular contexts, it is necessary to adopt a constitutive approach in order to delve into the underlying assumptions and processes that are found within language, cultural formations, and interactions within contexts (for communication as constitutive, see Putnam & Boys, 2006). In the communication as "constitutive of social realities" approach, there are several characteristics and assumptions. These include: talk and interaction bring realities into being; the focus is on the production of meanings in social action; participants rely on mindfulness that communication is always contextually, politically, and materially situated; human and non-human agents act upon each other (e.g., non-human agents might be promotion documents, design records, and so on); and human agents subscribe to understandings that the ambiguities, contradictions, and logics of difference in which order and disorder co-influence each other tend to operate as significant analytical frames as being normal and productive (e.g., Ashcraft, Kuhn, & Cooren, 2009; Brummans, Cooren, Robichaud, & Taylor, 2014; Brummans, Hwang, & Cheong, 2013; Robichaud & Cooren, 2011).

In taking a constitutive approach, findings from research and everyday lived experience regarding diversity and inclusion in academe can be pieced together and start to make sense. For instance, the men in engineering had participated in training and cohort orientation meetings that delineated the efforts toward and benefits of diversity and inclusion, particularly for encouraging the retention of women engineers. Although their language indicates that they "get it" at an intellectual level and for rational reasons (i.e., prestige of their cohort and program, innovativeness, diverse team work for employability), at the emotional and "irrational" or contradictory levels, they voiced quite different preferences and attitudes about women in engineering. Thus, they indicate that they engage in unintentional microaggressions that may harm efforts to build cultures of and policies for inclusion (e.g., Bond & Haynes, 2014), especially if not counteracted by majority allies for change and women and/or minorities in engineering programs or learning communities.

In this regard, training developed to increase diversity and promote inclusionary cultures can backfire when people believe detrimental stereotypes are common (and thus are perceived as socially acceptable), or when they are instructed not to think about stereotypes and difference (thus prompting individuals to be hyperaware of and enact bias; e.g., Duguid and Thomas-Hunt's experiments, reported in Grant & Sandberg, 2014, from *The International New York Times*). In other words, they can continue to constitute realities such that they are not the problem and even if they are biased, the context in which they live and work are the sites that warrant change, although such change would be difficult to accomplish. Furthermore, in online contexts such as job candidate selection and fit, when hiring staff personnel believe that they can act fairly and not think about certain identity categories, they become hypersensitive and act in biased ways (e.g., Berkelaar & Buzzanell, 2014, 2015).

Moreover, taking diversity work as constitutive means that people typically frame the need for diversity along the lines of morality, demography, and pragmatic or economic reasons (for legitimacy discourse, see Green, Li, & Nohria, 2009; Suchman, 1995; Suddaby & Greenwood, 2005). For instance, the comments made by the men in engineering implied that diversity and inclusion efforts were morally right and that they agreed with such efforts in principle (thus understanding the socially acceptable nature of their position). Yet these areas of morality, demography, and pragmatic or economic reasons tend not to delve into the multiple privileges, including white and male privilege, that male members of the academy may experience but not recognize because they are invisible and acknowledging them would mean that these men did not do anything to earn such privileges (e.g., Foster, 2013; Gutiérrez y Muhs et al., 2012).

These frames for diversity and inclusion needs may not be effective. This is not to say that these frames are not valuable and often provide persuasive rationales and legitimization criteria for diversity and inclusion work, but there are unaddressed dynamics. For instance arguments about what to do may be expressed through stories of unique exemplars couched as proof of diversity and inclusion intervention success (for a classic study on tokens and structural barriers to gender and diversity, see Kanter, 1977). Sometimes these frames link morality+demography+organizational success in ways that provide "feel good stories," such as cases where underrepresented group members succeed despite the odds, and where remedies for inequality are readily available and are used by members of dominant groups. In the case of men in engineering, their quotes attest to beliefs that educational environments such as engineering are "gender neutral," regardless of empirical evidence to the contrary.

As a final example, structures and D/discourses are constituted in every action and interaction, yet are malleable enough to open possibilities for change. In the United States, policies undergo revisions to best suit changing interests and needs with language and the policy formation process constituting quality of life and reasonable accommodations for individuals. The constitutive and design processes that have prompted changes designed to make workplaces more inclusive and family friendly actually enhance quality of work life for all members (e.g., Kanter & Roessner, 2003a, 2003b) and are desired especially by members of the Millennial generation (e.g., O'Connor & Raile, 2015) and increasingly by male scientists and engineers (Damaske, Ecklund, Lincoln, & White, 2014). Even so, although policies have been devised and implemented, employees might be wary of using them for fear of career disruption, business flow, and being marked as different (e.g., Kirby & Krone, 2002). Often the logics, language, and underlying assumptions are contradictory with caregivers' arguments for leaves that accommodate their interests and needs aligned with the ethics of care and their supervisors' logic aligned with the ethics of justice and managerialism, resulting in perceived inabilities to negotiate leaves (Liu & Buzzanell, 2004).

Designing Diversity and Inclusion for Equity

As one means of moving forward in diversity and inclusion efforts, I suggest that communication scholars and practitioners might view DEI as a design issue that incorporates intercultural harmony (see Buzzanell et al., in press). In this next section, I speak specifically about designing DEI and accountability practices to incorporate intercultural harmony.

Design practices consider problem setting and problem solving as iterative, recursive processes in which attempts at solutions often begin with practical phases such as identifying "user" interests and problem specifications. In these practices, designers work within specific contexts and ideally develop alternative and tested solution prototypes not simply "for" but "with" those for whom the designs are being developed. In short, design is a constitutive, messy process that starts and stops, restarts, and incorporates social and technical processes (Bucciarelli, 1996, 2010; Dossick & Neff, 2011; Radcliffe & Foxmire, 2014). As such, it is ideally suited to the sometimes irrational, complex nature of diversity and inclusion.

To engage in design thinking requires different mindsets and processes than are typically utilized in diversity and inclusion efforts. These mindsets and processes are generative, incorporate lessons from failures, embrace complexity, and keep prototyping and redesigning as people and contexts change (see Cross, 2008, 2011; Cross, Christiaans, & Dorst, 1996; Dorst, 2011; Dorst & Cross, 2001; IDEO, 2016). In human-centered or empathic design, there is movement from seeing design solely as solving problems using technical expertise to focusing on potential users as the sources of and co-experts in design processes (see Zoltowski, Oakes, & Cardella, 2012). As designs become more human-centered, designers gain greater understanding of potential users and of the context in all its multifaceted complexities—to the point where one achieves harmony. In design, harmony is not an end state, but a dynamic process that always requires more work to increase understanding, involves co-design with "users," creates empathic and ethical sensibilities and responses iteratively and dialogically (see also Kulich, 2014). Ideally, design should be a process of making parties vulnerable by questioning their reasons, historical-cultural understanding, and rich context as designers enter the worlds of users and of themselves as designers and situated human beings.

Because the rational solutions to diversity and inclusion have produced relatively few and sometimes ironic consequences, we look to design to develop different ways of achieving intercultural harmony. First, because of the contradictory results

of bias training, communication scholars can engage in effective message production by communicating that particular biases and associated actions are undesirable
and negative. After noting that all people experience stereotypes and biases, trainers
can conclude with statements like the "vast majority of people try to overcome
their stereotypic preconceptions" and can provide direct advice such as "don't
judge certain groups of people based on race or national origin." Trainers can
reinforce ideas that people want to conquer their biases and that there are benefits
to doing so (e.g., most people don't want to discriminate, and trainees should not
do so either; Grant & Sandberg, 2014). Encouraging people to correct their biases
can change the ways people view themselves and their agency.

Second, designing for intercultural harmony requires mindfulness (see Ting-
Toomey, 2014) and *guanxi* and *mianzi*. Servaes (2014) writes:

> It is fair to conclude that, in order to avoid conflict and strive for "harmony",
> *guanxi* (inter-relationships) and *mianzi* (face) are regarded as the two wings of
> harmony. In other words, "*guanxi* forms the structural pattern of the Chinese
> social fabric and mianzi is the operational mechanism that connects the nodes
> of *guanxi* network.
>
> *(Chen & Starosta, 1997, p. 5)*

These processes require active handling of conflict to achieve mutually acceptable solutions so that the long-term positive relationships can be sustained
(Leung et al., 2011). This active handling of conflicts means that disputes and
disagreements do not become intractable conflicts. Also, active handling means
that conflict is anticipated and built into design processes. Thus diversity and
inclusion work should include conflict management training, with mentoring
on how to enact inclusion every day, all the time. Mentoring would involve
formal systems for legitimacy, informal mentoring for relationships, and episodic
or spontaneous mentoring for the just-in-time support and insights that create
bonds of colleagiality and inclusion (Long, Buzzanell, Anderson, Batra, Kokini,
& Wilson, 2014).

Closing

Many of the speakers at the 2014 Shanghai Normal University Conference on
Intercultural Communication delved into intercultural conflict management from
similar stances albeit with different theoretical bases and constructs. For example,
the design processes as described in my chapter are inherently dialogic. These
processes resemble Jia's (2014) multicultural ethics, described as being for togetherness between self and other as a challenge to essentialist notions (being for self)
of ethics. Togetherness ethics are grounded in processes and creativity in which
boundaries are blurred and offer transformative spaces (Jia, 2014). In embracing
these ethics and dialogic assumptions, individuals and collectivities can better
understand the lack or failures of diversity and inclusion efforts not as isolated

problems but as wicked problems. At this point, diversity and inclusion can become DEI efforts that can require design thinking and activity to create and sustain truly inclusionary, harmonious, equitable, and accountable cultures (see Buzzanell, 2021; Buzzanell et al., in press).

References

Acker, J. (2006). Inequality regimes: Gender, class, and race in organizations. *Gender & Society*, 20, 441–464.

Allen, B.J. (2011). *Difference matters: Communicating social identity* (2nd ed.). Long Grove, IL: Waveland.

Alvesson, M., & Kärreman, D. (2011). Organizational discourse analysis—well done or too rare? A reply to our critics. *Human Relations*, 64, 1193–1202.

Arendt, C., Dohrman, R., Buzzanell, P. M., Rajan, P., O'Connor, E., Litera, N., & Armstrong, C. (2014, November 22). *Discourses of elitism and exclusion: Relating engineering self-efficacy and subtle sexism.* Paper presented to the Organizational Communication Association Division of the National Communication Association Conference held in Chicago, IL, November 19–23.

Ashcraft, K., Kuhn, T., & Cooren, F. (2009). Constitutional amendments: "Materializing" organizational communication. *The Academy of Management Annals*, 3(1), 1–64.

Bailyn, L. (1993). *Breaking the mold: Women, men, and time in the new corporate world.* New York, NY: The Free Press.

Barley, W., Leonardi, P., & Bailey, D. (2012). Engineering objects for collaboration: Strategies of ambiguity and clarity at knowledge boundaries. *Human Communication Research*, 38, 280–308.

Basford, T., Offermann, L., & Behrend, T. (2014). Do you see what I see? Perceptions of gender microaggressions in the workplace. *Psychology of Women Quarterly*, 38, 340–349.

Berkelaar, B., & Buzzanell, P. M. (2014). Cybervetting, person-environment fit, and personnel selection: Employers' surveillance and sensemaking of job applicants' online information. *Journal of Applied Communication Research*, 42, 456–476.

Berkelaar, B., & Buzzanell, P. M. (2015). Online employment screening and digital career capital: Exploring employers' use of online information for personnel selection. *Management Communication Quarterly*, 29, 84–113.

Bilge, S. (2010). Recent feminist outlooks on intersectionality. *Diogenes*, 225, 58–72.

Bond, M., & Haynes, M. (2014). Workplace diversity: A social-ecological framework and policy implications. *Social Issues and Policy Review*, 8, 167–201.

Brummans, B., Cooren, F., Robichaud, D., & Taylor, J. (2014). Approaches to the communicative constitution of organizations. In L. Putnam & D. Mumby (Eds.), *The Sage handbook of organizational communication: Advances in theory, research, and methods* (3rd ed., pp. 173–194). Los Angeles, CA: Sage.

Brummans, B., Hwang, J., & Cheong, P. (2013). Mindful authoring through invocation: Leaders' constitution of a spiritual organization. *Management Communication Quarterly*, 27(3), 346–372.

Bucciarelli, L. (1996). *Designing engineers.* Cambridge, MA: MIT Press.

Bucciarelli, L. (2010). Ethics and engineering education. *European Journal of Engineering Education*, 33, 141–149.

Buzzanell, P. M. (2011). Interrogating culture. *Intercultural Communication Studies*, 20(1), 1–16.

Buzzanell, P. M. (2012). How can we sustain commitments to the work and personal aspects of our lives? In A. Goodboy & K. Shultz (Eds.), *Introduction to communication studies:*

Translating communication scholarship into meaningful practice (pp. 317–323). Dubuque, IA: Kendall-Hunt.

Buzzanell, P. M. (2021). Designing feminist resilience. In S. Eckert & I. Bachmann (Eds.), *Reflections on feminist communication and media scholarship: Theory, method, impact* (pp. 43–58). Routledge.

Buzzanell, P. M. (2014). Reflections on global engineering design and intercultural competence: The case of Ghana. In X. D. Dai & G. M. Chen (Eds.), *Intercultural communication competence: Conceptualization and its development in contexts and interactions* (pp. 315–334). Newcastle upon Tyne, UK: Cambridge Scholars Publishing.

Buzzanell, P. M., Long, Z., Kokini, K., Anderson, L., & Batra, J. (2015). Mentoring in academe: Taking a feminist poststructural lens on stories of women engineering faculty of color. *Management Communication Quarterly, 29*, 440–457.

Buzzanell, P. M., Eddington, S., Pyatovskaya, E., & Mestrovich Seay, A. (in press). Design thinking and design communication for intercultural conflict management. In D. Busch (Ed.), *The Routledge handbook of intercultural mediation*. Routledge.

Chen, G. M., & Starosta, W. (1997). Chinese conflict management and resolution: Overview and implications. *Intercultural Communication Studies, 7*, 1–13.

Collins, P. H. (2000). *Black feminist thought: Knowledge, consciousness, and the politics of empowerment.* New York, NY: Routledge.

Conklin, J. (2006). *Dialogue mapping: Building shared understanding of wicked problems.* Chichester, UK: Wiley.

Crenshaw, K. W. (1988). Race, reform, and retrenchment: Transformation and legitimation in antidiscrimination law. *Harvard Law Review, 101*, 1331–1387.

Crenshaw, K. (1989/1993). Demarginalizing the intersection of race and sex: A black feminist critique of antidiscrimination doctrine, feminist theory and antiracist politics. In D. K. Weisberg (Ed.), *Feminist legal theory: Foundations* (pp. 383–395). Philadelphia, PA: Temple University Press.

Crenshaw, K. (1991). Mapping the margins: Intersectionality, identity politics, and violence against women of color. *Stanford Law Review, 43*, 1241–1299.

Cross, N. (2008). *Designerly ways of knowing.* Basel, Switzerland: Birkhauser.

Cross, N. (2011). *Design thinking: Understanding how designers think and work.* London, UK: Bloomsbury Academic.

Cross, N., Christiaans, H., & Dorst, K. (Eds.). (1996). *Analysing design activity.* Chichester, UK: John Wiley & Sons.

Damaske, S., Ecklund, E., Lincoln, A., & White, V. (2014). Male scientists' competing devotions to work and family: Changing norms in a male-dominated profession. *Work and Occupations, 41*, 477–507.

Davis, K. (2008). Intersectionality as buzzword: A sociology of science perspective on what makes a feminist theory successful. *Feminist Theory, 9*, 67–85.

Dougherty, D. S. (2011). *The reluctant farmer: An exploration of work, social class, and the production of food.* Leicester, UK: Troubador.

Dhamoon, R. K. (2011). Considerations on mainstreaming intersectionality. *Political Research Quarterly, 64*, 230–243.

Dorst, K. (2011). The core of "design thinking" and its application. *Design Studies, 32*, 521–532.

Dorst, K., & Cross, N. (2001). Creativity in the design process: Co-evolution of problem-solution. *Design Studies, 22*, 425–437.

Dossick, C., & Neff, G. (2011). Messy talk and clean technology: Communication, problem-solving and collaboration using Building Information Modelling. *The Engineering Project Organization Journal, 1*, 83–93.

Eddington, S., Corple, D., Buzzanell, P. M., Zoltowski, C. B., & Brightman, A. (2020). Addressing organizational cultural conflicts in engineering with design thinking. *Negotiation and Conflict Management Research*, 13, 263–284.

Fairhurst, G., & Putnam, L. (2014). Organizational discourse analysis. In L. Putnam & D. Mumby (Eds.), *The SAGE handbook of organizational communication* (3rd ed., pp. 271–295). London, UK: Sage.

Fiske, S. (2012). Managing ambivalent prejudices: Smart-but-cold and warm-but-dumb stereotypes. *The Annals of the American Academy of Political and Social Science*, 639, 33–48.

Foster, J. (2013). *White race discourse: Preserving racial privilege in a post-racial society*. Lanham, MD: Lexington.

Fotaki, M. (2013). No woman is like a man (in academia): The masculine symbolic order and the unwanted female body. *Organization Studies*, 34, 1251–1275.

Fyke, J., & Buzzanell, P. M. (2013). The ethics of conscious capitalism: Wicked problems in leading change and changing leaders. *Human Relations*, 66, 1619–1643.

Grant, A., & Sandberg, S. (2014, December 6). When talking about bias backfires. *The International New York Times*. Retrieved from www.nytimes.com/2014/12/07/opinion/sunday/adam-grant-and-sheryl-sandberg-on-discrimination-at-work.html?_r=0.

Grint, K. (2005). Problems, problems, problems: The social construction of "leadership". *Human Relations*, 58, 1467–1494.

Gray, B., Coleman, P., & Putnam, L. (2007). Intractable conflict: New perspectives on the causes and conditions for change. *American Behavioral Scientist*, 50, 1415–1429.

Green, S. E., Li, Y., & Nohria, N. (2009). Suspended in self-spun webs of significance: A rhetorical model of institutionalization and institutionally embedded agency. *Academy of Management Journal*, 52, 11–36.

Grint, K. (2005). Problems, problems, problems: The social construction of "leadership". *Human Relations*, 58, 1467–1494.

Gutiérrez y Muhs, G., Niemann, Y., González, G., & Harris, A. (Eds.). (2012). *Presumed incompetent: The intersections of race and class for women in academia*. Boulder, CO: Utah State University Press.

Hearit, L. B., & Buzzanell, P. M. (2016). Public understandings of women in STEM: A prototype analysis of governmental discourse from the C-SPAN Archives. In R. X. Browning (Ed.), *The C-SPAN archives: An interdisciplinary resource for discovery, learning, and engagement* (pp. 213–239). West Lafayette, IN: Purdue University Press.

Holloway, E. (2013). *Engineering students at typically invisible transition points: A focus on admissions and the sophomore year*. Unpublished dissertation, Purdue University, W. Lafayette, IN.

Holvino, E. (2010). Intersections: The simultaneity of race, gender and class in organization studies. *Gender, Work and Organization*, 17, 248–277.

IDEO. (2016). Retrieved from https://www.ideo.com.

Jia, Y.-X. (2014, December). The building of dialogic ethics in intercultural conflict management: An application of the Third Culture Theory to intercultural conflict management. Presentation at the Fourth International Conference of Intercultural Communication (ICIC), Foreign Languages College, Shanghai Normal University, Shanghai, China.

Kanter, R. M. (1977). *Men and women of the corporation*. New York, NY: Basic Books.

Kanter, R. M., & Roessner, J. (2003a). Deloitte & Touche (A): A hole in the pipeline. *Harvard Business School*, Case # 9–300–012.

Kanter, R. M., & Roessner, J. (2003b). Deloitte & Touche (B): Changing the workplace. *Harvard Business School*, Case # 9–300–013.

Kirby, E., & Buzzanell, P. M. (2014). Communicating work-life. In L. Putnam & D. Mumby (Eds.), *The SAGE handbook of organizational communication: Advances in theory, research, and methods* (3rd ed., pp. 351–373). Thousand Oaks, CA: Sage.

Kirby, E., & Krone, K. (2002). "The policy exists but you can't use it": Communication and the structuration of work-family policies. *Journal of Applied Communication Research*, 30, 50–77.

Kisselburgh, L., Berkelaar Van Pelt, B., & Buzzanell, P. M. (2009). Discourse, gender, and the meanings of work: Rearticulating science, technology, and engineering careers through communicative lenses. In C. Beck (Ed.), *Communication Yearbook* 33 (pp. 258–299). New York, NY: Routledge.

Klarsfeld, A. (Ed.). (2010). *International handbook on diversity at work: Country perspectives on diversity and equal treatment*. Cheltenham, UK: Edgar Elgar Publishing LTD.

Klarsfeld, A. (Ed.). (2014). *International handbook on diversity at work: Country perspectives on diversity and equal treatment* (2nd ed.). Cheltenham, UK: Edgar Elgar Publishing LTD.

Kossek, E., Dumas, T., Piszczek, M., & Allen, T. (2021). Pushing the boundaries: A qualitative study of how stem women adapted to disrupted work–nonwork boundaries during the COVID-19 pandemic. *Journal of Applied Psychology*, 106, 1615–1629.

Kulich, S. (2014). *Analyzing intercultural conflicts: Re-checking what's in our cases*. Presentation at the Fourth International Conference of Intercultural Communication (ICIC), Foreign Languages College, Shanghai Normal University, Shanghai, China.

Kuhn, T., Golden, A., Jorgenson, J., Buzzanell, P. M., Berkelaar, B., Kisselburgh, L., Kleinman, S., & Cruz, D. (2008). Cultural discourses and discursive resources for meaningful work: Constructing and disrupting identities in contemporary capitalism. *Management Communication Quarterly*, 22, 162–171.

Leung, K., Brew, F., Zhang, Z.-X., & Zhang, Y. (2011). Harmony and conflict: A cross-cultural investigation in China and Australia. *Journal of Cross-Cultural Psychology*, 42, 795–816.

Liu, M., & Buzzanell, P. M. (2004). Negotiating maternity leave expectations: Perceived tensions between ethics of justice and care. *Journal of Business Communication*, 41, 323–349.

Long, Z., Buzzanell, P. M., Anderson, L., Batra, J., Kokini, K., & Wilson, R. (2014). Episodic, network and intersectional perspectives: Taking a communicative stance on mentoring in the workplace. In E. Cohen (Ed.), *Communication Yearbook* 38 (pp. 387–422). New York, NY: Routledge.

Maranto, C. L., & Griffin, A. (2011). The antecedents of a "chilly climate" for women faculty in higher education. *Human Relations*, 64, 139–159.

Muhr, S. L., & Sullivan, K. (2013). "None so queer as folk": Gendered expectations and transgressive bodies in leadership. *Leadership*, 9, 416–435.

Mumby, D. (Ed.). (2010). *Reframing difference in organizational communication studies: Research, pedagogy, practice*. Thousand Oaks, CA: Sage.

Nicotera, A. M., & Clinkscales, M. C. (2010). Nurses at the nexus: A case study in structurational divergence. *Health Communication*, 25, 32–49.

Nicotera, A., & Mahon, M. (2013). Between rocks and hard places: Exploring the impact of structurational divergence in the nursing workplace. *Management Communication Quarterly*, 27, 90–120.

Nicotera, A. M., Mahon, M. M., & Zhao, X. (2010). Conceptualization and measurement of structurational divergence in the healthcare setting. *Journal of Applied Communication Research*, 38, 362–385.

O'Connor, A., & Raile, A. (2015). Millennials "get a 'real job'": Exploring generational shifts in the colloquialism's characteristics and meanings. *Management Communication Quarterly*, 29, 276–290.

Pearce, R., Wald, E., & Ballakrishnen, S. (2015). Difference blindness vs. bias awareness: Why law firms with the best of intentions have failed to create diverse partnerships. *Fordham Law Review*, 83 (2407). University of Denver Legal Studies Research Paper No.

15–08; Fordham Law Legal Studies Research Paper No. 2591478. Available at SSRN: http://ssrn.com/abstract=2591478.

Putnam, L., & Boys, S. (2006). Revisiting metaphors of organizational communication. In S. R. Clegg (Ed.), *Handbook of organization studies* (pp. 541–576). Thousand Oaks, CA: Sage.

Putnam, L., Jahn, J., & Baker, J. (2011). Intersecting difference: A dialectical perspective. In D. Mumby (Ed.), *Reframing difference in organizational communication studies: Research, pedagogy, and practice* (pp. 31–53). Thousand Oaks, CA: Sage.

Radcliffe, D., & Fosmire, M. (Eds.). (2014). *Integrating information into engineering design.* West Lafayette, IN: Purdue University Press.

Rittel, H., & Webber, M. (1973). Dilemmas in a general theory of planning. *Policy Sciences,* 4, 155–169.

Roberson, Q. (2006). Disentangling the meanings of diversity and inclusion in organizations. *Group & Organization Management,* 31, 212–236.

Robichaud, D., & Cooren, F. (Eds.). (2011). *Organization and organizing: Materiality, agency and discourse.* New York, NY: Routledge.

Servaes, J. (2014) Guanxi in intercultural communication and public relations. *Public Relations Review.* Available online: www.sciencedirect.com/science/article/pii/S0363811114001428.

Suchman, M. C. (1995). Managing legitimacy: Strategic and institutional approaches. *Academy of Management Review,* 20, 571–610.

Suddaby, R., & Greenwood, R. (2005). Rhetorical strategies of legitimacy. *Administrative Science Quarterly,* 50, 35–67.

Sue, D. (2010). *Microaggressions in everyday life: Race, gender, and sexual orientation.* Hoboken, NJ: Wiley.

Sue, D., Alsaidi, S., Awad, M., Glaeser, E., Calle, C., & Mendez, N. (2019). Disarming racial microaggressions: Microintervention strategies for targets, White allies, and bystanders. *American Psychologist,* 74, 128–142.

Ting-Toomey, S. (2011). Intercultural communication ethics: Multiple layered issues. In G. Cheney, S. May, & D. Munshi (Eds.), *Handbook of communication ethics* (pp. 335–352). New York, NY: Routledge.

Ting-Toomey, S. (2014, December). *Conflict Face-Negotiation Theory: Tracking its evolutionary journey.* Presentation to the International Conference of Intercultural Communication (ICIC), held at Shanghai Normal University, Shanghai, China.

Valian, V. (1998). *Why so slow? The advancement of women.* Cambridge, MA: MIT Press.

van den Brink, M., & Benschop, Y. (2012). Gender practices in the construction of academic excellence: Sheep with five legs. *Organization,* 19, 507–524.

Watzlawick, P., Beavin, J. H., & Jackson, D. D. (1967). *Pragmatics of human communication: A study of interactional patterns, pathologies and paradoxes.* New York, NY: Norton.

Werbner, P. (2013). Everyday multiculturalism: Theorising the difference between "intersectionality" and "multiple identities". *Ethnicities,* 13, 401–419.

Wingfield, A. H. (2009). Racializing the glass escalator: Reconsidering men's experiences with women's work. *Gender and Society,* 23, 5–26.

Wingfield, A. H., & Alston, S. R. (2014). Maintaining hierarchies in predominantly white organizations: A theory of racial tasks. *American Behavioral Scientist,* 58, 274–287.

Zoltowski, C., Oakes, W., & Cardella, M. (2012). Students' ways of experiencing Human-Centered Design. *Journal of Engineering Education,* 101, 28–59.

4

THE DEVELOPMENT OF INTERCULTURALITY AND THE MANAGEMENT OF INTERCULTURAL CONFLICT

Xiaodong Dai

Introduction

Intercultural communication takes place between people with differing cultural backgrounds. Conflicts often arise as a result of disparate social preferences and incompatible value orientations: the greater the cultural distance, the greater the likelihood that there will be tension and misunderstanding (Ting-Toomey, 2007, 2009). Intercultural communication scholars have investigated conflict management from diverse perspectives. For example, Worchel (2005) and Marsella (2005) addressed how culture shapes people's perception of reality and proffered viable ways of reaching mutual understanding and achieving peaceful co-existence. Ting-Toomey and Kurogi (1998) discussed the role of face in conflict situations and formulated a facework competence model. Most of the studies focus on describing intercultural differences and how these differences lead to intercultural conflicts. This chapter argues that in order to manage intercultural conflict effectively we need to turn our attention to the interactive process, and that the development of interculturality can provide us with a possible conflict management alternative. The discussion includes three parts: (1) the definition of the concept of interculturality; (2) a demonstration of how developing interculturality can help to manage intercultural conflict; and (3) the use of Sino-U.S. face conflict management as an example of the effective development of interculturality.

Defining Interculturality

Culture flows, intermixes, and evolves in the process of intercultural interaction, which blurs cultural boundaries and gives rise to interculturality. The concept of interculturality has been used in bilingual, bicultural education as well as in immigration policy studies. It is associated with ethnic, linguistic, and national conflicts.

DOI: 10.4324/9781003252955-6

In recent years, more and more scholars have begun to emphasize the positive values associated with the concept, such as mutual acknowledgment and respect (e.g., Dai, 2010; Mato, 2012). According to Zhu (2014), interculturality refers to the process in which people with differing cultural identities learn from each other, develop intercultural personhood, and mediate between different perspectives. From the perspective of intersubjectivity, I define interculturality as the multiple connections between cultures through which culturally different individuals endeavor to reduce cultural distance, negotiate shared meanings and mutually desired identities, and establish reciprocal relationships.

This definition is based on three assumptions. First, the development of interculturality is a dialogical process that involves two or more culturally different individuals. It is characterized by the interlocutors' desire to talk, to learn, and to establish connections with each other (Buber, 2002). The typical goals of interculturality include mutual understanding, relational transformation, self-growth, and communication pattern change (Heidlebaugh, 2008). The dialogue's emphasis on multivocality, open-endedness, mutuality, and meaning co-creation allows interlocutors to explore more fully the complexities of their counterpart's commitment and perspective as well as their own (Black, 2008).

The construction of interculturality concerns the two parties of cultural self and cultural other, each of whom assumes the role of a cultural agent. Self and other are existentially different and separate and relationally asymmetrical. They are relatively independent partners who live in different worlds, but try to develop mutuality and reciprocity, which demonstrates a synthesis of connection and distance (White, 2008). In an ideal state, self and other are equal, but due to the differences in power, knowledge, and wealth, the self sometimes dominates and is dominated by the other. The two parties are constantly in tension and are constantly struggling for recognition. However, the space between self and other remains open in the sense that "each party recognizes his or her dependence upon the other, and each can allow the judgment of the respective other to be valid as an objection against oneself" (Honneth, 2003, p. 12).

Second, individuals adapt to each other and negotiate their desired identities in the process of developing interculturality. Establishing intercultural connections suggests that individuals go beyond cultural boundaries and engage with people from other cultures. Through mutual adaptation they become re-socialized into a larger intercultural community and develop a more inclusive identity. According to Kim (2001, 2008), adapting to others is, first of all, a learning process. Individuals acquire new cultural elements and integrate them into their communicative scripts. They unlearn some of the old behavior and habits by adopting new responses in situations that previously would have evoked old ones (Kim, 2008, 2012).

When adapting to each other, individuals want to be recognized and included, but they also want to be autonomous and differentiated, so that both self-identification and mutual identification can be achieved. Intercultural identity negotiation operates with two basic dialectical principles: inclusion and differentiation (Brewer, 1991, 2003; Ting-Toomey, 2005). When intercultural communicators become progressively similar to each other, they diverge to accentuate differences. When they perceive that the differences prevent them from maintaining intercultural ties, they start to develop commonalities. Identification with both the culture of origin and the culture of contact constitutes an important component of the reconstructed identity (Ward, Bochner, & Furnham, 2001). Equilibrium is kept by correcting deviations from optimal distinctiveness (Brewer, 1999, 2003). The newly acquired identity which is broader than individuals' original cultural identity paves the way for the development of intercultural personhood and helps to improve intercultural relations (Kim, 2001, 2008, 2012).

Third, individuals endeavor to reach an intercultural agreement and establish productive relationships. In the intersubjective space, individuals communicate with each other with reference to the generalized other (Mead, 1967), which refers to a role model who provides people with common norms, rules, and patterns of behavior in a society (Charon, 1998). People in the same society share a similar perspective on social communication, since they define objects, other people, the world, and themselves from a generalized standpoint and anticipate the socially expected reactions of others (Shibutani, 1955).

In contrast, individuals from different societies employ different frames of reference in intercultural communication, a process in which the interculturally shared generalized other is yet to be negotiated. They approach the same world from diverse perspectives and make different or even contradictory interpretations. In order to have a meaningful dialogue across cultures, people negotiate intercultural agreements on the basis of cultural similarities and human universals.

When negotiating with cultural others, two basic human mechanisms help individuals to bridge the cultural gap, i.e., taking on the role of the other and the process of self-reflection. The ability to take on the role of the other is fundamental to human understanding and cooperation (Blumer, 1969; Morris, 1967). It allows us to see things from the perspective of our counterparts in interaction, which enables us to understand them, sympathize with them, and reach an agreement with them (Charon, 1998). Meanwhile the reflective mechanism urges us to examine our own weaknesses and search for other life possibilities. Once we come to realize the validity of their way of representing reality, we are ready to relate ourselves to cultural others and engage them in dialogues. In intercultural interactions we are exposed to new ideas and behavior, and our cultural inventory becomes enlarged and more elaborated with the borrowing of new words and the introduction of new categories or ideas. Thus, through mutual learning and cross-referencing we enhance each other and establish reciprocal relationships in the process of intercultural interaction embedded in the concept of interculturality (Tu, 2001).

Managing Intercultural Conflict in the Space of Interculturality

Conflicts take place when relational partners perceive incompatible ideas, emotions, needs, or goals (Collier, 1991). An effectively managed conflict allows both parties to better know their cultural differences, clarify misunderstandings, find out common needs, interests, and goals, and further strengthen relationships (Ting-Toomey & Oetzel, 2001). A mutually shared perspective, a common understanding on the root of the conflict, and a coordinated action are the key factors of successful intercultural conflict management (Dai & Chen, 2015; Harris and Moran, 1987; Ting-Toomey, 2009). Interculturality connects two cultures and creates a space where individuals with differing cultural identities adapt to each other to develop an intercultural perspective and foster intercultural personhood. The critical role of interculturality in conflict management is reflected in four aspects: (1) accommodating differences and cultivating a positive attitude to diversity; (2) developing an intercultural perspective and enhancing mutual understanding; (3) promoting mutual critique and working toward a rational solution; and (4) facilitating joint action and enhancing intercultural harmony.

Accommodating Differences and Cultivating a Positive Attitude to Diversity

Cultural differences in and of themselves do not necessarily result in conflict; it is how these differences are perceived and interpreted that may elicit intercultural conflicts (Marsella, 2005; Worchel, 2005). Samovar, Porter, and Stefani (2000) revealed that ethnocentrism is the salient characteristic that directly relates to intercultural communication. Individuals with an ethnocentric lens view things merely from their own perspective and see their own culture as the best one. They tend to deny other cultures, a behavior which often leads to misunderstanding, conflict, and hostility (Bennett & Bennett, 2004).

Interculturality links one culture with another. It embodies people's openness and the interactive nature of human relations. In the space of interculturality cultural differences have become relativized in relation to a shared world (Ajzner, 1994) and individuals are "dealing with a relational field, not with dual worlds" (Diamond, 1996, p. 310). Individuals with an ethnorelative lens recognize the value of cultural diversity. They are ready to accept differences, adapt to the other's perspective, and integrate the other's cultural element into their own to form a broadened worldview (Bennett & Bennett, 2004). The positive attitude to differences makes it possible for culturally dissimilar individuals to engage in a dialogue and explore the effective way to manage intercultural conflicts.

Developing an Intercultural Perspective and Enhancing Mutual Understanding

The effective management of intercultural conflict begins with identifying the root of the problem. Since culturally different individuals tend to be biased in evaluating conflict situations, they have to develop a shared perspective in order to reach mutual understanding. Interculturality opens up a space for culturally different individuals to relate to each other and to form interpersonal relationships. The sustained contact produces the need for intercultural adaptation. In the process of intercultural adaptation, individuals acquire new ideas, unlearn some of the old ideas, and develop an intercultural perspective (Kim, 2001, 2012). The intercultural perspective integrates both our own values and those of others, and it represents a new way of viewing the world. It enables individuals to transcend their mono-cultural lens and makes "judgments by the standards of more than one culture" (Evanoff, 2006, p. 422).

Individuals who have developed an intercultural perspective are able to see what mono-cultural persons are unable to see and have a more comprehensive view of a given phenomenon. An intercultural perspective not only broadens commu-nicators' vision, but also provides them with a shared frame of reference. When culturally different individuals interact, they tend to interpret the meaning with their own frame of reference. An intercultural perspective serves as an inter-culturally shared frame of reference that allows interactants to define things from a common standpoint and anticipate culturally expected reactions. With an inter-cultural perspective, individuals are capable of reaching a mutual understanding on the nature of the intercultural conflict, identifying where the problems are, and negotiating possible solutions (Dai, 2010; Dai & Chen, 2015).

Promoting Mutual Critique and Working toward a Rational Solution

Achieving mutual understanding in a conflict situation does not necessarily imply that people have reached an agreement on how to solve the problem. All com-munication takes place between people with different minds and different posi-tions. If we simply accept differences as they are, we will lose the chance to reject negative elements and explore better choices (Evanoff, 2006). If we impose our view on others, however, more conflicts will ensue.

Interculturality is a space where diverse perspectives intersect, and where culturally different individuals engage each other in dialogue. In this dynamic space, two basic competing forces—namely, convergence and divergence—are at work. While individuals converge to reach mutual understanding, they diverge to maintain self-identity. Culturally different individuals develop unity in diversity. When parties to a conflict negotiate in the space of interculturality, they view people with different ideas as colleagues who are capable of enligh-tening them—not as combatants or advocators. And the goal of argumentation in the conflict negotiation is to work out a solution that benefits both sides (Barge & Little, 2002). It allows the parties to mutually criticize each other and produce shared knowledge that enhances advanced cultural integration (Miike, 2010). In this synergistic approach to conflict, different positions are equally attended to and the expected goals are fully addressed. Because the solution is reached through critical reflection and peaceful argument, and because some of the cultural biases have been removed, it is more rational and workable than any of the original solutions proffered by the conflict parties.

Facilitating Joint Action and Enhancing Intercultural Harmony

After working out a possible solution to the problem, conflict parties need to take a joint action to determine whether the solution works interculturally. In social communication, individuals coordinate their actions through various social agreements which function to regulate individual behavior and promote the development of reciprocal relationships. People with similar mental models are always more likely to find shared gains and take joint actions (Liu, Friedman, Barry, Gelfand, & Zhang 2012). As stated above, interculturality fosters an intercultural perspective and cultivates intercultural personhood. The broadened intercultural perspective enables individuals to avoid the ethnocentric mindset by identifying their common interest and mutually desired outcome. An intercultural person is an ideal cultural mediator, who can access both his/her own and others' cultural frameworks and switch back and forth seamlessly between them (Ringberg, Luna, Reihlen, & Peracchio, 2010). Both the development of intercultural perspective and the cultivation of intercultural personhood help culturally differing individuals coordinate their actions in conflict management.

In addition, the extended intercultural personhood is also conducive to intercultural harmony. It transforms an individual's representation of the membership: they no longer belong to a separate cultural group but to a more inclusive intercultural one. As Brewer and Gaertner (2004) indicated, "With common ingroup identity, the cognitive and motivational processes that initially produced ingroup favoritism are redirected to benefit the former outgroups" (p. 306). The more individuals perceive themselves as one group, the more they are willing to cooperate with each other and work for their mutual interest (Reicher, 1982).

Sino-U.S. Face Conflict Management

Intercultural conflict may arise from inappropriate behavior or contradictory expectations. Face conflict is one of the mundane but difficult problems individuals need to deal with in intercultural communication. While face and facework are universal phenomena, how individuals define face and enact facework differs across cultures (He & Zhang, 2011; Ting-Toomey & Kurogi, 1998). In some situations, the differences are so great that they often lead to intercultural conflicts. The following section discusses how the development of interculturality helps to manage face conflict between the Chinese and Americans.

Face Conflict between the Chinese and Americans

There are differences between the Chinese and Americans not only in face definition but also in face orientation and communication behavior. For the Chinese, face is a person's social respectability (Cheng, 1986; He & Zhang, 2011), which is hierarchical, relational, and full of emotional and moral implications (Gao, 2006; Jia, 2001, Liu, 2011). According to He and Zhang (2011), respectability refers to "the quality of being considered morally correct and socially acceptable" (p. 2361). People need to meet the basic moral standard in order to have a face in Chinese society. Face is determined by a person's social status, family prestige, virtuous behavior, and personal competence in China (Jia, 2001; Liu, 2011). A person gains face when his/her performance exceeds social expectation. Face enhances one's own and one's family's social functioning. Losing face results in negative consequences ranging from the loss of symbolic resources to the loss of one's whole personhood and family disgrace. Face plays such an important role in social communication that the Chinese would use all possible means to maintain or save face (Chen, 2002; Hwang, 2011).

Due to the emphasis on harmonious relationships, the Chinese tend to show a great concern for other's face and mutual face. Chinese culture dictates that one is obliged to honor others' face and return the favor in social interaction. The strategies for giving face to others include *guanxi*, reciprocity, self-debasement, modesty, politeness, being obliging, and avoiding direct and open criticism (see Chen, 1997, 2000, 2011; Chen & Ma, 2002). In Chinese society, losing face often leads to anger, hatred, and hostility.

For Americans, face is the positive value a person claims for oneself in social communication (Bargiela-Chiappini, 2003; Goffman, 1967). It is relatively equal, individual, and rational. In American society, a person's face is judged by his/her ability, competitiveness, social performance, and achievements, and individuals tend to use open and aggressive ways to gain face (Ting-Toomey & Oetzel, 2001; Zhao, 2010). While gaining face improves one's social functioning, it does little to enhance the social image of other members of one's family. Jia (2001) pointed out that the loss of face in American society only means a decrease in social worth. It seldom leads to personal or family disgrace. Although American culture also requires its members to attend to others' face, unlike Chinese culture, it does so only so that each individual's self-mage can be enhanced (Bargiela-Chiappini, 2003; Chang, 2008; Jia, 2001).

Compared with Americans, the Chinese are more face-sensitive and more vulnerable with regard to face-keeping. In communication, the two parties often run into a face conflict due to the existence of a huge cultural gap (Ting-Toomey, 2009; Ting-Toomey & Kurogi, 1998; Ting-Toomey & Oetzel, 2001). More problematic is that when a face conflict arises, Americans tend to use more direct, confrontational, and dominating strategies to uphold face, while the Chinese tend to use more indirect and compromising strategies in an effort to save face (Ting-Toomey, 2005, 2015; Ting-Toomey & Kurogi, 1998). It is necessary for people from differing cultures to find an appropriate way to negotiate differences in order to effectively manage face conflict.

Face Conflict Management from the Perspective of Interculturality

From the perspective of interculturality, a positive attitude to differences, mutual understanding, mutual critique, and coordinated action are key to successful intercultural face conflict management. In the space of interculturality, the Chinese and

Americans can be connected to form a Sino–U.S. intercultural bond. Although both parties differ in face conception, face orientation, and face behavior, they can treat these differences as a way of approaching their shared reality. People learn more from those who differ from themselves than from those with a similar cultural perspective (Ting-Toomey & Oetzel, 2001), and face conflict between collectivistic Chinese and individualistic Americans creates an opportunity for intercultural learning, as well as mutual change and growth.

Under the rubric of interculturality, the Chinese and Americans are encouraged to adapt to each other in order to reach mutual understanding. Mutual adaptation requires both parties to acquire new cultural knowledge, a process which will broaden their vision and help them to develop an intercultural perspective. For example, through a broadened intercultural perspective, the Chinese can come to understand that Americans tend to perceive self as an independent, stable, unique, and free entity (Markus & Kitayama, 1991), and therefore face for Americans is an individual issue.

On the other hand, the Chinese view self as "connected, fluid, flexible and committed being who is bound to others" (Harb & Smith, 2008, p. 179), they therefore tend to take face as both an individual and relational issue, with more emphasis on the relational aspect (Chang, 2008; Jia, 2001). In terms of facework, Americans value social equality and individual initiative, and encourage inter-personal competition, hence they tend to use direct and horizontal facework and employ competing or dominating strategies in conflict situations. In contrast, the Chinese have large power distance and value interpersonal harmony, so they tend to use indirect and vertical facework and employ avoiding, obliging, or third party mediation strategies to deal with conflicts (Ting-Toomey, 2009, 2015; Ting-Toomey & Kurogi, 1998).

The fact that the Chinese and Americans have reached a mutual understanding does not imply that they have accepted one another's ways of coping with conflict. Interculturality promotes the engagement of the two parties in mutual critique, so that a workable solution can be reached. The American conception of face emphasizes individual rights, self-value, and I-image. Observed through an inter-cultural lens, it is rational and equal but it lacks communal warmth and its indivi-dualistic view of self precludes an adequate appreciation of the social basis of communication (Kim, 2000). The Chinese conception of face emphasizes the individual's obligation to others, collective value, and We-image. It is relational and full of human affection but it has little regard for social justice (Dai & Chen, 2014). Jia (2001) argued that this Chinese emotional and hierarchical view of face inculcates an inflated sense of vanity and social inequality. In Sino–U.S. face con-flict management, while the Chinese may incorporate rationality, equality, and individual agency into their conception of face, they can resist radical individualism and impersonalization, and strike a balance between rights and obligations. As for Americans, they may incorporate Chinese humanism and communalism, and at the same time resist excessive face emotion and hierarchical face-giving practices so as to cultivate healthy human relationships.

Effective face conflict management is achieved when two parties enact a mutually negotiated solution. With the development of interculturality, Americans and the Chinese no longer approach face from their respective cultural perspectives, but through an integrated overarching intercultural lens which enables them to identify their common interests and goals. Equally important is that they extend their cultural identity and develop their intercultural personhood. It blurs the intergroup boundary, reduces social bias, and facilitates intercultural cooperation. Both the development of an intercultural lens and the cultivation of an intercultural personhood provide them with a basis for joint actions in face conflict management.

Research has shown that the Chinese and Americans have a great opportunity to gain intercultural knowledge and cultivate similar value orientations and communication behavior in the globalizing society, which is characterized by sustained interactions and mutual influence (e.g., Egri & Ralston, 2004; Haslett & Leidel, 2015). In recent years American scholars have highlighted the interconnection of human societies and advocated relational self-conception (e.g., Carl & Duck, 2004; Gergen, 1999; Gordon, 2007). They have also gradually understood Chinese face-giving and been able to appreciate the hospitality they received from their Chinese friends (Perlmutter, 2007; Wang, 2009). In a similar way, many Chinese have begun to embrace the American conception of face by incorporating American rationalism into their facework, making use of direct ways of coping with interpersonal conflicts, and placing more emphasis on competence and ability in face gaining practices (He & Zhang, 2011; Pan, Chaffee, Chu, & Ju, 1994; Zhao, 2010).

Conclusion

Intercultural conflict management involves different cultural perspectives. Individuals need to mediate between their own and others' cultural systems, so that they can effectively solve their problems and improve their intercultural relationships. The development of interculturality offers us a viable way of managing intercultural conflicts. In the space of interculturality, culturally differing individuals relate to each other so as to form an intercultural union. They make mutual adaptations and extend their cultural horizons and identities in order to foster intercultural perspective and cultivate intercultural personhood. The broadened vision and the extended identity not only enable them to liberate themselves from narrow minded ethnocentrism, but also allow them to reach intercultural understanding, engage in mutual critique, negotiate intercultural agreements, and take a joint action to deal with their shared problems. Face conflict management experiences demonstrate that merely focusing on describing intercultural differences cannot remove intercultural tensions, and so we need to address the dynamic interactive process. It is through the sustained interaction that conflict parties clarify misunderstandings, rise above the ethnocentric mindset, work out possible solutions, and explore how they can co-exist harmoniously and achieve mutual growth.

References

Ajzner, J. (1994). Some problems of rationality, understanding, and universal ethics in the context of Habermas's theory of communicative action. *Philosophy of the Social Sciences*, 24, 466–484.

Barge, K. & Little, M. (2002). Dialogical wisdom, communicative practice, and organizational life. *Communication Theory*, 12, 375–397.

Bargiela-Chiappini, F. (2003). Face and politeness: New (insights) for old (concepts). *Journal of Pragmatics*, 35, 1453–1469.

Bennett, J. M. & Bennett, M. J. (2004). Developing intercultural sensitivity: An integrative approach to global and domestic diversity. In D. Landis, J. M. Bennett, & M. J. Bennett (Eds.), *Handbook of intercultural training* (pp. 147–165). Thousand Oaks, CA: Sage.

Black, L. W. (2008). Deliberation, storytelling, and dialogic moments. *Communication Theory*, 18, 93–116.

Blumer, H. (1969). *Symbolic interactionism: Perspective and method*. Englewood Cliffs, NJ: Prentice-Hall, Inc.

Brewer, M. B. (1991). The social self: On being the same and different at the same time. *Personality and Social Psychology Bulletin*, 17, 475–482.

Brewer, M. B. (1999). Multiple identities and identity transition: Implications for Hong Kong. *International Journal of Intercultural Relations*, 23, 187–197.

Brewer, M. B. (2003). Optimal distinctiveness, social identity, and the self. In M. R. Leary & J. P. Tangney (Eds.), *Handbook of self and identity* (pp. 480–491). New York, NY: The Guilford Press.

Brewer, M. B. & Gaertner, S. L. (2004). Toward reduction of prejudice: Intergroup contact and social categorization. In M. B. Brewer & M. Hewstone (Eds.), *Self and social identity* (pp. 298–318). Malden, MA: Blackwell.

Buber, M. (2002). *Dialogue* (R. G. Smith, Trans.). London, UK: Routledge.

Carl, W. J. & Duck, S. W. (2004). How to do things with relationships ... and how relationships do things with us. In P. Kalbfleisch (Ed.), *Communication Yearbook* (Vol. 28, pp. 1–34). Mahwah, NJ: Lawrence Erlbaum Associates.

Chang, Y. Y. (2008). Cultural "faces" of interpersonal communication in the U.S. and China. *Intercultural Communication Studies*, 17(1), 299–313.

Charon, J. M. (1998). *Symbolic interactionism: An introduction, an interpretation, an integration*. Upper Saddle River, NJ: Prentice Hall.

Chen, G. M. (Ed.). (1997). Chinese conflict management and resolution [Special Issue]. *Intercultural Communication Studies*, 7(1), 1–168.

Chen, G. M. (Ed.). (2000). Chinese conflict management in intercultural context [Special Issue]. *Intercultural Communication Studies*, 9(2), 1–175.

Chen, G. M. (2002). The impact of harmony on Chinese conflict management. In G. M. Chen & R. Ma (Eds.), *Chinese conflict management and resolution* (pp. 3–19). Westport, CT: Ablex.

Chen, G. M. (2011). Key concepts in understanding the Chinese [Special Issue]. *China Media Research*, 4(4), 1–106.

Chen, G. M. & Ma, R. (Eds.). (2002). *Chinese conflict management and resolution*. Westport, CT: Ablex.

Cheng, C.-Y. (1986). The concept of face and its Confucian roots. *Journal of Chinese Philosophy*, 13, 329–348.

Collier, M. J. (1991). Conflict competence within African, Mexican, and Anglo American friendships. In S. Ting-Toomey & F. Korzenny (Eds.), *Cross-cultural interpersonal communication* (pp. 132–154). Newbury Park, CA: Sage.

Dai, X. D. (2010). Intersubjectivity and interculturality: A conceptual link. *China Media Research*, 6(1), 12–19.

Dai, X. D. & Chen, G. M. (2014). The construction of national image in media and the management of intercultural conflict. In R. S. Fortner & P. M. Fackler (Eds.), *The handbook of media and mass communication theory* (pp. 708–725). Malden, MA: Wiley.

Dai, X. D. & Chen, G. M. (2015). On interculturality and intercultural communication competence. *China Media Research*, 11(3), 100–113.

Diamond, N. (1996). Can we speak of internal and external reality? *Group Analysis*, 29, 303–317.

Egri, C. P. & Ralston, D. A. (2004). Generation cohorts and personal values: A comparison of Chinese and United States. *Organization Science*, 15(2), 210–220.

Evannoff, R. (2006). Integration in intercultural ethics. *International Journal of Intercultural Relations*, 30, 421–437.

Gao, Y.-P. (2006). A new interpretation of Chinese concept of face. *Journal of Capital Normal University (Social Sciences Edition)*, 1, 55–60.

Gergen, K. (1999). *An invitation to social construction.* Thousand Oaks, CA: Sage.

Goffman, E. (1967). *Interaction ritual: Essays on face-to-face behavior.* New York, NY: Pantheon Books.

Gordon, R. D. (2007). Beyond the failures of Western communication theory. *Journal of Multicultural Discourses*, 2, 89–107.

Harb, C. & Smith, P. B. (2008). Self-construals across cultures: Beyond independence-interdependence. *Journal of Cross-Cultural Psychology*, 39, 178–197.

Harris, P. R. & Moran, R. T. (1987). *Managing cultural differences.* Houston, TX: Gulf.

Haslett, B. B. & Leidel, K. (2015) Work values in a changing global environment: Comparing Chinese and U.S. students. *Intercultural Communication Studies*, 24, 11–34.

He, M. & Zhang, S.-j. (2011). Re-conceptualizing the Chinese concept of face from a face-sensitive perspective: A case study of a modern Chinese TV drama. *Journal of Pragmatics*, 43, 2360–2372.

Heidlebaugh, N. J. (2008). Invention and public dialogue: Lessons from rhetorical theories. *Communication Theories*, 18, 27–50.

Honneth, A. (2003). On the destructive power of the third: Gadamer and Heidagger's doctrine of intersubjectivity. *Philosophy & Social Criticism*, 29, 5–21.

Hwang, K. K. (2011). Face dynamism in Confucian society. *China Media Research*, 7(4), 13–24.

Jia, W. S. (2001). *The remaking of the Chinese character and identity in the 21st century.* Westport, CT: Ablex Publishing.

Kim, Y. Y. (2000). On becoming intercultural. In M. W. Lustig & J. Koester (Eds.), *Among US: Essays on identity, belonging, and intercultural competence* (pp. 59–67). New York, NY: Addison Wesley Longman, Inc.

Kim, Y. Y. (2001). *Becoming intercultural: An integrative theory of communication and cross-cultural adaptation.* Thousand Oaks, CA: Sage.

Kim, Y. Y. (2008). Intercultural personhood: Globalization and a way of being. *International Journal of Intercultural Relations*, 32, 359–368.

Kim, Y. Y. (2012). From ascription to achievement: The case of identity adaptation and transformation in the globalizing world. In X. D. Dai, & S. J. Kulich (Eds.), *Intercultural adaptation (I): Theoretical explorations and empirical studies* (pp. 31–49). Shanghai, China: Shanghai Foreign Language Education Press.

Liu, J. F. (2011). Reexaming the definition of face. *Science of Social Psychology*, 26(2), 137–142.

Liu, L. A., Friedman, R., Barry, B., Gelfand, M. J., & Zhang, Z.-X. (2012). The dynamics of consensus building in intracultural and intercultural negotiations. *Administrative Science Quarterly*, 57, 269–304.

Markus, H. R. & Kitayama, S. (1991). Culture and the self: Implications for cognition, emotion, and motivation. *Psychological Review*, 98, 224–253.

Marsella, A. J. (2005). Culture and conflict: Understanding, negotiating, and reconciling constructions of reality. *International Journal of Intercultural Relations*, 29, 651–673.

Mato, D. (2012). Socio-cultural differences and intercultural communication in social participation experiences. *Intercultural Communication Studies*, 21(1), 101–116.

Mead, G. H. (1967). *Mind, self, & society: From the standpoint of a social behaviorist*. Chicago, IL: The University of Chicago Press.

Miike, Y. (2010). Culture as text and culture as theory: Asiacentricity and its raison d'être in intercultural communication research. In T. K. Nakayama & R. T. Halualani (Eds.), *The handbook of critical intercultural communication* (pp. 190–215). Oxford, UK: Wiley-Blackwell.

Morris, C. W. (1967). Introduction: George H. Mead as social psychologist and social philosopher. In G. H. Mead, *Mind, self, & society* (C. W. Morris (Ed.), pp. ix–xxxv). Chicago, IL: The University of Chicago Press.

Pan, Z. D., Chaffee, S. H., Chu, G. C., & Ju, Y. N. (1994). *To see ourselves: Comparing traditional Chinese and American cultural values*. Boulder, CO: Westview Press.

Perlmutter, D. D. (2007). *Picturing China in the American press*. Lanham, MD: Lexington Books.

Reicher, S. (1982). The determination of collective behavior. In H. Tajfel (Ed.), *Social identity and intergroup relations* (pp. 41–83). New York, NY: Cambridge University Press.

Ringberg, T. V., Luna, D., Reihlen, M., & Peraccchio, L. A. (2010). Bicultural-bilinguals: The effect of cultural frame switching on translation equivalence. *International Journal of Cross-Cultural Management*, 10, 77–92.

Samovar, L. A., Porter, R. E., & Stefani, L. A. (2000). *Communicating between cultures*. Beijing, China: Foreign Language Teaching and Research Press.

Shibutani, T. (1955). Reference groups as perspectives. *American Journal of Sociology*, 60, 562–569.

Ting-Toomey, S. (2005). Identity negotiation theory. In W. B. Gudykunst (Ed.), *Theorizing about intercultural communication* (pp. 211–234). Thousand Oaks, CA: Sage.

Ting-Toomey, S. (2007). Researching intercultural conflict competence. *Journal of International Communication*, 13(2), 7–30.

Ting-Toomey, S. (2009). Intercultural conflict competence as a facet of intercultural competence development. In D. K. Deardorff (Ed.), *The Sage handbook of intercultural competence* (pp. 100–120). Thousand Oaks, CA: Sage.

Ting-Toomey, S. (2015). Managing intercultural conflict effectively. In L. A. Samovar, R. E. Porter, E. R. McDaniel, & C. S. Roy (Eds.), *Intercultural communication: A reader* (pp. 355–366). Boston, MA: Cengage Learning.

Ting-Toomey, S. & Kurogi, A. (1998). Facework competence in intercultural conflict: An updated face-negotiation theory. *International Journal of Intercultural Relations*, 22, 187–225.

Ting-Toomey, S. & Oetzel, J. G. (2001). *Managing intercultural conflict effectively*. Thousand Oaks, CA: Sage.

Tu, W. M. (2001). The context of dialogue: Globalization and diversity. In G. Picco (Ed.), *Crossing the divide: Dialogue among civilizations* (pp. 49–96). South Orange, NJ: School of Diplomacy and International Relations, Seton Hall University.

Wang, L. X. (2009). To use Long as a foil: American imagination of China and the construction of national identity. In L. Li, X. L. You, & W. Y. Xie (Eds.), *Sino-Western cultural communication: A review and envision* (pp. 395–422). Shanghai, China: Shanghai People's Publishing.

Ward. C., Bochner, S., & Furnham, A. (2001). *The psychology of culture shock*. Hove, UK: Routledge.

White, W. J. (2008). The interlocutor's dilemma: The place of strategy in dialogic theory. *Communication Theory*, 18, 5–26.

Worchel, S. (2005). Culture's role in conflict and conflict management: Some suggestions, many questions. *International Journal of Intercultural Relations*, 29, 739–757.

Zhao, Y. (2010). A contrastive analysis on Sino-U.S. face concept: A focused study of university students. *Guizhou Social Sciences*, 10, 103–106.

Zhu, H. (2014). *Exploring intercultural communication: Language in action*. London, UK: Routledge.

5

TRANSFORMING CONFLICT THROUGH COMMUNICATION AND COMMON GROUND

Beth Bonniwell Haslett

Early views on conflict and conflict resolution approached conflict as something to be eliminated or, at the very least, hidden and suppressed. People have since come to realize that conflict is an inescapable part of life, and that, while it is a constant presence in our lives, it can be managed.

Communication plays an essential role in managing conflict. While conflicts can be settled by force, the consequences of using coercion and/or force are suffering and loss, and, given our weapons, can cause catastrophic damage. The stakes are extraordinarily high, especially in intercultural conflict, and we need to use communication and dialogue to resolve and manage conflict. Resolving intercultural conflict is particularly complex because of cultural differences in worldviews, communication styles and values. In addition, intercultural and interpersonal dialogue must involve those who are oppressed, victimized and treated unfairly as well as those who enjoy relative privilege (Sorrells, 2014).

Much scholarly attention has been devoted to analyzing various communicative strategies to resolve conflict and to assess different cultural styles in approaching conflict (Oetzel, Ting-Toomey, Matsumoto, Pan, Tikai, & Wilcox, 2001; Ting-Toomey, 2005; Ting-Toomey & Kurogi, 1998; Ting-Toomey, Gao, Trubisky, Yang, Kim, Lin, & Nishida, 1991). While such studies are very useful, an important new perspective on conflict has been emerging. This perspective involves searching for common ground on which to resolve disputes, and acknowledges the importance of community in both communication and culture. Both common ground and community rest fundamentally upon face—the respect accorded each human by virtue of their humanity. In communication, face is a basic component of effective interaction and forms the foundation for effective interpersonal and intercultural dialogue. It is through communication that humans establish culture, a shared way of life that is transmitted from generation to generation. In every culture, these shared ways of life provide a sense of common ground and

DOI: 10.4324/9781003252955-7

community that members identify with (G. M. Chen, 2004; L. Chen, 2011; Miike & Yin, 2015, Ury, 2000, 2009).

In what follows, we shall analyze how both communicative and cultural practices can foster the emergence of common ground and a sense of community. Next, we shall explore specific approaches that emphasize common ground and community as crucial components for managing intercultural conflict. There are several approaches that build upon community such as Dai's interculturality, Bauman's liquid modernity, Ury's Third Side and Haslett's development of face. From such perspectives on communication, culture and conflict management, strategies relying on communication and community for effective conflict management have emerged.

Culture

For many years, nation-states have defined cultures. And, to some degree, that holds true today, especially with regard to control of territories and disputes over that control. However, modernization and globalization have broadened the cultural landscape. Generally culture may be broadly defined as a shared way of life (values, beliefs and norms) transmitted from generation to generation (Schein, 1992). Increasingly, culture has become a "site of contestation where meaning-making is a struggle and not a static entity that remains fixed and stable" and thus people question "the ways that dominant perspectives, values and practices are privileged" (Sorrells, 2014, p. 162). Given the change and flux in cultural ideas, one's culture appears to be primarily determined by one's identification with a given set of cultural values (Chen, 2011; Chen, 2015; Collier, 2015; Haslett, 2012a, 2012b, 2014; Kim, 2008) because there are many different cultural groups within a given nation-state who may identify with other groups and nation-states (Lustig & Koester, 2010).

Immigration, migration and diasporas have introduced many different cultural groups into various nation-states. Nation-states themselves have become increasingly interconnected economically and politically (Bauman, 2000; Giddens, 1984, 1990). While we may tend to think of East versus West, or refer to Asia as a unified entity, there are important cultural values and practices that distinguish different Asian cultures. All cultures are hybrid in the sense that there have been cultural changes through cultural contact such as colonialism, economic ties, migration, immigration and the influence of modernization and globalization (Giddens, 1984). Miike and Yin (2015) point out that these influences need to be studied in order to appreciate the impact of such contact, and to understand the power balances between countries as a result of cultural contact.

Multiculturalism, as outlined by Karenga (2010), recognizes: (1) each culture's validity as being a valued way of living; (2) respects everyone's view; and (3) commits to a search for common ground among cultures and to sharing resources. Particularly important is the emphasis on seeing cultures as valid ways of living, each to be studied and explored in their own right—that is, in terms of their own cultural traditions and resources, rather than being judged by external standards.

Dimensions that measure differences across cultures (Hofstede, 2001) have also measured intracultural differences within a given nation-state. Although cultural differences exist, we also have studies of universal values that support the idea of shared human values and remind us of our interconnectedness. Schwartz and his colleagues uncovered four broad dimensions of universal value constructs (self-enhancement, openness to change, self-transcendence and conservatism). Self-enhancement incorporates power, achievement and hedonism; openness to change reflects the values of stimulation and novelty; self-transcendence reflects the values of universalism and benevolence and conservatism reflects the values of security, tradition and conformity. Cultures vary in terms of how important each value is (e.g., its priority) in influencing social practices (Schwartz, 1992; Schwartz & Barat, 2001). Spencer-Oatey (2007) concluded that analyzing values reveals the attributes that people may be "face sensitive to, and thereby offer partial reasons for people's sensitivities" (p. 651). It is essential to acknowledge that different values are weighted differently within and across cultures, situations and identities (Chen, 2011; Spencer-Oatey, 2005).

Carbaugh (2007) also notes the importance of understanding cultural structures, those "deeply felt," "commonly intelligible" and "widely accessible" tacit beliefs (p. 170). One must also understand cultural propositions, those underlying beliefs of a culture, and cultural premises, which enable one to recognize the significance of what is going on (Carbaugh, 2007, Spencer-Oatey, 2010).

Some cultural traditions incorporate philosophies of harmony and treating all with dignity and respect. There is a reciprocal bond between the individual and the community such that "the reciprocal interplay between self as center and self for others enables the self to become a center of relationships. As a center, personal dignity can never be marginalized and, as relationships, the spirit of consideration is never suppressed" (Tu, 2001, p. 26). The "ethics of duty consciousness in Asia obligates all parties of a community to work together for the common good and well-being of all members" (Miike & Yin, 2015, p. 458).

These Asiacentric perspectives reflect a view of the self, not as an autonomous individual, but as the center of an expanding and evolving web of relationships (Miike, 2010, 2015). On a universal level, such a web extends to viewing oneself as a part of humankind with connections to others, nature and a spiritual power. This inter-connectedness is expressed in Confucian terms by *tianrenheyi*, the Islamic tradition of *tawhid* and the Hindu perspective of *sarvodaya* (Miike & Yin, 2015). Such perspectives acknowledge basic humanity and dignity to be a fundamental right of every person, and by extension, so too is honoring the alternative cultural ways in which people live.

In these Eastern cultures, there are philosophies that emphasize recognizing our common survival and our dependency upon each other. In Buddhism, this recognition of mutual dependence is referred to as "dependent co-arising"; and it has different cultural manifestations and practices (in China as *yuan,* in Japan as *en* and in Korea as *yon*) (Miike & Yin, 2015). Many diversity programs in the United States, for example, recognize that despite many differences common human needs, such as security and adequate food, unite all.

In order to understand other cultures, we need to appreciate each culture's traditions from that culture's perspective (an emic perspective) rather than from external standards developed by outsiders (an etic perspective). This obligates us to examine the evolution of major philosophies and religions to understand the current cultural practices present in many societies (Kaplan, 2014). The past is a framework or lens through which greater insight into current issues can be achieved. This broadened frame of reference allows us to become global citizens, or as Dai (2012) expressed it, to display *interculturality*.

Cultures themselves represent shared values and ways of life, and from that shared base, common ground is established among members of that group. We can extend this common ground to incorporate all humans via shared universal values. These broader universal values can provide a basis for common ground and community among all, regardless of culture. As noted above, some Eastern cultures are already oriented to strong communal values and have traditions and social practices aligned with interconnectedness.

Communication

Culture and communication are inextricably linked because we learn our culture via communication, both verbal and nonverbal. And, in turn, culture shapes our communicative practices (Haslett, 2012b). While intercultural communication provides great challenges because of the lack of shared perspectives across interactants, it also provides an opportunity to learn and explore new ideas, and thus move beyond our own ethnocentrism (Dai, 2010; Ury, 2000, 2009).

Although Eurocentric models and perspectives on communication have dominated scholarly research, more recent scholarship has proposed alternative models which acknowledge multiculturalism and a desire to investigate cultural resources from the vantage point of native scholars. In particular, the emphasis on individuals, senders and receivers, and the direct, rational dialogues of Eurocentric models are being challenged (Asante, 1998; Chen & Starosta, 2003). Alternative models, such as Afrocentric and/or Asiacentric models, emphasize the we/community rather than the I/individual in communication and add a moral dimension of sincerity to our communication models (Miike, 2010; Miike & Yin, 2015). Such models do not merely suggest a collectivist orientation, but an orientation toward what benefits all; such an emphasis is very compatible with the deep structural aspects of face (i.e., trust, empathy, etc.). Such models also move from focusing on cultural differences to interculturality (Dai, 2010).

In order to communicate effectively, Miike and Yin (2015) argue that scholars need to look at communication-related terms ('communication' is a loan word from English), analyze world views and communicative purposes and examine all world systems of communication. Their approach greatly enlarges our views of communication and points the way toward meaningful intercultural dialogue. Miike and Yin (2015) note that *biaoda* (Chinese) and *hyogan* (Japanese) mean to make known, to make things sensible and observable. These processes emphasize subtlety and ambiguities on the part of speakers, and perceptiveness, reciprocity and introspection on the part of listeners. Varied strategies are pursued in expressing one's self, and written communication may be used as an important system of expression.

Communicative strategies also vary widely, frequently influenced by religion (Miike & Yin, 2015). For example, in Islamic cultures, people memorize the Quran which provides a common pool of information and communicative practices still in use today. In the Hindu tradition, communication is to know the inner self and one's connection to a supreme power (*Brahman* or the universal soul). Self-knowledge is the main purpose of communication, and greater self-knowledge leads to more effective communication. In Buddhism, communication reflects moving toward spiritual enlightenment (being one with the universe), removing excessive ego which is the source of much mental suffering and becoming a very compassionate individual (Brummans & Hwang, 2010). A Confucian perspective focuses on self-cultivation and self-transformation through communication with others: this leads to sensitivity to the emotions of others (Shuter, 2003).

Intercultural communication, as many scholars have noted, can be approached as a balancing act between differences and similarities. Chen and Starosta (2003) argued that effective communication is understanding "that differences exist in the similarity, and to pursue the unity from the differences" (p. 5). In China, "the middle way" acknowledges the balance that can be achieved between opposites rather than viewing opposites as intractable differences (Chen, 2004, 2015). In short, the situation is not *either/or* but *both/and*: Through balancing opposites, one finds new creative opportunity and harmony (see a very rich discussion of balancing opposites by Chung, 2011).

With this brief overview of the complexities of culture and of communication, we have found frameworks that support the idea of common ground and community. As noted, some cultural models are already oriented toward group and community. Communicative practices, framed by an Asiacentric or Afrocentric perspective, have also modeled practices for forming community and extending that to humankind generally.

Given this complexity of cultural and communicative practices, how can we establish effective strategies for conflict resolution? We now turn to explore the intersection of communication, culture and conflict as broadly conceptualized by Kozan (1997), based upon the distinctions between associative and abstractive cultures articulated by Edmund Glenn (1983). First, we briefly characterize conflict, and then move to a consideration of communication, culture and conflict.

Communication, Culture and Conflict Management

Conflict Management

Standard definitions of conflict rest upon the assumption of opposing interests in which each party views the other as blocking the achievement of their goals (Hocker & Wilmot, 2014). For conflict resolution, many strategies assume a zero-sum outlook in which parties either gain or lose, and win-win outcomes are very unlikely. Varying strategies, such as accommodation, compromise, avoidance and competition, have been developed to resolve conflict and studied cross-culturally. However, given cultural differences in worldviews and social practices, misunderstanding in handling intercultural conflict is likely because the same communicative strategy may be interpreted differently by different cultures (Haslett, 2014; Kozan, 1997).

Culture, Conflict and Conflict Resolution Strategies

In a very comprehensive overview of culture and conflict, Kozan (1997) utilized Glenn's model of associative and abstractive cultures (1983) to develop a holistic framework for contrasting conflict styles across different cultures. Associative cultures view knowledge as something gained through experience and feeling, and use par-ticularistic reasoning: such cultures are high-context cultures that look at the totality of experiences over time and thus rely upon a broadened frame of reference. In contrast, abstractive cultures rely upon shared, developed systems of knowledge and tend to be universalistic in their cognitive style. Communication is more specific and differentiated; distinctions are made between the individual and their work. Abstractive cultures are differentiated into two different types: neo-particularistic (emphasizing objectivity) and co-subjective (emphasizing universalistic principles).

Kozan developed three models of conflict and applied them to Glenn's cultural models. Glenn's associative model was integrated with a conflict style of harmony; neo-particularistic cultures with a confrontational conflict style; and co-subjective cultures with a regulative conflict style. Hofstede's collectivistic cultures were linked to Glenn's associative cultures, and abstractive cultures were linked to highly individualistic cultures with low uncertainty avoidance (confrontational style) or high uncertainty avoidance (regulative conflict style).

Kozan also employed an inclusive model of conflict processes including ante-cedent conditions (factors, such as past events and actions, influencing the current conflict event); thoughts and emotions surrounding the conflict, behavior in the current conflict and conflict outcomes. Also included were interventions by man-agers and third parties to help resolve disputes. The qualities and characteristics found in Kozan's analysis are found in Table 5.1.

Countries utilizing the *harmony* conflict model are collectivist cultures such as Japan and China. In the harmony model, conflict is minimized to preserve relationships and to maintain social and moral order. Groups rely on normative reasoning and exhibit positive emotion. With high power distance and high collectivism, there is a reduced perception of emotional intensity. Conflict styles emphasize accommodation and avoidance, with low competitiveness. The maintenance of face is highly valued, and there is concern for both self- and other-face. Conflict process concerns center upon following the appropriate rituals to preserve the social position and status of the conflict participants. The maintenance of long-term relationships is also important.

The *confrontational* model emphasizes fair play, mutual concessions and compromise, and is characteristic of abstractive, neo-particularistic cultures such as the United States. Aggressive pursuit of one's goals is acceptable and conflict is seen as natural, and even desirable. Negative emotions can be displayed, and confrontation and compromise are both strategies used to secure outcomes. Third party interventions are usually by those who have such intervention as an institutional responsibility.

TABLE 5.1 Three cultural models of conflict managementx

Antecedent Conditions	Low competitiveness due to observance of mutual obligations	Highly competitive work environment due to individualistic goals	Low competitiveness due to extensive rules and procedures
Thoughts	Holistic definition of conflict in particular-istic terms	Analytical defini-tion of conflict in terms of sub issues	Analytical definition of conflict in terms of universalistic principles
Emotions	Suppression of nega-tive emotions	Expression of nega-tive emotions	Expression of nega-tive emotions
Behavior	Avoidance and accommodation	Confrontation and compromise	Avoidance or forcing
Outcome criteria	Face-saving concerns	Due process concerns	Due process concerns
No managerial third parties	Frequent, intrusive, informal	Infrequent, plan-ned, non-intrusive	Formal appeal sys-tems, adjunctive
Managerial intervention	Mediatorial	Facilitative or autocratic	Restructuring or laissez-faire
Third-party emphasis	Harmony, shame	Reason, fairness (equity)	Reason, general principles (equality)

Source: Kozan, 1997, p. 358.

Finally, a *regulative* model focuses on conflict resolved primarily by universal rules and principles. Rules help contain conflict and create shared meanings through the use of universal principles. The rights and responsibilities of various roles help remove emotions from the conflict. A major emphasis is on finding the right principles to be applied in any given situation. Avoidance and/or authoritative command are strategies used to resolve conflict and negotiation follows fairly rigid processes. Procedural justice is very important as due process must be followed: countries following these principles include Russia, France, Great Britain and Spain.

Of course, these models reflect ideal types of conflict resolution models and most cultures will follow more than one model. For example, Kozan suggested that the harmony model operates differently in cultures that are expressive versus more reserved, and people-oriented rather than primarily respect-oriented. Arab and Latin American countries would exemplify expressive and people-oriented cultures while China and Japan would reflect more reserved and respect-oriented cultures. Within culture variation may also be significant with different situations, issues, groups of people and frames of reference involved in conflict. Kozan also noted that the use of a particular strategy may be viewed very differently by dif-ferent cultures and thus single strategy comparisons, like studying avoidance over different cultures, might lead to misleading conclusions.

As such, studying conflict resolution across different cultures is a very complex issue, particularly in light of different historical contexts, and with different cogni-tive frames of reference being applied. While some studies found differences across cultural styles in handling conflict, similarities in conflict strategies can also be noted, such as those suggested by Kozan. For example, a comparative study by Terpstra-Tong and Ralston (2002) found that both the United States and a number of Eastern countries preferred to use reason or rational persuasion and soft tactics over hard tactics in their upward influence strategies. Tjosvold and Wang (2013) suggested that framing conflict as incompatible actions helps lay a foundation for cooperative goals and leads to managing conflict.

Kozan's perspective categorizes cultures into different orientations toward conflict: cultures may have approaches based on harmony, competition or regulation. As such, Kozan presents a complex portrait of both similarities and differences in handling conflict. However, recent thinking has moved beyond such contrasts to focus on more broadly-based global needs for interconnections. Much of this thinking recognizes the need for global recognition and cooperation on issues that threaten our very survival, such as global warming, ethnic cleansing, poverty and so forth. We next turn to these models, based on communication and community, in resolving conflict. One such model, the Third Side, has been effectively used in intercultural conflicts such as the Palestinian conflict, Serbia, Northern Ireland and other areas of global tension.

Transforming Conflict through Communication and Community

The importance of communication (dialogue) in conflict management has long been recognized as a critical element in managing conflict. Yet, at times, communicative differences, as well as the conflict issues themselves, seem to be major issues of contention. However, the models discussed here demonstrate the way in which dialogue can be constructively used to manage conflict. In these processes, we face the challenges of globalization, postmodernity and increasing uncertainty. The noted sociologist Zygmunt Bauman discusses the global influence of these forces, and provides a worldwide context in which intercultural conflicts occur.

Bauman: A World View on Postmodernity and Cultural Challenge

Bauman (2000) suggested that globalization is a major world factor in which nation-states must confront change. As Sorrells (2014) noted:

> *globalization* is ... the complex web of economic, political and technological forces that have brought people, cultures, cultural products, and markets, as well as beliefs, practices and ideologies into increasingly greater proximity to and con/disjunction with one another within inequitable relations of power ... it is used to address both the *contested processes* that contribute to and the vastly *inequitable conditions* of living in our contemporary 21st century world.
>
> *(pp. 144–145, emphasis in original)*

Both Bauman and Sorrells share concerns about social justice and constructive conflict management which includes all participants in a dialogue for intercultural communication and understanding.

Bauman (2000) argued that the world has moved from a heavy commodity (hardware) orientation to an information orientation (software). Globalization has created heightened uncertainty and insecurity, with nation-states increasingly unable to provide services for their citizens; as such, Bauman argued for an increased movement toward collective social and political policies. In Bauman's opinion, we experience an

> individualized, privatized version of modernity, with the burden of pattern-weaving and the responsibility for failing falling primarily on the individual's shoulders. It is the patterns of dependency and interaction whose turn to be liquefied has now come. They are now malleable to an extent unexperienced by, and unimaginable for, past generations.
>
> *(2000, pp. 7–8)*

Individuals are more able to determine their own particular paths and increasingly separated from any sense of shared public interest. Furthermore, people have significant choice and can seek their own identity, dependent only on their own resources, and, thus, people have moved to a consumerist lifestyle. Through the processes of globalization, there is an increasing divide between wealth and poverty, and with an individual's responsibility becoming increasingly private, collective action has become difficult.

The challenges of such a fragmented, individualist world may be met, Bauman suggests, by a community orientation in which there is joint negotiation and reconciliation, and in which all voices are heard. As Bauman (2000) noted, in the present state of liquid modernity, the value of beliefs can be established in a multidialogue in

> which all voices will be admitted, and in which all possible comparisons and juxtapositions will be made in good faith and with good intentions. In other words, the acknowledgement of cultural difference is for the sake of this argument the beginning rather than the end of the matter.
>
> *(p. 60)*

Bauman's worldview presents multiple challenges to managing our lives as well as our conflicts. However, the call for collective action, a sense of common ground and concern for all, is one that has great appeal. In what follows, we will discuss the work of several scholars who have presented approaches to establishing common ground which provides a basis for intercultural cooperation.

Dai's Interculturality

According to Dai (2010), individuals must go beyond their own cultural boundaries to establish intercultural connections with others. Both intersubjectivity and interculturality involve establishing relationships between self and other. Such connections may develop on an *individual* level where the individual distinguishes himself/herself from others; on an *interpersonal* level in developing relationships with others; on the *collective* level in which the self-interacts with larger groups and, lastly, on a *humanity* level when the self is viewed as belonging to the human species.

Whereas intersubjectivity within the same culture relies on shared cultural knowledge, in intercultural communication the understanding of the other is based upon cultural overlaps between the two interactants and human universals. Inter-subjectivity is transformed into interculturality through experience with others in varied contexts; over time, these intercultural agreements broaden one's worldview.

Among human commonalities, Dai noted that:

> people in all cultures desire beauty, want to be respected and pursue happiness. In essence, they have similar life worlds and similar needs .... More importantly, they all possess communicative reason—the ability to criticize and argue with others, and can learn from each other, perfect each other and reach agreement across cultures.
>
> *(2010, p. 16)*

Through the ability to understand the other, and to think reflectively about the other and our interactions, we broaden our understanding of others and appreciate new points of view and behavior (Kim, 2008).

An intercultural orientation relies upon both local and foreign knowledge as a frame of reference. As Dai noted, intercultural persons

> no longer take their own value for granted and interpret things merely from one cultural perspective, but rather view things from both their and others' cultural lens and try to synthesize the local and foreign knowledge into an extended intercultural frame of reference.
>
> *(2010, p. 17)*

This interculturality provides a broader platform for dialogue, enhances mutual understanding and helps turn differences into creative interactions. Interculturality is particularly important in conflict resolution. As Dai noted, within interculturality,

> people will find it easier to locate where a problem lies and work out *a mutually acceptable way to solve it* ... in the intercultural way of thinking, difference is not only legitimized, but also appreciated and treated as a dialogue promoter.
>
> *(2010, p. 18, emphasis added)*

Ury's Third Side

William Ury is an internationally renowned negotiator who has assisted in managing conflict in many troubled sites around the world, such as Northern Ireland, the Middle East and Africa. His forty years of working in this area has led him to develop and refine an approach to conflict termed the Third Side (Ury, 2000, 2009; www.thethirdside.org). He has found that all cultures follow elements of this approach in some fashion: the heart of this approach is community and reflects the common heritage of humankind. More specifically, the Third Side involves a community of concerned people, both within and without the conflict arena, who try to contain the conflict and create constructive resolutions for conflict. Creating a "Third Side"—a common ground—helps disputants to focus upon a shared problem rather than confronting each other. Third Side strategies try to move the dialogue to a place of creative exchange where new options and perspectives help create a new shared perspective on a common problem.

Underlying this perspective are several assumptions about conflict and approaches to conflict. First, conflict is natural and healthy, and may in fact be necessary for progress and coping with injustice. Second, the Third Side (3S) attempts to transform how conflict is expressed and to utilize constructive skills such as debate and dialogue to manage conflict. Third, the surrounding community acts as a container for creative exchanges. Fourth, one can reflect upon the 3S process at any point in a conflict, searching for an understanding of all sides of a particular conflict. And fifth, many different roles can be played in the 3S process but all require courage, preparation, knowledge, skill, coordination and creativity (www.thirdside.org).

According to Ury, there are three stages at which conflict can be transformed from a destructive to a constructive process. At the initial stage of *latent tensions,* steps can be taken to try and prevent escalation of the conflict. In the next stage of *overt conflict,* steps may be taken to resolve the conflict. And finally, in the stage of *struggling over power,* steps can be taken to contain the conflict.

At the initial stage of tension, a variety of tensions may arise out of frustrated needs, limited knowledge, poor skills in communication and weak relationships among the community. People acting as *providers* may assist in meeting basic human needs such as food, safety, identity and freedom. *Teachers* may help people learn new perspectives, skills and values so other alternatives, besides violence, are available. *Bridge-builders* help create and strengthen relationships within the community and across disputing parties.

During the second stage of overt conflict, people may play important roles as *mediators* when they discuss the dispute and try to encourage parties to really evaluate what they want and why, and then suggest possible alternative approaches. An *arbiter* has the right to settle a dispute and different people may serve as arbiters, such as teachers, parents or a manager. *Equalizers* use their influence to try to democratize power and collectively act to empower those who are unrepresented and weak. Finally, the wounds from conflict may be very deep and *healers* take an active role in helping people deal with emotions arising from the conflict. Ury suggests that conflicts cannot truly be fully resolved until damaged relationships have begun to heal.

The final stage of containment involves people participating as witnesses, referees and peacekeepers. *Witnesses* act to observe and act on conflict, and draw attention to the conflict and related violence. *Referees* essentially set the rules for fighting fairly: fighting can help clear the air, but it should be done in a way that minimizes harm. When the limits on fighting have been breached, *peacekeepers* need to intervene and stop violent, harmful conflict.

The 3S process may develop and be established over years, and progress may be slow and uneven. Many people can play different roles in this process and at multiple levels. Community support is drawn from insiders who have close ties and vested interests in the dispute, as well as from the outside community who can support and facilitate conflict management. The 3S process has been successfully used on multiple levels, including peer conflict, parent-child conflict, organizational conflict and conflicts between countries and ethnic groups. Thus, the process is effective on multiple levels with individuals as well as groups of varying sizes.

Constructive handling of conflict also involves the ability to reframe the situation—to see it in a new light, and thus open up new, alternative ideas and proposals. People are encouraged to think about *what* they want but also about *why* they want it.

After reframing, Ury suggested that we try to build a golden bridge, not for our opponents to retreat as suggested by Sun Tzu, but to view it as a bridge for both parties to advance and meet.

Every individual can learn negotiation skills and employ the 3S process. Ury argues that it is necessary to "Go to the balcony". In essence, you remove yourself from the conflict and view it as if it were being acted out on stage. You step back and look at the conflict from a distance and ask yourself how the conflict might be viewed differently.

First, you need to *stop*: step away, take time out, relax and clear your mind, and think about the conflict process. Second, it is important to *look*: look at your initial reaction to take sides and ignore that, and then name your emotions rather than venting them. Finally, *listen*: listen to hear your emotions, and to understand what is going on. These three steps are essential in the 3S process and enable one to be more open to new ideas and creative solutions.

In Ury's experience, the emergent will of the community is a critical component in managing conflict—the will to deal constructively, not destructively, with conflict. Through trust, being perceived as impartial, and displaying respect, people can make significant improvement in managing conflict constructively. Another important ingredient is understanding the history surrounding the conflict and the cultural differences that may be involved. As he noted, in his experience, peace involves dealing with our deepest differences, and from this great things and new solutions may emerge (Ury, 2009).

Many studies of conflict have focused on alternative conflict styles and strategies followed by different cultures, but the Third Side concept, as can readily be seen, moves beyond this by reconceptualizing the process of conflict and conflict management. Ury's conflict management strategies involve both establishing common ground and utilizing multiple communicative roles. Both Dai's discussion of interculturality and Bauman's liquid modernity are important in establishing larger frames of reference for interacting across culturally different individuals and societies.

Goffman's model of face also echoes many of the themes Ury has developed in the concept and practice of the Third Side. Mutual themes include reframing, respect and multiple points of view. In what follows, we will discuss face as a concept for approaching constructive conflict management, and a set of communicative practices that support face. It is argued that face is a universal practice found in all cultures and, when extended to intercultural dialogue and conflict management, will provide a foundation for establishing common ground and transforming intercultural conflict management. While face is a universal value, cultures vary in how they do facework (Bargiela-Chiappini & Haugh, 2009).

Goffman's Model of Face

Goffman acknowledged culture as a fundamental frame for interaction and further utilizes frames as a way of establishing particular contexts for interaction. As he observed:

> Frames are a central part of a culture and are institutionalized in various ways. They are subject to change historically …. Whatever the idiosyncrasies of their own motives and interpretation, they [individuals] must gear their participation into what is available by way of standard doings and standard reasons for doing those doings
>
> *(1981, p. 63)*

Those standard doings and standard reasons are frames that characterize a culture's social practices. It is through interaction "that our understandings of our own long-term relationships and commitments, and of our society's widely institutionalized enterprises, will be subject to confirmation and undermining during these [interactive] occasions" (Goffman, 1981, p. 68). Frames are like a "filtering process through which societal-level values and principles of conduct are transformed and refocused so as to apply to the situation at hand" (Gumperz, 2001, p. 217). These frames can also be laminated (re-interpreted) and thus offer new frameworks for interpretation and action (Goffman, 1974).

Face is supported tacitly, without apparent effort, so that face itself does not become a focus of attention in interaction. In effective interaction, participants display respect for the encounter through demeanor (an appropriate attitude) and deference (appropriate recognition of status) in interaction. Interactants are vulnerable to face threats which can lead to embarrassment and/or shame. As Ho (1994) pointed out, reciprocity is an integral aspect of face and people themselves may lose face by failing to give face to others. As such, face represents the "reciprocated compliance, respect, and/or deference that each party expects from, and extends to, the other party" (Ho, 1976, p. 883; Hu, 1944).

Both Goffman and Ho suggested that face is critical in acknowledging the meaningfulness of our actions as human beings. All humans have a moral right to the claim of a basic, decent face.... It is the minimum, irreducible, and inviolate face that one must maintain for adequate functioning as a social being. The loss of this basic face would seriously threaten the integrity of one's social being or, worse, one's acceptability as a member of human society.

(Ho, 1994, p. 279)

Ho also observed that face is "far more profound than just politeness, embarrassment, or impression management .... At rock bottom, face as the integrity of one's social being is not something that has to be earned, but is an inalienable right to human dignity" (p. 277). Being treated with dignity, when interacting with others, is at the heart of Goffman's concept of face and is how we present our saneness and competence as social beings.

Goffman pointed out that the "maintenance of face is a condition of interaction, not its objective" (1967, p. 12). Face is focused on others in displaying deference:

Concern for face is a pervasive social sanction ... it is a powerful mechanism underlying other-directedness, that is, acting in ways that reflect a high degree of sensitivity for how one's actions are perceived and reacted to by others ... to maintain face, to avoid losing face, and to regain face lost are essential for effective social functioning.

(Ho, 1994, pp. 272–273)

Ting-Toomey (1994) suggested that "[f]ace involves the claimed sense of self-respect or self-dignity in an interactive situation. Facework involves the verbal and nonverbal negotiation aspects of face maintenance, face claim, and face expectation" (p. 3).

Face also applies to groups and the group face may, at times, take precedent over individual face (as it may in Asian countries) (see Haugh, 2007, 2009; Sifianou & Tzanne, 2011). According to Goffman, "It is as if face, by its very nature, can be saved in a certain number of ways, and as if each social grouping must make its selection from this single matrix of possibilities" (1967, p. 13).

Thus, face may embrace a wide range of behavior, and different face needs may emerge in different contexts and with different participants. Scholars have developed a range of facework strategies that reflect how individuals manage face. People try to sustain a viable image of themselves over diverse contexts and in order to sustain a viable image "footwork, or rather self work, will be continuously necessary" (Goffman, 1971, p. 185). In fact, Goffman noted that "Each person, subculture, and society seems to have its own characteristic repertoire of face-saving practices. It is to this repertoire that people partly refer when they ask what a person or culture is 'really' like" (1971, p. 185).

Because all cultures utilize face in interaction but may vary in how facework is enacted, a major task is to understand how face is viewed in different cultures— what are the important components of face? For example, cultures may vary in terms of their concern for self-face, mutual face or other-face. Ting-Toomey

(1994) found that face and facework varied across the cross cultural dimensions of individualism and collectivism. Conflict strategies also varied as a function of concern for self-face, other-face and mutual face (Ting-Toomey, 1994, 2005; Ting-Toomey & Kurogi, 1998). Using face-negotiation theory, self-construals and national culture were found to influence face and facework strategies (Oetzel et al., 2001). Haugh (2009) observed that face can also "involve an awareness of one's position within a network ... [and] be associated with groups as well as individuals" (p. 209).

Cultures strongly influenced by Confucianism assign degrees of face to different social categories such as priest, teacher or business person. Hu (1944) observed two aspects to face in China, *mien-tzu* (achievement or external accomplishments) and *lien* (moral character, an internal characteristic). Lim (2004) found four universal aspects of face in Korea: decency, integrity, nobility and capability. Koreans desire to demonstrate that they are a group of "exemplary and honorable human beings" (p. 65) and, in conflict, use strategies relying on relational holism (Kim, Kim, & Lim, 2013). Chen (2001) noted that harmony is a very strong aspect of communication in China, and to avoid conflict Chinese follow strategies such as self-restraint/self-discipline, reciprocity, indirect expression of disapproval, establishing face for opponents and emphasizing particularistic relationships.

There appears to be considerable variation in how face is conceptualized and in the communicative strategies used to honor face (Ting-Toomey & Oetzel, 2002). Thus, while face is universal, the requirements of face are culturally specific. Knowledge of appropriate face needs is thus a subject for research and rests upon the values of the cultural group being studied (Kim & Nam, 1998). To manage intercultural communication and conflict, interactants must possess knowledge of one another that incorporates history, cultural values and social practices like face.

In managing conflict, it is particularly important to express respect for others and face provides the motivation for establishing that respect. For Goffman, face emerges through interaction and depends upon the response of others. As such, for Goffman,

> situations are rituals calling for cooperation in keeping up the momentary focus of attention and thus giving respect both to the persons who properly take part and to the situational reality as something worth a moment of being treated seriously.
>
> *(Collins, 2004, p. 24)*

Holtgraves observed that, for Goffman,

> face is a more basic and more abstract construct that is entailed in the projection of any identity or line .... Face, therefore, is not an objective of interaction but rather a condition for interaction, or a ritual constraint. Moreover, because face (and deference) can be given only by others, it is each other person's best interest to maintain the other's face. Acting with demeanor (supporting one's own face)

entails acting with deference (supporting the other's face) ... facework is (and must be) a cooperative venture.

(1992, p. 142)

Equity among participants in an interaction is established by orienting toward others as well as oneself, and observing mutual face is a primary way in which to establish these mutual concerns.

Among interactants,

the concern for face exerts a reciprocated constraint upon each member of the social network ... and it is a powerful mechanism underlying other-directedness, that is, acting in ways that reflect a high degree of sensitivity for how one's actions are perceived and reacted to by others.

(Ho, 1994, p. 272)

Through face, in the display of appropriate demeanor and deference, humans enact the cultural and social practices that constitute their daily lives (Hu, 1944). As such, face is constitutive of interaction—a necessary condition for interaction itself.

Goffman observed that any group

must mobilize their members as self-regulating participants in social encounters. One way of mobilizing the individual for this purpose is through ritual: he is taught to be perceptive, to have feelings attached to self and a self expressed through face, to have pride, honor, and dignity, and to have tact and a certain amount of poise.

(1967, p. 44)

Conflict management may especially rely on the qualities of dignity, tact and poise since conflict itself may challenge participants' dignity.

Intercultural interactions are complex. Underlying tacit assumptions about communicative practices are not shared and, indeed, may conflict across cultures. In addition, such cultural practices may be largely hidden and out-of-our-awareness. Past sociohistoric conflicts and antagonism may also complicate honoring face in intercultural communication because such problems may influence present day situations (Giddens, 1984, 1990; Kim, 2007; Sifianou, 2012).

Communicative Premises

Face reflects the sacredness and sanity of human beings, irrespective of social or cultural groups. However, how face is conceptualized and how facework is carried out varies across cultures. Nevertheless, core communicative premises underlie universal face which is present in every encounter. These premises support effective intercultural communication as well as conflict management. These premises, comprising both nonverbal and verbal dimensions of communication (Haslett, 2014), include:

1.   Acknowledging mutual face by honoring both self and other face; a viable self-other orientation is a marker of intercultural identity (Kim, 2009);
2.   Displaying trust which supports the routines of social life and social interaction (Goffman, 1983a);
3.   Displaying respect;
4.   Displaying empathy and affect (Goffman, 1983b);
5.   Acknowledging plurality of beliefs, values and behaviors in the search for common ground;
6.   Acknowledging equity in participation across participants—all have voice. Equity implies being aware of privilege/disadvantage across cultures and individuals (Chen, 2011; Sorrells, 2014).

Fundamentally, these premises outline communicative principles for honoring face—the dignity of social beings—in interaction across the wide variation in human behavior, attitudes and cultural practices. While these principles are not necessarily exhaustive, they represent an excellent base for establishing face for both effective intercultural communication and conflict management. Furthermore, these premises honor the sense in which Goffman developed the concept of face.

In what follows, I suggest some communicative practices that support these communicative principles. As a departure point, I believe that *mindfulness* is a necessary, but not sufficient, condition for effective intercultural communication and conflict management. All of the principles outlined above, and the associated communicative practices outlined below, rely on thoughtful, non-judgmental analysis of one's own cultural scripts as well as those of others. I agree with Langer's (1989) conceptualization of mindfulness which involves being aware of multiple categories or perspectives; being open to new information and being able to form new categories in which to perceive and make sense of the world. Despite differences we must find cooperative, collaborative ways in which to live and to interact, and mindfulness will assist in achieving constructive collaboration.

Face is supported by the following verbal and nonverbal communication practices.

1.   *Respect.* Respect is supported by the display of appropriate deference (acknowledging the other's face) and of demeanor (the projection of an appropriate attitude toward one's self and toward the situation) (Goffman, 1955, 1956). By displaying consideration and respect, individuals may create a sense of moral obligation for others to reciprocate and thus encourage continued dialogue (Patriotta & Specdale, 2009). The ability to display appropriate deference and demeanor rests upon knowledge of the cultural practices of interactants and especially being aware of your own cultural practices (Stadler, 2013; Ting-Toomey et al., 1991). In the context of conflict management, there must be commitment to the relationships in intercultural encounters—a willingness to persevere across difficulties and disappointments to reach some common ground (Ury, 2000, 2009).

2. *Trust.* Trust incorporates the most basic bedrock of universal face—we recognize our own and other's personhood and acknowledge a shared sense of social reality and mutual vulnerability. While the bases for trust will vary across cultures, we must begin conflict management—intercultural or not—with a fundamental trust in mutual dignity and with an acknowledgment of mutual vulnerability among participants. In discussing trust in Goffman's work, Comte (2008) concluded that trust "constitutes a universal social datum and an elementary precondition for social exchanges and the cooperation between individuals" (p. 375).

3. *Communion as expressed in empathy and affect.* Face also engenders affect such as shame, embarrassment, pride and so forth (Goffman, 1956, 1967, 1983a, 1983b). Conflict frequently involves strong emotion and emotional regulation plays an important role in effective intercultural communication (Guerrero, 2013). Matsumoto, LeRoux, Robles and Campos (2007) suggested that critical thinking, adaptability, openness and conflict resolution are hampered if emotions are not regulated (i.e., if negative emotions are not controlled). A key to empathy is the capacity to take another's perspective, and observing universal face will be very useful in this respect. It is also critical to acknowledge emotions such as fear, anger, shame and loss in managing conflict and to establish a climate in which such emotions may be expressed and understood (Abu-Nimer, 2001; Meyer, 2001).

4. *Plurality of beliefs.* Intercultural encounters require a high degree of adaptability because many of our taken-for-granted beliefs and assumptions do not apply in intercultural contexts. Some of the dialectic tensions residing in intercultural conflicts, such as the dialectic of privilege/disadvantage or present-future/past-history, are present within cultures as well (Martin & Nakayama, 1999). Such tensions may be highlighted in intercultural conflicts and a basic respect for diverse perspectives must exist. Through reframing contexts in conflict settings, common ground and flexible communicative practices may emerge. As Xiao (2014) suggested, a "common ground of cross-cultural understanding is that which is constructed by two cultural parties who are willing to communicate with each other and make efforts to reach a certain state of mutual understanding" (p. 8).

5. *Openness in communication.* Another key communicative practice rests upon open communication. Being open to others rests upon being non-judgmental because being non-judgmental lessens vulnerability and risk for all participants.

6. *Equity among interactants.* Goffman's concept of face is based upon the moral rights and obligations people owe one another by virtue of being human and being involved in a social world. That is, we treat others and are treated by others with dignity, tact and reciprocity: we need to find ways of living together that honor all voices and multiple cultural practices.

Generally, this chapter has argued for reframing our approaches to conflict management by focusing on what unites us, as humans. Honoring face should be an important part of this process because face is a cultural universal. Part of the knowledge we need to learn about one another is an understanding about how facework functions across different cultures (Hwang, 2011; Ting-Toomey et al., 1991). There is a growing appreciation of common ground and how this common ground may provide a basis for constructive conflict management. Such views are already displayed in many Eastern cultures that are based on community and harmony among cultural members. And scholarly work, such as that of Dai, Bauman, Haslett, and Goffman, outlines ways in which differing cultures and mindsets can reach common ground through broadened perspectives and a fundamental respect for all humans. Finally, effective conflict management programs, like Ury's Third Side, give us communicative strategies and hope for managing conflict even in the most difficult, intractable conflicts.

While these principles and practices may seem idealized and unrealistic, they are goals worth working toward because they increase the opportunities for successful conflict management. As Kaplan (2014) observed,

> Cooperative social action is the proverbial twofer. It focuses the community on addressing needed projects and simultaneously breaks down barriers by creating friendships among participants as they collaborate. Participants derive a sense of accomplishment from their work. Communication and mutual respect are promoted as they collaborate.
>
> *(p. 200)*

With community, communication and respect, truly remarkable progress can be made toward managing conflict and building a sustainable future.

References

Abu-Nimer, M. (2001). Conflict resolution approaches: Western and Middle Eastern lessons and possibilities. In P. Chew (Ed.), *The conflict and culture reader* (pp. 230–235). New York, NY: New York University Press.

Asante, M. K. (1998). *The Afrocentric idea.* Philadelphia, PA: Temple University Press.

Bargiela-Chiappini, F. & Haugh, M. (2009). *Face, communication and social interaction.* London, UK: Equinox.

Bauman, Z. (2000). *Liquid modernity.* Cambridge, UK: Polity.

Brummans, B. H. J. M. & Hwang, J. (2010). Tsu Chi's organizing for a compassionate world: Insights into the communicative praxis of a Buddhist organization. *Journal of International and Intercultural Communication, 3*(2), 136–163.

Carbaugh, D. (2007). Cultural discourse analysis: Communication practices and intercultural encounters. *Journal of Intercultural Communication Research, 36,* 167–182.

Chen, G. M. (2001). Toward transcultural understanding: A harmony theory of Chinese communication. In V. H. Milhouse, M. K. Asante, & P. G. Nwosu (Eds.), *Transcultural realities: Interdisciplinary perspectives on cross-cultural relations* (pp. 55–70). Thousand Oaks, CA: Sage.

Chen, G. M. (2002). The impact of harmony on Chinese conflict management. In G. M. Chen & R. Ma (Eds.), *Chinese conflict management and resolution* (pp. 3–19). Westport, CT: Ablex.

Chen, G. M. (2004). The two faces of Chinese communication. *Human Communication*, 7(1), 27–36.

Chen, G. M. (2015). An alternative view of identity. In L. Samovar, R. Porter, E. McDaniel, & C. Roy (Eds.), *Intercultural communication: A reader* (pp. 61–69). Boston, MA: Cengage Learning.

Chen, G. M. & Starosta, W. J. (2003). Asian approaches to human communication: A dialogue. *Intercultural Communication Studies*, 3, 97–109.

Chen, L. (2011). Cultural identity as a production in process. *Journal of Asian Pacific Communication*, 21, 213–237.

Chung, J. (2011). Chi (qi) process: The interplay of opposites in selected communication contexts. *Chinese Media Research*, 7(4), 85–92.

Collier, M. J. (2015). Cultural identity and intercultural communication. In L. Samovar, R. Porter, E. McDaniel & C. Roy (Eds.), *Intercultural communication: A reader* (pp. 53–60). Boston, MA: Cengage Learning.

Collins, R. (2004). *Interaction chains*. Princeton, NJ: Princeton University Press.

Comte, M. (2008). Little naked pangs of the self: The real performance of the self and the function of trust in Goffman's action theory. *International Review of Sociology*, 18, 375–392.

Dai, X. D. (2010). Intersubjectivity and interculturality: A conceptual link. *China Media Research*, 6(1), 12–19.

Giddens, A. (1984). *The constitution of society*. Berkeley, CA: University of California Press.

Giddens, A. (1990). *The consequences of modernity*. Cambridge: Polity Press.

Glenn, E. S. (1983). *Man and mankind: Conflict and communication between cultures*. Rahway, NJ: Ablex.

Goffman, E. (1955). On face-work: An analysis of ritual elements in social interaction. *Psychiatry: Journal for the Study of Interpersonal Processes*, 18(3), 213–231.

Goffman, E. (1956). Embarrassment and social organization. *The American Journal of Sociology*, 62, 264–271.

Goffman, E. (1967). *Interaction ritual: Essays on face-to-face behavior*. Garden City, NY: Doubleday, Anchor Books.

Goffman, E. (1971). *Relations in public: Microstudies of the public order*. New York, NY: Basic Books.

Goffman, E. (1974). *Frame analysis*. New York, NY: Basic Books.

Goffman, E. (1981). *Forms of talk*. Oxford, UK: Blackwell.

Goffman, E. (1983a). The interaction order. *American Sociological Review*, 48, 1–17.

Goffman, E. (1983b). Felicity's condition. *American Journal of Sociology*, 89(1), 1–53.

Guerrero, L. K. (2013). Emotion and communication in conflict interaction. In J. Oetzel & S. Ting-Toomey (Eds.), *The Sage handbook of conflict communication* (pp. 105–131). Thousand Oaks, CA: Sage.

Gumperz, J. (2001). Interactional sociolinguistics: A personal perspective. In D. Schiffrin, D. Tannen & H. Hamilton (Eds.), *The handbook of discourse analysis* (pp. 215–228). Oxford, UK: Blackwell.

Haslett, B. (2012a). A structurational interaction approach to investigating culture, identity and mediated communication. In P. Cheong, J. Martin & L. Macfadyen (Eds.), *New media and intercultural communication: Identity, community and politics* (pp. 39–59). New York, NY: Peter Lang.

Haslett, B. (2012b). *Communicating and organizing in context: The theory of structurational interaction*. New York, NY: Routledge.

Haslett, B. (2014). A face model of intercultural communicative competence. In X. D. Dai & G. M. Chen (Eds.), *Intercultural communicative competence: Conceptualization and its development in cultural contexts and interactions* (pp. 118–143). Newcastle upon Tyne, UK: Cambridge Scholars Publishers.

Haugh, M. (2007). The discursive challenge to politeness theory: An interactional alternative. *Journal of Politeness Theory*, 3, 295–317.

Haugh, M. (2009). Face and interaction. In F. Bargiela-Chiappini & M. Haugh (Eds.), *Face, communication, and social interaction* (pp. 1–30). London, UK: Equinox.

Ho, D. (1976). On the concept of face. *American Journal of Sociology*, 81, 867–884.

Ho, D. (1994). Face dynamics: From conceptualization to measurement. In S. Ting-Toomey (Ed.), *The challenge of facework* (pp. 269–285). Albany, NY: SUNY Press.

Hocker, J., & Wilmot, W. W. (2014). *Interpersonal conflict* (14th ed.). New York, NY: McGraw Hill.

Hofstede, G. (2001). *Culture's consequences: Comparing values, behaviors, institutions, and organizations across nations*. Thousand Oaks, CA: Sage.

Holtgraves, M. (1992). The linguistic realization of face management: Implications for language production and comprehension, person perception, and cross-cultural communication. *Social Psychology Quarterly*, 55, 141–159.

Hu, H. C. (1944). The Chinese concepts of "Face." *American Anthropologist*, 49–50, 61–64.

Hwang, K.-K. (2011). Face dynamism in Confucian society. *China Media Research*, 7(4), 13–24.

Kaplan, H. R. (2014). *Understand conflict and change in a multicultural world*. New York, NY: Rowman & Littlefield.

Karenga, M. (2010). *Introduction to Black studies*. Los Angeles, CA: University of Sankore Press.

Kim, J. Y., & Nam, S. H. (1998). The concept and dynamics of face: Implications for organizational behavior in Asia. *Organization Science*, 9(4), 522–534.

Kim, S. Y., Kim, J., & Lim, T. S. (2013). The impact of relational holism on conflict management styles in colleagueship and friendship: A cross-cultural study. *Studies in Communication Sciences*, 13, 58–66.

Kim, Y. Y. (2007). Ideology, identity, and intercultural communication: An analysis of differing academic conceptions of cultural identity. *Journal of International Communication Research*, 36, 237–253.

Kim, Y. Y. (2008). Intercultural personhood: Globalization and a way of being. *International Journal of Intercultural Relations*, 32(4), 359–368.

Kim, Y. Y. (2009). The identity factor in intercultural competence. In D. Deardorf (Ed.), *The Sage handbook of intercultural competence* (pp. 53–65). Thousand Oaks, CA: Sage.

Kozan, M. K. (1997). Culture and conflict: A theoretical perspective. *The Journal of Conflict Management*, 8(4), 337–360.

Langer, E. (1989). *Mindfulness*. Cambridge, MA: Perseus.

Lim. T.-S. (2004). Towards an Asian model of face: The dimensionality of face in Korea. *Human Communication*, 11, 53–66.

Lustig, M. & Koester, J. (2010). *Intercultural competence*. New York, NY: Allyn & Bacon.

Martin, J. & Nakayama, T. (1999). Thinking dialectically about culture and communication. *Communication Theory*, 1, 1–25.

Matsumoto, D., LeRoux, J. A., Robles, Y., & Campos, G. (2007). The intercultural adjustment potential scale (ICAPS) predict adjustment above and beyond personality and general intelligence. *International Journal of Intercultural Relations*, 31, 747–759.

Meyer, M. (2001). To set right: *Ho'oponopono*, a native Hawaiian way of peacemaking. In P. Chew (Ed.), *The conflict and culture reader* (pp. 176–181). New York, NY: New York University Press.

Miike, Y. (2010). An anatomy of Eurocentrism in communication scholarship: The role of Asiacentricity in de-Westernizing theory and research. *China Media Research*, 6(1), 1–11.

Miike, Y. (2015). "Harmony without uniformity": An Asiacentric worldview and its communicative implications. In L. A. Samovar, R. E. Porter, E. R. McDaniel, & C. Roy (Eds.),
Intercultural communication: A reader (14th ed., pp. 27–41). Boston, MA: Cengage Learning.

Miike, Y. & Yin, J. (2015). Asiacentricity and shapes of the future: Envisioning the field of
intercultural communication in the globalization era. In L. A. Samovar, R. E. Porter, E.
R. McDaniel, & C. Roy (Eds.), *Intercultural communication: A reader* (pp. 449–465). Boston,
MA: Cengage Learning.

Oetzel, J., Ting-Toomey, S., Matsumoto, Y., Pan, X., Tikai, J., & Wilcox, R. (2001). Face
and facework in conflict: A cross-cultural comparison of China, Germany, Japan and the
United States. *Communication Monographs*, 68(3), 235–258.

Patriotta, G. & Specdale, S. (2009). Making sense through face: Identity and social interaction in a consultancy task force. *Organization Studies*, 30, 1227–1248.

Schein, E. (1992). *Organizational culture and leadership*. San Francisco, CA: Jossey-Bass.

Schwartz, S. H. (1992). Are there universals in the structure and content of values: Theoretical advances and empirical tests in 20 countries. In M. Zanna (Ed.), *Advances in
Experimental Social Psychology*, 25, 1–65. New York, NY: Academic Press.

Schwartz, S. H. & Barat, A. (2001). Value hierarchies across cultures: Taking a similarities
perspective. *Journal of Cross Cultural Psychology*, 32, 268–290.

Shuter, R. (2003). Ethics, culture and communication: An intercultural perspective. In L. A.
Samovar, R. E. Porter, E. R. McDaniel, & C. Roy (Eds.), *Intercultural communication: A
reader* (10th ed., pp. 449–455). Belmont, CA: Wadsworth Learning.

Sifianou, M. (2012). Disagreements, face and politeness. *Journal of Pragmatics*, 44, 1554–1564.

Sifianou, M. & Tzanne, A. (2011). Conceptualizations of politeness and impoliteness in
Greek. *Intercultural Pragmatics*, 7(4), 661–687.

Sorrells, K. (2014). Intercultural praxis: Transforming intercultural competence for the 21st
century. In X. D. Dai & G. M. Chen (Eds.), *Intercultural communication competence: Conceptualization and its development in cultural contexts and interactions* (pp. 144–168). Newcastle-
upon-Tyne, UK: Cambridge Scholars Publishing.

Spencer-Oatey, H. (2005). (Im)Politeness, face and perceptions of rapport: Unpackaging
their bases and interrelationships. *Journal of Politeness Research*, 1, 95–119.

Spencer-Oatey, H. (2007). Theories of identity and the analysis of face. *Journal of Pragmatics*,
39, 639–656.

Spencer-Oatey, H. (2010). Intercultural competence and pragmatics research: Examining the
interface through studies of intercultural business discourse. In A. Trosberg (Ed.), *Pragmatics across languages and cultures* (pp. 189–216). Berlin, Germany: Mouton.

Stadler, S. (2013). Cultural differences in the orientation to disagreement and conflict. *China
Media Research*, 9(4), 66–75.

Terpstra-Tong, J. & Ralston, D. (2002). Global understanding of upward influence strategies. *Asia Pacific Journal of Management*, 18, 373–404.

The Third Side. (2015). www.thirdside.org.

Ting-Toomey, S. (1994). Face and facework: An introduction. In S. Ting-Toomey (Ed.),
The challenge of facework. Albany, NY: SUNY Press.

Ting-Toomey, S. (2005). The matrix of face: An updated face-negotiation theory. In
W. Gudykunst (Ed.), *Theorizing about intercultural communication* (pp. 71–92). Thousand
Oaks, CA: Sage.

Ting-Toomey, S., Gao, G., Trubisky, P., Yang, Z., Kim, H., Lin, S-L., & Nishida, T.
(1991). Culture, face maintenance, and styles of handling interpersonal conflict: A study
in five cultures. *The International Journal of Conflict Management*, 2(4), 275–296.

Ting-Toomey, S. & Kurogi, A. (1998). Facework competence in intercultural conflict: An
updated face-negotiation theory. *International Journal of Intercultural Relations*, 22, 187–225.

Ting-Toomey, S. & Oetzel, J. (2002). Cross-cultural face concerns and conflict styles: Current status and future directions. In W. Gudykunst & B. Mody (Eds.), *Handbook of international and intercultural communication* (2nd ed., pp. 143–163). Thousand Oaks, CA: Sage.

Tjosvold, D. & Wang, L. (2013). Developing a shared understanding of conflict: Foundations for Sino-Western mediation. *China Media Research*, 9(4), 76–84.

Tu, W. (2001). The global significance of local knowledge: A new perspective on Confucian humanism. *Sung Kyun Journal of East Asian Studies*, 1, 22–27.

Ury, W. (2000). *The Third Side: Why we fight and how we can stop*. New York, NY: Penguin Books.

Ury, W. (2009). From the boardroom to the border: Negotiating for sustainable agreements. Presentation, November 18, Joan B. Kroc Institute for Peace and Justice, University of San Diego.

Xiao, X. (2014). Constructing common ground for cross-cultural communication. *China Media Research*, 10(4), 1–9.

6

CONFLICT FACE-NEGOTIATION THEORY

Tracking Its Evolutionary Journey

Stella Ting-Toomey

Introduction: A Brief Background

The conflict Face-Negotiation Theory (FNT) , developed by Stella Ting-Toomey (1985, 1988, 2005a, 2015a) explains the culture-based, individual-based, and situational factors that shape communicators' tendencies in approaching and managing conflicts in diverse situations. The outcome components of the FNT also address the competence components and criteria that are needed to arrive at an intercultural harmonizing state. The meaning of "face" is generally conceptualized as how we want others to see us and treat us and how we actually treat others in association with their social self-conception expectations. In everyday interactions, individuals are constantly making conscious or semi-conscious choices concerning face-saving, face maintenance, and face-honoring issues across interpersonal, workplace, and international contexts. While *face* is about a claimed sense of social interactional identity *in situ,* "facework" is about verbal and nonverbal behaviors that protect/save self-face, other-face, mutual-face, or communal-face.

The researching of facework can be found in a wide range of disciplines such as anthropology, psychology, sociology, linguistics/English as a second language, management, international diplomacy, and human communication studies. The concept of face has been used to explain linguistic politeness rituals, apology acts, embarrassment situations, requesting behaviors, and conflict interactions, among others. The basis of the conflict FNT was influenced by Hsien Chin Hu's (1944) anthropological essay on "The Chinese Concept of 'Face'," Erving Goffman's (1955) sociological article on "On Face-Work," and Penelope Brown and Stephen Levinson's (1987) linguistics monograph on "Politeness."

Intercultural conflict refers to the perceived or actual incompatibility of cultural values, situational norms, goals, face orientations, emotions, scarce resources, styles/processes, and/or outcomes in a face-to-face (or mediated) context within

DOI: 10.4324/9781003252955-8

a socio-historical embedded system. The study of intercultural conflict communication involves, at least in part, cultural group membership differences and face-identity dissonances (Ting-Toomey & Oetzel, 2013). Intercultural harmonization can be experienced by increasing our awareness and knowledge of how different cultural perspectives enact various face concerns and engage in different conflict styles. The stage of intercultural harmony can be attained by integrating culture-sensitive knowledge, mindfulness, and adaptive facework practice in managing the problematic conflict situation skilfully and arriving at a peace-building state with luminosity.

The objective of this chapter is to track the evolutionary journey of the conflict FNT and highlighting some of the key research findings along its 34 plus years (see Ting-Toomey, 1985; Zhang, Oetzel, Ting-Toomey, & Zhang, 2019) of historical development. The chapter is organized in three sections. First, the core assumptions and key conditions of the conflict FNT are identified. Second, essential FNT constructs and their associated cross-cultural conflict research patterns are summarized. Third, recent research trends are reviewed and future directions of the conflict FNT are offered. While I cannot name all the scholars who have worked diligently on facework research within the human communication discipline and across different disciplinary arenas, I want to acknowledge their inspirational ideas here and also recommend readers to check out some of the citations included in my original writings in the past 30 plus years. Since the objective of this chapter is to track the evolutionary journey of the conflict FNT, I will predominantly include theoretical and research studies under the umbrella of the conflict FNT.

Culture, in this chapter, is defined as a learned system of traditions, symbolic patterns, and constructed and negotiated meanings that fosters a particular sense of shared community-hood, identity-hood, and interaction habits among the aggregate members of a community (Ting-Toomey & Chung, 2022; Ting-Toomey & Dorjee, 2020). While a system-level aggregate membership culture (i.e., the "normative culture") exists due to the historical socialization-adaptation process, there is also an individualized "subjective culture" within and between individuals in a cultural milieu. Both cultural and individual conditioning factors in conjunction with macro-micro situational factors shape intercultural conflicting and harmonizing pathways, processes, and outcomes. The conference themes—intercultural conflict and intercultural harmony—are viewed as twin dialectical concepts interwoven with the rhythms of discordance and balance spiralling forward throughout an intercultural conflict life cycle until they reach a positive symbiotic state.

Conflict Face-Negotiation Theory: Core Assumptions and Key Conditions

Conflict Face-Negotiation Theory: Core Assumptions

In 1985, the introductory conflict face-negotiation theoretic framework emphasized the functional connection between Edward T. Hall's (1976, 1983) low-context and high-context cultural schema with different conflict styles (Ting-Toomey, 1985).

Altogether, eight theoretical propositions were introduced. For example, two (Propositions 5 and 6) theoretical propositions stated: P5: Individuals from low-context cultures tend to use direct, confrontational conflict attitude and style, and P6: Individuals from high-context cultures tend to use indirect/tactful, non-confrontational attitude and style.

In 1988, the formal seed version of the conflict FNT became available—with five core assumptions and 12 theoretical propositions—stating the relationship between individualism-collectivism (Hofstede, 1991, 2001; Triandis, 1995, 2002) and self-face concern and other-face concern issues. Four particular facework types were also identified: self-concern and other-concern autonomy face ("negative face"), and self-concern and other-concern approval face ("positive face") maintenance strategies. Furthermore, specific conflict communication styles were delineated: dominating versus smoothing/obliging, and direct closure-orientation versus indirect avoidance style (Ting-Toomey, 1988). A cultural variability framework of "I-identity" and "We-Identity" cultures was used to connect culture-level analysis with face concerns and conflict styles. For example, two propositions (Propositions 9 and 10) stated: P9: Members of individualistic, low-context cultures tend to use more dominating or controlling strategies to manage conflict than do members of collectivistic, high-context cultures; and P10: Members of collectivistic, high-context cultures tend to use more obliging or smoothing strategies to manage conflict than do members of individualistic, low-context cultures;

In 1998, a second formal rendition of the conflict FNT with seven assumptions and 32 propositions was issued (Ting-Toomey & Kurogi, 1998) in which the importance of investigating individual-level factors with face concern issues and conflict styles was focused on in particular. In addition, the three key conflict content competence dimensions (i.e., culture-sensitive knowledge, mindfulness, and conflict interaction skills), together with the four facework competence criteria (i.e., perceived appropriateness, effectiveness, mutual adaptability, satisfaction) were incorporated. In the 2005a version (see Ting-Toomet, 2005a), based on the results of several large, cross-cultural conflict data sets, a third formal version of the conflict FNT was presented. The third version of FNT retained the seven core assumptions and an updated 24 theoretical propositions (scaled back from the 32 propositions of Version 2) (Ting-Toomey, 2005a). The propositions that were eliminated dealt primarily with the power distance value dimension and role status orientations in conjunction with conflict styles and tactics.

In retrospect, the inconsistent cross-cultural empirical research results on small/large power distance value dimension and face concern issues could be a methodological artifact due to the use of college student samples. To illustrate, in many of the Asian collectivistic cultures (e.g., in China, Japan, and South Korea), and in contrast to U.S. college student samples, many Asian students were full-time college students without the actual work experiences of a hierarchical workplace system, thus the power distance value dimension results were often attenuated. Later research work by other intercultural scholars (see, for example, Merkin's conflict work, 2006) did uncover more robust differences on the power distance value issues with cross-cultural workplace conflict messages.

More specifically, the seven core assumptions of the conflict FNT (Ting-Toomey, 2005a; Ting-Toomey & Kurogi, 1998) are as follows: (1) people in all cultures try to maintain and negotiate face in all communication situations; (2) the concept of face is especially problematic in emotionally-threatening or identity vulnerable situations when the situated identities of the communicators are called into question; (3) the cultural value spectrums of individualism-collectivism and small/large power distance shape facework concerns and styles; (4) individualism and collectivism value patterns shape members' preferences for self-oriented face concern versus other-oriented or mutual-oriented concern; (5) small and large power distance value patterns shape members' preferences for horizontal-based facework versus vertical-based facework; (6) the value dimensions, in conjunction with individual, relational, and situational factors influence the use of particular facework behaviors in particular cultural scenes; and (7) intercultural facework competence refers to the optimal integration of knowledge, mindfulness, and communication skills in managing vulnerable identity-based conflict situations appropriately, effectively, and adaptively.

Conflict Face-Negotiation Theory: Key Conditions

It appears that when an individual's face image is being threatened in a conflict situation, she or he would likely experience identity-based frustrations, emotional vulnerability, anger, defensiveness, hurt, or even vengeance. The threats to face can be on a group membership level or an individual level. In the 2005a third version of conflict FNT, the following conditions were posited concerning the valence direction of an intercultural *face threatening process (FTP)*: First, the more important the culturally appropriate facework rule that is violated is, the more severe the perceived FTP. Second, the larger the cultural distance between the conflict parties, the greater the mistrust or misunderstanding is that cumulates in the FTP. Third, the more important the perceived conflict topic or imposition of the conflict demand is, as interpreted from distinctive cultural angles, the more severe the perceived FTP is. Fourth, the more power the conflict initiator has over the conflict recipient, the more severe the perceived FTP by the recipient. Fifth, the more harm or hurt the FTP produces, the greater the time and effort needed to repair the FTP. Self-face concern becomes incrementally more salient if several of these conditions are present in a face-threatening process.

For example, individuals are likely to move toward self-face saving and ingroup communal-face saving emphasis as they perceive the escalation of the various face-threatening conditions directed at them or their salient ingroups. Cultural worldview perspectives, individual personality tendencies, relational parameters, and situational pressures frame the underlying interpretations of what count as a severe intercultural "face-threatening" interaction episode.

Conflict Face-Negotiation Theory: Essential Constructs and Key Research Findings

Due to space limitation, this section reports the research findings related to the conflict FNT from 2000 to 2015a, for earlier FNT-related conflict research results, consult the overview articles about the FNT versions in 1998 and 2005a (Ting-Toomey, 2005a; Ting-Toomey & Kurogi, 1998) and theoretical variations and research articles in: Ting-Toomey and Cole (1990: intergroup facework diplomatic communication—Cuban Missile Crisis case study); Ting-Toomey, Gao, Trubisky, Yang, Kim, Lin, and Nishida (1991: a five-culture study—China, Korea, Japan, Taiwan, the U.S.); Trubisky, Ting-Toomey, and Lin (1991; a two-culture study—Taiwan and the U.S.); Cocroft and Ting-Toomey (1994: Japan and the U.S.); Ting-Toomey (1994: an edited book on cross-cultural facework); and Gao (1998) and Gao and Ting-Toomey (1998: a co-authored book on Chinese communication patterns).

The struggle for face respect or face deference in a conflict episode consists of three facets: (a) locus of face—concern for self, other, or both, plus communal-face; (b) face valence—whether face is being defended, maintained, or honored, and (c) temporality—whether face is being restored or proactively protected. Locus of face is the primary dimension of face that has been tested extensively and also this face facet shapes the direction of the subsequent conflict messages (Ting-Toomey, 2005a; Ting-Toomey & Takai, 2006).

Self-face is the protective concern for one's own image when one's own face is threatened in the conflict situation. *Other-face*, on the other hand, is the concern to accommodate the other conflict party's image in the conflict crisis situation. *Mutual-face* is the concern for both parties' images and/or the "identity expectancy image" of the relationship (Ting-Toomey & Kurogi, 1998). *Communal-face* is the concern to uphold ingroup membership face in assessment of ingroup/outgroup face expectancies and reactions (see, for example, Ting-Toomey & Cole, 1990, on intergroup diplomatic communication; Dorjee, Baig, and Ting-Toomey, 2013, on honor killing; and Dorjee and Ting-Toomey, 2020, on community conflict complexity; see also other scholarly conceptualizations of face concern and facework, for example, Bond, 1992; Chen, 2014).

Cross-Cultural Conflict Face Concern Variations: Research Findings

More specifically, in a direct empirical test of the theory (Oetzel, Garcia, & Ting-Toomey, 2008; Oetzel, Myers, Meares, & Lara, 2003; Oetzel & Ting-Toomey, 2003; Oetzel, Ting-Toomey, Masumoto, Yokochi, Pan, Takai, & Wilcox 2001; Ting-Toomey, Gao, Trubisky, Yang, Kim, Lin, & Nishida, 1991), the research program investigated the underlying assumption of the conflict FNT that underscores face is an explanatory mechanism for cultural membership's influence on conflict behavior. For example, in Oetzel et al.'s (2001) international study, a questionnaire was administered to 768 participants in four national cultures (China, Germany, Japan, and the U.S.) in their respective languages asking them to recall and describe a recent interpersonal conflict with someone with "equal status or higher status," or with someone who is "very close or not very close." However, since the situational characteristics did not have a strong effect on conflict behavior in the college student respondents, results were reported as overall findings of the testing of the conflict FNT.

The major findings of the set of studies were as follows: First, cultural individualism-collectivism had a direct effect on conflict styles, as well as mediated effects through self-construal and face concerns. Second, *self-face concern* was associated positively with dominating style and *other-face concern* was associated positively with avoiding and integrating styles. Third, German respondents reported the frequent use of direct-confrontive facework strategies and did not care much for avoidance facework tactics; Japanese respondents reported the use of different pretending strategies to act as if the conflict situation did not exist; Chinese respondents engaged in a variety of avoiding, obliging, and passive aggressive facework tactics; and the U.S. American respondents reported the use of upfront expression of feelings and remaining calm as facework strategies to handle problematic conflict situations.

In another study, Zhang, Ting-Toomey, Dorjee, and Lee (2012) tested the conflict FNT in intimate relationship settings. They discovered that in intimate relationship conflicts in China and the U.S, research evidence supported the notion that Chinese individuals tend to prefer a loyalty conflict response in intimate relationship conflicts, and U.S. individuals tend to prefer the action-orientation exit strategy or overt anger expression strategy in dealing with emotional transgression issues.

Cross-Cultural Facework Strategies and Conflict Styles: Research Findings

Facework is the communication strategies used to uphold, support, and challenge self-face and other-face identity issues in a conflict situation. Facework is linked closely with identity and relationship conflict goals. Facework can refer to the identity-sensitive verbal and nonverbal messages of a broad conflict style. It can also stand alone or apart from an interactive conflict negotiation process as facework behaviors can be enacted before, during, or after a conflict confrontation process.

Three broad types of facework have been identified in research: dominating, integrating, and avoiding (Oetzel, Ting-Toomey, Yokochi, Masumoto, & Takai, 2000). *Dominating facework* includes being aggressive, defending a position, and expressing an opinion. *Integrating facework* includes problem-solving, displaying identity respect, private discussion of the conflict, apologizing, and remaining calm with self-discipline during the conflict. *Avoiding facework* includes pretending that the conflict does not exist, passive aggressive sabotaging tactics, giving in to the other's position, and utilizing a third party to help manage the conflict situation (Oetzel et al., 2000; Ting-Toomey & Oetzel, 2001).

While facework strategies can be used as pre-emptive, ongoing, or retrospective maneuvers to explain away a conflict situation, conflict styles refer to the patterned conflict communication responses used during a conflict episode. The five-style conflict model represents one way of conceptualizing these different conflict style tendencies (Rahim, 1983, 1992). The *dominating style* (or *competitive/controlling) style* emphasizes conflict tactics that push for one's own position above and beyond the other person's interest. The dominating style includes aggressive, defensive, controlling, and intimidating tactics. The *avoiding style* involves dodging the topic, the other party, or the situation altogether. This style includes behavior ranging from glossing over the topic and denying that conflict exists, to leaving the conflict scene. The *obliging (or accommodating) style* is characterized by great concern for the other person's conflict interest above and beyond one's own conflict interest. Individuals tend to use the obliging style when they value their relationship more than their personal conflict goal. They tend to either smooth over the conflict or give in to the wishes of their conflict partners. The *compromising style*, however, involves a give-and-take concession approach to reach a mid-point agreement concerning the conflict issue. In using the compromising style, individuals tend to use fairness appeals, trade-off suggestions, or other quick, short-term solutions. It is an intermediate style resulting in some gains and some losses for each party (Rahim, 1983, 1992). Finally, the *integrating (or collaborative) style* reflects a commitment to find a mutual-interest solution and involves great concern for both self-interest and the other person's interest in the conflict situation. In using an integrative style, individuals tend to use non-evaluative descriptive messages, qualifying statements, and mutual-interest clarifying questions to seek common-ground solutions. This is the most time-consuming style of the five conflict styles and is least practiced in workplace conflict situations.

It was also repeatedly noted in the 1988 to 2005a multiple versions of FNT development that in the U.S.-centric conflict style research literature, obliging and avoiding conflict styles are often described as being negatively disengaged (i.e., either acting *too passively* or acting *indifferently* or *fleeing* from the conflict scene altogether with no active resolutions). However, according to multiple cross-cultural research data sets, many Asian and Latin collectivists (see, for example, Ting-Toomey et al., 1990; see also Oetzel et al., 2001; Oetzel, Ting-Toomey, Chew-Sanchez, Harris, Wilcox, & Stumpf, 2003) do not necessarily perceive obliging and avoiding conflict styles as negative. For example, collectivists often use these two conflict communication styles to maintain other-face interests and ingroup harmony. From the collectivistic cultural lens, obliging and avoiding conflict styles can be viewed as two very constructive, face-sensitive conflict styles in either building relationship rapport or buying more time to handle the conflict appropriately and effectively.

In addition, from the U.S.-centric individualistic conflict style lens, the use of compromising conflict style is an expedient way of giving-up something to achieve a 50–50, middle-of-the-road solution that leaves both conflict parties potentially frustrated. However, for collectivists, the "compromising style" is often viewed as a long-term conflict commitment strategy to gain trust and build further relationship favors (see conflict style critique discussion in Ting-Toomey, 1988, 2005a; Ting-Toomey & Oetzel, 2002; see also Kim & Leung, 2000).

Moreover, in expanding the five-style conflict model to be inclusive of ethnic pluralism issues in a heterogeneous society, three tested, cross-cultural conflict styles were added to the classic five styles of managing conflicts: emotional expression, third-party help, and passive-aggressive neglect style (Ting-Toomey et al., 2000). *Emotional expression* refers to the reliance of emotions and gut-level responses to guide conflict management approach and style. *Third-party help* involves the seeking of third-party help to give advice and mediate the escalating conflict episode. Lastly, *neglect* refers to the use of passive aggressive conflict tactics to side-step the conflict but at the same time get an emotion arousal reaction from the other conflict party.

In testing the conflict FNT within the pluralistic U.S. culture, multiethnic conflict research has uncovered distinctive conflict interaction styles in relationship to particular cultural/ethnic identity salience issues (Ting-Toomey, 1986, 2005b; Ting-Toomey, Yee-Jung, Shapiro, Garcia, Wright, & Oetzel, 2000). To illustrate, in the U.S. cultural context, results revealed that Latino American and Asian American respondents tended to use more avoidance and seeking third-party help conflict strategies than African Americans; and that Asian Americans also used more avoidance tactics than European Americans. African American females also tended to confront intimate relationship conflicts more readily than European American females. More interestingly, individuals who identified strongly with the mainstream U.S. culture used more integrating, compromising, and emotionally expressive conflict strategies than individuals who identified weakly with the larger U.S. culture. Concurrently, individual respondents who indicated strong ethnic identity heritage affiliations also expressed a higher use of productive integrative conflict style than respondents who revealed weak ethnic identity affiliations.

In addition, bicultural individuals (i.e., those individuals who identified strongly with both the larger mainstream U.S. culture and also their ethnic group membership) also tended to use more integrating and compromising conflict strategies than marginal identity individuals. In addition to testing cultural and ethnic identity distinctiveness issues, in the early and mid-2000s, the conflict FNT research program also focused on testing the individual-level prediction of face concerns and conflict styles in diverse relationship types (e.g., interpersonal relationship type, family relationship type, and workplace relationship type) and negotiated situations (e.g., ingroup versus outgroup situations, and role status difference and power imbalance situations).

Independent versus Interdependent Self-Construal, Face Emphases, and Conflict Responses: Research Findings

Self-construal is one's overall personality self-image and is composed of an independent and an interdependent self (Markus & Kitayama, 1991, 1998). The independent construal of self involves the view that an individual is a unique entity with an individuated repertoire of emotions, cognitions, and motivations. In comparison, the interdependent construal of self involves an emphasis on the importance of relational or ingroup interdependence. Self-construal is the individual-level equivalent of the cultural variability dimension of individualism-collectivism (Gudykunst, Matsumoto, Ting-Toomey, Nishida, Kim, & Heyman, 1996; Oetzel, Garcia, & Ting-Toomey, 2008; see also a summary critique of individualism-collectivism, Ting-Toomey, 2010a, 2010b). However, both dimensions of self exist within each individual and co-vary with particular facework situations, regardless of cultural identity. The manner in which individuals conceive of their overall self-image—independent versus interdependent selves or both—should have a profound influence on the expectancies of what constitute appropriate or inappropriate conflict communication responses in a wide variety of situations across a diverse range of cultures. In a more recent study, the role of relational self-construal was also added to test the face concern issues in emotional infidelity conflict situations in China and the U.S. (Q. Zhang et al., 2012).

In a cross-national conflict study in four nations, Oetzel and Ting-Toomey (2003) found that independent self-construal is associated positively with self-face concern and the use of dominating/competing conflict strategies. Interdependent self-construal, on the other hand, is associated positively with other-face concern and the use of avoiding and integrating conflict tactics. Bicultural construal individuals also manifested a wider range of conflict style tactics than the other three construal types (i.e., high independent self, high interdependent self, and ambivalent self: Ting-Toomey & Oetzel, & Yee-Jung, 2001). In addition, R. Zhang et al. (2012) also revealed that respondents with high independent self-construals preferred the exit and anger voice responses, and respondents with high relational self-construals preferred the use of integrative conflict style and third-party help conflict style.

In sum, the overall findings in testing conflict FNT revealed that individualistic cultural members and independent self-construal types have more self-face concern and less other-face and mutual-face concerns than collectivists and interdependent types. In comparison, collectivistic cultural members and interdependent types have more other-face emphasis in managing conflicts with others than individualists and independent self-construal types (Oetzel et al., 2001; Oetzel et al., 2008).

While research studies in the 1990s and early 2000s have focused on testing the relationship between the value dimensions of culture-based individualism-collectivism to face concern strategies and conflict styles, the mid-2000s conflict studies to current times have rediscovered the spectrums of small and large power distance values and related these value dimensions to facework expectancies and practices. For example, Merkin (2006) has integrated the small/large power distance value dimension to the individualism-collectivism value dimension in explaining face-threatening response messages and conflict styles in multiple cultures. She found that high-status individuals from large power distance cultures tended to use both direct and indirect facework strategies to deal with face-threatening situations—depending on whether they were delivering positive or negative messages. Furthermore, Kaushal and Kwantes (2006) uncovered that the dominating conflict style of "high concern for self/low concern for others" was positively associated with both vertical individualism and vertical collectivism. The notion of "face" or "claimed social interactive identity" is considered a key domain out of the several domains of the larger competent power distance facework negotiation process.

In fact, Ting-Toomey and Oetzel (2013; see also Smith, Dungan, Pederson, & Leung, 1998; Triandis, 1995), in combining both individualism-collectivism and small/large power distance value patterns, identified four predominant international workplace conflict approaches: impartial, status-achievement, benevolent, and communal. The *impartial approach* reflects a combination of an individualistic and small power distance value orientation; the *status-achievement approach* consists of a combination of an individualistic and large power distance value orientation; the *benevolent approach* reflects a combination of a collectivistic and large power distance value orientation; and the *communal approach* consists of a combination of collectivistic and small power distance value orientation. Depending on whether the international employees are encountering unequal status conflicts or equal status conflicts, different face concerns and conflict styles are predicted. In recent years, Leung and Cohen (2011) proposed the use of the CuPS approach (Culture x Person x Situation) in which within-culture and between-culture variations on cultural and individual differences concerning concepts of dignity, honor, and face can be explained in combination with various situational priming experiments.

Conflict Face-Negotiation Theory: Recent Research Status and Future Directions

Recent research testing (2010–2019) on the conflict FNT include the following themes: face-sensitive conflict emotions, interpersonal transgressions and forgiveness, intergenerational face and the dark side of face, and measurement methodological issues of various face concern constructs.

Conflict FNT: Recent Research Trends

Face-Sensitive Emotions

Zhang, Ting-Toomey, and Oetzel (2014) linked emotion to the theoretical assumptions of the conflict FNT and probed the critical role of anger, compassion, and guilt in understanding the complex pathways of their relationships with self-construal, face concerns, and conflict styles in U.S. and Chinese cultures.

Results revealed that in both U.S. and Chinese cultures anger was associated positively with independent self-construal, self-face concern, and the competing style, and compassion was associated positively with interdependent self-construal, other-face concern, and the integrating, compromising, and obliging styles. Guilt was related positively with interdependent self-construal and the obliging style in the U.S., and with interdependent self-construal and the avoiding style in China.

Research findings also indicated that, overall, emotion mediated the effects of self-construal and face concerns on conflict styles in both cultures, but cultural differences also emerged. The effects of self-construal were mediated through face concerns more than emotions in the U.S. However, the effects of self-construal were mediated via both face concerns and conflict emotions in China (Q. Zhang et al., 2014). The researchers explained this interesting research finding through the individualized lens of the independent self-construal personality as a strong, stand-alone trait in shaping self-face concern in dealing with conflict issues in the U.S. However, for independent-self cultural members in China, the emotion of anger (i.e., feeling *irritated, angry, annoyed,* and *aggravated*) fully mediates self-face concern and competitive conflict style. It appears that when aggravated anger was finally experienced and triggered in a conflict cycle, the Chinese respondents displayed a strong tendency to protect self-face from hurt or embarrassment, and this emotion of anger also prompted the use of a dominant competitive outlook in the conflict face-negotiation situation (Q. Zhang et al., 2014).

Conflict Forgiveness

This particular cross-cultural forgiveness study (Q. Zhang, Oetzel, Ting-Toomey, & J. Zhang, 2019) probed the dynamic nature of emotions and the perceived face threat in the forgiveness and reconciliation processes in China and the U.S..

The major findings of the research were as follows: (1) Chinese participants reported more relationship-oriented forgiveness than U.S. participants; (2) relative to pre-forgiveness, results indicated less post-forgiveness anger and more compassion in both the U.S. and Chinese samples—thus, some cross-cultural commonalities; (3) initial anger had a negative association with forgiveness, but initial compassion had a positive association with forgiveness in both cultures; (4) perceived face threat had a positive relationship with initial anger and a negative relationship with initial compassion in both cultures; (5) anger was negatively correlated, and compassion was positively correlated, with reconciliation in both cultures; and (6) the hypothesized Structural Equation Model (SEM) had a good fit with the data in both cultures; thus, perceived face threat evokes initial emotions (i.e., anger and compassion), which influences forgiveness, and in turn counter-influences emotions (i.e., anger and compassion), which then affects reconciliation. Overall, the findings of the study contributed to an understanding of the reactive emotions of anger and compassion in shaping interpersonal amends and reconciliation. The strength of fit of the SEM in both China and the U.S. paints a more complete picture of the direct path between forgiveness and reconciliation and the mediated paths among perceived face threats, emotions, and reconciliation (Q. Zhang et al., 2019).

In sum, according to the research findings, forgiveness is an essential step to achieve reconciliation in both individualistic and group-based cultures. Alternatively, softening or reframing the perceived face threat event in the relationship, and developing empathy and compassion for the transgressor may also activate the beginning step for the forgiveness and reconciliation processes. The results offered some evidence for the fifth condition proposed in the FNT's FTP: "Fifth, the more harm or hurtful the FTP produces, the more time and effort is needed to repair the FTP …. Self-face concern becomes incrementally more salient if several of these conditions are present in a face-threatening communication process" (Ting-Toomey, 2005a, p. 77). The findings of this cross-cultural China-U.S. forgiveness study paved the initial steps for testing the FTP conditions.

From a functional paradigm research lens, a recent methodological study (n = 1003 research participants) in testing FNT in five nations (i.e., China, Taiwan, Uganda, Ethiopia, and the U.S.) emphasized the importance of establishing cross-cultural measurement equivalence issues on facework behaviors (Fletcher, Nakazawa, Chen, Oetzel, Ting-Toomey, Chang, & Zhang, 2014; see also Oetzel, Ting-Toomey, Yokochi, Masumoto, & Takai, 2000). Interested readers can also track the various measurement scales for operationalizing self-construals, face concerns, and conflict styles in the following sources: Ting-Toomey et al. (1991), Ting-Toomey and Oetzel (2001), Oetzel and Ting-Toomey (2003).

Multiple theoretical variation and methodological approaches have been used to test and extend the theory. The author welcomes the testing, extension, and modification of the FNT theory via the tripartite research paradigms of functional-interpretive-critical approaches. Depending on the research questions asked, the testing of the theory itself can draw from any of the paradigms, and also a mixed-method framework—provided the rationale and the logical reasoning process of using a particular method is in alignment with the spirit of the FNT core assumptions, propositions, and conditions.

Intergenerational Face and the Dark Side of Face

In a recent study, from an interpretive paradigm lens, Baig, Ting-Toomey, and Dorjee (2014) used conflict FNT as a guiding framework in exploring how the South Asian Indian term *izzat* relates to the meaning construction of *face* in intergenerational contexts in the U.S. Based on a qualitative design approach, the twin objectives of the research were: to explore the meanings of *izzat* among Asian Indian Americans; and to understand how the motif of *izzat* serves as a potential source of intergenerational conflict. Interview data and thematic analysis results revealed six interpretive themes: Respect as a performance ritual, staging family face, reacting to complex *izzat* emotions, managing face boundaries in embarrassing situations, dispelling grounds for gossip, and identity acculturation change process and *izzat* socialization.

Participants viewed *izzat* primarily as related to family respect and embarrassment situations. They also used active concealment and diversion facework strategies to ward off potential *izzat* face-threatening encounters. Overall, differences in *izzat* were contextualized in terms of ethnic family socialization process and the identity change process between the older generation and the younger Asian Indian American generation in the multiethnic U.S. society.

In flipping face on its head, Dorjee, Baig, and Ting-Toomey (2013) explored the dark side of face in analyzing an "honor killing" case study with a conjoint social ecological perspective (SEP) and the FNT (see Oetzel, Ting-Toomey, & Rinderle, 2006; Oetzel, Ting-Toomey, & Willow, 2013; Ting-Toomey & Oetzel,

2013). Informed by this integrative perspective, a true life horrific case story of honor killing—"Miss Banaz Mahmod's Honor Killing Story in the U.K."—was systematically analyzed. Miss Banaz Mahmod's story illustrates intercultural issues such as the ethnocentric lens and insensitivity, and taboo intercultural relationship development. It also reveals intergroup membership issues such as traditional family role expectations, gender role inequality, ingroup community reactions, social justice and injustice issues, and historical intergroup hostility factors.

In particular, the conflict FNT worked well with SEP in the honor killing story given its theoretical focus on the dark side of face concerns, facework strategies, and group membership identity honor and vulnerability issues. *Honor* is a face concern issue that involves the emotions of pride and shame, and honor killing is a drastic face restoration strategy. Thus, to restore family pride and communal honor, the father Mr. Mahmod felt he had seemingly no choice but to order paid assassins to murder his own daughter in a brutal and violent manner. He hoped to restore some semblance of family face reputation and ingroup communal honor. In essence, the misnomer term of "honor killing" constitutes a heinous narrow-range cultural and moral struggle and that challenges universal human conscience and human rights.

Thus, it is imperative that intercultural researchers should pay responsive and responsible attention to the theorizing and researching process of integrating the study of *moral face* or ethics into the development of conflict FNT (Ting-Toomey, 2011; Ting-Toomey & Oetzel, 2013). In short, honor killing represents the abyss of the cultural dark side of facework (Dorjee et al., 2013; see also R. Zhang & Ting-Toomey, 2014 for an integrative SEP and FNT case study analysis on "Anna Mae He's Chinese Adoption Story, 1999–2009").

Conflict FNT: Future Research Directions

In the evolutionary journey of the conflict Face-Negotiation Theory (FNT) development, five master summary points can be made here: First, the study of *face* is an intoxicating metaphor that spans a wide terrain of academic disciplinary boundaries and covers a wide range of communication phenomenon of interest. Second, the advancement of the FNT can only be made by instilling a strong sense of situational complexity and identity complexity in its further evolutionary phases. Third, the progress of the FNT is dependent highly on rigorous and also creative cross-cultural comparative testing, intercultural and intergroup facework encounters testing, and developmental-longitudinal testing methodologies.

Fourth, FNT is considered to be a theory-research-practice conceptual framework to be used in multiple applied settings such as intercultural communication training, conflict peace-building training, mediation training, to name a few examples (see, for example, Ting-Toomey, 2004, 2007a, 2007b, 2009a, 2009b, 2009c). Indeed, more research studies need to be designed to probe the pre-training, process-training, and post-training effects of increased face knowledge, enhanced ethnorelative view, and improved facework skills practice. Fifth, the themes of situated identity negotiation, facework emotions, conflict styles, ingroup/outgroup convergence/divergence facework issues, and the role of mindfulness need further investigation in gaining a fuller picture of the Face-Negotiation Theory into the mid-21st century.

Identity Negotiation and Facework

Given the within-identity diversity in any contemporary society, attention should also be paid to the differentiated sociocultural identity membership issues in the conflict negotiation process. For example, Kim-Jo, Benet-Martinez, and Ozer (2010) found that Korean and European American monocultural respondents tended to use more obliging conflict style and competitive conflict style, respectively. However, the most intriguing conflict style finding was associated with the Korean American bicultural group. The Korean American respondents tended to use significantly more competitive conflict style than Korean nationals and a similar amount to European Americans, and, simultaneously, also used more avoidance conflict style than Korean nationals in conflict resolution.

The researchers theorized that some cultural individuals, in this case, the Korean American respondents, may actually adhere more strongly to their ethnic heritage root values than insider members of their heritage country (Kim-Jo et al., 2010). However, this explanation alone does not account for the competitive style of the Korean American participants. Instead, Briley, Morris, and Simonson's (2005) research findings on Hong Kong bicultural individuals and the chameleon nature of biculturalists and their adaptive impression management skills may explain the bicultural code-switching conflict mode—from the use of avoidance style to the use of competitive communication style and other adaptive facework strategies (see also A. Toomey, Dorjee, Ting-Toomey, 2014, for bicultural intergroup conflict strategies). Thus, more FNT-related conflict research on the different situationally competent facework strategies that biculturalists used in a multiethnic society may also yield a more complex picture of how bicultural and nimble facework strategies are being deployed in diverse conflict competence arenas (see also Ting-Toomey, 2005b; and the edited book on "intercultural communication competence," Dai & Chen, 2014).

Facework Emotions

While recent research studies have focused on investigating the relationship between face concerns and the emotions of anger, compassion, and guilt, in an actual conflict negotiation situation, mixed and blended emotions of anger, sadness, guilt, shame, contempt, fear, and hope may underlie the different self-face concern and other-face concern conflict moves. Theoretically, careful attention can be paid to the expanded role of emotion in unpacking the relationship between self-construal and the emotional appraisal process in a conflict situation. Research-wise, the mediating links of primary (e.g., perceived conflict goal salience/relevance) and secondary (e.g., future expectancy for things to get better or worse) emotional appraisal processes between face concerns and conflict styles could be further tested across a wide range of cultures.

Furthermore, the recently identified conflict emotional sets (i.e., vulnerable, fearful, hostile, flat, self-conscious, and positive; Guerrero, 2013) can also add in-depth complexity to the study of conflict emotions and facework strategies in different individuals, situations, and cultures. Conceptual and operational definitions of "conflict emotions experienced" versus "conflict emotions expressed" in an intercultural or intergroup face-vulnerable conflict situation need to be further unpacked.

Conflict Styles Revisit and Unpacking

Consistent results have revealed that individualists and independent self-construals are related to dominating/competing conflict style, and that collectivists and interdependent self-construals are related to avoidance and obliging, and to integrative and compromising conflict styles, respectively. It seems reasonable to propose that more cultural/ethnic indigenous perspectives are needed to unpack the meaning conceptualizations and situational dynamics of the when, what, and how of using "competition," "avoidance," "compromise," "avoidance," and the enactment of different "harmonizing" styles in different conflict management situations. By playing close attention to cultural pluralistic voices in conceptualizing taken-for-granted conflict style constructs, the research domain of global and domestic cross-cultural conflict styles can be enriched and further expanded.

For example, inconsistent conflict style findings on passive aggressive conflict style and third-party consultation help (i.e., the results were inconsistent in terms of their relationship to self-face concern or other-face concern) will need more culturally-responsive, well-conceptualized and well-designed intercultural/intergroup conflict research studies. Various culturally-grounded understudied concepts such as "eating bitter" or "enduring" conflict style, "self-other paradoxical" style, "know thy enemy" style, and "harmony repairing" style (to name a few of the Chinese conflict-related concepts) can help to expand the existing conflict style vocabulary in the mainstream U.S. conflict style literature. An integrative hour-glass emic plus etic perspective could offer us a fuller picture of the derived stories, meanings, and dynamic situations on the various core constructs related to the conflict FNT.

Intergroup Facework Convergence/Divergence Issues

While 30 plus years of FNT testing have focused primarily on *cross-cultural comparative* facework style analysis, more research studies are needed to look at the face convergence and divergence processes in *intercultural* or *intergroup-level* conflict negotiation processes (Ting-Toomey & Dorjee, 2014, 2020). Videotaped interaction analysis method, experimental studies, intergroup discourse analysis studies, mixed-method tools, and real-life macro-micro intergroup conflict case studies may yield more fruitful research in advancing the conflict FNT in the next decade.

In addition, the study of language usage in code-switching between "saving-face" and "giving face" and in the context of perceived ingroup/outgroup situations may yield some deep insights in the role of language (or bilingual code-switching) and facework enactment, ingroup/outgroup facework adaptive change process, and what constitutes constructive or hurtful facework appraisal outcome. Indeed, well-planned research studies on the meaning construction of face and the use of diverse verbal and nonverbal facework messages in different intergroup situations (e.g., intergroup manager-employee performance appraisal situation, or intercultural romantic conflict situation) would yield further insights into intergroup-interpersonal relationship turning point processes.

Mindfulness and Intercultural Harmony

Intercultural facework competence is really about the mindful management of emotional frustrations and conflict interaction struggles due primarily to cultural or ethnic group membership differences. It means having the necessary culture-based knowledge, open-minded ethnorelative attitude, and operational skills to mindfully "mind the mind" and make the commitment to see things from a different light. It means paying exquisite attention to identity-based communication issues and con-jointly creating a harmonizing peace-building pathway and destination that can be sustained at the macro and micro levels of conflict resolution practice.

In a recent theorizing effort, a three-faceted prism of mindfulness was introduced (Ting-Toomey, 2009a, 2009b, 2009c, 2015b). The threefold mindfulness prism includes: being present in the immediate time and space orientation, meta-cognition awareness, and affective attunement. Intercultural conflict competence/incompetence perception is often formed based on the criteria of perceived communication appropriateness, effectiveness, and adaptability and filtered through the three facets of mindfulness. Mindful transformation is the incremental spiritual awakening process in understanding how our own cultural worldviews and value system shape our conflict responses and gut-level reactions and, simultaneously, realizing that there are alternative worldviews and value system that frame our cultural partners' conflict lens and meanings. Dynamic conflict practitioners practice constructive conflict management skills such as cultural de-centering, watchful noticing, mindful listening, creative reframing, astute verbal and nonverbal code-switching, respectful mutual-face attunement, and inclusive community-dialogue skills. Through an intentional practice of some of these peace-building conflict communication skills, interpersonal harmony can be attained and intrapersonal tranquility can be realized (see Ting-Toomey, 2004, 2007b, 2009a).

Future research also needs to pay more attention in terms of how mindful transformation can be fostered and induced from an ethnocentric state to an eth-norelative state, or from a mindless-incompetence stage to a mindful-competence awareness stage (Ting-Toomey, 2014; Ting-Toomey & Chung, 2022). We need more research studies to capture the subtle mind-shift process, emotional arousal process, body-mindfulness awakening process, and behavioral adaptation process in moving individuals from a dysfunctional-polarized conflict state to an interdependent consciousness state. More collaborative research effort among international and domestic diversity researchers could help to expand the repertoires of understanding intersecting identity complexity, mindfulness, intergroup facework, conflict styles, and facework emotions from globally diverse ethnic/racial membership groups, plus globally diverse gender variation viewpoints.

To conclude, the multiple pathways of testing the conflict FNT have been an emotionally exhilarating and intellectually rewarding journey. While I cannot name all the specific names in this closing paragraph, I want to thank many of my former and present students, colleagues, and international scholars and friends for collaborating with me and also being willing to let me collaborate with them on many of the FNT-related research projects. In my FNT work, I am blessed with their illuminating light and support and I count myself very lucky to be constantly uplifted by their collective wisdom, inspiration, and grace. I am oftentimes amazed and in awe, playful yet focused, questioning and reflecting, searching and researching again—in the collaborative journey of fine-tuning and expanding this perpetually-in-motion work-in-progress theory, namely, the conflict FNT.

References

Baig, N., Ting-Toomey, S., & Dorjee, T. (2014). Intergenerational narratives on face: A South Asian Indian American perspective. *Journal of International & Intercultural Communication*, 7, 127–147.

Bond, M. (1992). *Beyond the Chinese face: Insights from psychology*. Hong Kong, China: Oxford University Press.

Briley, D., Morris, M., & Simonson, I. (2005). Cultural chameleons: Biconstruals, conformity motives, and decision making. *Journal of Consumer Psychology*, 15, 351–362.

Brown, B. (1977). Face-saving and face-restoration in negotiation. In D. Druckman (Ed.), *Negotiations: Social-psychological perspectives* (pp. 275–299). Beverly Hills, CA: Sage.

Brown, P., & Levinson, S. (1987). *Politeness: Some universals in language usage*. Cambridge, UK: Cambridge University Press.

Cai, D. A., & Fink, E. L. (2002). Conflict style differences between individualists and collectivists. *Communication Monographs*, 69, 67–87.

Chen, G. M. (2014). The two faces of Chinese communication. In M. Asante, Y. Miike, & J. Yin (Eds.), *The global intercultural communication reader* (pp. 273–282). New York, NY: Routledge.

Cocroft, B., & Ting-Toomey, S. (1994). Facework in Japan and the United States. *International Journal of Intercultural Relations*, 18, 469–506.

Dai, X. D., & Chen, G. M. (Eds.). (2014). *Intercultural communication competence: Conceptualization and its development in cultural contexts and interaction*. Newcastle upon Tyne, UK: Cambridge Scholars Publishing.

Dorjee, T., Baig, N., & Ting-Toomey, S. (2013). A social ecological perspective in understanding 'honor killing': An intercultural moral dilemma. *Journal of Intercultural Communication Research*, 42, 1–21.

Dorjee, T., & Ting-Toomey, S. (2020). Understanding intergroup conflict complexity: An application of the socioecological framework and the integrative identity negotiation theory. *Journal: Negotiation and Conflict Management Research*, 13, 244–262.

Earley, P. C. (1997). *Face, harmony, and social support: An analysis of organizational behavior across cultures*. New York, NY: Oxford University Press.

Fletcher, C. V., Nakazawa, M., Chen, Y.-W., Oetzel, J., Ting-Toomey, S., Chang, S.-J., & Zhang, Q. (2014). Establishing cross-cultural measurement equivalence of scales associated with face-negotiation theory: A critical issue in cross-cultural comparisons. *Journal of International & Intercultural Communication*, 7(2), 148–169.

Gao, G. (1998). An initial analysis of the effects of face and concern for "other" in Chinese interpersonal communication. *International Journal of Intercultural Relations*, 22, 467–482.

Gao, G., & Ting-Toomey, S. (1998). *Communicating effectively with the Chinese*. Thousand Oaks, CA: Sage.

Goffman, E. (1955). On face-work: An analysis of ritual elements in social interaction. *Psychiatry: Interpersonal and Biological Processes*, 18, 213–231.

Gudykunst, W. B., Matsumoto, Y., Ting-Toomey, S., Nishida, T., Kim, K. S., & Heyman, S. (1996). The influence of cultural individualism-collectivism, self construals, and individual values on communication styles across cultures. *Human Communication Research*, 22, 510–543.

Guerrero, L. K. (2013). Emotion and communication in conflict interaction. In J. G. Oetzel & S. Ting-Toomey (Eds.), *The Sage handbook of conflict communication* (2nd ed., pp. 105–131). Thousand Oaks, CA: Sage.

Hall, E. T. (1976). *Beyond culture*. New York, NY: Doubleday.

Hall, E. T. (1983). *The dance of life*. New York, NY: Doubleday.

Hofstede, G. (1991). *Culture and organizations: Software of the mind*. London, UK: McGraw-Hill.

Hofstede, G. (2001). *Culture's consequences: Comparing values, behaviors, institutions, and organizations across cultures* (2nd ed.). Thousand Oaks, CA: Sage.

House, R., Hanges, P., Javidan, M., Dorfman, P., & Gupta, V. (Eds.). (2004). *Culture, leadership, and organizations: The GLOBE study of 62 societies*. Thousand Oaks, CA: Sage.

Hu, H. C. (1944). The Chinese concept of "face." *American Anthropologist*, 46, 45–64.

Kaushal, R., & Kwantes, C. (2006). The role of culture and personality in choice of conflict management strategy. *International Journal of Intercultural Relations*, 30, 579–603.

Kim, M. S., & Leung, T. (2000). A multicultural view of conflict management styles: Review and critical synthesis. In M. Roloff (Ed.), *Communication Yearbook 23* (pp. 227–269). Thousand Oaks, CA: Sage Publications.

Kim-Jo, T., Benet-Martinez, B., & Ozer, D. (2010). Culture and interpersonal conflict resolution styles: Role of acculturation. *Journal of Cross-Cultural Psychology*, 41, 264–269.

Leung, A. K.-Y., & Cohen, D. (2011). Within- and between-culture variation: Individual differences and the cultural logics of honor, face, and dignity cultures. *Journal of Personality and Social Psychology*, 100(3), 507–526.

Markus, H. R., & Kitayama, S. (1991). Culture and self: Implication for cognition, emotion, and motivation. *Psychological Review*, 98, 224–253.

Markus, H. R., & Kitayama, S. (1998). The cultural psychology of personality. *Journal of Cross-Cultural Psychology*, 29, 63–87.

Merkin, R. (2006). Power distance and facework strategies. *Journal of Intercultural Communication Research*, 35, 139–160.

Oetzel, J. G., Garcia, A., & Ting-Toomey, S. (2008). An analysis of the relationships among face concerns and facework behaviors in perceived conflict situations: A four-culture investigation. *International Journal of Conflict Management*, 19, 382–403.

Oetzel, J. G., Myers, K., Meares, M., & Lara, E. (2003). Interpersonal conflict in organizations. Explaining conflict styles via face-negotiation theory. *Communication Research Reports*, 20, 106–115.

Oetzel, J. G., & Ting-Toomey, S. (2003). Face concerns in interpersonal conflict: A cross-cultural empirical test of the face-negotiation theory. *Communication Research*, 30, 599–624.

Oetzel, J. G., Ting-Toomey, S., Chew-Sanchez, M., Harris, R., Wilcox, R., & Stumpf, S. (2003). Face and facework in conflicts with parents and siblings; A cross-cultural comparison of Germans, Japanese, Mexicans, and U.S. Americans. *Journal of Family Communication*, 3, 67–93.

Oetzel, J. G., Ting-Toomey, S., Masumoto, T., Yokochi, Y., Pan, X, Takai, J., & Wilcox, R. (2001). Face behaviors in interpersonal conflicts: A cross-cultural comparison of Germany, Japan, China, and the United States. *Communication Monographs*, 68, 235–258.

Oetzel, J. G., Ting-Toomey, S., & Rinderle, S. (2006). Conflict communication in contexts: A social ecological perspective. In J. G. Oetzel & S. Ting-Toomey (Eds.), *The Sage Handbook of Conflict Communication* (pp. 727–739). Thousand Oaks, CA: Sage.

Oetzel, J. G., Ting-Toomey, S., & Willow, J. A. (2013). Conflict communication in contexts: Organizing themes and future directions. In J. G. Oetzel & S. Ting-Toomey (Eds.), *The Sage handbook of conflict communication* (2nd ed., pp. 815–829). Los Angeles, CA: Sage.

Oetzel, J. G., Ting-Toomey, S., Yokochi, Y., Masumoto, T., & Takai, J. (2000). A typology of facework behaviors in conflicts with best friends and relative strangers. *Communication Quarterly*, 48, 397–419.

Rahim, M. A. (1983). A measure of styles of handling interpersonal conflict. *Academy of Management Journal*, 26, 368–376.

Rahim, M. A. (1992). *Managing conflict in organizations* (2nd ed.). Westport, CT: Praeger.

Smith, P. B., Dugan, S., Peterson, M. F., & Leung, K. (1998). Individualism, collectivism and the handling of disagreement: A 23 country study. *International Journal of Intercultural Relations*, 22, 351–367.

Ting-Toomey, S. (1985). Toward a theory of conflict and culture. In W. Gudykunst, L. Stewart, & S. Ting-Toomey (Eds.), *Communication, culture, and organizational processes* (pp. 71–86). Beverly Hills, CA: Sage.

Ting-Toomey, S. (1986). Conflict communication styles in black and white subjective cultures. In Y. Kim (Ed.), *Current research in interethnic communication* (pp. 75–88). Beverly Hills, CA: Sage.

Ting-Toomey, S. (1988). Intercultural conflicts: A face-negotiation theory. In Y. Kim & W. Gudykunst (Eds.), *Theories in intercultural communication* (pp. 213–235). Newbury Park, CA: Sage.

Ting-Toomey, S. (Ed.). (1994). *The challenge of facework: Cross-cultural and interpersonal issues.* New York, NY: State University of New York–Albany Press.

Ting-Toomey, S. (2004). Translating conflict face-negotiation theory into practice. In D. Landis, J. Bennett, & M. Bennett (Eds.), *Handbook of intercultural training* (3rd ed., pp. 217–248). Thousand Oaks, CA: Sage.

Ting-Toomey, S. (2005a). The matrix of face: An updated face-negotiation theory. In W. B. Gudykunst (Ed.), *Theorizing about intercultural communication* (pp. 71–92). Thousand Oaks, CA: Sage.

Ting Toomey, S. (2005b). Identity negotiation theory: Crossing cultural boundaries. In W. Gudykunst (Ed.), *Theorizing about intercultural communication* (pp. 211–233). Thousand Oaks, CA: Sage.

Ting-Toomey, S. (2007a). Researching intercultural conflict competence: Some promising lenses. *Journal of International Communication*, 13, 7–30.

Ting-Toomey, S. (2007b). Intercultural conflict training: Theory-practice approaches and research challenges. *Journal of Intercultural Communication Research*, 36, 255–271.

Ting-Toomey, S. (2009a). Facework collision in intercultural communication. In F. Bargiela-Chiappini & M. Haugh, M. (Eds.), *Face, communication and social interaction* (pp. 227–249). London, UK: Equinox Publications.

Ting-Toomey, S. (2009b). Intercultural conflict competence as a facet of intercultural competence development: Multiple conceptual approaches. In D. K. Deardorff (Ed.), *The Sage handbook of intercultural competence* (pp. 100–120). Thousand Oaks, CA: Sage Publications.

Ting-Toomey, S. (2009c). A mindful approach to managing conflicts in intercultural-intimate couples. In T. A. Karis & K. Killian (Eds.), *Intercultural couples: Exploring diversity in intimate relationships* (pp. 31–49). New York, NY: Routledge/Taylor & Francis Group.

Ting-Toomey, S. (2010a). Applying dimensional values in understanding intercultural communication. *Communication Monographs, 77*, 169–180.

Ting-Toomey, S. (2010b). Intercultural mediation: Asian and Western conflict lens. In D. Busch, C.-H. Mayer, & C. M. Boness (Eds.), *International and regional perspectives on cross-cultural mediation* (pp. 79–98). Frankfurt am Main, Germany: Peter Lang.

Ting-Toomey, S. (2010c). Intercultural conflict interaction competence: From theory to practice. In M. Guilherme, E. Glaser, & M. C. Mendez-Garcia (Eds.), *The intercultural dynamics of multicultural working* (pp. 21–40). Bristol, UK: Multilingual Matters.

Ting-Toomey, S. (2011). Intercultural communication ethics: Multiple layered issues. In G. Cheney, S. May, & D. Munshi (Eds.), *The ICA handbook of communication ethics* (pp. 335–352). Mahwah, NJ: Lawrence Erlbaum Publishers.

Ting-Toomey, S. (2012). Understanding intercultural conflict: Multiple theoretical insights. In J. Jackson (Ed.), *The Routledge handbook of language & intercultural communication* (pp. 279–295). New York, NY: Routledge.

Ting-Toomey, S. (2014). Managing identity issues in intercultural conflict communication: Developing a multicultural identity attunement lens. In V. Benet-Martinez & Y.-Y. Hong (Eds.), *The Oxford handbook of multicultural identity: Basic and applied psychological perspectives* (pp. 485–506). New York, NY: Oxford University Press.

Ting-Toomey, S. (2015a). Facework/Facework negotiation theory. In J. Bennett (Ed.), *The Sage encyclopedia of intercultural competence* (Volume 1, pp. 325–330). Los Angeles, CA: Sage.

Ting-Toomey, S. (2015b). Mindfulness. In J. Bennett (Ed.), *The Sage encyclopedia of intercultural competence* (Volume 2, pp. 620–626). Los Angeles, CA: Sage.

Ting-Toomey, & Chung, L. (2022). *Understanding intercultural communication* (3rd ed.). New York, NY: Oxford University Press.

Ting-Toomey, S., & Cole, M. (1990). Intergroup diplomatic communication: A face-negotiation perspective. In F. Korzenny & S. Ting-Toomey (Eds.), *Communicating for peace: Diplomacy and negotiation across cultures* (pp. 77–95). Newbury Park, CA: Sage.

Ting-Toomey, S., & Dorjee, T. (2014). Language, identity, and culture: Multiple identity-based perspectives. In T. Holtgraves (Ed.), *The Oxford handbook of language and social psychology* (pp. 27–45). New York, NY: Oxford University Press.

Ting-Toomey, S., & Dorjee, T. (2020). *Communicating across cultures* (2nd ed.). New York, NY: The Guilford Press.

Ting-Toomey, S., Gao, G., Trubisky, P., Yang, Z., Kim, H. S., Lin, S. L., & Nishida, T. (1991). Culture, face maintenance, and styles of handling interpersonal conflict: A study in five cultures. *The International Journal of Conflict Management, 2*, 275–296.

Ting-Toomey, S., & Kurogi, A. (1998). Facework competence in intercultural conflict: An updated face-negotiation theory. *International Journal of Intercultural Relations, 22*(2), 187–225.

Ting-Toomey, S., & Oetzel, J. G. (2001). *Managing intercultural conflict effectively*. Thousand Oaks, CA: Sage Publications.

Ting-Toomey, S., & Oetzel, J. G. (2002). Cross-cultural face concerns and conflict styles: Current status and future directions. In W. B. Gudykunst & B. Mody (Eds.), *Handbook of international & intercultural communication* (2nd ed., pp. 143–163). Thousand Oaks, CA: Sage.

Ting-Toomey, S., & Oetzel, J. G. (2013). Culture-based situational conflict model: An update and expansion. In J. G. Oetzel & S. Ting-Toomey (Eds.), *The Sage handbook of conflict communication* (2nd ed., pp. 763–789). Los Angeles, CA: Sage.

Ting-Toomey, S., Oetzel, J. G., & Yee-Jung, K. (2001). Self-construal types and conflict management styles. *Communication Reports*, 14, 87–104.

Ting-Toomey, S., & Takai, J. (2006). Explaining intercultural conflict: Promising approaches and directions. In J. G. Oetzel & S. Ting-Toomey (Eds.), *The Sage handbook of conflict communication* (pp. 691–723). Thousand Oaks, CA: Sage.

Ting-Toomey, S., Yee-Jung, K., Shapiro, R., Garcia, W., Wright, T., & Oetzel, J. G. (2000). Ethnic/cultural identity salience and conflict styles in four U.S. ethnic groups. *International Journal of Intercultural Relations*, 24, 47–81.

Toomey, A., Dorjee, T., & Ting-Toomey, S. (2013). Bicultural identity negotiation, conflicts, and intergroup communication strategies. *Journal of Intercultural Communication Research*, 42, 112–134.

Triandis, H. C. (1995). *Individualism and collectivism*. Boulder, CO: Westview.

Triandis, H. C. (2002). Individualism and collectivism. In M. Gannon & K. Newman (Eds.), *Handbook of cross-cultural management* (pp. 16–45). New York, NY: Lawrence Erlbaum.

Trubisky, P., Ting-Toomey, S., & Lin, S.-L. (1991). The influence of individualism-collectivism and self- monitoring on conflict styles. *International Journal of Intercultural Relations*, 15, 65–84.

Zhang, Q., Oetzel, J., Ting-Toomey, S., & Zhang, J. (2019). Making up or getting even? The effects of face concerns, self-construal, and apology on forgiveness, reconciliation, and revenge in the U.S. and China. *Communication Research*, 46, 503–524.

Zhang, Q., Ting-Toomey, S., & Oetzel, J. G. (2014). Linking emotion to the conflict face-negotiation theory: A U.S.-China investigation of the mediating effects of anger, compassion, and guilt in interpersonal conflict. *Human Communication Research*, 40, 373–395.

Zhang, R., & Ting-Toomey, S. (2014). Analyzing an intercultural conflict case study: Application of a social ecological perspective. In M. Hinner (Ed.), *Chinese culture in a cross-cultural comparison* (pp. 485–510). Frankfurt, Germany: Peter Lang/PL Academic Research.

Zhang, R., Ting-Toomey, S., Dorjee, T., & Lee, P.(2012). Culture and self-construal as predictors of relational responses to emotional infidelity: China and the United States. *Chinese Journal of Communication*, 5, 137–159.

7

THE ART AND DISCIPLINE OF NONVIOLENCE

An Intercultural Praxis Approach to Conflict in the Neoliberal Global Context

Kathryn Sorrells

As I write this chapter, the experience and impact of Covid-19 looms large in every community around the globe. The pandemic has underscored our awareness of global interdependence and amplified intercultural conflicts in unprecedented and paradoxical ways. As nation-states attempt to shut down borders and wealthy nations hoard vaccines, it becomes clearer and clearer the pandemic knows no borders and stockpiling by wealthy nations only prolongs the pandemic. As communities, particularly low-income countries, minorities, communities of color and immigrants across the globe are disproportionately impacted, the wealthiest among us increase their wealth exponentially. National and global responses to the pandemic have laid bare the ideological and material conditions at the core of our neoliberal global society. Neoliberalism valorizes capital and profits over human life and human needs; extracts, exploits and discards everything—people, the environment, culture, life and death—through the marketplace; and uses differences in culture, race, gender, class, religion, nationality and documentation status to magnify and justify systemic inequities, instigate and exacerbate conflict and maintain systems of power and control.

During all the injustices experienced through the pandemic, flagrant incidents of racialized anti-Black state violence triggered massive protests in the U.S. A multiracial coalition, masked against the coronavirus, supported the movement for Black Lives demanding racial, economic and gender justice in the summer of 2020. Calls for intersectional justice echoed around the globe from Palestine to France and from Russia to Tunisia to Hong Kong. Amidst intensified intercultural conflict, neoliberal global crises and appeals for intersectional justice, we must ask: What is at the core of these crises and what radical vision is needed to address them? What role can intercultural communication play?

In this chapter, I draw attention to the global crises and concomitant conflicts we face as a result of neoliberal globalization and reveal the distinctly interconnected,

DOI: 10.4324/9781003252955-9

contradictory and inequitable conditions in which intercultural communication occurs today. I propose the art and discipline of nonviolence, as practiced by Dr. Martin Luther King, as a critical theoretical and methodological approach to address the various forms of violence that underpin intercultural conflicts in the neoliberal global context. Referred to as the triple evils, Dr. King saw "racism, economic exploitation and militarism" as interconnected forms of violence existing in a vicious cycle (King, 1967). The art and discipline of nonviolence works against the triple evils on intrapersonal, interpersonal and movement levels to break down barriers and create what Dr. King called the "beloved community." The principles of nonviolence are highlighted within the intercultural praxis model (Sorrells, 2022) to provide a framework of analysis, reflection and action regarding intercultural conflict in personal and social contexts. A scenario is introduced to illustrate how the intercultural praxis model, informed by the philosophy and methodology of nonviolence, provides a process to address intercultural conflict and move toward reconciliation, harmony and the beloved community.

Intercultural Conflict in the Neoliberal Context

Over the past 40 years, neoliberal economic and political policies have coalesced with rapid advances in communication and transportation technologies to dramatically accelerate interactions and inter-relations among people from diverse cultures and locations. The coronavirus pandemic and global economic fallout that followed deepened our awareness and embodied experience of global interdependence and inter-reliance. It also exposed the ideological and material crises at the core of our neoliberal global society (Giroux, 2021). Neoliberalism is a form of political economy that endeavors to restore the class power of the global economic elite. The political project of neoliberalism promotes free-markets and reduced government intervention and regulation, shifts responsibility from the government/public sector to individuals and privatizes public spaces, goods and services as well as industries and resources (Harvey, 2005, 2016). Neoliberalism reveres capital, profit and property over human life and needs. The mandates by nation-states and leaders to re-open their economies in the midst of a raging pandemic at the expense of the lives and well-being of those on the front line and the most vulnerable, the elderly and the poor clearly illustrate the logic of neoliberalism.

The living conditions in the neoliberal global context include elevated uncertainty, polarization and conflict. Increased displacement and labor migration, magnified economic inequity and insecurity, greater risks from climate and health crises along with real and perceived ethnic, racial and religious tension have led to a backlash against globalization in recent years. Anti-immigrant, protectionist and populist rhetoric and policies, fueled by job insecurity, xenophobia and long histories of racism, have given rise to new forms of ethnic, racial and religious nationalism, isolationism and violence around the world. Despite the promises or perhaps, precisely because of the unfulfilled promises of liberal capitalism and democracy for universal prosperity and individual human rights, we are living in "the age of anger" as defined by public intellectual

Pankaj Mishra (2016), where "authoritarian leaders manipulate the cynicism and discontent of furious majorities" (para 7). Conservative, right-wing politicians and authoritarian leaders across the globe arouse and harness populous anger, discontent and resentment—responses to the contradictory conditions of neoliberal globalization—to advance ethnonationalist movements predicated on anti-immigrant/anti-minority, White supremacist/ethno-supremacist and anti-democratic rhetoric, practices and policies (Michelson & de Orellana, 2022; Mishra, 2017).

Increased economic inequity resulting from neoliberal globalization has created a political arena where those most disadvantaged economically are now, more than ever, targeted as the "problem," or "cause of discontent." The disproportionate impact of the pandemic on women all over the world, particularly women of racial/ethnic minorities as well as poor and migrant women graphically demonstrates how gender, class, race/ethnicity, nationality and documentation status are exploited through neoliberalism magnifying pre-existing economic, social and health disparities and inequities while further concentrating privilege and wealth among the few. Prior to the pandemic, the gap between the wealthy and the poor had increased within countries and around the world. In 2020, the world's 2,153 billionaires controlled the same wealth as 4.6 billion people or 60 percent of the world's population and the unpaid labor of women—cooking, cleaning, caring for children and the elderly—continues to be "the 'hidden engine' that keeps the wheels of our economies, businesses, and societies moving" (Oxfam, 2020).

Historians Man, Paik and Pappademos (2019) argue militarism and capitalism have been deeply connected since the forced trafficking of human bodies during the colonial period. The enmeshed relationship has evolved such that militarism stabilizes capitalism, suppresses any anti-capitalist movements globally and standardizes policies and practices of human destruction. The militarization of the police, similar to the militarization of borders and cities around the world, engages brutal rhetoric, policies, tactics and equipment to contain economic and social issues, while further normalizing an inhumane culture of violence and death, an erosion of civil liberties and the destruction of human rights. "Militarization has become a central feature of the pandemic age and points to the dominance of warlike values in society" (Giroux & Filappakau, 2020). In the course of the pandemic, language, culture and media, have been further weaponized and militarized.

The coronavirus pandemic and responses to it exemplify the crises and concomitant conflicts of neoliberalism—magnified inequity, exploitation and disparities based on race/ethnicity/gender/religion/class/nationality, increased climate-driven migration, displacement and ecological destruction, a global rise of ethnonationalism, militarism and the culture of violence and death. In his speech, "The Three Evils of Society," Dr. Martin Luther King (1967), spoke powerful words that, five decades later, provide wisdom for the world:

> So, we are here because we believe, we hope, we pray that something new might emerge in the political life of this nation which will produce a new man, new structures and institutions and a new life for mankind. I am

convinced that this new life will not emerge until our nation undergoes a radical revolution of values … Our only hope today lies in our ability to recapture the revolutionary spirit and go out into a sometimes hostile world, declaring eternal opposition to poverty, racism and militarism.

The Art and Discipline Nonviolence

Nonviolent struggle, also called civil resistance or nonviolent resistance, is the most powerful philosophy and methodology for social change developed in the 20th century with roots in pre-history (Ackerman & Duvall, 2000; Lawson, 2022). Often misunderstood as pacifism, nonviolent struggle is anything but passive. Proponents and practitioners of Gandhian nonviolence fundamentally define it as strong resistance, even militant resistance. While the term "nonviolence" states what it is not, Gandhi used the word *satyagraha,* translated as "holding to truth," "truth force" or "soul force" to express the positive and transformative power of nonviolence. Reverend James M. Lawson (2022) speaks of nonviolence as a force more powerful:

> From the perspective of Gandhi, nonviolence is the use of power to try to resolve conflicts, injuries, and issues in order to heal and uplift, to solidify community, and to help people take power into their own hands and use their power creatively. Nonviolence makes the effort to use power responsibly. It's personal, and that's why Gandhi spoke of it as a way of life, a lifestyle that determines all of our relationships with one another, the way we deal with our families, friends, and neighbors.
>
> *(p. 31)*

An important tenet of Jainism, Hinduism and Buddhism, *ahimsa,* "non-injury" or "nonviolence," draws on a basic premise that all living beings have a spark of divinity or spiritual energy, that harm to others harms oneself and violence begets violence in a karmic cycle. Practiced by individuals and collectives throughout history, the art and discipline of nonviolence, as a form of personal and political resistance for social transformation, was systematically applied by Mohandas Gandhi in the struggle for independence in India and by Dr. Martin Luther King, Bayard Rustin, James Lawson, John Lewis and others during the Civil Rights Movement from the mid-1950 to the early 1970s in the U.S. (Ackerman & Duvall, 2000; Lawson, 2022).

Gandhi's notion of nonviolence was grounded in the power of the individual, what peace activist and scholar, Michael Nagler (2020), calls "person power." Gandhi understood individuals as autonomous yet interconnected beings on diverse paths toward the fullest development of their humanity. Empowering individuals with tools and strategies for nonviolence is at the center of building constructive programs that benefit the community and larger scale movements of nonviolent resistance. Based on Gandhian principles, Nagler (2020), along with a group of activists, outline five steps to enhance the development of the inner peace necessary for "person power." The first step calls upon people to avoid the violence disseminated through mass media. In his teaching, Reverend James Lawson invited students to examine their relationship to violence, the myths and stories they have been told, their personal experiences of violence and the violent messages consumed through the media on a daily basis. The goal is to uncover the tragic and traumatizing impact of violence on our daily lives while also debunking myths that romanticize and valorize violence. These efforts challenge the ways violence has been normalized and prepare one to focus on learning about nonviolence, which is step two. A deep and long history, tradition, philosophy and methodology of nonviolence exists (Lawson, 2022), which is rarely taught in schools and yet is gaining traction through nonviolent movements for climate justice and for racial/intersectional justice such as Black Lives Matter. As we re-orient toward nonviolence, Nagler (2020) notes, "It's hard to imagine anything more practical, both for our own well-being and the reformation of society, than the ability to transform our anger into nonviolent power" (p. 55).

Grounding one's knowledge and understanding of nonviolence in a spiritual practice is the third step. Practices of mindfulness, mediation, prayer or similar practices build the capacity and pathways in our bodies and minds to shift fear and anger into creativity, compassion and courage. The discipline to still the mind and transform anger, hatred and fear into constructive energy is critical for the discipline of nonviolence. The fourth step in developing a personal relationship with and practice of nonviolence involves prioritizing relationships. Building and sustaining relationships challenges modern tendencies toward isolation and reinforces our connections to and inter-reliance on each other. Creating strong, trustful and enduring relationships is part of the art of nonviolence laying the foundation for Dr. Martin Luther King's "beloved community." The fifth step in the art and discipline of nonviolence is to enact the change you want to see in the world. "The sovereign remedy for demoralization and lack of dignity—which, as we know, are a potent cause of violence—is to align our personal capacities with what's needed by our community and, indeed, by the whole world" (Nagler, 2020, p. 58). Through these steps that address the discipline of the body, mind and spirit, we, in creative collaboration with others, become the "soul force," "the force more powerful" of nonviolence (Lawson, 2022; Nagler, 2020).

As Peter Ackerman and Jack Duvall (2000) describe in cases studies in their book, *A Force More Powerful: A Century of Nonviolent Conflict,* nonviolent resistance or civil resistance has had widespread success in toppling totalitarian regimes, repelling occupying armies and dismantling political systems that deny human rights. From Russia in the early 1900s to Indian independence to the U.S. Civil Rights Movement to the labor movement that transformed Poland in the 1980s, a "worldwide march toward a fresh understanding of power: that real power derives from the consent of those it would control, not from the threat of violence against them" emerged in the 20th century (Ackerman &

Duvall, 2000, p. 2). While most societies in the neoliberal global context valorize, romanticize and normalize violence and many, including political scientists, assume that opposition movements choose violent methods over non-violent ones because they are more effective, this is simply not the case. In a study of violent and nonviolent resistant movements from 1900 to 2006, Erica Chenoweth and Maria Stephens (2021) found that nonviolent campaigns were successful 53 percent of the time as compared to 26 percent for violent campaigns.

To challenge the efficacy of violence and to work toward nonviolent solutions, Dr. Martin Luther King described three ways people in conflict within uneven relationships of power can address their situation of exploitation or oppression. There are those who would surrender to the conditions that exist, assuming it is better to live with things the way they are rather than go through the challenge and hardship to change the old order. This method of acquiescence, where the struggle has been given up, is, according to Dr. King, a cowardly way lacking morals. A second way for people to respond is to rise up with violence and hatred. Dr. King acknowledges that violence can bring a temporary sense of victory but, he claims, will never bring enduring peace. In the end, violence creates more problems. As poet, scholar and revolutionary Audre Lorde (1984) stated: "For the master's tools will never dismantle the master's house. They may allow us to temporarily beat him at his own game, but they will never enable us to bring about genuine change" (p. 110). For King, using violence was both impractical and immoral ending in destruction for everyone. Those in positions of power know how to deal with violence and generally have much greater resources to mobilize violence; on the other hand, they do not know how to deal with nonviolence.

Dr. King argues for a third way, the way of nonviolence, where the means and ends cohere. The means of nonviolence is the goal or the ideal in process; thus, with a nonviolent approach, there is alignment between the means and ends. *Ahimsa* or non-injury is at the center of the discipline of nonviolence, which means eschewing physical violence, resisting retaliation and refusing to hate your enemy. Hate is destructive for the one who hates as for the one who is hated. Thus, Dr. King called for *agape*, the Greek notion of love that extends understanding, good-will and redemption to all humankind. The method of nonviolence stands with determination against injustice, hates the systems that are oppressive while simultaneously striving to understand and humanize the person upholding the unjust system. The capacity to inflict violence and suffering is met with the capacity to endure suffering. Physical force is met with soul force exposing the opponent's or opponents' weaknesses. Suffering can act as a catalyst to change the opponent or opponents even when reason fails. The end result of nonviolence is reconciliation and redemption with the purpose of creating the beloved community. Love rebuilds community and defeats injustice (King, 1957).

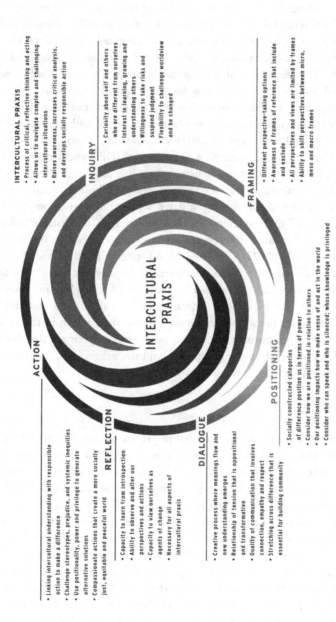

INTERCULTURAL PRAXIS MODEL
KATHRYN SORRELLS, PH.D.

INTERCULTURAL PRAXIS
- Process of critical, reflective thinking and acting
- Allows us to navigate complex and challenging intercultural situations
- Raises awareness, increases critical analysis, and develops socially responsible action

INQUIRY
- Curiosity about self and others who are different from ourselves
- Interest in learning, growing and understanding others
- Willingness to take risks and suspend judgment
- Flexibility to challenge worldview and be changed

FRAMING
- Different perspective-taking options
- Awareness of frames of reference that include and exclude
- All perspectives and views are limited by frames
- Ability to shift perspectives between micro, meso and macro frames

ACTION
- Linking intercultural understanding with responsible action to make a difference
- Challenge stereotypes, prejudice, and systemic inequities
- Use positionality, power and privilege to generate alternative solutions
- Compassionate actions that create a more socially just, equitable and peaceful world

REFLECTION
- Capacity to learn from introspection
- Ability to observe and alter our perspectives and actions
- Capacity to view ourselves as agents of change
- Necessary for all aspects of intercultural praxis

DIALOGUE
- Creative process where meanings flow and new understanding emerges
- Relationship of tension that is oppositional and transformative
- Quality of communication that involves connection, empathy and respect
- Stretching across difference that is essential for building community

POSITIONING
- Socially constructed categories of difference position us in terms of power
- Consider how we are positioned in relation to others
- Our positioning impacts how we make sense of and act in the world
- Consider who can speak and who is silenced; whose knowledge is privileged

INTERCULTURAL PRAXIS

INFOGRAPHIC BY JESSICA ARANA

FIGURE 7.1 Intercultural praxis model

Integrating Nonviolence with the Intercultural Praxis Model

I turn now to intercultural praxis, a process of critical, reflective, engaged thinking and acting that enables us to navigate the complex, contradictory and challenging intercultural spaces we inhabit interpersonally, communally and globally. The principles of nonviolence are integrated into the praxis model strengthening the tools, resources and goals of the model. Exercised within specific and concrete temporal and spatial contexts that necessarily engender historical and sociopolitical as well as local and global conditions, intercultural praxis underpinned by nonviolence invites us to practice a way of being, thinking, analyzing, reflecting and acting in the world with regard to cultural differences. Cultural differences based on nationality, region, ethnicity, race, gender, class and religion, to name a few, are real. Differences manifest in language, dress, behavior, attitudes, beliefs, values, histories and worldviews. The challenge in intercultural communication is not just about cultural differences; differences are always and inevitably situated within relations of power. Thus, a central intention of the intercultural praxis model is to understand and address the intersection of cultural differences and hierarchies of power in intercultural interactions (Sorrells, 2022). To understand intercultural praxis, I offer six interrelated points of entry into the process: Inquiry, Framing, Positioning, Dialogue, Reflection and Action. The purpose of engaging in intercultural praxis is to raise our awareness, increase our critical analysis and develop a mindset and methods for socially responsible nonviolent action in the neoliberal global context. All six ports of entry into intercultural praxis are interconnected and interrelated. As each is foregrounded, hold the others in mind and consider how they inform the foregrounded port of entry.

Inquiry

Inquiry, as a port of entry for intercultural praxis, means a desire and willingness to know, to ask, to find out and to learn. In a more pragmatic sense, curious inquiry about those who are different from ourselves leads us to engagement with others. While it may sound simple, inquiry also requires that we are willing to take risks, allow our own way of viewing and being in the world to be challenged and, perhaps, changed, and that we are willing to suspend judgments about others in order to see and interpret others and the world from different points of view. Inquiry also refers to a process of examining oneself, and clarifying one's values, beliefs and commitments. What is my relationship to violence? How can I ground my engagement with self and others in nonviolence? How are we as individuals developing our practice of *satyagraha*,? In line with mindfulness or mindful approaches to intercultural communication and conflict, introduced by Stella Ting-Toomey (1999), inquiry involves an attunement to one's own as well the other person's assumptions, understanding and emotions in relation to the interaction or conflict (Ting-Toomey, 1999; Ting-Toomey & Oetzel, 2001).

When using the intercultural praxis model to guide group-based discussions or community-based nonviolent resistance, *inquiry* is central to *focus* as a first step described by Lawson (2022), which includes investigation and education of oneself, one's group and one's community. What do we need to know about the situation or conflict? What resources do we have to learn about the issue? What does the issue, conflict or injustice look like from a variety of different angles?

Framing

The port of entry "framing" suggests a range of different perspective-taking options that we can learn to make available and need to be aware of in intercultural praxis. First, the concept and action of framing (Goffman, 1974; Lakoff, 2004) connotes that our perspectives, our views on ourselves, others and the world around us are always and inevitably both constrained and enabled by frames. We see things through individual, cultural, national and regional frames or lenses that necessarily include some things and exclude others. This process of "highlighting" and "hiding" not only impacts our everyday perceptions of the world, but our frames also represent and advance certain dominant or oppositional interests. Hence, frames serve political ends, as well as sense-making functions. Dr. King's principle that "nonviolence seeks to win friendship" and "nonviolence seeks to defeat injustice, not people" (King Center, n.d.) here. In relation to framing as a point of entry into intercultural praxis, we may disagree with, find intolerable and even hate certain frames of references, for example, ones that reproduce what Dr. King called the triple evils—economic injustice, militarism and racism—yet, the goal is to fight against the injustice without demonizing or dehumanizing the people.

Secondly, at times it is very important to narrow the frame and focus on the particular and very situated aspects of an interaction, event or exchange. Take, for example, a conflict between two people from different cultures. It is important to look at the interactional dimension between the individuals or the micro frame highlighting differences in communication styles, how nonverbal communication may be used differently, the ways in which the two people may perceive their identities differently based on cultural belonging and the ways in which the two may have learned to enact conflict differently based on their respective enculturation. However, in order to fully understand the particular intercultural misunderstanding or conflict, it is also necessary to view the incident, event or interaction from a broader, intermediate or meso frame. As we extend the frame, we may see a history of conflict and misunderstanding between the two groups that the individuals represent; we may observe historical and/or current patterns of inequities between the two groups. As we broaden further to a macro frame, we may also map out broader geopolitical, global relations of power that shed light on the particular and situated intercultural interaction, misunderstanding or conflict (Sorrells, 2022).

Positioning

Positioning as a point of entry into intercultural praxis invites us to consider how we are positioned in terms of power in relation to others. The world is stratified by socially constructed hierarchical categories based on culture, race, class, gender, nationality, religion, age, geographic location and physical abilities among others. Like the lines of longitude and latitude that divide, map and position us geographically on the Earth, these hierarchical categories position us and the groups we belong to socially, politically and materially in relation to each other and in relation to structures and configurations of power. Positioning, as a way to enter into intercultural praxis, directs us to interrogate who can speak and who is silenced both historically and today; whose language is spoken and whose language is trivialized or denied; whose actions have the power to shape and impact others and whose actions are dismissed, unreported and marginalized. In other words, whose cultural norms, practices, worldviews and values are upheld as "normal," as "human nature" and as "central" to the human story and whose are marginalized, disparaged and even annihilated. Being cognizant of positioning in the intercultural praxis model means we take stock of intersectional systemic inequities in whatever form and leverage our positionality, our advantages, privileges and resources, whether based on education, class, region, citizenship, language, gender or race, to challenge inequities and create more inclusive, equitable and just homes, workplaces, communities and societies.

In the first step, *focus*, in the process of nonviolent resistance and in preparation for the second step, *negotiation*, working together within one's group or community to examine and understand the dynamics of power that need to be addressed, how and who to negotiate with and the levers of power to be pressured to create change requires an understanding of relationships of power (Lawson, 2022). "Person power," used individually and collectively in the long tradition of nonviolence, aligns with positioning as we understand who we are, where we have come from and how we can mobilize our resources for repair, reconciliation and the "beloved community."

Dialogue

Dialogue has long occupied a normative place in philosophy, theology and communication studies (Buber, 1958; Arnett, 1999). The word "dialogue" is derived from the Greek word *dialogos. Dia*" means "through," "between" or "across" and *logos* refers to "word" or "the meaning of the word" as well as "speech" or "thought." Anthropologist Crapanzano (1990) suggests that dialogue necessarily entails both an oppositional and a transformative dimension. Given the differences in power and positionality in intercultural interactions, engagement in dialogue is necessarily a relationship of tension that "is conceived as a crossing, a reaching across, a sharing if not a common ground of understanding …" (p. 277). Cognizant of differences and the tensions that emerge from these differences, the process of dialogue invites us to stretch ourselves—to reach across and to exceed our grasp—to imagine, experience and creatively engage with points of view, ways of thinking, being and doing and beliefs different from our own while accepting that we may not fully understand or may not come to a common agreement or position.

Dialogue is a foundational tenet of the art and discipline of *satyagraha*, nonviolence or soul force. Dialogue with oneself and community ground the practice in one's experiences, knowledge and truths and those of the community. Dialogue as outlined here is a form of radical listening, understanding and accountability. While dialogue is often oppositional particularly in the negotiation phase of nonviolent civil resistance, Dr. King reminds us of the creative and transformative power of engaging in nonviolent dialogue:

> Nonviolence resists violence to the spirit as well as the body. Nonviolent love is active, not passive. Nonviolent love does not sink to the level of the hater. Love restores community and resists injustice. Nonviolence recognizes the fact that all life is interrelated.
>
> *(King Center, n.d.)*

Reflection

While cultures around the world differ in the degree to which they value reflection and the ways in which they practice reflection, the capacity to learn from introspection, to observe oneself in relation to others and to alter one's perspectives and actions based on reflection is a capacity shared by all humans. Many cultures, including the dominant culture of the U.S., place a high value on doing activities and accomplishing tasks, which often leaves little space and time for reflection. However, reflection is a key feature of intercultural praxis and the development of nonviolence, "*satyagraha* as well as in the steps of *focus, negotiation, direct-action* and *follow-up*, the four steps in the practical application of nonviolence (Lawson, 2022).

The late Brazilian educator and activist Paulo Freire (1998) notes in his book, *Pedagogy of Freedom*, that critical praxis "involves a dynamic and dialectic movement between 'doing' and 'reflecting on doing'" (p. 43). Reflection is what informs our actions. Reflection that incorporates critical analyses of intercultural issues on the micro, meso and macro levels, that considers multiple cultural frames of reference, that recognizes our own and others' positioning, as well as the role of historical and current systemic inequities enables us to act in the world in meaningful, effective, and socially responsible ways. As Freire observes, reflection can itself serve a political function insofar as it intervenes in uninformed actions that may otherwise be normalized as "the way things are" and "the way things must be." By disengaging from the taken-for-granted and non-reflexive flow of everyday actions, knowledge systems and value commitments, it becomes possible to re-position and re-frame and re-structure what may be oppressive conditions or relations of power.

Action

Influenced by the work of Paulo Freire (2000), the concept of intercultural praxis refers to an on-going process of thinking, reflecting and acting. Intercultural praxis is not only about deepening our understanding of ourselves, others and the world in which we live. Rather, intercultural praxis means we turn our increased understanding into responsible and liberatory action to make a difference in the world—to create a more socially just, equitable and peaceful world. Each of us takes multiple and varied actions, individually and collectively, that have intercultural communication dimensions and implications every day of our lives. We take action when we go to work, when we speak out (or not) about inequity, discrimination and misuses of power. Watching or reading the news is an action that affords opportunities to understand how cultural and national interests shape, limit and bias the news we receive. Our consumption of products, food and entertainment are all actions. When we know who has labored to make the goods we consume and under what conditions, we confront ourselves and others with the choices we make through our actions. We take action when we make decisions about who we develop friendships and long-term relationships with and when we choose not to be involved. What informs our choices and actions? What are the implications of our actions?

When we feel strongly enough about an issue, we are moved to organize and take collective action. Nonviolent resistance can take many forms. In his book, *The Politics of Nonviolent Action,* Gene Sharpe's (1973) outlines nearly 200 techniques for nonviolent action ranging from persuasive dialogue to demonstration, marches and boycotts. Methods of nonviolent struggle are carried out to maintain pressure on negotiations so the desired outcomes can be researched. Lawson often says there is more protest today than ever there was in the past. The problem, however, is that the struggle is not sustained in an organized manner. Protracted struggle must be waged strategically with intention and moral grounding (Lawson, 2022, p. 47). From everyday actions to collective civil resistance, intercultural praxis informed by inquiry, framing, positioning, dialogue and reflection can be the catalyst for personal change as well as social and global transformation.

Case Study: Intercultural Praxis Approach

In the course of the Covid pandemic, experiences of intercultural conflict among family members, co-workers, political parties, public officials and constituents, employees and corporate owners, law enforcers and citizens, health professionals and public officials multiplied, often magnifying existing tensions and conflicts within families, communities and nations around the globe. The following scenario illustrates the layered and multidimensional aspects of intercultural conflicts in the neoliberal global context. The intercultural praxis model informed by the philosophy and methodology of nonviolence provides a process of analysis and set of strategies to address the intercultural conflict and move toward reconciliation, harmony and the beloved community.

> Weeks before the extended-family gathering for the holidays, invitations were sent out by email, phone and text. The event was planned at the home of the European-American parents, Evelyn and Roger, who live in a wealthy neighborhood near a large city in northern California in the U.S. The couple enjoyed

hosting family and friends on holiday occasions operating from a "big-tent," inclusive philosophy. Their son, Michael, who lived in South Korea for two years and is fluent in Korean and his wife, Da-Hee, who he met in South Korea, their three-year-old son and Da-Hee's parents, referred to as Eomma (mother in Korean) and Appa (father in Korean), who were visiting from South Korea were invited. Evelyn and Roger, the English-only speaking parents and Eomma and Appa, the Korean-only speaking parents had met once before at the wedding in South Korea. The Eomma and Appa's older daughter, Da-Som, her African-American husband, Kobi, and their four-year-old daughter, who lived nearby, were also invited. Kobi's parents, who live in Ghana, had hoped to come but were unable to travel to the U.S. due to Covid restrictions and lack of access to vaccine in their country. As the holiday approached, Kobi's two sisters decided to travel to California from New York City and were invited to the gathering too.

As the day of the gathering drew closer and concerns over Covid variants heightened, the hosts, Richard and Evelyn, wanted everyone to get boosted or take a Covid test before attending. While most of the attendees were already boosted, in the interest of protecting his parents and his wife's parents, Michael vehemently insisted that Eomma and Appa—recently arrived from South Korea where boosters were not yet available—get boosted. Michael's insistent approach expressed in an angry conversation with his parents-in-law added to their hesitancy to get the vaccine booster in the U.S. Michael also made it clear the siblings of Kobi had to get boosted or tested. While Eomma and Appa did reluctantly get the vaccine booster shot, they decided to have their holiday celebration with Da-Som and Kobi only. After many conversations between Michael and Da-Hee and other family members, Michael apologized to Eomma and Appa and sent an apologetic text to Kobi, but none of them responded. Evelyn and Richard were upset by what felt like a rebuke by those who did not attend and were concerned this set of incidents would have a long-term impact on the extended family relations.

As with any scenario or lived experience, we cannot possibly understand all the motives, underlaying conditions, assumptions and tensions that enable and constrain interactions; yet, we can begin to sort through and make sense of some of the intercultural issues using the intercultural praxis model informed by the art and discipline of nonviolence. It is useful to couple *inquiry* and *reflection* in the praxis model allowing us to question and contemplate ideas, feelings and actions in nonjudgmental and receptive ways. Applying the practice of nonviolence begins here in relation to ourselves and others. Dr. King's first principle is that nonviolence is a way of life for courageous people, which actively and adamantly resists evil mentally, emotionally and spiritually (King Center, n.d.).

Inquiry as a port of entry into the praxis model invites us to be curious about ourselves and others; to be interested in learning and being changed by our interactions; to be willing to take risks as well as be flexible and courageous enough to examine our ways of being, thinking and viewing the world and to be changed by our interactions.

What questions emerge after reading the scenario? What perspective was most understandable or relatable for you and why? The position that seems "right" or "makes sense" is likely the worldview or cultural frame that aligns with your own. Noting what seems "normal" and then challenging yourself to understand other perspectives or cultural frames presented is central to the intercultural praxis process.

What tools and mechanisms are available to develop the peace of mind and "person power" that Gandhi imagined and practiced? How can we equip ourselves to manage the anger, fear and deep dislike or even hate that may arise—either from the immediate issues or ones layered over history—in our intercultural interactions? How can we choose a different path, as Dr. King suggests, from either opting out or turning to violence? How can we engage the principle of nonviolence that seeks to win friendships and understanding? How can our path from the start engage a way of being—of mutual respect and friendship—that practices and embodies the outcome of the "beloved community"—a place of redemption, reconciliation and love?

Framing and *positioning* are deeply interrelated in most all situations and particularly in conflict situations. The frames we use to make sense of our experiences are informed by our positionality. Our cultural frames are developed through the people we interact with, the stories and experiences we share, the media we consume and the meanings we construct with others. Thus, our positionality—where we are positioned within hierarchical structures of power—in terms of nation, region, language, socio-economic class, race, gender and religion—shape the frames and standpoints from which we make sense of any situation. For example, the European-American host family may not perceive themselves as being situated in a position of power; yet, as the ones hosting, they are on home territory, which inevitably creates a position of advantage in relation to others who are invited into their space, their rituals and their family. Additional dimensions such as class, race and nationality substantiate the European-American position of power in relation to others in this scenario. Their access to vaccines and boosters is clearly an advantage and privilege as compared to the parents who were not able to attend from Ghana and the parents from South Korea who had not yet been able to receive a booster. Their cumulative advantages, amassed from continents and accrued over centuries, yet experienced in this very local and particular moment, may have obfuscated their awareness of their power, which, is quite apparent to the others. Dr. King reminds us in his third principle that nonviolence seeks to defeat injustice and not people. The goal is to question, challenge and dismantle underlying assumptions, practices, norms, policies and structures that maintain and promote injustice, not to denigrate or defeat people.

Eomma and Appa may have felt like "outsiders" as visitors to the U.S. and self-conscious about their inability to speak English. The situation highlights the language supremacy of English globally. Few would expect the U.S. couple to speak Korean but often non-English speakers are expected to learn English, which is another unrecognized advantage for those who grow up speaking English. The South Korean parent's "otherness" may also feel accentuated by differences beyond language that accompany traveling into new cultural territory including differences

in food, norms and behavior—especially during a holiday season. Given the hege-
mony of the U.S. media globally, the South Korean parents were probably aware
of holiday customs in the U.S.; however, knowing about them and being prepared
to or wanting to be immersed in them, given the choice, is a different matter.
Would spending a holiday with their in-laws occur in their cultural context? While
a big tent philosophy is experienced as inclusive in the hosts' culture, what deeper
inquiry, reflection and re-framing could occur so everyone feels included? How
can expectations, assumptions and practices be re-framed to account for the ways
people are positioned differently?

Eomma and Appa were particularly offended and upset by their son-in-law's
demand that they get boosted or tested. They might have had reservations about
the booster vaccination in the U.S. and doubts about the health care system in
general in the U.S., which could have made them hesitant and anxious. Through
inquiry and reflection about the sources of their reservations, we may reveal how
inextricably intertwined assumptions are with framing and positioning. Despite
remarkable evidence to the contrary, the notion of U.S. superiority and excep-
tionalism persists in the U.S. Beyond their reluctance about the health care system,
the South Korean parents were most surprised and upset by the way their son-in-
law talked to them, his intensity and relentlessness. The son-in-law's behavior was
based on concern for the health of both sets of parents; however, the intensity with
which he confronted the South Korean parents was experienced by them as highly
disrespectful. While they complied and got boosted, how much did this encounter
influence their decision not to attend the gathering? What role did differences in
cultural conflict styles play in the decision not to attend the event? What role did
the rank of the daughters—younger vs. older—play? How did Kobi, the African-
American man, feel about the demand by Michael, his European-American
brother-in-law, to make sure his sisters were boosted or tested? Given the racialized
terrain embedded in the U.S. over centuries, how did the commanding message
impact on his African-American brother-in-law and his family?

The intercultural praxis entry points of framing and positioning encourage
shifting from micro, meso and macro frames when analyzing intercultural conflicts
(Sorrells, 2022). As illustrated here, the micro frame focuses our attention on the
immediate interpersonal relationships highlighting cultural orientations to conflict,
communication styles, language barriers, assumptions, perceptions and values. The
meso or intermediate frame broadens our view to address the ways cultural group
prejudices, cultural histories and identities, as well as group-based forms of systemic
oppression such as ethnocentrism, racism and sexism may impact intercultural
conflicts as illustrated in the scenario. The meso frame brings issues of privilege and
advantage, for example, those of the European-American family in the scenario,
and the ways tensions may be exacerbated by historical patterns of inequity such as
the tense relationship between the African-American and European-American son-
in-law into view. The macro or geopolitical frame expands our viewpoint to
include the impact of media and discourse as well as geopolitical inequities that
impact intercultural conflict. For example, the macro frame brings into focus the

widely disparate access in the context of neoliberal globalization to vaccines and boosters for countries around the world as illustrated in the scenario. If everyone had had equal access to vaccines and boosters, how might the conflict in the intercultural scenario have changed? Developing the ability to move between frames enhances our understanding of a particular issue or conflict providing depth and dimensionality where the cumulative impact of histories—for example, systemic inequities over time—are made visible and connections between the local and the global are revealed.

Dialogue and Action

Dialogue, grounded in a sense of connection, empathy and respect, might have benefited all participants in the scenario. Dialogue informed by inquiry into cultural assumptions, an understanding of how cultural frames impact our assumptions and how positionality shapes our frames and perspectives would probably have led to different outcomes. From the outset, questions such as the following may have been helpful: How would each of the family like to celebrate the holiday? If we plan to gather together, how can we set it up to be as inclusive as possible? And, what is the most effective way to communicate restrictions or guidelines for joining the event? Who can communicate restrictions and guidelines most successfully? For example, might it have been better to invite Da-Hee to talk with her parents about getting boosted? And would engaging Da-Som in the conversation about booster shots for Kobi's family along with Kobi have led to a different outcome? Asking questions, reflecting on one's positionality in relation to others and the impact on others are forms of action that are important when engaging in intercultural praxis. To engage in dialogue purposefully and meaningfully, participants must listen to the experiences and perspectives of others—without judgment, defensiveness or expectation.

Dialogue did occur between family members at the end of the incidents described in the scenario, which was probably helpful in repairing the hurt caused and making those concerned aware of important questions about cultural assumptions, frames and positionality. How much more helpful might it have been if dialogue informed by inquiry, framing, positioning and reflection had been engaged in? The intercultural praxis model can be used to prepare for intercultural situations that are likely to contain conflict, provide a guide for analysis and action while involved in the intercultural situation or conflict and also function as an assessment tool to consider how we can learn from the interaction. If the European-American family had reflected on their positionality in the situation, this may, along with dialogue, have led to questioning their privileges, challenging assumptions they may have had that enabled discrimination, and that upheld systems of inequity. Michael, the European-American son, at the hub of relationships, may have realized the pivotal role he played or could have played in nurturing relationships and intercultural understanding with this constellation of people. He took the first steps toward reconciliation in apologizing for his angry outburst. With his increased awareness of his positionality as a White male in the U.S., how could he have leveraged his privilege, positionality and power to create more inclusive, equitable and better relationships within this extended family? What actions could each member have taken to create the healthy, safe and inclusive network of support and love within this multicultural extended family?

In his fourth principle, Dr. King states that a nonviolent approach embraces suffering as a tool of education and transformation (King Center, n.d.). Suffering, in the context of nonviolence as a way of life, includes discomfort and distress caused by arguments and disagreements, the pain and sorrow from loss and exclusion as well as the suffering inflicted on the body through brutal and violent tactics of oppression. Staying in difficult dialogues, whether with family members who disagree and are hurt or defensive as in the scenario, with colleagues or community members in conflict or among nations who struggle to care for their citizens during a pandemic, is a way of embracing hardship or suffering as a means of growth, learning and change. How could each extended family member re-write the script for this scenario based on the principles of nonviolence? How could each family member take the concern and distress they may have felt as an opportunity to learn and transform?

Dr. King's fifth principle—nonviolence chooses love over hate—informs our actions in the intercultural praxis model. What would it look like if each person in the scenario approached each other with love? Dr. King is not referring to romantic or sentimental love; rather, *agape* love is full of understanding, goodwill and redemption for all. This love is the moral imperative that demands accountability and truth-telling regarding uneven and oppressive relations of power. Dr. King argued, "Agape is the willingness to go to any length to restore community … Therefore, if I respond to hate with a reciprocal hate I do nothing but intensify the cleavages of a broken community" (King, 1958, p. 105). What lengths are we willing to go to for our local community? For our global community? As noted in the scenario, access to vaccines against the coronavirus is extremely inequitable around the globe. The World Health Organization (2022) argues vaccine equity *is* within the world's reach. The issue is a matter of sharing technology, ensuring equitable distribution and recognizing that no one is safe until the whole world is vaccinated. However, illustrating the ideological and material crises at the core of our neoliberal global society, high income nations representing one fifth of the global adult population are stockpiling doses and biotech companies refuse to share their technologies (Goldhill, 2021; Nebehay & Mason, 2021). The unequal access to vaccines impacted the extended family in the scenario in various ways. Would any family member or others feel strongly enough about this issue to organize with others to take collective action to end vaccine inequity?

> Nonviolence is trying to use the power that life gives you in ways that solve problems and heal and transform you and change and transform others. Everyone has the gift of creation and the gift of power … Nonviolence insists that the power each of us has, the power that we often give to our

governments, is a power that, used rightly, can turn violence into nonviolence, can turn cruelty into kindness, can turn untruth into truth, can turn war into peace and justice.

(Lawson, 2022, p. 80)

Conclusion

In this chapter, I drew attention to the global crises and concomitant conflicts we face as a result of neoliberal globalization and addressed the distinctly interconnected, contradictory and inequitable conditions in which intercultural communication occurs today. The art and discipline of nonviolence, as practiced by Dr. Martin Luther King was proposed as a critical theoretical and methodological approach to address the violence that underpins intercultural conflicts in the neoliberal global context. "Person power" is understood as nonviolence grounded in individuals who are autonomous yet interconnected each on a path toward their fullest humanity. This power, *satyagraha* or "soul force," cultivated through the discipline of nonviolence in intrapersonal, interpersonal and inter-group situations, has the power to dismantle the three evils of racism, poverty and militarism and create the beloved community. The principles of nonviolence were highlighted within the intercultural praxis model to provide a framework of analysis, reflection and action regarding intercultural conflict on interpersonal and social levels. A scenario was introduced to illustrate how the intercultural praxis model informed by the philosophy and methodology of nonviolence provides a roadmap for moving intercultural conflict toward reconciliation and the beloved community. In a speech titled "Remaining Awake Through a Great Revolution" at the National Cathedral in Washington, D.C. on March 31, 1968 just days before his assassination, Dr. King proclaimed, "We shall overcome because the arc of the moral universe is long but it leans toward justice."

References

Ackerman, P. & Duvall, J. (2000). *A force more powerful: A century of nonviolent conflict*. New York, NY: Palgrave.

Arnett, R. A. (1999). *Dialogic civility in a cynical age: Community, hope, and interpersonal relationships*. Albany, NY: State University of New York Press.

Buber, M. (1958). *I and thou* (R. G. Smith, Trans.). New York, NY: Scribner.

Chenoweth, E. & Stephens, M. (2021). *Civil resistance. What everyone needs to know*. New York, NY: Oxford University Press.

Crapanzano, V. (1990). On dialogue. In T. Marahão (Ed.). *The interpretation of dialogue* (pp. 269–291). Chicago, IL: University of Chicago Press.

Freire, P. (1998) *Pedagogy of freedom: Ethics, democracy, and civic courage*. Lanham, MD: Rowman & Littlefield.

Freire, P. (2000). *Pedagogy of the oppressed*. New York, NY: Continuum.

Giroux, H. A. (2021). *Race, politics, and pandemic pedagogy: Education in a time of crisis*. New York, NY: Bloomsbury Academic.

The Art and Discipline of Nonviolence 131

Giroux, H. A. & Filappakau, O. (2020). *Militarism in the age of the pandemic.* Retrieved from https://www.e-ir.info/2020/04/22/militarization-in-the-age-of-the-pandemic-crisis.

Goffman, E. (1974). *Frame analysis: An essay on the organization of experience.* London, UK: Harper & Row.

Goldhill, O. (2021). We have enough Covid vaccines for most of the world. But rich countries are stockpiling more than they need for boosters. Retrieved from https://www.statnews.com/2021/12/13/we-have-enough-covid-vaccines-for-most-of-world-but-rich-countries-stockpiling-more-than-they-need.

Harvey, D. (2005). *A brief history of neoliberalism.* Oxford, UK: Oxford University Press.

Harvey, D. (2016). *Neoliberalism is a political project: An interview with David Harvey.* Retrieved from https://www.jacobinmag.com/2016/07/david-harvey-neoliberalism-capitalism-labor-crisis-resistance.

King, M. L. (1957). *Nonviolence and racial justice.* Retrieved from https://kinginstitute.stanford.edu/king-papers/documents/nonviolence-and-racial-justice#fn6.

King, M. L. (1958) *Stride toward freedom: The Montgomery circle.* New York, NY: Harper & Row.

King, M. L. (1967). The three evils of society. Retrieved from https://mlkglobal.org/martin-luther-king-speeches.

King, M. L. (1968, March 31). *Remaining awake through a great revolution.* Retrieved from https://www.youtube.com/watch?v=SLsXZXJAURk.

King Center. (n.d.). *The King philosophy—Nonviolence 365.* Retrieved from https://thekingcenter.org/about-tkc/the-king-philosophy.

Lakoff, G. (2004). *Don't think of an elephant: Know your values and frame the debate.* White River Junction, VT: Chelsea Green.

Lawson, J. M. (2022). *Revolutionary nonviolence: Organizing for freedom.* Oakland, CA: University of California Press.

Lorde, A. (1984). *Sister outsider: Essays and speeches.* Berkeley, CA: Crossing Press.

Michelson, N. & de Orellana, P. (2022). *Global nationalism: Ideas, movements and dynamics in the twenty-first century.* London, UK: World Scientific Europe.

Mishra, P. (2017). *The age of anger: The history of the present.* New York, NY: Farrar, Straus & Giroux.

Nagler, M. N. (2020). *The third harmony: Nonviolence and the new story of human nature.* Oakland, CA: Berrett-Koehler.

Nebehay, S. & Mason, J. (2021). *WHO warns against vaccine hoarding as power countries go without.* Retrieved from https://www.reuters.com/business/healthcare-pharmaceuticals/who-warns-against-vaccine-hoarding-poor-countries-go-without-2021-12-09.

Oxfam. (2020, January 20) World's billionaires have more wealth than 4.6 billion people. Oxfam International. Retrieved from https://www.oxfam.org/en/press-releases/worlds-billionaires-have-more-wealth-46-billion-people.

Sharpe, G. (1973). *The politics of nonviolent action.* Boston, MA: Porter Sargent.

Sorrells, K. (2022) *Intercultural communication: Globalization and social justice* (3rd ed.). Thousand Oaks, CA: Sage.

Ting-Toomey, S. (1999). *Communicating across cultures.* New York, NY: Guilford.

Ting-Toomey, S. & Oetzel, J. G. (2001). *Managing intercultural conflict effectively.* Thousand Oaks, CA: Sage.

World Health Organization. (2022). Vaccine equity. World Health Organization. Retrieved from https://www.who.int/campaigns/vaccine-equity.

8

MULTICULTURAL IDENTITY AND CONFLICT COMMUNICATION COMPETENCE IN THE 21ST CENTURY

Min-Sun Kim and Yoshiko Kameo

Increased cultural diversity in different settings calls for adapting to the unfamiliar environment and learning to work and live productively with people from different cultural backgrounds (Chen & Starosta, 1997). Miller and Steinberg (1975) distinguish between pseudo conflicts and simple conflicts. Simple conflicts stem from incompatible goals, while pseudo conflicts arise from a communicative misunderstanding between parties. Intercultural communication is generally characterized by different expectations (because of cultural values and norms) between interaction partners. Therefore, the potential for pseudo conflicts is greater in intercultural relationships than in intracultural ones (see Lee & Rogan, 1991).

Conflict as a concept can help explain many aspects of social life, such as conflicts of interests, social disagreement, and fighting between individuals and groups, organizations, or nations (Kim & Leung, 2000). Although conflict tends to be a negative experience caused by abnormally difficult circumstances, it can provide numerous opportunities for psychological growth through empathy, creative understanding, and insight. Often, it is not the content of conflict that creates tensions or frictions; instead, the cultural style creates uncertainty and anxiety in the conflict encounter situation (Ting-Toomey, 1988).

Given that cross-cultural interactions are burgeoning, there has never been such a great need for knowledge about conflict styles in different cultures to cope with conflicts at the cultural interfaces. Cross-cultural conflict is a topic with a growing body of literature. Utilizing a national or ethnic culture approach (e.g., Nomura & Barnlund, 1983), many studies have sought to describe the differences in style use between members of different cultures and to understand the differences in conflict handling between cultures (Chua & Gudykunst, 1987).

So far, findings of intercultural conflict management have been mainly concerned with comparing different styles among people of different nationalities, ethnicities, gender, age, or cultural orientations (Boonsathorn, 2007; Ghadamosi, Baghestan, &

DOI: 10.4324/9781003252955-10

Al-Mabrouk, 2012). Research indicates that individuals from collectivistic cultures are more likely to prefer compromising or integrative conflict management styles. In contrast, those from more individualistic cultures may value a dominating style (see Kim, 2017). However, when a whole culture, society, or individual is cast in specific dichotomous categories, subtle differences and qualitative nuances that may be more characteristic of these social entities are glossed over (Kim, 2002). Also, when cultures and individuals are categorized in binary terms, this inevitably makes good/bad comparisons of conflict management styles.

In the past, our understanding and definition of identity evolved significantly. Whether through immigration, sojourning, marriage, adoption, or birth, a wide range of people is actively carrying the frame of references of two or more cultures (see Bennett, 1993). Biculturals or multiculturals emerge from cultural mixing between groups, between individuals with different cultural orientations, and within individuals with different cultural orientations. Increasing numbers of people find that the conflicts do not arise between different groups but between different cultural values, attitudes, and expectations within themselves (Phinney, 1989). We are yet to know much about such individuals' distinctive multicultural experiences and their competencies and skills to improve the effectiveness of multicultural conflict management. This chapter aims to develop an understanding of multicultural identity as a part of psychological growth that benefits intercultural conflict communication competence.

While in the past literature bicultural individuals were considered to exhibit various components of intercultural sensitivity, acquisition of multicultural identity can be seen as a natural process of human growth involving a radical shift of personal perspectives and maturation of vision. Multicultural persons are not simply sensitive to other cultures or knowledgeable about cultural differences. Rather, they can be defined by psycho-cultural patterns of identity that are significantly different from the relatively static forms of self-process found in the usual culture-typed identity patterns. Further, the recognition that cultural diversity exists within multicultural individuals can bring about social change by challenging many accepted assumptions about intercultural conflict management. In the following section, we will review past approaches to cross-cultural conflict management. Then, pointing toward the path beyond comparing culture-typed individuals, we will explore conceptual frameworks of multicultural experiences and the implications for conflict communication competence.

Past Research on Cross-Cultural Conflict Management

Problems of cross-cultural conflict are particularly acute in today's world. Viewing conflict as cultural behavior helps explain why disputes over seemingly similar issues can be handled so dissimilarly in different cultures (Kim, 2017). Conflict researchers have proffered a plethora of different definitions for conflict. Simons (1972) defines conflict as a state of social relationship in which conflicting interests between two or more parties give rise to a struggle between them. Ting-Toomey

(1985) calls it a form of intense interpersonal and intrapersonal dissonance or tension between two or more interdependent parties based on incompatible goals, needs, desires, values, beliefs, and attitudes. In this chapter, the domain of conflict will be limited to interpersonal conflict.

Interpersonal conflict may be handled by various styles of behavior. There have been many attempts to measure interpersonal conflict management styles, adapted to study intercultural conflict styles. Five proposed conflict styles were organized on a two-dimensional grid, beginning with Blake and his associates (Blake & Mouton, 1964). These styles and dimensions were then renamed several times, and several instruments were devised to measure the styles.

For several decades, the Dual Concern model has been a popular method of organizing five conflict styles on a grid formed by the dimensions of seeking one's concerns and seeking those of the other party (Blake & Mouton, 1964; Thomas & Kilmann, 1978). Although the two-dimensional Managerial Grid has profoundly influenced most conflict style theorists, the factor structures of the instruments have been disparate, inconsistent, or unclear (e.g., Kim, Lee, Kim, & Hunter, 2004). Conflict categories have been located within dimensional structures that are researcher-defined and researcher-salient (Nicotera, 1993).

Research on Cross-Cultural Conflict Management

Many cross-cultural communication researchers have frequently adopted conflict styles based on the two assumed dimensions. There have been numerous cross-cultural comparison studies of different conflict management strategies, most studies utilizing a national or ethnic culture approach (Kim, 2017). Research on conflict management across cultures indicates differences in conflict styles used in individualistic and collectivistic cultures. The findings in the cross-cultural conflict literature reveal that collectivists value harmonious interpersonal relationships with others (Cathcart & Cathcart, 1976), showing concern for face-saving (Nomura & Barnlund, 1983) and preferring indirect styles of dealing with conflict (Chua & Gudykunst, 1987; Ohbuchi & Takahashi, 1994). Overall, the findings reported in the cross-cultural conflict literature show that, compared with individualists, collectivists value harmonious interpersonal relationships with others, prefer indirect or avoiding styles of dealing with conflict and show concern for face-saving (Kim, 2017).

In the mainstream U.S. context, open controversy and preference for direct (dominating) conflict communication styles have been considered normal and beneficial for decision-making (Kim, 2002). Consequently, the models relying on Blake and Mouton's (1964) work, which was created in the Western cultural context, conceptualize avoiding (or withdrawal style) as either negative or destructive ("lose-lose" style). The flavor of various scales is that confrontation is more desirable than avoidance (Kim, 2002).

However, avoidance of conflict can help the individual control his/her emotion and allow the passive expression of discontentment without the dangers of a direct challenge. Specifically, as with inferences regarding silences, avoidance of conflict can be seen as negative politeness—being nice to others by not imposing. The benefit of using avoidance strategies comes from being understood without putting one's meaning on record. Likewise, the work in this area has been biased by the individualistic assumption that confrontation is more desirable than avoidance, which restricts a complete understanding of the conflict phenomenon (Kim, 2002).

Furthermore, most intercultural conflict communication research has focused on the preferred communication styles of "culture-typed" individuals. Prior work on intercultural conflict management presumes, implicitly or explicitly, that cultural categories are linear and exclusive. The dichotomized way of representing cultural differences leads to unjustifiable generalizations and ignores the subtleties and frequent contradictions inherent in many national/ethnic cultures. For instance, while individualism and collectivism were initially believed to represent endpoints lying on the single dimension (e.g., Hofstede, 1980), both individualist and collectivist orientations may coexist within individuals and cultures.

Using multicultural perspectives, we can seek to understand new and creative ways of managing intercultural conflict. Sampson (1988) has argued that the reality of globalization and a shrinking world will force just such a rethinking of the nature of the individual. Moving toward research trends that focus on hybrid identities is a reasonable response to contemporary social changes, such as increasing cultural diversity, interdependence, and widespread demands for democratic participation in the construction of social reality (Kim, 2002).

Understanding Multicultural Identity

Accelerated changes in the modern world compel us to take cognizance of the dynamic nature of individuals' cultural identity and conflict communication competence (Kim, 2017). Multicultural or multiethnic groups live in the same country, and cultural or co-cultural diversity can be found within ethnic groups. As individuals' cultural identities can no longer be described as static, it is common for individuals to internalize more than one culture, live in culturally mixed environments, speak multiple languages, and retain transnational or global ties. Thus, there is an increasing need for researchers to examine how bicultural or multicultural individuals (henceforth called interchangeably "bicultural" and "multicultural") process their identities from many aspects (Heo & Kim, 2013). Cultural identity is generally difficult to define, and multicultural identity may be even more ambiguous. The following section will clarify the psychological process of being bi- or multicultural.

Bicultural Individuals and Global Identity: Who are They?

Facilitated by the internet, language, products, and the media, globalization has given rise to a new crop of multicultural individuals who are identified with a global culture or multiple cultures worldwide (Hong, Wan, No, & Chiu, 2015). Multiculturals increasingly emerge from cultural mixing between groups, as well as individuals with different cultural orientations (West, Zhang, Yampolsky, & Sasaki, 2017).

Many researchers have attempted to define biculturals as individuals who live at the juncture between two cultures (Park, 1928; Stonequist, 1935) and those who internalize more than one culture (Chen, Benet-Martínez, & Bond, 2008) by endorsing both independent and interdependent self-construals (Kim et al., 1996). Furthermore, biculturals are conceptualized as those who can function in two cultures (Phinney & Devich-Navarro, 1997), retain their ethnic identity while adjusting to the mainstream cultural identity (Berry & Kim, 1988), and maintain a local identity linked to the global culture (i.e., global identity) (Eytan, 2004).

Migration has been a prime factor in accelerating biculturalism in the modern world. Previous research has studied acculturation strategies that new immigrants utilize when they move from their home country to new cultures (Berry & Kim, 1988; Sussman, 2000). In addition to the new immigrants' experiences of becoming multiculturals, some researchers argue that globalization greatly and predominantly affects individual and national psychology and thus results in bicultural identities or hybrid identities (Arnett, 2002). Global interconnection and shared responsibility in our communities have produced the concept of global citizenship or a transnational identity (Dwyer, 1999). Croucher (2004) argues that "globalization intensifies the need for cosmopolitanism or for an awareness of being citizens of the world" (p.189). Migration has increased under globalization, so both trends towards biculturalism should be simultaneously considered (see Heo & Kim, 2013).

Several researchers have noted that transformative cultural identities such as bicultural or hybrid identities are continuing to emerge (Arnett, 2002). As the world shrinks, individuals have more opportunities to come into contact with global cultures without migrating, resulting in "global consciousness" (Arnett, 2002, p. 777). With a sense of belonging to cosmopolitan culture and an awareness of the global culture, those with global consciousness do not need to move to other places to experience cultural differences.

Multicultural Identity: "Transcending Cultural Boundaries"

There is increasing credence given to the idea of a multicultural personality shaped and contoured by the stresses and strains resulting from cultural interweaving at both the macro and microcultural levels (Heo & Kim, 2013). Seemingly, a multicultural style evolves when the individual can negotiate the conflicts and tensions inherent in cross-cultural contacts. Then, the multicultural person may represent an affirmation of individual identity at a higher social, psychological, and cultural integration level. Multiculturalism suggests a human being whose identifications and loyalties transcend the boundaries of nationalism and whose commitments are pinned to a larger vision of the global community (Adler, 1998), sometimes called an "international," "transcultural," "multicultural," "cosmopolitan" or "intercultural" individual.

The implications of a bicultural perspective in identity acquisition are that it allows for a more fluid cultural exchange between groups. Rather than placing groups in a hierarchy of dominance, the idea behind a bicultural viewpoint is that biculturalism allows culture to be a choice rather than one imposed on an individual (Kim, 2002). Different groups of individuals probably integrate and experience the combination of their national and ethnocultural group membership in different ways (Berry, 2003). They might, for example, differ in the extent to which they blend both identities in their sense of self and to what extent they view both their cultural identities as compatible (Haritatos & Benet-Martínez, 2002; Huynh, Nguyen, & Benet-Martinez, 2011).

Research has highlighted biculturals' challenging and stressful experiences but has also drawn attention to the beneficial outcomes it might have (Vivero & Jenkins, 1999). For example, bicultural individuals might need to reconcile dual group loyalties, combine potentially contrasting norms and values, and experience identity conflict. Bicultural identity has also been associated with relatively good well-being and psychological and sociocultural adjustment (Berry, 1997; Nguyen & Benet-Martínez, 2013).

There have been historical shifts in identifying biculturalism, from viewing biculturals as marginals to viewing them as biculturals who integrate multiple cultural identities (Heo & Kim, 2013). The previous concept, "marginal man," is concerned with how mainstream groups or in-groups see the ethnocultural or outgroups. On the other hand, acculturation theory highlights individuals' attitudes toward adapting to new cultures by examining how individuals possess dual or multiple cultural identities and engage in active cultural frame switching. Some researchers contend that transformative identities such as bicultural or hybrid identities have emerged due to globalization (Heo & Kim, 2013). In this framework, biculturals combine local culture with global culture rather than the majority culture.

As research on biculturalism has grown, researchers have begun to acknowledge that the construct of biculturalism is more complex and multidimensional. A more recent approach to bicultural identity is based on a cognitive or internal process. Several attempts have been made to explain biculturalism. LaFromboise, Coleman, and Gerton (1993) discussed the way each individual integrates culture into his/her identity to a different extent. Based on a brief description of biculturals, monocultural individuals are those individuals who have never internalized other cultures other than their own (native) culture. Biculturals and monoculturals are different in terms of the degree of cognitive structure. While monoculturals have only one set of cultural knowledge structures, bicultural individuals possess two or more separate and complete sets of knowledge and cognitive systems for each culture (Luna, Ringberg, & Peracchio, 2008). In short, bicultural individuals have a more complex understanding of what it means to be a member of two cultures (Benet-Martínez, Leu, Lee, & Morris, 2002).

Hong, Morris, Chiu, and Benet-Martinez (2000) found that biculturals exhibit characteristically East Asian behaviors when primed with East Asian cues, while Hong Kong and Chinese American biculturals exhibit characteristically Western behaviors when primed with Western cultural lines. The same being participants seemed to access multiple cultural meaning systems and switch between culturally appropriate behaviors depending on the context.

Overall, the formation of bicultural identity may be thought of as a process similar to ego identity formation over time, as people explore and make decisions about the role of cultural identity in their lives. Phinney (1989) examined commonalities across various models and proposed a progression from an unexamined ethnic identity through a period of exploration to an achieved or committed ethnic identity, which is characterized by an exploration of one's cultural identity search. This stage is similar to the moratorium status described by Marcia (1980) and "encounter" by Cross (1978), or "awakening," according to Kim (2015). Several authors have noted the additive element of biculturality or multiculturality, suggesting that the acculturation process need not substitute new cultural values for old ones. Instead, acculturation may add new conflict communication behaviors that allow cultural-frame-of-reference shifting (Dyal & Dyal, 1981). Saltzman's (1986) "150 percent person" represents just such a culturally expanded individual.

The common thread running through the above models is that individuals begin with an unexamined racial or ethnic identity. The individual is then challenged by experiences that make race or ethnicity more problematic. To resolve the conflict, individuals initiate an introspection of their own ethnic or racial identities. This search leads individuals to value their racial, ethnic, or minority group membership and integrate it with other identities. These models suggest that bicultural individuals develop a deeper understanding and appreciation of their cultural identity. This culmination may require resolution or coming to terms with two or more extremes of cultural identifications (Heo & Kim, 2013).

This awareness of living on the margins of at least two cultures eliminates being overly on a single culture for identity ("culture-typed"). Instead, bicultural individuals tend to be constructive in dealings with culturally diverse others. In applying the notion of bicultural identity to "multicultural scientists," Adler (1998) notes that the multicultural identity is based not on belongingness, which implies the person is neither totally part of nor apart from the culture; but on the boundary.

This new type of person is multicultural because he/she embodies a core process of self-verification, which is different from a social-psychological style culture-typed identity. According to Anderson (2003), we are usually satisfied with the concept of maturity as having grown up within a culture to fit a particular society's roles, rules, norms, and expectations. The kind of maturity called multicultural identity acquisition is more about growing up beyond the culture within which one has grown up. Individuals with multicultural identities know that societal structures are one of many ways to manage human interaction. Such a shift can be seen as a facet of spiritual growth.

It is an identity based not on "belongingness," which implies either owning or being owned by a culture, but on a style of self-consciousness capable of negotiating new formations of reality (Adler, 1998).

According to Berger and Berger (1973), the multicultural person is a "homeless mind," a condition which, though allowing great flexibility, does not allow anything permanent and unchanging to develop. This homelessness is at the heart of his/her motivational needs. The multicultural person is starved of ideas and feelings that give coherence to his/her world and provide structure and form to the search for the universal and absolute, defining the perpetual quest. Like great philosophers in any age, the multicultural person can never totally accept the demands of any single culture, nor are they free from the conditioning of their own culture (Berger & Berger, 1973). The degree to which they can continually modify the frame of reference and become aware of the structures and functions of a group may very well be the critical factor in the extent to which the multicultural person can truly function successfully between cultures (Adler, 1998).

Toward Multicultural Conflict Communication Competence

Cultural competence refers to the capacity to function in a different culture or a culturally diverse environment and enable understanding, adaptation, communication, and coordination in those environments (Ang, Van Dyne, & Koh, 2006). In the past, there have been attempts to explore to what extent group leaders must be equipped with an ever-increasing level of cultural knowledge, personal awareness, and intervention skills to respond effectively to conflict (Loode, 2011). For instance, it was recommended that group leaders continually examine and identify their own cultural biases and how they impede the effective facilitation of intercultural group conflict. Therefore, skills and knowledge-based interventions in multicultural groups were emphasized by focusing on practical examples and case studies from clinical and supervision experiences.

On the other hand, many cross-cultural conflict communication researchers have typically investigated the variations in the communication strategies between Westerners and East Asians. As mentioned earlier, this approach encourages a conceptualization of cultural meaning systems as being unchanging, stereotypical, and internalized worldviews (Berry, Poortinga, Segall, & Dasen, 1992). Along the way, a handful of researchers began to investigate how individuals who endorse independent and interdependent self-construals use different communication strategies within and between cultures (Kim et al., 1996; Yamada & Singelis, 1999).

Biculturalism and corresponding bicultural communication competence place little emphasis on assimilating and more focus on making choices between their communication patterns (Kim, 2002). Given the inadequacy of a bipolar construct of self-construals in characterizing individual variations in behavior across cultures, Kim et al. (1996) proposed and tested the multidimensional framework of self-construal types (bicultural, marginal, independent, and interdependent). They found that biculturals were the most adaptive in communication situations in unfamiliar settings. Heo and Kim (2013) found that certain individuals ("biculturals") had both highly developed independent and interdependent self-construals, the possession of which enabled these biculturals to cope better, with less stress, in cultural environments foreign to their own.

Biculturals and monoculturals seem to differ in their level of cognitive complexity of two or more cultures. Biculturals have richer, more complex knowledge about what it means to be a member of each of the two cultures

(Benet-Martínez, Lee, & Leu, 2006). The crucial component of bicultural communication competence is drawing on diverse cultural-specific experiences and knowledge of an explicit and tacit nature to understand and interpret one's behavior and that if others using cultural frame switching (Hong et al., 2015). In a multicultural setting, this involves developing behavioral flexibility and attributional, cognitive, and behavioral complexities to comprehend the nature of another culture (Clausen & Keita, 2016). Therefore, bicultural individuals may develop (1) high cognitive flexibility in acculturating into a new culture and show (2) high behavioral flexibility. These two crucial components of multicultural conflict competence will be elaborated on below.

Cognitive Flexibility: Flexible Deployment of Cultural Knowledge

In its early conceptualization in sociology, cognitive flexibility was defined as the readiness with which the person's concept system changes selectively in response to appropriate environment stimuli (Scott, 1962). To be cognitively flexible, an individual must be aware that there are options and alternatives available in any situation, be willing to adapt to the situation, and have the competence to be flexible (Martin & Rubin, 1995). Findings from Harrison, Wilson, Pine, and Chan (1990) identified that increased cognitive flexibility is one of the advantages experienced by ethnic minority children in the United States because those children gain an ability to negotiate the demands of the two cultures.

Ethnographic research often reveals that bicultural individuals develop cognitive flexibility while acculturating into a new culture. Previous research has theorized that cognitive flexibility may have an essential function in the significant part of the bicultural experience (LaFromboise et al., 1993). Kim and Omizo (2006) claimed cognitive flexibility might be an essential element of bicultural competence. It can mirror the capability of bicultural individuals to manage and resolve potential conflicts as they try to function in two different cultural norms. The term refers to the ability to draw on the dynamic interaction of cultural knowledge and cross-cultural skills of behavioral flexibility and cross-cultural communication to effect cultural frame switching and apply metacognition for mediating conflicts to motivate a multicultural team toward a given organizational outcome (Clausen & Keita, 2016; Hong et al., 2000).

Cultural frame-switching (Hong et al., 2000) is a good example of flexible and discriminative cultural knowledge being used to take advantage of grasping experiences in a changing sociocultural milieu. Reflectivity, sensitivity, and flexibility define the conceptual core of cultural competence. By the same token, multicultural individuals become aware of the culture-centric nature of their own cultural beliefs as they expose themselves to ideas from foreign cultures. They may gradually attempt to weave seemingly inconsistent ideas from diverse cultures into their own cultural lives. In doing so, they may become a creative and generative agent in complicated conflict situations.

Prior research on the bicultural or "constructive marginal" individual has shown that these individuals have an integrated, multicultural frame of reference. They exercise personal choice in forming their clear boundaries and are secure in the new identity that they create, which incorporates various cultural frames of reference (Bennett, 1993). Thus, these bicultural individuals are relatively secure with their newly established self-concept, and they are comfortable shifting between different frames of reference. The ability to comfortably shift between cultural frames of reference requires the bicultural individual to display empathy for others (Bennett, 1993). To effectively function with others of a differing cultural orientation, the bicultural individual needs to constantly put him/herself in the shoes of another. Thus, it is evident that bicultural individuals may successfully transition between cultures because they can display empathy with individuals of different cultural frames of reference.

Various pieces of research have examined and supported biculturals' ability to frame switch between cultures, to manage dual cultural systems, or to move between interpretive frames, in multiple domains: language assessment (Schwartz et al., 2014), attribution (Bennett, 1993), personality (Ramirez, 1984), self-construals (Kim et al., 2004), among others. Many of those studies employed a variety of cultural and linguistic/language-mediated priming methods to test the robustness of the cultural frame shifting effects or cultural frame activation across samples. It is assumed that when primed with Western cultural cues, bicultural individuals are more likely to act in a characteristic Western manner. In contrast, when primed with East Asian cues, those individuals tend to exhibit East Asian ways.

Alternating bicultural individuals identify with two different cultures and switch between them in response to particular social and cultural context demands (LaFromboise et al., 1993). In other words, they develop two or more separate frames or scripts for understanding their cultures and can adjust their role to their specific cultural environment. When provided with the appropriate cultural cue, alternating biculturals activate the appropriate cultural frame and respond accordingly. These alternators are likely to employ strategies such as problem-solving, coping, human relational, communication, and incentive motivation according to their cues embedded in the surroundings and use them in the appropriate context (Ramírez-Esparza, Gosling, Benet-Martínez, Potter, & Pennebaker, 2006).

In addition to possessing dual cognitive structures of knowledge of cultural beliefs, values, norms, and habits for social interactions within multicultural settings, biculturals can integrate and switch behaviors between cultural schemas for bicultural efficacy and facilitate cross-cultural communication (LaFromboise et al., 1993).

Bicultural individuals function within an ethno-relative perspective (Benet-Martinez et al., 2002). The bicultural individual believes that knowledge is gained primarily from context rather than from the dictates of one cultural authority. This requires the cultural sensitivity component of self-monitoring. Gudykunst, Yoon, and Nishida (1987) defined self-monitoring as self-control guided by situational cues to social appropriateness. The fact that biculturals are attuned to situational cues rather than a stable cultural dictate leads to the justifiable assumption that the bicultural individual engages in adequate self-monitoring, a component of intercultural sensitivity, which generates creative responses to conflict situations.

Also, their commitment to ethnorelativism seems to foster their ability to empathize with individuals of different cultural frames of reference. It also prompts them to attend to situational cues to monitor their behavior and suspend judgment about the opinions of others, prompting highly innovative ways of engaging in intercultural conflict management. Bicultural individuals with two or more cultural frames that are applicable to diverse situations can be helpful when developing international and multicultural competencies, notably in challenges associated with conflict resolution and improving communication effectiveness (Kane & Levina, 2017; Schindler, Reinhard, Knab, & Stahlberg, 2016).

Behavioral Flexibility: Adaptability

Adaptability seems to be an essential key variable in bicultural communication competence. Adaptability focuses on the ability of the communicator to be flexible in the use of conversational strategies with a variety of people in different situations. A bicultural person who identifies with both independent and interdependent characteristics may develop a repertoire of strategies and use them to adapt to the demands of different contexts. Having a repertoire of individualistic and collectivistic cultural experiences allows one to adjust more adequately in differing situations. On the other hand, the culture-typed person may feel that certain conversational styles are inconsistent with internalized culture-role standards, thus leading to psychological discomfort.

Bicultural individuals may also demonstrate more adaptive behavior and exhibit higher levels of various types of competence than culture-typed individuals. Therefore, an individual with highly developed interdependent and independent characteristics may acquire a broader range of strategies from which to choose, thus demonstrating greater communication competence (Kim & Leung, 2000). Bicultural individuals may develop a repertoire of conflict communication strategies and styles in different situations and contexts. This adaptability may give biculturals more competence than monocultural individuals who feel that certain communication styles are inconsistent with internalized cultural role standards (Kim, 2012).

Because bicultural individuals may be able to identify to a high degree with both independent and interdependent characteristics, they may be free from cultural pressure to restrict their strategy choices to stereotypic roles. Thus, bicultural individuals are more likely than marginal or culture-typed individuals to display conversational adaptability across situations. Similarly, bicultural individuals may be well aware of "appropriate" communication styles in different cultural contexts, showing high flexibility for behavioral adaptation. According to Kim (2002), this vision of people as multi-faceted also seems to coincide with such concepts as the "universal person" (Walsh, 1973), "multicultural person" (Adler, 1998), and "international person" (Lutzker, 1960). Adler (1998) defines the unique characteristics of the multicultural person as being neither totally a part of nor apart from their culture. They may be better able to make deliberate choices in specific situations and maintain a dynamic balance between avoidance and confrontation rather than being bound by the culturally imposed emphases on communicative behaviors (Kim, 2017). Consequently, multicultural individuals may be able to reconcile conflicts posed by competing conflict management styles and achieve a high level of communication competence.

The consciousness of one's own cultural identity has been called a state of dynamic betweenness by Yoshikawa (1988). The suggestion here is one of continual and comfortable movement between cultural identities. An integrated, multicultural existence is maintained, where the conscious, deliberate choice-making of communication management strategies prevails. Emerging findings in multicultural studies reveal that bicultural individuals possess dual cultural schemas or cognitive structures of knowledge of cultural beliefs, values, norms, and habits for face-to-face social interactions within cultural environments, the ability to integrate and switch behaviors between cultural schemas for bicultural efficacy, and communicate across cultures (LaFromboise et al., 1993).

In the Cultural Identity Model proposed by Sussman (2000), cultural identity is dynamic and can be additive (gaining identification with a new culture) without being subtractive (losing cultural identification). This competency uses cultural, language, and behavioral adaptability for cross-cultural interaction to adopt appropriate and effective verbal and nonverbal communication in multicultural teams (Hong, 2010). Behavioral adaptability involves decoding multicultural team members' behaviors and adopting appropriate self-depiction strategies that reflect the context (Clausen & Keita, 2016).

Sparrow (2000) defines a bicultural individual as having a chameleon-like ability to blend in and become harmonious in different settings with the experience of alternating between cultural meaning systems. Biculturalism may also have important implications for society (Berry, 2003). As findings from a meta-analysis indicate, biculturalism is positively linked with better sociocultural and psychological adaptation (Nguyen & Benet-Martínez, 2013). This suggests greater productivity and achievement and fewer interpersonal conflicts, which, in turn, lead to greater national or global success and well-being enhanced by biculturalism or multiculturalism public policy (Leung, Maddux, Galinsky, & Chiu, 2008).

Conclusion

In this chapter we explored the multicultural approaches to conflict management behaviors from the standpoint of bicultural and multicultural identity acquisition. As people struggle to come to terms with cultural pluralism, there is increasing recognition of the identity challenges in the life of bicultural or multicultural individuals and their potential conflict communication patterns. Bicultural competence characterizes a dynamic interaction of cultural frame switching and cross-cultural communication skills of behavioral flexibility. While a benefit of biculturalism is often argued theoretically and empirically, there is a lack of comprehensive response to the effects of biculturalism on intercultural conflict management. There are important research questions to be addressed, such as the role of bicultural identity in communication flexibility and changes in communication patterns.

This chapter aims to understand further people's bicultural identity experiences and corresponding conflict management behaviors. In earlier times it may have been natural for individuals to closely identify with their culture of origin—to accept the views and ways of their respective societies and to consider them as part of their heritage spontaneously. Deliberate confinement to a single culture is not salvation but injurious provincialism. The proprietary discourse of "my" culture versus "yours" has, in principle, become obsolete.

Over the last decade the dominant factor of cultural variability in intercultural conflict communication research has been perceiving the self as either individualistic or collectivistic (Kim & Miyahara, 2018). The ongoing process of globalization and changes in information and communication technologies bring us all into a daily confrontation with realities different from our own (Matthews, 2000). Traditionally, there has been a tendency to take the view that only a few people will ever make it into the state of individual maturity devoid of intrapsychic conflict by transcending cultural conditioning. Developing bicultural or expanded selves in a multicultural society may be viewed as an asset because such a perspective diminishes rigid culture-typed (and culturally-conditioned) conflict communication behaviors. Bicultural individuals develop cultural frame switching, cultural sensitivity, cognitive/behavioral communication flexibility, etc. which are key for success in today's increasingly globalized and mobile world. Therefore, it is possible to view these bicultural individuals as ideal cultural mediators in miscommunication and intercultural conflicts within communities, nations, and internationally.

There is a critical knowledge gap about how a bicultural's unique experience of frame switching leads to easy adaptation to situationally salient cultural contexts and appropriate conflict management styles (Roberts & Beamish, 2017). With today's multicultural world enhanced by immigration, refugees, sojourners, and advanced communication and technology, more individuals are required to interact with others from different cultures. In such a society, more people will actively carry or maintain more than one cultural frame of reference. In other words, biculturalism permits the individual to gain a dynamic relationship between two cultural memberships which leads to bicultural conflict communication competence.

Biculturalism issues are not only taking center stage in countries across the world but are also growing in importance across multiple research and functional domains (Chu, White, & Verrelli, 2017). Given that cross-cultural interactions are burgeoning, there has never been such a need for knowledge about conflict styles in different cultures. The very openness of a genuinely multicultural society precludes establishing such things as ethnic, racial, or cultural "identities" (Bramann, 1999). As multiculturalism is an increasingly significant psychological and cultural phenomenon, the necessity to make independent, individual choices (in conflict situations) is an inevitable part of living in the modern world (Bramann, 1999).

Future research could provide important insights into the process by which bicultural individuals' competencies and skills could be used for multicultural conflict effectiveness. More work will foster recognition of biculturals' distinctive experiences and related implications within multicultural conflict management and the use of their competencies and skills to improve the effectiveness of multicultural communication. Continuous conceptual refinement and various ways of testing theories will yield a further understanding of intercultural conflict communication processes and desirable outcomes. Using multicultural perspectives, we can continue to understand new and creative ways of managing intercultural conflict.

References

Adler, P. S. (1998). Beyond cultural identity: Reflections on multiculturalism. In M. J. Bennett (Ed.), *Basic concepts of intercultural communication* (pp. 225–245). Yarmouth, ME: Intercultural Press.

Anderson, W. T. (2003). *The next enlightenment: Integrating East and West in a new vision of human evolution.* New York, NY: St Martin's Press.

Ang, S., Van Dyne, L., Koh, C. (2006). Personality correlates of the Four-Factor Model of Cultural Intelligence. *Group & Organization Management,* 31(1), 100–123. doi:10.1177/1059601105275267.

Arnett, J. J. (2002). The psychology of globalization. *American Psychologist,* 57(10), 774–783.

Benet-Martínez, V., Lee, F., & Leu, J. (2006). Biculturalism and cognitive complexity. *Journal of Cross-Cultural Psychology,* 37(4), 386–407.

Benet-Martínez, V., Leu, J., Lee, F., & Morris, M. W. (2002). Negotiating biculturalism: Cultural frame switching in biculturals with oppositional versus compatible cultural identities. *Journal of Cross-Cultural Psychology,* 33(5), 492–516. https://doi.org/10.1177/0022022102033005005.

Bennett, M. J. (1993). Towards ethnorelativism: A developmental model of intercultural sensitivity. In R. M. Paige (Ed.), *Education for the intercultural experience* (pp. 21–71). Yarmouth, ME: Intercultural Press.

Berger, P. & Berger, B. (1973). *The homeless mind.* New York, NY: Random House.

Berry, J. W. (1997). Immigration, acculturation, and adaptation. *Applied Psychology: An International Review,* 46, 5–68. http://dx.doi.org/10.1111/j.1464-0597.1997.tb01087.x.

Berry, J. W. (2003). Conceptual approaches to acculturation. In K. M. Chun, P. B. Organista, & G. Marín (Eds.), *Acculturation: Advances in theory, measurement, and applied research* (pp. 17–37). Washington, DC: American Psychological Association.

Berry, J. W. & Kim, U. (1988). *Acculturation and metal health.* In P. Dasen, J. W. Berry, & N. Sartorius (Eds.), *Health and cross-cultural psychology* (pp. 207–236). Newbury Park, CA: Sage.

Berry, J. W., Poortinga, Y. H., Segall, M. H., & Dasen, P. R. (1992). *Cross-cultural psychology: Research and applications.* Cambridge, UK: Cambridge University Press.

Blake, R. R. & Mouton, J. S. (1964). *The managerial grid.* Houston, TX: Gulf Publishing.

Boonsathorn, W. (2007). Understanding conflict management styles of Thais and Americans in multinational corporations in Thailand. *International Journal of Conflict Management,* 18, 196–221. doi:10.1108/10444060710825972.

Bramann, J. K. (1999) *Multiculturalism and personal identity.* Preliminary draft of the Philosophical Forum presentation for 26 October, available online at http://faculty.frostbury.edu/phil/forum/multicult.htm.

Cathcart, D. & Cathcart, R. (1976). A Japanese social experience and concept of groups. In L. A. Samovar & R. E. Porter (Eds.), *Intercultural communication: A reader* (pp. 58–66), Belmont, CA: Wadsworth.

Chen, G. M. & Starosta, W. J. (1997). A review of the concept of intercultural sensitivity. *Human Communication*, 1, 1–16.

Chen, S. X., Benet-Martínez, V., & Bond, M. H. (2008). Bicultural identity, bilingualism, and psychological adjustment in multicultural societies: Immigration-based and globalization-based acculturation. *Journal of Personality*, 76(4), 803–838.

Chu, E., White, F. A., & Verrelli, S. (2017). Biculturalism amongst ethnic minorities: Its impact for individuals and intergroup relations. *Australian Journal of Psychology*, 69(4), 229–236. https://doi.org/10.1111/ajpy.12153.

Chua, E. & Gudykunst, W. B. (1987). Conflict resolution styles in low- and high-context cultures. *Communication Research Reports*, 5, 32–37.

Clausen, L. & Keita, M. H. (2016). Bicultural resourcefulness in global management: From education to corporate collaboration. *Copenhagen Journal of Asian Studies*, 34(1), 58–80. https://doi.org/10.22439/cjas.v34i1.5192.

Cross, W. E. (1978). The Thomas and Cross Models of Psychological Nigrescence: A review. *Journal of Black Psychology*, 5, 13–31. http://dx.doi.org/10.1177/009579847800500102.

Croucher, S. (2004). *Globalization and belonging*. Lanham, MD: Rowman & Littlefield Publishers.

Dwyer, C. (1999). Migrations and diasporas. In P. Cloke, P. Crang, & M. Goodwin (Eds.), *Introducing human geographies* (pp. 287–295). London, UK: Arnold Publishers.

Dyal, J. A. & Dyal, R.Y. (1981). Acculturation, stress and coping: Some implications for research and education. *International Journal of Intercultural Relations*, 5, 301–328.

Eytan, A. (2004). Globalization and biculturalism. *British Journal of Psychiatry*, 184, 362–363.

Ghadamosi, O., Baghestan, A. G., & Al-Mabrouk, K. (2012). Gender, age and nationality: Assessing their impact on conflict resolution styles. *Journal of Management Development*, 33, 245–257. doi:10.1108/JMD-02-2011-0024.

Gudykunst, W. B., Yoon, Y. C., & Nishida, T. (1987). The influence of individualism-collectivism on perceptions of communication in ingroup and outgroup relationships. *Communication Monographs*, 54, 295–306.

Haritatos, J. & Benet-Martínez, V. (2002). Bicultural identities: The interface of cultural, personality, and socio-cognitive processes. *Journal of Research in Personality*, 36, 598–606.

Harrison, A. O., Wilson, M. N., Pine, C. J., & Chan, S. Q. (1990). Family ecologies of ethnic minority children. *Child Development*, 61, 347–362.

Heo, H. H. & Kim, M. S. (2013). Outcome-oriented and process-oriented frameworks on biculturalism. *Journal of Intercultural Communication*, 31. http://immi.se/intercultural.

Hofstede, G. (1980). *Culture's consequences: International differences in work related values*. Beverly Hills, CA: Sage.

Hong, H. (2010). Bicultural competence and its impact on team effectiveness. *International Journal of Cross-Cultural Management*, 10(1), 93–120. doi:10.1177/1470595809359582.

Hong, Y., Morris, M., Chiu, C. Y., & Benet-Martínez, V. (2000). Multicultural minds: A dynamic constructivist approach to culture and cognition. *American Psychologist*, 55, 709–720.

Hong, Y., Wan, C., No, S., & Chiu, C-Y. (2015). Multicultural Identities. In S. Kitayama, & D. Cohen (Eds.), *Handbook of cultural psychology* (pp. 323–345). New York, NY: Guilford.

Huynh, Q.-L., Nguyen, A.-M. D., & Benet-Martínez, V. (2011). Bicultural identity integration. In S. J. Schwartz, K. Luyckx, & V. L. Vignoles (Eds.), *Handbook of identity theory and research* (pp. 827–842). Springer. http://dx.doi.org/10.1007/978-1-4419-7988-9_35.

Kane, A. A. & Levina, N. (2017). 'Am I still one of them?': Bicultural immigrant managers navigating social identity threats when spanning global boundaries. *Journal of Management Studies*, 54(4), 540–577. doi:10.1111/joms.12259.

Kim, B. S. & Omizo, M. M. (2006). Behavioral acculturation and enculturation and psychological functioning among Asian American college students. *Cultural Diversity and Ethnic Minority Psychology*, 12, 245–258. https://doi.org/10.1037/1099-9809.12.2.245.

Kim, M. S. (2002). *Non-Western perspectives on human communication: Implications for theory and practice*. Thousand Oaks, CA: Sage.

Kim, M. S. (2012). World peace through intercultural research. *International Journal of Intercultural Relations*, 36, 3–13.

Kim, M. S. (2017). Intercultural conflict. In Jon Nussbaum (Ed.), *Oxford research encyclopedia of communication*. New York, NY: Oxford University Press.

Kim, M. S., Hunter, J. E., Miyahara, A., Horvath, A., Bresnahan, M., & Yoon, H. J. (1996). Individual- vs. culture-level dimensions of individualism and collectivism: Effects on preferred conversational styles. *Communication Monographs*, 63, 29–49.

Kim, M. S., Lee, H. R., Kim, I. D., & Hunter, J. E. (2004). A test of a cultural model of conflict styles. *Journal of Asian Pacific Communication*, 14, 197–223.

Kim, M. S. & Leung, T. (2000). A multicultural view of conflict management styles: Review of past research and critical synthesis. In M. Roloff (Ed.), *Communication yearbook 23* (pp. 227–269). Thousand Oaks, CA: Sage.

Kim, M. S., & Miyahara, A. (2018). Intercultural communication. In K. H. Youm & N. Kwak (Eds.), *Korean communication, media, and culture: An annotated bibliography* (pp. 227–254). Lanham, MD: Lexington Books.

Kim, Y. Y. (2015). Finding a "home" beyond culture: The emergence of intercultural personhood in the globalizing world. *International Journal of Intercultural Relations*, 46, 3–12. doi:10.1016/j.ijintrel.2015.03.018.

LaFromboise, T., Coleman, H. L. K., & Gerton, J. (1993). Psychological impact of biculturalism: Evidence and theory. *Psychological Bulletin*, 114, 395–412.

Lee, H. & Rogan, R. (1991). A cross-cultural comparison of organizational conflict management behaviors. *The International Journal of Conflict Management*, 2, 181–199.

Leung, A., Maddux, W., Galinsky, A., & Chiu, C. (2008). Multicultural experience enhances creativity: The when and how. *American Psychologist*, 63(3), 169–181.

Loode, S. (2011). Navigating the unchartered waters of cross-cultural conflict resolution education. *Conflict Resolution Quarterly*, 29, 65–84. doi:10.1002/crq.21037.

Luna, D., Ringberg, T., & Peracchio, L. (2008). One individual, two identities: Frame switching among biculturals. *Journal of Consumer Research*, 35(2), 279–293.

Lutzker, D. (1960). Internationalism as a predictor of cooperative behavior. *Journal of Conflict Resolution*, 4, 426–430.

Marcia, J. E. (1980). Identity in adolescence. *Handbook of Adolescent Psychology*, 9, 159–187.

Martin, M. M. & Rubin, R. B. (1995). A new measure of cognitive flexibility. *Psychological Reports*, 76, 623–626.

Matthews, G. (2000). *Global culture/Individual identity*. London: Routledge.

Miller, G. R. & Steinberg, M. (1975). *Between people: A new analysis of interpersonal communication*. Chicago, IL: Science Research Associates.

Nguyen, A.-M. D. & Benet-Martínez, V. (2013). Biculturalism and adjustment: A meta-analysis. *Journal of Cross-Cultural Psychology*, 44, 122–159. http://dx.doi.org/10.1177/0022022111435097.

Nicotera, A. M. (1993). Beyond two dimensions: A grounded theory model of conflict-handling behavior. *Management Communication Quarterly*, 6, 282–306.

Nomura, N. & Barnlund, D. C. (1983). Patterns of interpersonal criticism in Japan and the United States. *International Journal of Intercultural Relations*, 7, 1–18.

Ohbuchi, K. & Takahashi, Y. (1994). Cultural styles of conflict management in Japanese and Americans: Passivity, covertness, and effectiveness of strategies. *Journal of Applied Social Psychology*, 24, 1345–1366.

Park, R. E. (1928). Human migration and the marginal man. *American Journal of Sociology*, 5, 881–893.

Phinney, J. S. (1989). Stages of ethnic identity development in minority group adolescents. *Journal of Early Adolescence*, 9, 34–49.

Phinney, J. & Devich-Navarro, M. (1997). Variations in bicultural identification among African American and Mexican American adolescents. *Journal of Research on Adolescence*, 7(1), 3–32.

Ramirez, M. (1984). Assessing and understanding biculturalism-multiculturalism in Mexican-American adults. In J. Martinez & R. Mendoza (Eds.), *Chicano psychology* (pp. 77–94). Orlando, FL: Academic.

Ramírez-Esparza, N., Gosling, S. D., Benet-Martínez, V., Potter, J. P., & Pennebaker, J. W. (2006). Do bilinguals have two personalities? A special case of cultural frame switching. *Journal of Research in Personality*, 40(2), 99–120. https://doi.org/10.1016/j.jrp.2004.09.001.

Roberts, M. J. & Beamish, P. W. (2017). The scaffolding activities of international returnee executives: A learning based perspective of global boundary spanning. *Journal of Management Studies*, 54(4), 511–539. doi:10.1111/joms.12266.

Saltzman, C. E. (1986). One hundred and fifty percent persons: Models for orienting international students. In R. M. Paige (Ed.), *Cross-cultural orientation: New conceptualizations and applications* (pp. 247–268). Lanham, MD: University Press of America.

Sampson, E. E. (1988). The debate on individualism: Indigenous psychologies of the individual and their role in personal and societal functioning. *American Psychologist*, 43, 15–22.

Schindler, S., Reinhard, M.-A., Knab, M., & Stahlberg, D. (2016). The bicultural phenomenon: The interplay of group prototypicality and cultural identity switching. *Social Psychology*, 47(5), 233–243. doi:10.1027/1864-9335/a000276.

Schwartz, S. J., Benet-Martínez, V., Knight, G. P., Unger, J. B., Zamboanga, B. L., Des Rosiers, S. E., Stephens, D. P., Huang, S., & Szapocznik, J. (2014). Effects of language of assessment on the measurement of acculturation: Measurement equivalence and cultural frame switching. *Psychological Assessment*, 26(1), 100–114. https://doi.org/10.1037/a0034717.

Scott, W. A. (1962). Cognitive complexity and cognitive flexibility. *Sociometry*, 25, 405–414. https://doi.org/10.2307/2785779.

Simons, H. W. (1972). Persuasion in social conflicts: A critique of prevailing conceptions and a framework for future research. *Speech Monographs*, 39(4), 227–247. https://doi.org/10.1080/03637757209375763.

Sparrow, L. M. (2000). Beyond multicultural man: Complexities of identity. *International Journal of Intercultural Relations*, 24, 173–201.

Stonequist, E. V. (1935). The problem of the marginal man. *The American Journal of Sociology*, 41(1), 1–12.

Sussman, N. M. (2000). The dynamic nature of cultural identity throughout cultural transitions: Why home is not so sweet. *Personality & Social Psychology Review*, 4(4), 355–373.

Thomas, K. W. & Kilmann, R. H. (1978). Comparison of four instruments measuring conflict behavior. *Psychological Reports*, 42, 1139–1145.

Ting-Toomey, S. (1985). Toward a theory of conflict and culture. In W. B. Gudykunst, L. P. Stewart, & S. Ting-Toomey (Eds.), *Communication, culture, and organizational processes* (pp. 71–86). Ting-Toomey Beverly Hills, CA: Sage.

Ting-Toomey, S. (1988). Intercultural conflict styles: A face negotiation theory. In Y. Y. Kim & W. B. Gudykunst (Eds.), *Theories in intercultural communication* (pp. 213–235). Newbury Park, CA: Sage.

Vivero, V. N. & Jenkins, S. R. (1999). Existential hazards of the multicultural individual: Defining and understanding "cultural homelessness." *Cultural Diversity and Ethnic Minority Psychology*, 5, 6–26.

Walsh, J. E. (1973). *Intercultural education in the community of man*. Honolulu, HI: University of Hawaii Press.

West, A. L., Zhang, R., Yampolsky, M., & Sasaki, J. Y. (2017). More than the sum of its parts: A transformative theory of biculturalism. *Journal of Cross-Cultural Psychology*, 48(7), 963–990. https://doi.org/10.1177/0022022117709533.

Yamada, A.-M. & Singelis, T. M. (1999). Biculturalism and self-construal. *International Journal of Intercultural Relations*, 23(5), 697–709.

Yoshikawa, M. J. (1988). Cross-cultural adaptation and perceptual development. In Y. Y. Kim & W. B. Gudykunst (Eds.), *Cross-cultural adaptation: Current approaches* (pp. 140–148). Newbury Park, CA: Sage.

9

DE-WESTERNIZING THE CONFLICT MANAGEMENT MODEL

Is "Avoidance" Really that Bad?

Akira Miyahara

Introduction

Conflict is a frequently and extensively studied area of research in various academic disciplines: anthropology, business, history, peace studies, political science, psychiatry, psychology, sociology, etc. Whether interpersonal, small-group, organizational, intercultural, or a combination of all, conflict, a social situation where people's individual, relational, and even national goals are at stake, serves the field of communication as a "test ground" for communication competence in various cultures, as it forces the participants to deploy and utilize to the fullest extent their knowledge and skills in communication, thus reflecting the norms, traditions, and societal changes that all influence people's daily communication practices in their respective cultures. Studying the outcomes of cross-cultural comparisons of conflict communication behavior can contribute not only to a better understanding of the communication behavior that is deemed effective and appropriate, but offer pragmatic suggestions concerning mutually effective and satisfactory management of conflict across cultures. An accurate understanding of people's communication behavior, particularly in conflicting situations, thus holds an important key to fruitful academic advancement in the communication field as well as to the practical benefit thereof.

Given the predominantly Western approach so far adopted in most communication studies, it is not surprising that theories, concepts, and research methods applied in conflict studies have their origins in the Euro-American academic traditions. One theoretically and pragmatically proven lesson from conflict is that it has more potentially positive than negative effects, and therefore we must constructively cope with it rather than avoid it. Conflict, if dealt with effectively, at least in many Euro-American social contexts, is expected to bring about positive outcomes to the parties involved. As early as in the 1950s US sociologists argued that conflict is a sign of a healthy

DOI: 10.4324/9781003252955-11

relationship as it contributes to the bonding of personal ties within a group and preservation of group identity and morals (Coser, 1956). Communicative dimensions
such as assertiveness have been viewed as a measure of social competence that is highly
valued by Americans as it contributes to "effective" management of conflict situations,
but not by the Japanese (Singhal & Nagao, 1993).

Avoiding a conflict is, on the other hand, thought to be a lose-lose situation, and
therefore the most ineffective strategy. Western and particularly US scholars have
maintained that for independent individuals directly confronting conflict is viewed
as a productive and successful strategy, if they communicate in an open and honest
way, respecting and challenging one another, and a tangible solution is agreed
upon (e.g., Cupach & Canary, 1997). For conflict to have a positive outcome, the
people in a conflict situation must communicate in an "open and honest" way and
"challenge one another," a mode of communication emphasized in many Western
cultures as healthy and competent, but not necessarily endorsed in some Asian
cultures, where conflict and, especially, open confrontation are to be avoided at all
costs. It is noteworthy that Western researchers have also warned against the negative
impact of conflict on human relationships. Cupach and Canary (1997), for instance,
stress that for people who are interdependent, conflict is a face-threatening process in
which a discussion of substantive issues is prioritized over relational and face issues
and relational and group feelings are not properly considered.

In the Western communication studies it is considered that, if treated in a
"competent" manner such as open and honest discussions of issues, conflict is a
potentially positive experience, but it may have a devastating effect if people place
more value on human relationships than the issues that are the cause and/or effect
of the conflict. Such bi-polar and dichotomous analyses have played pivotal roles in
intercultural and cross-cultural communication studies, as they facilitate the process
of inquiry whose goals are to identify and investigate Western and Eastern people's
communication behaviors that seem to be at extreme ends of a continuum.
Okabe, a prominent Japanese scholar in rhetoric, advanced a vivid warning
against oversimplified and overgeneralized explanation by "paired opposites"
applied to East-West, analytical-synthetic, and direct-indirect dichotomies (2005).

Such dichotomous East vs. West inquiries have also served researchers and
practitioners as a conveniently simplified generalization of "Asia" as though it is a
unified group of cultures. It has been speculated, for example, that the conflict
behaviors of Chinese and Japanese managers are more or less the same since both
cultures are considered as collectivistic and high-context as they both inherit
Confucian teachings as the cornerstone of their social and moral codes (Chiu,
Wong, & Kosinski, Jr., 1998). The researchers have reported some findings that
seem contradictory to and inconsistent with what has been believed to be "typical"
Asian communication behaviors. Chiu et al. (1998), for example, reported that
Japanese managers tended to employ more assertive styles than the People's
Republic of China (PRC) Chinese managers do in dealing with conflict situations,
even though they are both expected to be influenced by Confucian principles. Lee,
Nakamura, Chung, Chun, Fu, Liang and Liu (2013) have also reported intra-Asia

differences in couples' conflict behaviors among five Asian cultures, China, Hong Kong, Japan, Korea, and Taiwan, as responses from Korean and Japanese partici-pants indicated a preference for subtler and less direct strategies than those chosen in other parts of Asia. Some Western researchers have also started resonating with their Eastern (Asian) counterparts about the inadequacy and even inaccuracy of applying cultural dimensions to various cultures by the nation, in addition to applying Western concepts to non-Western cultures (Canary & Lakey, 2013).

In today's globally diversifying society, where people with different and often conflicting cultural standards come into daily contact, their communication tactics in conflict situations provide researchers with an excellent pool of topics for inquiries. Semlak (1982) argued that the plurality of American institutions is one characteristic that forms a basis for conflict. We must be aware that conflict may be a generally Western, and particularly US, way of identifying a communication situation as such. Conflict takes place more commonly in a pluralistic society than in a more uniform one, and, therefore, it may not be such a theoretically meaningful or practically fertile concept to study in Eastern cultures as in the West.

Ontological assumptions of and views on a relational phenomenon called "conflict" may not be universally agreed upon, and it may be situated quite differently in social practices across cultures depending on the philosophies and people's perceptions of it. What may appear to be a conflicting situation in culture A may not hold the same significance in culture B, and its nature, consequences, and positive/negative effects need to be viewed in a completely different light. The ultimate purpose of cross-cultural studies in any discipline, communication in particular, is to identify similarities and differences between cultures, which in turn inform students and practitioners of the behavioral, attitudinal, and cognitive aspects of conflict. Moreover, in addition to academic findings and practical suggestions to manage conflicts in a satisfactory fashion being a favorable outcome of cross-cultural studies in the age of globalization, Wang and Shen (2000) emphasized the importance of learning about ourselves. Globalization has forced people to come face to face with not only "others," but also with themselves: who they are, what "place" they have in this community, and where they are heading (p. 26).

The first purpose of this chapter is to outline the tendencies of research conducted about Japanese people's conflict behavior. Some "obstacles" will be discussed that have made fair and emic studies of Japanese conflict behavior difficult. Secondly, I will characterize the Japanese conflict management style identified as "avoiding" and "withdrawing" and other terms that have negative connotations on the Western and US standards. While avoiding or withdrawal in a conflict situation is often regarded as the most ineffective and the least desirable strategy, it is not only accepted but encouraged in many Japanese contexts and in fact often utilized by people in various forms as a manifestation of "air-reading" (ku'uki wo yomu). Several specific commu-nication behaviors associated with air-reading will be introduced along with Japanese people's motives for using them. Finally, I will introduce the "dark" side of air-reading. If Japanese people blindly conform to the cultural values that seem to be accepted as an important part of communication competence in Japan, they will deprive themselves of opportunities to be competent communicators and to grow as responsible global citizens. I argue that while air-reading may be an effective and necessary strategy in social situations, once it becomes the only way to cope with a conflict, it may have more drawbacks than positive consequences both individually and relationally.

Tendencies of Japanese Conflict Studies

Western Domination of Science and Theorizing

Given the long tradition of philosophies of science in the West being driven by scholars' enthusiastic and vigorous endeavors to build, test, modify, and re-build robust theoretical explanations of happenings by clarifying causal relationships between objects, phenomena, and events, conflict has been primarily studied by Western researchers. Wang and Shen (2000) argue that:

> Western science is an activity of constructing theories through mathematically structured language to formulate knowledge to serve humanity's objective in explaining and controlling the world. Lacking in logical mathematical structures, Asian philosophers have followed a different line of development that provides us with neither theory in the Western sense nor conceptualization.
>
> (p. 19)

Theorizing is a Western mode of thinking after all! Onishi and Bliss (2006) echoed the same contention in the field of communication; Western theories and empirical studies predominate in the literature on conflict management, as the scholarship in this domain started in the West.

The dual concern model, a typical and very popular Western mode of theorizing conflict management communication strategies, is applied to conflict communication studies with regard to self, productivity, and goal achievement, and concern for the other, relationship, and harmony. The dual concern model has been advanced and applied to Asian contexts and has served numerous Western and Asian researchers as the theoretical foundation for their conflict communication studies (e.g., Moriizumi, 2016; Singhal & Nagao, 1993). These, in turn, have produced an abundance of results by means of empirical and quantitatively validated research designs.

While the Western theories of conflict management have produced useful and meaningful results, their shortcomings have also been highlighted. Anedo (2012), for example, argued that the Western model of conflict does not place as much emphasis on the human relationship aspect of conflicts, as the interpersonal constructs are overtaken by concern for the outcomes in a conflict situation and not the relationship per se. Given the strong emphasis on human relationships in any situation including conflict in Japanese culture, lack of sufficient consideration of the relationship aspects prior to, during, and after conflict, if it took up the same meaning as in the Western cultures, and were it ever to be studied in Japan in the same way, any "theory" to account for the mechanism, nature, and consequences of conflict would not have the necessary authority that a theory is required to have to be identified as "good" and "useful."

Other more productive theoretical constructs applied to conflict studies, especially in intercultural communication, are the notions of individualism-collectivism on the cultural level, independent vs. interdependent self-construals on the individual level, and low- and high-context communication, the attributes associated with these bipolar characteristics, respectively. These communication concepts and classifications of Japanese people into the collectivistic, interdependent, and high-contextual categories have produced a great number of studies, whose findings have made a considerable contribution to a better understanding of Japanese communication behavior, formerly regarded as mysterious, exotic, and even inscrutable. These same concepts, however, have been recently criticized as oversimplistic, ethnocentric, and even utterly wrong.

Hendry (1992) stated that much of the ideology is based on fairly fundamental misinterpretations of the concepts, both by Japanese commentators of the Western notions, and by Western commentators of the Japanese situation. In part, the criticism is a plea for a move away from the oversimplified classification of Japanese society as, for example, collectivistic as opposed to individualistic or a "consensus" society. Oyserman, Coon, and Kemmelmeier (2002) conducted extensive meta-analyses of the studies that had used individualism-collectivism as a main construct to identify and classify conflict management strategies in cultures across the world. They reported findings contradictory to the traditional characterizations associated with the culture groups. European Americans were not more individualistic than African Americans, or Latinos, and not less collectivistic than the Japanese or Koreans.

Chiu et al. (1998) found that the Japanese tended to be more assertive than the Chinese in their approach to handling conflict. In Onishi and Bliss's study (2006) Japanese participants had a stronger preference for competing than the Hong Kong Chinese, and Ting-Toomey et al. (1991) also reported that the Japanese used avoidance strategies less than the Chinese and Taiwanese. Cai and Fink (2002) stressed their doubt about using the "five-style" conflict management model in any circumstances, as they found that avoiding was preferred by individualists rather than by collectivists. They also found that collectivists preferred compromising and integrating more than individualists did, whereas individualism and collectivism showed no significant preference either way for the obliging style, all of which challenged the long-held beliefs about individualists' and collectivists' ways of handling conflicts.

A brief examination of research studies indicates that such popular and seemingly theoretically sound models as individualism-collectivism, independent vs. interdependent self-construals, and low- vs. high-contextual communication do not seem to fully or accurately capture the characteristics of non-Western cultures in general, and Japanese culture in particular, in managing conflicts. This demonstrates that while the Western theories and concepts may account for the features of Japanese conflict communication to a certain extent, more culture-specific explanation is in need.

Nihonjinron *as a source of the illusion of Japanese uniqueness*

In addition to the concepts and theories imported from the West, another "obstacle" that has hindered accurate descriptions of Japanese conflict communication is *Nihonjinron,* a genre of arguments about Japanese cultural and racial uniqueness advanced by Japanese intellectuals over the decades. Being collectivistic, inter-dependent, high-contextual, and harmony-oriented all seem to fit and reinforce the "unique" characteristics attributed to Japanese conflict communication by the authors of *Nihonjinron.* The scholars who supported the *Nihonjinron* argument and those who subscribed to the primary principles of it believed in the exclusive peculiarity and uniqueness of Japanese culture to the extent that they contended that one has to be born Japanese in order to truly understand and be part of Japanese culture.

Ever since Ruth Benedict's anthropological work (1946) on Japanese culture in the 1940s the abundance of literature on Japanese social practices has celebrated the "uniqueness" and "peculiarity" of the Japanese. This phenomenon has intri-gued a number of communication researchers with the result that it has initiated and increased the number of research studies in which the Japanese are chiefly compared to a vastly different group of people, i.e., US Americans, most of the results of which have confirmed and reinforced the traditional beliefs. Conflict management communication is one such category in which the Japanese have been classified as "collectivists," as opposed to the Americans who have been classified as individualists, and both demonstrate the "typical" communication behaviors commonly associated with the respective groups.

In recent years the tendency to classify the Japanese as unique along with many arguments about their social practices have been criticized as biased, imbalanced, or simply wrong. For example, Takano (2008) advanced his argument that classifying the Japanese as collectivists is nothing but an illusion. He offers thorough empirical and historical evidence to claim that even though there has been "scientific" support for the classification including the pivotal studies by Hofstede, Triandis, and Markus and Kitayama which almost uniformly state that Japan is collectivistic on the cultural level and interdependent on the individual level, it would be an illusion to believe that the Japanese are by nature collectivistic. However, Takano does not clearly state what cultural and individual feature best illustrates and describes the Japanese. Takeuchi (1995) analyzed Japanese people's social behavior with "socio grammar," a set of emic concepts or Japan-centric yardsticks, and advanced his argument that even though the social characteristics identified as being "uniquely Japanese" are often attributed to the people's collectivistic tendencies which manifest themselves in "groupism," "conformity and harmony," and "priority on collective above indivi-dual goals," that is a very superficial observation, and Japanese people's social beha-vior is driven primarily by pursuit of their self-centered objectives. Yamagishi (2002), with his strong objection to categorizing the Japanese as a group-harmony-oriented people, stated that it is the "implicit ingroup regulations" and "mutual and voluntary policing" (p.37) that keep the Japanese from behaving in a way that harms group benefits, and that the Japanese have no choice but to conform to the group objectives, which gives an appearance of collectivistic tendencies. Yamagishi further claims that believing the Japanese mindset encourages them to pursue group goals at the expense of self-goals leads to grave misunderstandings by foreign observers and the Japanese themselves.

Japanese Conflict Avoidance Viewed from the Japanese Perspective

Japanese communication in conflict situations needs to be viewed and examined in its own light in order to inform researchers and practitioners of Japanese characteristics and, more importantly, the social and psychological motives of people that underlie them. Outcome-oriented rather than relationship-based understanding of conflict has often been valued in conflict studies by Western researchers. While securing, increasing, and improving the outcome of communication is important in the West, such an outcome-centered view of communication may not be regarded as important or even worth potentially risking good relationships in the East. The ontological orientation of conflict in relation to human relationship may be fundamentally different in Eastern and Japanese culture.

I have so far argued that Japanese conflict communication is *not* what we have been led to believe, but I have not presented any discussion of what *it is*. The motives and intentions that drive the Japanese to seek strategies in which they strive for mutually satisfactory dealings in situations of conflict have not been sufficiently discussed by either Japanese or Western communication researchers. "Avoidance" as seen in Japanese conflict situations is not tantamount to lack of ability to deal with a potential dissension that would end up completely ignoring or running away from the conflict, but it may be an elaborate manifestation of Japanese people's profound desire to maintain human relationships. Anedo (2012) argued that some important questions to be answered in the Western model of conflict management communication are left unanswered such as: "Avoiding conflict actually takes some skill and vigilance, so why would one bother" (p. 19)?

The rest of this chapter explores the nature and various dimensions and types of Japanese conflict avoidance communication with a preliminary list of the avoidance tactics. I will ultimately argue that avoiding conflict in their interpersonal communication should not be regarded as a bad social practice in Japanese culture as it is a reflection of people's careful, sensitive, and considerate perception of the others involved as well as the idiosyncrasies of the social situations, hence an important part of their social competence. I will conclude with the potentially negative impact of avoiding conflict on the learning process of communication competence necessary to live in the globalizing world and in Japanese local communities.

Although Asian cultures have been often cast in one category of "Asian," which is generally considered to prefer non-confrontational conflict strategies over direct and open exchanges of ideas, a number of subtle but important differences that have masked the characteristics of each culture have been reported by researchers. One such finding, as Ohbuchi and Takahashi (1994) found, is a particularly strong tendency to avoid conflict among the Japanese, who are motivated by both their desire to preserve relationships and their perceptions of shared responsibility. Ikeda and Richey (2012) presented their argument that even though Japan has been thought of as a Confucian society for a long time, in comparison to other Asian nations, the Confucian values with regard to people's hesitancy to be non-conformist in a group, and their public aspect of Confucian values, are significantly less strong in the Japanese culture. Sueda (2021) presented her argument, citing conflict objectives: "instrumental," "relational," and "self-presentational," stressing that for the Japanese the priority may be different with relational and self-pre-sentational goals preceding instrumental ones. Sueda went on to claim that the Japanese feel secure as long as they maintain the balance between shame, a negative feeling that accompanies rejection and failure, and pride which is enhanced by a sense of self-esteem that arises when one accepts the given situation and successfully plays the given role, two important feelings associated with face. If, however, one of these feelings receives too much weight or pressure in a situation, something needs to be done to retain the equilibrium.

Some researchers have recently addressed the positive aspects of avoidance, identifying some important goals avoidance helps achieve, thus calling avoidance "strategic" rather than inactive (e.g., Wang, Fink, & Cai, 2013). Ohbuchi and Takahashi (1994) identified "keeping conflicts covert" as an intention to avoid risking harming a relationship, adding that it involves "actors' self-control or self-regulation of personal desires because they must maintain a polite public appearance, while privately tolerating frustration"(p. 1363). Researchers have identified a variety of interpersonal concerns that motivate avoidance, including Caughlin and Golish (2002) who found that self-protection, relationship protection, and conflict circumvention motivate topic avoidance. While the Japanese do seem to avoid confrontations by resorting to a variety of strategies, their motives cannot be explained by applying the Dual-Concern model. Nakatsugawa and Takai (2013) ela-borately argued that for the Japanese "avoidance" or "withdrawal" is not a manifesta-tion of a combination of low self- and other-concern, instead it comes from their desire to protect themselves. Contrary to the belief that the Japanese avoid direct confrontations to maintain group harmony, they seem to have a strong motivation to preserve their face by avoiding conflict, a reflection of their interest in protecting themselves. Some college students in their study stated that they would employ avoidance strategies, as they wished to be evaluated by others as a person who can successfully assess the situation, obviously coming from self-centered need and not from concerns for group harmony or for other face, previously believed to be the primary motive for avoidance strategies.

With their concern for self-protection the Japanese have been known to adopt what may appear to their Western and even some Asian observers to be "double standards." The clear and strategic distinction between their private and public face (e.g., Hendry, 1992), their use of *hon'ne* and *tatemae* (gut feelings and façade), or resorting to the dis-tinguished manipulation of *omote-ura* (front-back) communication behavior (e.g., Sin-ghal & Nagao, 1983) all of which give the impression that the Japanese are not sincere or honest, are interpersonal communication tactics employed across social contexts including but not limited to conflict situations. Since the 1980s many scholars in Japanese management have identified *nemawashi* as one strategy that the Japanese resort to when they anticipate serious differences of opinion in a formal setting such as company meetings. Befu (1990) associates *nemawashi*, a metaphoric term originally referring to gardeners wrapping roots when transplanting a tree, with a behind-the-scenes strategy to work on differences of opinion by touching base with all those people involved. March (1988) asserted that *nemawashi* is "the practice of preliminary and informal sounding out of people's ideas about a course of action before a formal proposal is drawn up" (p. 27). If people have strong objections to a proposal, or new ideas to improve a proposal, *nemawashi* makes it possible for these to be discovered in advance, making the acceptance of the final, formal proposal more certain.

Along the same line of conflict-avoidance strategies, pre-giving, or rewarding someone before they comply with a request, is another indirect strategy to help prevent clashes of ideas from surfacing. While arguing gift-giving is a clear manifestation of the *on-giri* (favor-obligation) reciprocity, Befu (1990) stressed that gift-giving becomes complete only after it is followed by a return gift whose value is carefully calculated even by the wrapping paper of a famous and expensive department store. Such subtle and meticulous gift exchange helps preserve the giver's and returner's faces (pp. 224–225). Gift-giving accompanied by calculated return as a strategy to help prevent conflict from emerging is a social practice totally foreign to Western observers of Japanese interpersonal communication, who would view it as a form of bribery.

Nemawashi, gift-giving and return, along with the use of *hon'ne-tatemae* (gut feelings-façade), and *ura-omote* (back-front) reflecting the distinction of *uchi-soto* (inside-outside) mentality, are all communication tactics that the Japanese use as conflict preventative measures. If and when Japanese have no choice but to face differences in objectives, interests, and opinions, they deploy an assortment of strategies in order to avoid engaging in direct confrontation. Lebra (2007) succinctly stated that "it is not that Japanese never risk confrontations but that, as long as harmony, or the appearance of harmony, is to be maintained, non-confrontational modes must be exhausted first" (p. 99). Sueda (2021) asserted that the motives for interpersonal behavior in that process can be manifested in various forms such as lying (pretend), acknowledging the situation that originally caused the feeling of difficulty that subsequently led to a sense of shame, accepting and justifying it, forgiving, and self-reflection. Nakanishi (2013) argued that even in medical disputes, situations where decisions and disagreements may cause life-threatening consequences, dialogue-facilitative mediation including a third party has been considered to be an effective method of conflict resolution, as many patients do not seek legal settlements, but instead an "appropriate response to their feelings and emotions, and sincere explanation of the accidents" (p. 1). To realize such a process the dialogue-facilitative model mainly focuses on information sharing and transformation of perspectives, unlike typical mediation models in which problem-solving is pursued. The objective is to make both patients and doctors reconstruct their perspective of realities on adverse medical events or problems through sympathetic conversations, aided by a mediator.

Other specific communication tactics in a dissenting or potentially confrontational situation that the Japanese often use have been sporadically observed to be effective, although they had been absorbed under the general rubric of avoiding, dismissed in Western conflict literature as only of value in trivial disputes (Anedo, 2012). To illustrate, Anedo (2012) listed obey publicly and disobey privately, ignoring, and constructive diplomacy with an emphasis on face giving, tolerance, and forgiving as involving a less direct approach to dealing with conflict. Oetzel et al. (2001) found that the Japanese used pretend, give in, and remain calm strategies more than the Chinese and the defend strategy, stressing that while both the Japanese and the Chinese value other-face and harmony, the ways in which the two cultures avoid confrontation are different.

Lebra (2007) listed refusing to respond and remaining silent which can be taken in Japanese culture as a sign of sincerity but not in China, and argued that they are manifestations of a range of reactions to the conflict, from denial, *enryo* (social reserve) or simple withdrawal, acquiescence, and reluctant compliance in Japan.

Another tactic that the Japanese often use not only to avoid direct confrontations but also to soothe an existing or emerging conflict is apology, a communication behavior that would be shunned in many Western, if not Eastern cultures since it immediately means that the ongoing problems are all automatically attributed to the apologizer. A Japanese psychologist, Enomoto (2014), argued that a simple utterance of "*sumimasen*," literally translated as "cannot end," expressing the interlocutor's feeling that "whatever I may do or say is not enough to end what has happened, but I am sorry" (p. 61). As long as the parties involved in a conflicting situation admit that the fault is not ascribed to a particular individual present in the situation, but is due to the circumstances or to the relationship between the parties, they have agreed that there is room for improvement of the situation. Enomoto contended that there is no need for the Japanese to be engaged in win-lose exchanges of claims such as a debate, which involves them in fierce and cold-blooded logical battles. Barkley (2019) claimed that in an "Apology Press Conference" in Japan where executives apologize for scandals caused by their companies' carelessness, negligence, illegal dealings, immoral behavior of individual members, etc. that are beyond the executives' responsibility or ability to keep the organizations under their managerial control, the executives must first and foremost express their remorse in an apologetic manner. Official and public apologies are duly expected even from foreign executives operating in Japan. Barkley showed that Western theories in crisis communication do not apply to Japanese contexts.

The strategies and tactics along with their underlying motives and intentions which many Japanese share are thus hardly understood as being logical and consistent. As far as the Japanese are concerned the principal value they share in living as ethical and conscientious members of their communities, and on which the various communication tactics are based, is their positive attitude toward *ku'uki wo yomu* (reading the air). The final section of this chapter explores the concept and

TABLE 9.1 Tactics the Japanese use to avoid conflict

Avoidance tactics	Brief descriptions
Accept and acknowledge	Mutually accepting that there are differences leads to calmness.
Accept appropriate responses to emotions and feelings	Knowing that both parties share feelings, yet knowing nothing could be done, helps.
Apology	Not necessarily accepting the blame, but expressing remorse that the parties cannot mutually agree on issues, puts both parties on an equal footing.
Compliance	Give in, expecting to be viewed as being fair-minded and just.
Dialogue	Sincere information sharing helps soothe hurt feelings.
Forgive	Show generosity and how big-hearted one is.
Give in	Conceding, while at the same time expecting the other to do the same.
Ignore	Limited to small issues, but helps pave the way toward big ones.
Justify	Accepting it is nobody's fault or responsibility, but has just happened.
Mutual justification	Agreeing on causes and reasons for the differences draws parties closer together.
Pretend	Shelving the potential conflict, focusing on the "here and now."
Refusal to respond	Ignore differences, hoping the other party can interpret it as "no."
Remain calm	Losing one's temper is the worst thing to do in any situation, so stay calm.
Seek explanation	Accept sincere attitudes toward the conflict from the other party.
Self-reflect	Review and see what you could/should have done.
Silence	Accompanied by other nonverbal signs like averting eyes, and hissing sounds, silence provides parties with a "moment filled with nothing."
Third party	Problem is not solved, but left in someone else's hands.
Tolerance	Shows long-term commitment to issues and relationship.

practice of air-reading that has not been sufficiently explored either by Japanese or Western scholars of interpersonal, intercultural, or conflict communication.

Bright and Dark Sides of "Air-Reading"

The most important consideration for many Japanese in their social relationships including conflict is the value they place on *ku'uki* or literally "air," a concept and practice that deserves to be given more attention by communication scholars. The concept of *ku'uki* or simply *ki* has been introduced by some commentators, historians, and scholars in limited disciplines such as journalism (e.g., Ito, 2006), but it has not received due regard from communication researchers. What gives rise to the concept of *ku'uki* as an important element in interpersonal relationships is that of "*ma*" (間 = between-ness) or "space." The word for a person in Japanese is 人間, the first character referring to a human in its crude sense, more as a *homo sapiens*, and it is only because it is followed by the second character 間 that it becomes a person situated in a given space and time in human community. A baby born as a *homo sapiens* grows to be a person in relation to others. The "air," though obviously invisible, yet indispensable for any human survival, fills the atmosphere of the community and strongly influences the social surroundings as a climate in which we live, and particularly of voicing of opinions thus serving as *ku'uki* in and around any human relationship. The ability to read the air in an accurate and appropriate way is the most important social skill necessary to be socialized as a person.

Whatever one does or says that harms the air of a community, be it a dyadic relationship, a small group of several members, an organization, a town, or even possibly the entire nation, is regarded as an act that violates the norms that have held the fragile community together. While communication competence has been ranked the most important skill to have in order to enter the workforce and have a successful career in a business organization in Japan for decades, one of the most important specific skills required is said to be that of "*ku'uki wo yomu*" or "reading the air." A variety of skills conducive to cohesiveness and mutual commitment to achieving organizational goals is understandably a more important requisite for the members than their individual academic or professional achievements which would make them stand out from the rest. A candidate's positive attitude toward going along with the organizational community is a top priority at job interviews and thereafter in Japan.

In addition to being important in organizational settings such as businesses, reading the air plays an important role in communication competence, especially when there is a delicate power balance to be maintained. If, for instance, a person with less power due to age, experience, and status openly challenges another person with much more expertise and status in front of a lot of people, then that person would be criticized for not being able to read the air, even though, or especially when, what he/she said was logically sound. In this situation, if the younger and therefore less powerful person mindfully avoids voicing his/her opinion, thereby avoiding any conflict, it is said that he/she has successfully and accurately read the air and thus the entire group has been able to sustain its harmony. While such interpersonal interactions may be common in a work context in Western cultures, they are extended to relationships between people of the same age, experience, and status as well in Japan, for example in a class in school, and even close friendships. The motive in these situations is attributed to people's attitude toward maintaining harmonious interpersonal relationships.

Several writers have endorsed the positive influence of air-reading as it helps the Japanese express and further enforce their conscientious, harmony-concerned, and community-based ethos. Enomoto (2014) compared Japanese and Western modes of communication, characterizing the former as purporting to co-establish and co-maintain the air of cooperation and mutual understanding by obscuring the differences between parties, whereas the Euro-Americans value the differences and subsequent attempts to contest the issues and convince one another through direct confrontations of ideas and persuasion. Ishii (1984) and Miike (2003) advocated *enryo-sasshi* or reservation and consideration for others, manifested in "reading another's mind," a form of air-reading, as a tactic that facilitates and increases the positive outcomes of non-confrontational Japanese interpersonal communication. The other-oriented, considerate, humble, indirect, and ingratiating Japanese attitudes, backed up by the value they put on *enryo-sasshi*, air-reading, and conflict-avoiding intentions, especially in customer-valued contexts, manifest themselves in extensive honorifics, which sound excessive and redundant at times, and lengthy circumlocutory expressions that appear to be displays of politeness and hospitality to foreigners.

However, given that conflict avoidance, especially circumventing direct confrontations, is not driven by Japanese people's collectivistic and interdependent features as previously believed, but by their self-interest and preservation of identity, all these elaborate and seemingly polite expressions are used by the Japanese as tools for self-protection as they secure, establish, and maintain their place in the community. Yamagishi (2002) argued that while Japanese may often give the impression that they place organizational goals above their individual goals, and appear to possess collectivistic work ethics, their real motive comes from within themselves, as a result of their calculation that their individual happiness and satisfaction along with tangible rewards such as income and benefits will increase as long as they suppress their personal needs, feelings, and contentions. Nakatsugawa and Takai (2013) stated that "the self-protective intent in avoiding attacks or accusations is obviously highly self-concerned, thus the dual concern model falls short in explaining Japanese intentions within interpersonal conflict" (p. 54). Some conflict avoidance strategies such as conforming and apologizing require highly trained skills and a conscious effort to accurately and appropriately read the cues that surround interpersonal relationships, however, many Japanese do not always actively utilize such skills. Instead, they retreat to a silent and non-active mode even in a situation where there is not even a remotely probable reason for conflict, such as being asked basic questions in class.

Critics of current Japanese society take this criticism one step further. Reizei (2006), for example, argued that Japanese people's high-contextual use of language functions only in so far as the users somehow make a connection between a communication context at a previous time and a subsequent occasion. People today only use superficial expressions and "hyper honorifics" in order to protect their self-interest, so they are unable to connect the two contexts that are separated by time. When this happens the Japanese language with its subtle expressions that hint at the speaker's intentions without giving details stops functioning and thus "suffocates" without the air that would normally fill the communication context. *Ku'uki wo yomu* is a competent communication behavior only when it is used to fill the gap between two situations. Unless it is used to connect two contexts, people's justification for reading the air and refraining from saying anything is nothing but self-defense.

Given such discrepancies between true and genuine intentions of self-protection, and actual façade of politeness and consideration for others that serves the communicators' self-satisfaction, there are potentially serious drawbacks to air-reading that need careful consideration. What appears to be considerate, polite, and reserved behavior, all consequences of air-reading in most situations, may be doing more harm than good to individuals as well as the community to which they belong. One such negative consequence resulting from the discrepancies between the façade and the true intentions is the Japanese people's frustration at the need to maintain psychological balance. Pressured to obey publicly in a conflict situation, yet privately voicing opposing opinions to friends and associates they trust, many Japanese feel the stress arising from not being able to be themselves in difficult situations. Such an internal dilemma may be expressed in a very rude manner when they find themselves in an outgroup where they have far less need to be concerned about how they are viewed by others than in an ingroup setting.

Hirata and Warschauer (2014) harshly criticized the negative influence of Japanese people's affection for maintaining harmony. Whereas harmony has contributed mightily to the nation's prosperity and brought people together to fight for the survival of the nation after the terrible defeat of the war, harmony is the enemy of flexibility, openness, and, increasingly, innovation. Flexibility, openness to diversity, and innovation are essential in today's globalizing world. Devotion to consensus comes with resistance to innovation. Loyalty to authority figures comes with an unwillingness to challenge them. Without natural outlets for expression, conflicts go unresolved.

As long as it is carried out in a healthy outcome-oriented fashion, a clash of ideas can be a source of "good" decisions. By suppressing individual opinions, Japanese may be depriving themselves of opportunities to discuss issues at hand for genuinely constructive decisions. Furthermore, once people get used to not voicing their opinions, thereby ensuring their comfort as well as harmony with others, they will not only miss opportunities to practice speaking their minds, but also end up having no opinion at all. Although air-reading may have great potential to help avoid unnecessary conflicts and destructive human relationships, it can also have a greater detrimental influence on people's acquisition and enhancement of constructive and mutually satisfactory management of conflict. The chances of these negative consequences becoming reality may not be high at the moment but are likely to become so, especially because the Japanese often celebrate their own seemingly considerate, hospitable, and polite façade, which is derived from their respect for *ku'uki wo yomu* communication.

Conclusion

This chapter has outlined the tendency for communication researchers to apply theories and concepts about conflict developed and tested in the Western domain to non-Western cultures, particularly Japan. The applicability of such theoretical constructs as collectivism-individualism and interdependent and independent self-construals has been an issue debated by communication researchers. The Japanese, who are concerned about other-face, harmonious relationships, and self-protection, have been known for their various tactics to avoid conflict. However, the priority of their concerns has been questioned, as their goal of self-protection may be the driving force behind Japanese reservation and politeness. I have highlighted the value the Japanese put on "*ku'uki wo yomu*" as the main source of motivation. While their seemingly humble, reserved, and hospitable communication has played an important role in maintaining fragile interpersonal relationships, as well as the peaceful running of business organizations and even the country, air-reading communication is not without its drawbacks. Once it becomes a versatile tactic across social contexts, it may deprive the Japanese of an opportunity to view conflict as a healthy and constructive exchange of ideas. The consequences of blindly employing conflict avoiding communication tactics may be more damaging than temporary interpersonal clashes.

In today's globalizing world where interdependent, intercultural communication plays an increasingly crucial role, researchers must define and redefine not only Asian communication but also social sciences by collaborating in an attempt to overhaul theories, concepts, and methodologies that have been commonly accepted as constituting the research paradigm for human communication which is profoundly influenced by the philosophies in the respective cultures. Miike (2017), a strong advocate of Asia-centric views on human communication, argued for the need to understand people's communication behavior in light of the respective cultural, especially religious backgrounds, and reviewed the ontological and epistemological orientations of representative Asian religions, focusing on their influence on people's social practices. Ishii (1998), who has emphasized the necessity to build Asian theories of communication, introduced the Buddhist principle of *en*, "predetermined connection", and argued that it should be integrated as an important component of a larger whole such as a community, using the essential principle of general systems theory stating that "the holistic systems view of human relationships is relatively Eastern in orientation" (p. 115). The lack of Asian theories of communication is "mission unaccomplished" (Wang & Shen, 2000, p. 15), thus collaboration among Asian and between Asian and Western researchers is an urgent need.

References

Anedo, O. (2012). A cultural analysis of harmony and conflict: Towards an integrated model of conflict styles. *Unizik Journal of Arts and Humanities*, 13(2), 16–52. doi:10.4314/ujah.v13i2.2

Barkley, K. (2019). Cultural differences in crisis communication: Western theory and the Japanese context. Ph.D. dissertation, Seinan Gakuin University.

Befu, H. (1990). Conflict and non-Western bureaucracy in Japan. In S. N. Eisenstadt & E. Ben-Ari (Eds.), *Japanese models of conflict resolution* (pp. 213–238). London: Kegan Paul International.

Benedict, R. (1946). *The chrysanthemum and the sword: Patterns of Japanese culture*. Boston, MA: Houghton Mifflin.

Cai, D. & Fink, E. L. (2002). Conflict style differences between individualists and collectivists. *Communication Monographs*, 69(1), 67–87. doi:10.1080/03637750216536

Canary, D. & Lakey, S. (2013). *Strategic conflict*. New York, NY: Routledge.

Caughlin, J. P., & Golish, T. D. (2002). An analysis of the association between topic avoidance and dissatisfaction: Comparing perceptual and interpersonal explanations. *Communication Monographs*, 69, 275–295. doi:10.1080/03637750216546

Chiu, R. K., Wong, M., & Kosinski, F., Jr. (1998). Confucian values and conflict behavior of Asian managers: A comparison of two countries. *Social Behavior and Personality*, 26(1), 11–22. doi:10.2224/sbp.1998.26.1.11

Coser, L. A. (1956). *The functions of social conflict*. New York, NY: The Free Press.

Cupach, W. R. & Canary, D. J. (1997). *Competence in interpersonal conflict*. Long Grove, IL: Waveland Press.

Cupach, W. R., Canary, D. J., & Spitzberg, B. H. (2010). *Competence in interpersonal conflict*. Long Grove, IL: Waveland Press.

Enomoto, H. (2014). *Dibeito ga nigate, dakara Nihonjin wa sugoi* (Bad at debates, and therefore the Japanese are a wonderful people). Tokyo: Asahi Shinsho.

Hendry, J. (1992). Individualism and individuality: Entry into a social world. In R. Goodman & K. Refsing (Eds.), *Ideology and practice in modern Japan* (pp. 55–71). London: Routledge.

Hirata, K. & Warschauer, M. (2014). *Japan: The paradox of harmony*. New Haven, CT: Yale University Press.

Ikeda, K. & Richey, S. (2012). *Social networks and Japanese democracy: The beneficial impact of interpersonal communication in East Asia*. London: Routledge.

Ishii, S. (1984). Enryo-Sasshi communication: A key to understanding Japanese interpersonal relations. *Cross Currents*, 11(1), 49–58.

Ishii, S. (1998). Developing a Buddhist *en*-based systems paradigm for the study of Japanese human relationships. *Japan Review (Bulletin of the International Research Center for Japanese Studies)*, 10, 109–122.

Ito, Y. (2006). *Iken fuudo, "ku'uki," minshu shugi* (Opinion climate, "air" and democracy). *Media Communication* (Keio University Journal of Media Communication), 56, 3–27.

Lebra, T. (2007). *Identity, gender, and status in Japan. The collected papers of twentieth-century Japanese writers on Japan, Vol. 2*. Folkstone, UK: Global Oriental.

Lee, W. L., Nakamura, S., Chung, M. J., Chun, Y. C., Fu, M., Liang, S. C., & Liu, C. L. (2013). Asian couples in negotiation: A mixed-method observational study of cultural variations across five Asian regions. *Family Process*, 52(3), 499–518. doi:10.1111/famp.12040.

March, R. M. (1988). *The Japanese negotiator: Subtlety and strategy beyond Western logic*. Tokyo: Kodansha International.

Miike, Y. (2003). Japanese Enryo-Sasshi communication and the psychology of Amae: Reconsideration and reconceptualization. *Keio Communication Review*, 25, 93–115.

Miike, Y. (2017). Non-Western theories of communication: Indigenous ideas and insights. In L. Chen (Ed.), *Handbooks of communication science, Vol. 9: Intercultural communication* (pp. 67–97), Boston, MA: De Gruyter.

Moriizumi, S. (2016). What do I say next? Social status differences, self-construals, and partner's response messages in interpersonal conflict styles. *Japanese Journal of Communication Studies*, 45(1), 71–91. doi:10.20698/comm.45.1_71

Nakanishi, T. (2013). Communication model in medical dispute resolution in Japan. *Yamagata Medical Journal*, 31(1), 1–8.

Nakatsugawa, S. & Takai, J. (2013). Keeping conflict latent: "Salient" versus "non-salient" interpersonal conflict management strategies of Japanese. *Intercultural Communication Studies*, 22(3), 43–60.

Oetzel, J. G., Ting-Toomey, S., Masumoto, T., Yokochi, Y., Pan, X., Takai, J., & Wilcox, R. (2001). Face and facework in conflict: A cross-cultural comparison of China, Germany,

Japan, and the United States. *Communication Monographs*, 68(3), 235–258. doi:10.1080/03637750128061

Oetzel, J. G., Ting-Toomey, S., Yokochi, Y., Masumoto, T., & Takai, J. (2000). A typology of facework behaviors in conflicts with best friends and relative strangers. *Communication Quarterly*, 48, 397–419. doi:10.1080/01463370009385606

Ohbuchi, K. & Takahashi, Y. (1994). Cultural styles of conflict management in Japanese and Americans: Passivity, covertness, and effectiveness of strategies. *Journal of Applied Social Psychology*, 24(15), 1345–1366. doi:10.1111/j.1559–1816.1994.tb01553.x

Okabe, R. (2005). *Researching Japanese rhetorical theory and practice: Rhetorically "barren" or "fertile"?* Paper presented at the annual Conference of the International Communication Association, New York City, May 26–30.

Onishi, J. & Bliss, R. E. (2006). In search of Asian ways of managing conflict. *International Journal of Conflict Management*, 17(3), 203–225. doi:10.1108/10444060610742326

Oyserman, D., Coon, H. M., Kemmelmeier, M. (2002). Rethinking individualism and collectivism: Evaluation of theoretical assumptions and meta-analyses. *Psychological Bulletin*, 128(1), 3–72. doi:10.1037/0033–2909.128.1.3

Reizei, A. (2006) *"Kankei no ku'uki" "ba no ku'uki"* (*Ku'uki* surrounding relationships and *ku'uki* of the situation) in Japanese. Tokyo: Kodansha Gendai Shisho.

Semlak, W. D. (1982). *Conflict resolving communication: A skill development approach.* Prospect Heights, IL: Waveland Press.

Singhal, A. & Nagao, M. (1993). Assertiveness and communication competence: A comparison of the communication styles of American and Japanese students. *Asian Journal of Communication*, 3, 1–18. doi:10.1080/01292989309359570

Sueda, K. (2021). *Komyunikeishon sutadiz: Aidentiti to face kara mita keshiki* (Communication studies: Views from identity and face). Tokyo: Shin'yosha.

Takano, Y. (2008). *Shuudanshugi to iu sakkaku: Nihonjinron no omoi chigai to sono yurai* (An illusion called "collectivism": Misunderstanding about *Nihonjinron* and its origins) Tokyo: Shin'yosha.

Takeuchi, Y. (1995). *Nihonjin no koudou bunpou: Nihonjin rashisa no kaitaishinsho* (Socio grammar of Japanese people's behavior: A new approach to deconstructing "Japaneseness"). Tokyo: Toyokeizai.

Ting-Toomey, S., Gao, G., Trubisky P., Yang, Z., Kim, H. S., Lin, S. L., & Nishida, T. (1991). Culture, face maintenance, and styles of handling interpersonal conflict: A study in five countries. *International Journal of Conflict Management*, 2(4), 275–296. doi:10.1108/eb022702

Wang, G. & Shen, V. (2000). East, West, communication, and theory: Searching for the meaning of searching for Asian communication theories. *Asian Journal of Communication*, 10, 14–32. doi:10.1080/01292980009364782

Wang, Q., Fink, E. L., & Cai, D. A. (2012). The effect of conflict goals on avoidance strategies: What does not communicating communicate? *Human Communication Research*, 38, 222–252. doi:10.1111/j.1468–2958.2011.01421.x

Yamagishi, T. (2002). *Kokoro dekkachi na Nihonjin* (Hyper conscious Japanese). Tokyo: Nihon Keizai Shimbun.

10

THE *YIN* AND *YANG* OF CONFLICT MANAGEMENT AND RESOLUTION

A Chinese Perspective

Guo-Ming Chen

Introduction

Globalization has shrunk the world and greatly enhanced close interaction and con‐ nectivity in every aspect of human society, in which the acceleration of local and global cooperation and competition has become a norm rather than an exception of human life in the twenty-first century. It is thus important for global citizens to understand, recognize, and accept cultural differences, because the lack of cultural awareness and proper ways to address cultural differences in interaction will inevitably lead to unrealistic expectations, frustrations, conflicts, and failure in establishing a positive relationship between people from different cultures.

Conflict management and resolution as an important concept, both in theory and practice, has been studied by scholars from different disciplines for decades. With the impact of globalization, conflict becomes more intricate due to the dynamic nature of culture in the process of managing and resolving the conflict. In other words, culture and conflict have an interdependent relationship. Hence, to understand the way one's counterparts think and act based on their cultural orientation becomes a prerequisite for maintaining a peaceful world.

Chen and Starosta (2005) indicated that culture exerts its influence on human behaviors, including conflict management, through cultural context, language usage, and reasoning process. Studies from Hall (1976) and Ting-Toomey (1985) showed that people in high-context and low-context cultures have different com‐ munication styles and adopt different strategies in conflict management. The dif‐ ferent communication styles caused by cultural orientation are demonstrated in linguistic expressions particularly, as some cultures tend to be more direct in verbal expression, while others are more indirect and try to avoid confrontation in order to maintain a harmonious atmosphere in interaction (Ma, 1996). In addition, the linear or logical versus nonlinear or intuitive reasoning process between West and

DOI: 10.4324/9781003252955-12

East was also found to increase misunderstanding and conflict in intercultural communication (Kaplan, 1966).

Thus, the determinate role culture plays in the process of conflict management is indisputable. However, this significant role of culture in human interaction has led some scholars to stabilize the nature of culture by neglecting its dynamic attribute. That is, scholars tend to treat culture as an independent variable in the process of research without seeing the constant change and variation of culture (Chen, 2011a; Lommer & Adamopoulos, 1997). Therefore, it is necessary to explore the dynamic relationship between culture and human behaviors in general and conflict management in specific. This chapter attempts to face this problem by addressing two key issues: (1) to argue that communication is contextually dependent and therefore an emic approach should be taken to better understand members of a cultural group, and (2) to analyze the *yin* and *yang* or the dynamic nature of conflict behaviors from the cultural perspective.

Communication is Contextually Dependent

Because every culture has its own unique traits and heritage, scholars always assume that human communication is contextually dependent, and therefore an emic approach should be taken to better understand the cultural conventions and behaviors of a specific cultural group. In other words, in order to know members of a cultural group one has to examine the group from its own perspective. This culture specific approach is well illustrated with the paradigmatic assumptions of Eastern and Western cultures (see Figure 10.1).

The figure indicates that ontologically Eastern cultures take a holistic view of human communication, in which everything is running like a river without a beginning and an end, and the interactant is submerged in the wholeness of the universe as a member of the collectivistic network of relationships. In contrast, Western cultures hold an atomistic view of human communication by treating the interactant as a discrete self, thus individualism becomes a dominant value of society. Accordingly, Eastern and Western cultures are distinct from each other in terms of axiological, epistemological, and methodological assumptions. The axiological assumptions are especially useful for understanding the differences in conflict behaviors between Easterners and Westerners. It shows that the East emphasizes a harmonious relationship, while the West is confrontational in social interaction. Reflected in the process of conflict management, Easterners tend to be indirect and subtle in expressing themselves and avoid conflict by accommodating their counterparts' needs. In contrast, Westerners are direct and expressive in a conflict, which denotes a more dominant and divisive style in social interaction.

Abundant empirical studies have confirmed the sharp differences between East and West based on the paradigmatic assumptions. For example, a series of studies by the present author have demonstrated that Chinese people stress the importance of relationships, face, harmony, reciprocity, and credibility in a business negotiation (Chen & Chen, 2002); show self-restraint/self-discipline, indirect expression of disapproval, saving or making face for counterparts, reciprocity, and particularistic relationship in

Ontology	
East	West
Holistic	Atomistic
submerged collectivistic	discrete individualistic

Axiology		Epistemology		Methodology	
East	West	East	West	East	West
Harmonious	Confrontational	Interconnected	Reductionistic	Intuitive	Logical
indirect subtle adaptative consensual agreeable	direct expressive dialectical divisive sermonic	reciprocity we hierarchical associative ascribed	independent I equal free will achieved	subjective nonlinear ambiguous ritual accommodative	objective linear analytical justificatory manipulative

FIGURE 10.1 The paradigmatic assumptions of Eastern and Western cultures
Source: Chen & An, 2009, p. 204.

order to pursue a conflict-free or harmonious interaction (Chen, 2002). More specifically, Chen (2011b) sorted out nine key concepts, namely, harmony, face, interrelation, favor, reciprocity, politeness, rites, predestined relation, and hierarchy, that manifestly distinguish the Chinese from the Westerners in the process of communication or conflict management. Similarly, studies on U.S. American cultural values and conflict management have been done for many years (e.g., Barnlund, 1989; Glen & Glen, 1983; Kohls, 1984; Pribram, 1949; Stewart, 1972).

The contrasting paradigmatic assumptions between East and West not only stipulate clear differences between the two cultural groups that reinforce the need for an emic or culturally specific approach for the study of conflict management in both intracultural and intercultural contexts, but also provide a convenient tool for learning about one's own and others' cultures. However, the approach also suffers from the problem of oversimplifying the trait of a culture and dichotomizing cultural values. It tends to suggest that an unbridgeable discrepancy or insurmountable gap exists between Eastern and Western cultures (Chen, 2009a), which, as previously indicated, treats culture as a static or independent variable by neglecting its dynamic nature in the process of human interaction. This problem inevitably leads to the pessimistic belief that conflicts between cultures are unavoidable, and the management or resolution of intercultural conflicts is doomed to be difficult, though not impossible. Therefore, it is critical to go beyond the limitation of the static view by exploring the dynamic nature of culture in order to reach mutual understanding between cultural groups.

Dynamic Nature of Conflict Behaviors

It is commonly agreed that culture constantly changes due to the impact of technological inventions, natural and man-made calamities, and cross-border contacts (Chen & Starosta, 2005). From the perspective of human interaction the dynamic nature of culture can be more specifically displayed intraculturally by internal variations and interculturally by the continuum nature of cultural values.

Internal Variations of Culture

Geography and ethnicity are two important factors accounting for the internal variations of a culture. China and the U.S. are good examples. Both countries are vast geographically and are multiethnic, multiracial, and multi-religious societies. The multicultural fabric of society represents the intricate and diverse nature of conflict behaviors from different ethnic groups within the same country. The impact of geographic structure is also reflected, especially in China, in the different dialects used and in the various communication styles of people in different regions, such as North vs. South and East vs. West. Thus, it is important to understand that when referring to conflict behaviors in a culture, e.g., Chinese or American conflict management, it usually indicates the conflict behaviors of the dominant group in the culture, such as the Han ethnic group in China and the white Protestants of Anglo-Saxon ancestry (WASP) in the U.S.

The intracultural dynamic of human interaction is also revealed in the ambivalence of cultural practice. As Chen (2004) pointed out, there are two faces of Chinese communication, which show the internal diversity of Chinese culture. According to Chen, highlighted in the paradigmatic assumptions (see Figure 10.1), harmony is the core value of Chinese culture, which leads the Chinese to pursue a conflict free interaction by demonstrating an indirect communication style manifested in nonassertive, non-argumentative, and non-confrontational behaviors and heavy reliance on an intermediary in the process of conflict management (Jia, 2002; Ma, 1992). This is the first or public face of Chinese culture, which gives people the impression that Chinese people are always polite and accommodative in interaction. However, Chen explained that the other face of Chinese communication is quite contrary to the first one. It reflects the power game Chinese people play when harmony is challenged, or when needs are incompatible in a conflict situation (Hwang, 1987; Leung & Chan, 2003).

In other words, when the harmonious state of interaction is in jeopardy or face is lost, the Chinese can show sharp aggressive behaviors or raw emotion in public, or act fiercely and ferociously in competing for scarce resources (Chen, 2002). This second face or the dark side of Chinese culture is often neglected by scholars when studying Chinese communication behaviors. Such a confrontational style directly involved in a conflict is also commonly applied to outgroup members in Chinese society. It further forms the strategic aspect of Chinese communication for gaining the compliance of one's counterparts in a conflict situation. Chen (2004) argued that this side of Chinese communication is much more dynamic compared to the first face which is regulated by a set of explicit rules of interaction, and it "suggests that the Chinese are far beyond the superficial perception as being conservative, polite, humble, and self controlled, but can also be much more humane as being artful, crafty, cunning, deceitful and sly in interaction" (p. 32).

In addition, cultural context is another factor that influences conflict management. In a study of conflict management in a joint venture company in China, Liu and Chen (2000) found that although Chinese managers tended to adopt a collaboration strategy more frequently than a control strategy, they used a control strategy more often than a non-confrontation strategy. Moreover, Liu, Chen, and Liu (2006) found that cultural practices in state-owned enterprises were more influenced by group orientation both in workers' behaviors and in leadership style as compared to joint venture enterprises. Sheer's (2000) study on conflict in China's international export trading also showed that the types of conflict were mainly decided by the trading culture, and the conflict process was as strongly influenced by economic and political environments.

Continuum of Cultural Values

Interculturally, as indicated previously, the dichotomy problem of cultural values reflects a static view of culture and creates a gap in understanding between cultural groups. Chen (2009a) criticized the dichotomy view of culture as the tumor of intercultural communication, which makes effective management of intercultural conflicts impossible. As Chen argued, cultural values should be treated as a continuum or degree rather than being categorized as type. An either-or distinction should not be applied to study cultural values, as indicated in Figure 10.2. Instead,

East	VS.	West
Holistic	OR	Atomistic
Harmonious	OR	Confrontational
Interconnected	OR	Reductionistic
Intuitive	OR	Logical

FIGURE 10.2 The either-or view of paradigmatic assumptions between East and West
Source: Chen, 2009a, p. 403.

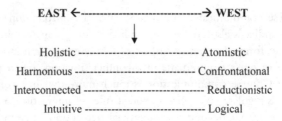

EAST ←---------------------------------→ WEST

Holistic --------------------------------- Atomistic
Harmonious -------------------------------- Confrontational
Interconnected -------------------------------- Reductionistic
Intuitive -------------------------------- Logical

FIGURE 10.3 The continuum view of cultural values based on paradigmatic assumptions
Source: Chen, 2009a, p. 403.

it should look like the explication in Figure 10.3 from the perspective of paradigmatic assumptions.

Treating cultural values as a continuum shows the dynamic nature of culture by demonstrating the differences and similarities between cultures simultaneously. Cultural differences provide a good opportunity for cultural groups to understand one another; only through understanding that cultural similarities exist can intercultural conflicts be appropriately managed. Figure 10.4 can be used to explain the existence of cultural similarities and differences simultaneously.

Figure 10.4 is drawn from Chen, Ryan, and Chen's (2000) study which compared determinants of conflict management between the Chinese and Americans. It shows mean scores of six factors, between the Chinese and Americans, that were identified as the key variables influencing Chinese conflict management. Of the practices that scholars commonly use, only those factors showing significant differences in terms of mean scores were interpreted in the study in the belief that difference is the norm for dealing with the comparison between Eastern and Western cultures. However, if

	Americans	Chinese
Factors	Mean	Mean
Severity	*6.22	5.56
Credibility	5.28	5.02
Relation	5.12	5.19
Power	4.14	4.40
Seniority	*3.76	4.52
Face	*3.44	4.23

Note. * $p < 0.05$.

FIGURE 10.4 Similarities and differences of cultural values between nations
Source: Chen, Ryan, and Chen, 2000, p. 168.

culture is treated as a continuum concept, we can see the overlapping part or similarities of the two cultures. This allows us to further interpret or reinterpret the results of the same study in Figure 10.4. That is, in addition to the differences shown in severity, seniority, and face in the process of conflict management, we first can see that the rank order of the six factors is quite similar; and second, no significant difference was found in three other variables, namely, credibility, relation, and power. Thus, from the perspective of conflict management the two cultures will not be as illustrated in Figure 10.5, which demarcates the two cultures as two completely separate entities. The mutual exclusiveness of the two cultures gives no opportunity for the two groups to penetrate into each other. This also means conflict is inevitable and the management of conflict is doomed to fail.

Instead, a more appropriate and accurate view of different cultures should be like the one demonstrated in Figure 10.6, which shows differences and similarities (i.e., the overlapping area or the diamond shape in the figure) between the two cultural groups. The mutual inclusiveness or similarity between the two cultures is where we see hope and the possibility of effective management and resolution of a conflict through

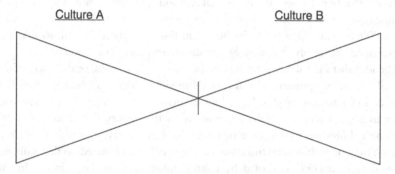

FIGURE 10.5 The mutual exclusiveness of the two cultures

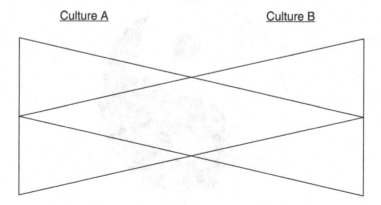

FIGURE 10.6. The mutual inclusiveness of the two cultures

interaction, though a complete identification between the groups remains an extremely difficult task to accomplish.

Yin and Yang of Conflict Management and Resolution

The mutual inclusiveness view of cultures is best epitomized by the Chinese *tai chi* model (see Figure 10.7). The model stipulates a oneness of two separate but interdependent interactants, represented by *yin* (the white color) and *yang* (the dark color) forces. The dark eye in the white area and the white eye in the dark area indicate similarities between the two sides, which produce the potentiality of mutual inclusiveness through interaction. The model allows the two parties to interpenetrate, interfuse, and mutually transform, while personal identity is still sustained. It also dictates that a conflict can only be resolved through the correspondence of the two parties in a mutually inclusive, though opposite, situation.

More specifically, the model lays down the foundation of effective Chinese conflict management and resolution. It prescribes that conflict should be treated as a holistic system, which is formed by the dynamic and dialectic interaction between the two parties. It argues that without the interaction the two parties cannot develop individually, though each party possesses its own identity (Chen, 2006, 2009b). A conflict has to be bound in this interrelated holism, so that it can be managed and resolved creatively, constructively, and harmoniously.

The idea that the balance is found but the distinction remains, or the effect of unity as well as diversity promoted by the *tai chi* model, is highly applicable when facing conflicts in contemporary globalizing human society. As Chen (2015a) pointed out, in order to build a cohesive global community in the twenty-first century people of differing cultures must cultivate a new sense of community, in which a mindset of multicultural or multi-contextual co-existence needs to be fostered, so that ambiguity, uncertainty, and conflicts caused by cultural differences can be reduced. In other words, intercultural conflict in the new global community is an infinite boundary

FIGURE 10.7 The *tai chi* model of conflict management

game which aims to continue to play the game, on the basis of dynamic flexibility or fluidity of the interacting context, rather than to play in order to win (Carse, 1986).

Conclusion

The increasing interaction among cultural groups due to the impact of globalization not only has made the relationship between conflict and culture more interdependent and complicated, but also demands a new way of studying conflict management and resolution from a more dynamic perspective. Traditionally, many scholars tended to neglect variations or the dynamic nature of culture that inevitably led to the dichotomy problem when dealing with cultural values. This static view of culture in turn affects how scholars perceive the nature of human interaction, and how they investigate the topic of conflict management and resolution in research.

In addition to supporting the argument that human communication is contextually or culturally dependent, this chapter further emphasizes the importance of examining human interaction in general and conflict management specifically from a dynamic perspective. The dynamic view allows the present author to reinterpret the findings of previous studies, which improves the problem of overlooking the potential similarities between cultures by treating cultural values as a continuum. It also provides an opportunity for people of differing cultures to interpenetrate and mutually transform without losing their own identity, as indicated by the Chinese *tai chi* model, in the process of interaction or conflict management. As Chen (2015b) advocated, the new era of human society, knitted by a close interconnected global network, should be an age of "different approaches contribute to the same end," rather than an age of "when Greek meets Greek then comes the tug of war" (p. 470). Only through the mindset of multicultural coexistence can the approach of "seeking common ground while keeping differences" be employed when dealing with conflicts, so that a productive and successful global community can be built.

References

Barnlund, D. S. (1989). *Communication style of Japanese and Americans: Images and reality*. Belmont, CA: Wadsworth.

Carse, J. P. (1986). *Finite and infinite game: A vision of life as play and possibility*. New York, NY: Ballantine.

Chen, G. M. (2002). The impact of harmony on Chinese conflict management. In G. M. Chen & R. Ma (Eds.), *Chinese conflict management and resolution* (pp. 3–19). Westport, CT: Ablex.

Chen, G. M. (2004). The two faces of Chinese communication. *Human Communication, 7*, 25–36.

Chen, G. M. (2006). Asian communication studies: What and where to now. *The Review of Communication, 6*(4), 295–311.

Chen, G. M. (2009a). Beyond the dichotomy of communication studies. *Journal of Asian Communication, 19*(4), 398–411.

Chen, G. M. (2009b). Toward an *I Ching* model of communication. *China Media Research, 5*(3), 72–81.

Chen, G. M. (2011a). Theorizing contextuality of intercultural communication. *Journal of Communication Research and Practice*, 1(2), 13–24.

Chen, G. M. (2011b). An introduction to key concepts in understanding the Chinese: Harmony as the foundation of Chinese communication. *China Media Research*, 7(4), 1–12.

Chen, G. M. (2015a). Theorizing global community as cultural home in the new century. *International Journal of Intercultural Relations*, 46, 73–81.

Chen, G. M. (2015b). Seeking common ground while accepting differences through tolerance: U.S.-China intercultural communication in global community. In L. A. Samovar, R. E. Porter, E. R. McDaniel, & C. S. Roy (Eds.), *Intercultural communication: A reader* (pp. 465–471). Boston, MA: Cengage Learning.

Chen, G. M. & An, R. (2009). A Chinese model of intercultural leadership competence. In D. K. Deardorff (Ed.), *The SAGE Handbook of intercultural competence* (pp. 196–208). Thousand Oaks, CA: Sage.

Chen, G. M. & Chen, V. (2002). An examination of PRC business negotiations. *Communication Research Reports*, 19, 399–408.

Chen, G. M., Ryan, K., & Chen, C. (2000). The determinants of conflict management among Chinese and Americans. *Intercultural Communication Studies*, 9, 163–175.

Chen, G. M. & Starosta, W. J. (2005). *Foundations of intercultural communication*. Lanham, MD: University Press of America.

Glen, E. S. & Glen, C. G. (1983). *Man and mankind: Conflict and communication*. New York, NY: Ablex.

Jia, W.-S. (2002). Chinese mediation and its cultural foundation. In G. M. Chen & R. Ma (Eds.), *Chinese conflict management and resolution* (pp. 289–295). Westport, CT: Ablex.

Kaplan, R. B. (1966). Cultural thought pattern in inter-cultural education. *Language Learning*, 16, 1–20.

Kohls, L. R. (1984). *The values Americans live by: Introduction*. Washington, DC: Meridian House International.

Hall, E. T. (1976). *Beyond culture*. Garden City, NY: Anchor.

Hwang, K. K. (1987). Face and favor: The Chinese power game. *American Journal of Sociology*, 92(4), 944–974.

Leung, T. K. & Chan, R. (2003). Face, favor and positioning – a Chinese power game. *European Journal of Marketing*, 37(11/12), 1575–1598.

Liu, S. & Chen, G. M. (2000). Assessing Chinese conflict management styles in joint ventures. *Intercultural Communication Studies*, 9, 71–88.

Liu, S., Chen, G. M., & Liu, Q. (2006). Through the lenses of organizational culture: A comparison of state-owned enterprises and joint ventures in China. *China Media Research*, 2(2), 15–24.

Lommer, W. J. & Adamopoulos, J. (1997). Culture as antecedent to behavior. In J. W. Berry, Y. H. Poortinga, & J. Pandey (Eds.), *Handbook of cross-cultural psychology* (Vol. 1, pp. 43–84). Needham Heights, MA: Allyn & Bacon.

Ma, R. (1992). The role of unofficial intermediaries in interpersonal conflict in the Chinese culture. *Communication Quarterly*, 40, 268–279.

Ma, R. (1996). Saying "yes" for "no" and "no" for "yes": A Chinese rule. *Journal of Pragmatics*, 25(2), 257–266.

Pribram, K. H. (1949). *Conflicting patterns of thought*. Washington, DC: Public Affair Press.

Sheer, V. C. (2000). Conflict processes in China's international export trading: Impact of the Chinese culture and the trading culture. *Intercultural Communication Studies*, 9(2), 47–69.

Stewart, E. C. (1978). *American cultural patterns: A cross-cultural perspective*. Pittsburgh, PA: Intercultural Communication Network.

Ting-Toomey, S. (1985). Toward a theory of conflict and culture. In W. B. Gudykunst, L. P. Stewart, & S. Ting-Toomey (Eds.), *Communication, culture, and organizational processes* (pp. 71–86). Beverly Hills, CA: Sage.

11

A CHINESE MODEL OF CONSTRUCTIVE CONFLICT MANAGEMENT

Yiheng Deng and Pamela Tremain Koch

Introduction

China's influence in the world has grown tremendously in recent decades. Previously most of the research focused on Westerners who were working and investing in China, but now the Chinese are increasingly working and investing overseas. Intercultural exchanges and their associated conflicts are common not only in foreign-based companies in China, but also in Chinese corporations which have offices in foreign countries. Hence, research that seeks to understand how conflict occurs in these intercultural workplaces continues to be very important. Leaders need to know how to derive positive benefits from intercultural conflict as well as how to restrict negative repercussions.

Acquisition of knowledge about intercultural conflict management, however, is hampered in two ways. First, Western theories have generally been applied to the Chinese context with little adaptation. Although useful in enabling cross-cultural comparisons, this approach is problematic because it does not incorporate native Chinese concepts and hence does not lead to a deep understanding of Chinese conflict behaviors. The problem is illustrated by the Western focus on direct conflict approaches that are likely to lead to beneficial outcomes (Rahim, 1983; Thomas & Kilmann, 1978). Since it is widely acknowledged that Chinese culture prioritizes harmony and conflict avoidance, these positive conflict outcomes are often thought difficult to achieve in the Chinese context as avoidance is known to have primarily negative outcomes. As Leung, Koch, and Lu (2002) indicated, "No matter the culture, avoidance and repression of conflict is as dysfunctional as domineering and imposition in the long run" (p. 215).

Fortunately, emic Chinese theory has grown in recent years (e.g., Hwang, 1998; Leung, Koch & Lu, 2002). However, although these emic understandings represent a significant step forward, research could be further advanced by merging etic and

DOI: 10.4324/9781003252955-13

emic understandings (Lin, 2010; Stahl & Tung, 2015). In this chapter, we attempt to develop a model which incorporates existing etic theory with Chinese emic concepts. We believe that it is important not only to understand Chinese conflict tendencies, but also to develop strategies to enable constructive conflict management in cross-cultural contexts.

This chapter integrates Western and Chinese models of conflict management to develop a framework of constructive conflict management applicable to cross-cultural interactions in Western companies in China and in Chinese companies in the West. We draw upon early research in cooperation and competition (Deutsch, 1949, 1968), more recent research that identifies relational and task aspects of conflict (e.g., Amason & Schweiger, 1997; De Dreu & Weingart, 2003; Jehn, 1997), and Chinese emic concepts such as face, *guanxi* (interrelations), and seniority. Combined with more recent research (Tjosvold & Sun, 2001; 2003; 2004), this new model may illustrate that constructive conflict management in the global workplace is viable for the Chinese.

Culture and Conflict Management

Collectivism and Conflict Management

Many early studies found that cultures differ in conflict handling styles (e.g., Elsayed-EkJiouly & Buda, 1996; Lee & Rogan, 1991; Miyahara et al., 1998; Oetzel,1998; Pearson & Stephan, 1998; Ting-Toomey et al., 1991; Trubisky, Ting-Toomey, & Lin, 1991). A common finding concerning intercultural conflict is that collectivists are less confrontational than their individualistic counterparts (e.g., et al.; Ting-Toomey, 1999; Ting-Toomey et al., 2000; Tse et al., 1994; Yuan, 2010). Nonetheless, some results found this difference varies according to the context (e.g., Cai & Fink, 2002; Koch & Deng, 2009; Liu & Chen, 2000; Peng, He, & Zhu, 2000; Wang, Jing & Klossek, 2007). Cai and Fink (2002), for example, studied cultural values at the individual level and conflict strategy choice and found little difference in strategy choice except for the dominating style. Their results indicated that although actual strategy use was similar, *perceptions* of these strategies differed.

Chinese Culture and Conflict Management

The extant literature primarily describes Chinese culture as conflict-avoidant (Chen, Liu, & Tjosvold, 2005; Liu & Chen, 2000; Ting-Toomey, 2010; Ting-Toomey & Kurogi, 1998), a tendency related to the importance of relationships in this collectivist society (Friedman, Chi, & Liu, 2006; Yuan, 2010). The tendency is often attributed to Confucian values, in particular the emphasis on harmony (Chen & Chung, 1994; Leung et al., 2002), which is thought to be so important that all other goals are subordinate to it.

Several factors have been identified that influence conflict in Chinese culture. For example, Chen, Ryan, and Chen (1999) picked out six conflict management factors, namely, face, *guanxi*, seniority, power, credibility, and severity of the conflict. The authors found that American and Chinese students ranked the importance of these six factors similarly. Chinese students ranked them in the order of severity of conflict, *guanxi*, credibility, seniority, power, and face; while American students ranked them in the order of severity of conflict, credibility, *guanxi*, power, seniority, and face. The similar ranking appears contrary to the dichotomized view of the two cultures. However, several differences were also found, with Chinese students being more authoritarian than American students. Chinese students scored face and seniority as significantly more important, while American students rated severity of the conflict significantly more important. One caveat to the findings, however, is that all the Chinese participants were students at an American university and were potentially influenced by accommodation to the dominant American culture.

A series of studies by Tjosvold and Sun (2000, 2001, 2003) confirm the distinction between relational and task conflict (Jehn, 1997). When the Chinese experience affronts to personal face, this greatly magnifies the relational aspects of conflict and increases the possibility of negative outcomes. While this appears to indicate that conflict can be particularly detrimental in China, they found this does not have to be the case. Drawing upon Deutsch's classic research on cooperative and competitive conflict (1949, 1968, 1990), they found that disagreement was not necessarily face threatening. In fact, participants did not feel personally slighted when others disagreed with their position, even when the disagreement was strongly worded. Hence, although relationships need to be protected, productive disagreements are possible.

Although the Chinese and Westerners do not interact in the same way, classic conflict theory (Deutsch, 1949, 1968, 1990) can help us understand Chinese conflict behaviors. For example, despite the fact that showing respect or focusing on cooperative goals may not be identical in all cultures (Wall Jr., 1990; Westwood & Chan, 1995), Tjosvold and Sun's studies (2000, 2001, 2003, 2004) indicate that open discussion and the exploration of opposing views are possible and constructive in the Chinese context if face is protected, a cooperative context is in place, coercion is avoided, and warm, non-verbal affect exists.

A significant question is whether Western conflict theories can be applied to the Chinese context. As indicated above, Tjosvold and Sun (2000, 2001, 2003) found that Deutsch's (1949, 1968, 1990) classic conflict theory was useful. Tjosvold and Wong (2004) proposed that the cooperative management of conflict can lead to better decisions and increase innovation in both collectivist and individualist cultures. They argued that in a suitable context Chinese values could contribute to managing conflict in a productive way, because the cooperative conflict can lead to innovation in a team. One way this might happen cross-culturally is via the creation of a "third culture" or "cultural tuning" (Leung et al., 2005), in which a new, common framework is created when differing cultural groups come together. Tjosvold and Wong (2004) indicated cultural tuning has three components. First, participants need to take a holistic perspective of cultural norms, motives, and cognitive processes of conflict management across all participants' cultures. Next, all cultural groups need to make mutual, synergistic efforts to deal with conflicts and to strengthen relationships. Finally, the parties involved need to reflect and learn from prior conflicts.

Constructive Conflict Management in the Chinese Context

Lin (2010) argued that emic and etic studies need to be integrated to better understand Chinese conflict management. Chinese culture and Chinese conflict management processes need to be understood and linked to general conflict research. Lin pointed out that Chinese research could greatly contribute to the advance of global conflict management studies.

Chinese Values

To understand Chinese conflict management, researchers must understand the influence of collectivism, Confucianism, and face on Chinese behaviors. Although collectivism has often been associated with the avoidance in a conflict (e.g., Leung et al., 2002), Morris et al. (1999) found that the preference for the avoidance strategy is primarily due to Confucian ethics rather than collectivistic values. Lin (2010) concurred that the collectivism explanation has been overused, and that other cultural concepts, such as Confucianism, might provide an alternative explanation.

Confucian values have strongly influenced Chinese conflict management (Leung et al., 2002). Confucianism emphasizes a harmonious balance between opposing and complementary forces (Hwang, 1998). Hwang (1998) concluded that the factor that ultimately determines Chinese conflict management is how important harmony and personal goals are in the process of conflict. Thus, Hwang proposed pursuing versus discarding personal goal and maintaining versus ignoring interpersonal harmony to plot Chinese conflict resolution behaviors.

However, it is questionable whether all conflict avoidance behaviors are due to Confucian influence. Leung, Koch, and Lu (2002) pointed out that while Confucianism emphasizes harmony and East Asians engage in conflict avoidance more than Westerners, classic Confucian teachings did not equate harmony with conflict avoidance. Thus, a multidimensional understanding of harmony is needed to understand Chinese conflict behaviors. They proposed a dualistic model of harmony, incorporating instrumental and value harmony, which contributes to an emic Chinese model of conflict behaviors (see Figure 11.1). In this model, harmony behavior may occur because good relationships are valued as an end in themselves (value harmony) or harmony behaviors may occur because they help people obtain other, unrelated goals (instrumental harmony). In the former case, harmony is sought because it is a moral imperative. In the latter, harmony is used to manipulate relationships for other ends. The true Confucian harmony prototype is value harmony. Confucian teachings do not encourage avoidance if festering conflict remains untreated. On the other hand, instrumental harmony does lead to conflict avoidance, as other instrumental goals drive the relationship.

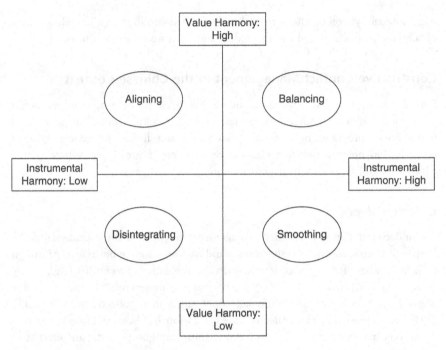

FIGURE 11.1 Emic Chinese model of conflict behaviors
Source: Leung et al., 2002, p. 212.

In Figure 11.1, prototypical conflict behaviors are displayed in a 2 x 2 framework distinguished by the extent to which instrumental harmony and value harmony are prized. When value harmony is high and instrumental harmony is low, individuals are willing to sacrifice personal goals in order to maintain harmonious relationships. The authors labeled this conflict style as aligning. When both value and instrumental harmony are high, individuals engage in balancing the conflict. When both are low, the conflict style is called disintegrating, as relationships are likely to be severed. In the final quadrant, individuals pursue instrumental harmony and ignore value harmony, which is labeled as smoothing, where superficial harmony is maintained in order to achieve personal goals.

Among the four conflict styles, balancing is similar to the collaborating or integrating style identified by Western scholars, where both relationship and task are taken into consideration. Both the balancing and collaborating/integrating styles aim to reach a win-win outcome of conflict resolution, which was called cooperative conflict by Deutsch (1949). The overlap between Western theories and the Chinese concept of balancing indicates that traditional Confucian values support managing conflict in a cooperative, open, and constructive fashion (Leung & Tjosvold, 1998).

Face is the third concept that must be considered in dealing with a conflict in Chinese society. Much research has indicated an association between face and

Chinese conflict management (e.g., Hwang, 1998; Jia, 1998; Oetzel & Ting-Toomey, 2003; Oetzel et al., 2001; Ting-Toomey & Kurogi, 1998; Ting-Toomey et al., 1991). Ting-Toomey and Kurogi's (1998) face negotiation theory prioritizes face as a central explanatory mechanism influencing conflict management styles. Ting-Toomey and Kurogi believe that face can also be used to understand conflict in Western cultures, "people in all cultures try to maintain and negotiate face in all communication situations ... (although) cultural variability, individual-level variables, and situational variables influence cultural members' selection of one set of face concerns over others" (p. 600).

Hwang (1998) treated harmony as the axis, and face and *guanxi* as the two wings of his theoretical model. Superficially, face and *guanxi* may hinder the open discussion of conflict due to the interdependent self-construal associated with both concepts. However, face and *guanxi* can also contribute to the formation of cooperative conflict. Both concepts have instrumental and value dimensions. Superficial face caring, for example, includes the maintenance of a perfunctory harmony, which decouples politeness from the Confucian ideal of benevolence.

While other factors such as power, reciprocity, group membership, and seniority are also important, harmony, *guanxi*, and face are the three major concepts in Chinese conflict management (Chen & Starosta, 1997). In addition to Confucianism and collectivism, the three concepts provide a foundation for understanding Chinese conflict management, though there are other traditional schools of thoughts, e.g., Daoism, Moism, communist ideology, legalism, and Buddhism illustrated in Figure 11.2, that also influence Chinese conflict behaviors (Lin, 2010).

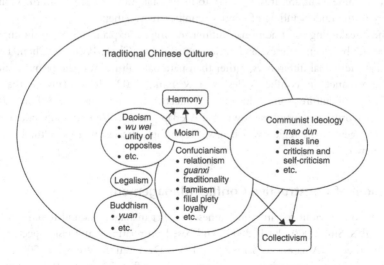

FIGURE 11.2 Components of Chinese culture that influence conflict behaviors
Source: Lin, 2010, p. 79.

Constructive Conflict Management in Chinese Society

Factors influencing conflict styles are further complicated by particular relationships in collectivistic cultures (Hofstede, 1980), which includes the status levels of conflicting parties. As Brew and Cairns (2004) mentioned, "divergence between Western expatriates and East Asian host-nationals in conflict management was mainly due to the power-distance dimension" (p. 331). They found that East Asian host nationals were more likely to use an indirect approach with their superiors and a direct approach with subordinates compared to expatriates from Australia. The finding is consistent with Hwang's model (1998), which indicates that in Chinese conflict management it is important to protect the face of those with a higher status.

Koch and Koch (2007) also found that increasing collective orientations resulted in less cooperation in out-group settings. Moreover, other studies show that the Chinese were more likely to pursue conflict with out-group members than with in-group members, and when conflicts occur, they were more likely to choose confrontational strategies with out-group members (Hwang, 1998; Leung, 1988; Ting-Toomey, 2005; Triandis, 2001). Hwang (1998) pointed out that three kinds of interpersonal relationship are crucial for understanding Chinese conflict management strategies: vertical in-group, horizontal in-group, and horizontal out-group. These relationships incorporate the status and group membership attributes in the process of conflict management.

Unfortunately, most studies have relied on traditional values to understand Chinese communication behaviors. As Hall (1973) stipulated, culture is not static, but "is about emergence, change and transformation" (p. 4). Lin (2010) also argued that, in addition to traditional influences, more recent influences such as communism also contribute to modern Chinese culture. It is necessary to incorporate new influences on the Chinese culture to the understanding of Chinese conflict management.

The weakening of traditional influences might explain research findings of similarities between Chinese and American students (Chen, Ryan, & Chen, 1999), and that individual differences, rather than national culture, was the primary source of the variance in conflict styles (Cai & Fink, 2002). It is plausible that the dichotomy of culture as individualism vs. collectivism is not valid (Cai & Fink, 2002). In other words, evidence has shown that overlaps exist in Western and Chinese conflict management strategies, which gives hope for a successful cross-cultural conflict management model.

A Model of Constructive Conflict Management

Drawing on previous research on Chinese conflict management and resolution (e.g., Tjosvold & Sun, 2000, 2001, 2003), and based on relational and task aspects of the conflict theory (Amason & Schweiger, 1997; De Dreu & Weingart, 2003; Jehn, 1997) as well as competitive and cooperative conflict (Deutsch, 1949,1968), the model of constructive cross-cultural management is proposed (see Figure 11.3). The model aims to describe processes by which conflict with Chinese may develop,

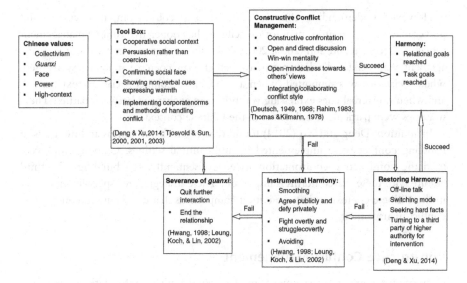

FIGURE 11.3 Model of cooperative conflict management with Chinese

escalate, or resolve. It maps out a path that will help people understand the conflict process, so that successful conflict management can be achieved. The following sections delineate the model of cooperative conflict management with Chinese specified in Figure 11.3.

Central Chinese Values

Previous studies provide insights into the understanding of Chinese central values, including collectivism, face, *guanxi*, and power. These values influence the tools used to promote constructive conflict management and the acceptance of conflict management practices. As indicated in previous research, as collectivists the Chinese have a tendency toward conflict avoidance, particularly when dealing with those of higher status. Protecting and giving face is important to maintain relationships or *guanxi* with in-group members.

The Strategic Toolbox

Although some research indicates that the Chinese tend to use a conflict avoidance style, Tjosvold and Sun (2000, 2001, 2003) found that the use of several conflict tools tends to increase the likelihood of constructive conflict practices, and conflict resulting in a successful outcome. Moreover, Leung et al. (2002) found that the application of these strategic tools reveals that direct conflict communication does not need to violate Confucian principles, but rather can build on them. Consequently, the Western cooperative conflict management theory can be promoted in the Chinese context.

However, understanding Chinese values such as collectivism, face, *guanxi*, and power may provide nourishment for or facilitate the cooperative conflict management processes. Tjosvold and Sun (2000, 2001, 2003) found that cooperative conflict management was facilitated when persuasive rather than coercive strategies were used, when social face was supported, when a cooperative conflict social context existed, and when nonverbal cues expressing warmth were exchanged between parties. These strategies were particularly influential in the Chinese context.

In addition, Deng and Xu (2014) found that when shared norms and methods of handling conflict were implemented in multicultural settings, Chinese employees used the constructive confrontation style. Consequently, the building of a third culture with these shared norms is important. These strategies are especially important in the Chinese context as they are critical components that contribute to constructive conflict management.

Constructive Conflict Management

Constructive conflict management involves constructive confrontation, open and direct discussion, a win–win mentality, open-mindedness towards others' view, and integrating/collaborating conflict style (Deutsch, 1949, 1968; Rahim, 1983; Thomas & Kilmann, 1978). Research has shown that open discussion and charity toward others consistently leads to better conflict outcomes (e.g., Chen, Liu, & Tjosvold, 2005; Leung et al., 2002; Tjosvold & Sun, 2001), though compromise, while not optimal, is still considered an acceptable conflict management style.

Success and Failure in Conflict Management

Successful cooperative conflict management leads to positive results because, first, harmony, which is central to Chinese traditional culture, is maintained; second, significant task goals are accomplished, or partially accomplished in the case of compromise. These two aspects of conflict are embedded more deeply in the relational focus of Chinese culture than in that of the West (Amason & Schweiger, 1997; De Dreu & Weingart, 2003; Jehn, 1997). A Chinese model of conflict management demands that true harmony is not only contingent upon the successful management of relationship goals, but is also contingent upon the successful management of task goals.

Unsuccessful conflict management may result in three outcomes. First, it may lead to instrumental harmony or the smoothing strategy where superficial harmony is used to achieve personal goals (Leung et al., 2002). In this situation, the Chinese may use the "obey publicly and defy privately" (Hwang, 1998, p. 29), or "fight overtly and struggle covertly" (Hwang, 1998, p. 31) strategy. In Western culture and sometimes also in China, this may involve an avoiding strategy, in which people refuse to admit that conflict exists (Rahim, 1983; Thomas & Kilmann, 1978). Second, unsuccessful conflict management may result in severance of the relationship. This occurs when *guanxi* is damaged and interactants may "tear off their faces" (Hwang, 1998, p. 27) as there is no longer any concern to protect or build up the face of the other.

Finally, there is the possibility of restoration. While harmony might not be immediately achieved, alternative methods may be used to repair the relationship. Deng and Xu (2014), for example, found that Chinese employees in a Sino-U.S. company developed coping strategies when constructive confrontation was difficult. This includes switching conflict management modes, seeking hard facts, resorting to off-line talk, and turning to a third party of higher authority to intervene. If successful, it may repair relationships and restore harmony, or the conflict may revert to instrumental harmony or complete severance.

Conclusion

Although conflict avoidance is often treated as the primary strategy used by the Chinese, studies have shown that this is not the only available tool (Tjosvold, Hui, & Law, 1998; Tjosvold, Nibler, & Wan, 2001). As Leung, Koch, and Lu (2002) argued, "Open discussion and cooperation do lead to better problem-solving and more positive outcomes. Openness has been found to be valued and useful in conflicts among Chinese" (p. 215). Traditional Chinese values derived from Confucianism dictate that real harmony should be integrated with benevolence and righteousness. This harmony is the foundation of cooperativeness and constructive conflict management.

Constructive conflict management in a multicultural workplace is possible for the Chinese because research has indicated that Chinese cultural values (e.g., harmony) do not necessarily lead to an avoiding style (Leunget al., 2002). Cai and Fink (2002) showed that the influence of collectivism on an individual psychological level (i.e., allocentrism) may be more influential than the impact of national level collectivism. This may be particularly true in a multinational corporation context where the company may attenuate the influence of national culture. In addition, while harmony was valued in traditional Chinese culture, it is not necessary to be antagonistic to open-minded discussion and the integration of the views of others. On the contrary, the pursuit of true harmony has the potential to foster a cooperative social environment. Furthermore, studies have found that the Western concept of cooperative conflict management can be applied to Chinese culture (Tjosvold & Sun, 2000, 2001, 2003; Tjosvold & Wong, 2004).

Multinational corporations in China would do well to incorporate Chinese values into their conflict management toolbox. It would help to create a healthy third culture (Casmir, 1993) and shared corporate norms for workplace conflict management. The strategies include the affirmation of social face, expressing warmth nonverbally, and the use of persuasive rather than coercive strategies; they help to create a cooperative environment in which the Chinese feel more comfortable participating in an open discussion (Tjosvold & Sun, 2000, 2001, 2003). These studies serve as a good starting point for exploring the possibility of constructive conflict management in the Chinese context.

In addition, the call for indigenous studies advocated by scholars such as Hwang (2000) and Lin (2010) is still relevant to the study of Chinese conflict management. We find research in the West can be useful in the Chinese context. In the same manner, we believe that Chinese concepts and theories have much to contribute to understanding the research in the West, as traditional Chinese concepts such as *guanxi* and face have been applied beyond the Chinese culture. We also believe that etic studies continue to be useful. Both emic and etic research are important when Chinese society is undergoing rapid and complex changes.

Finally, the model proposed in this chapter is subject to challenge. More studies need to be done to test the validity of the model, so that a solid theory can be developed to better understand factors affecting intercultural conflict management with the Chinese.

References

Amason, A. C. & Schweiger, D. M. (1997). The effects of conflict on strategic decision making effectiveness and organizational. In C. De Dreu & E. Van de Vliert (Eds.), *Using conflict in organizations* (pp. 101–115). London, UK: Sage.

Baxter, L. A. (1984). An investigation of compliance—gaining as politeness. *Human Communication Research*, 10(3), 427–456.

Brett, J. M., Tinsley, C. H., Shapiro, D. L., & Okumura, T. (2007). Intervening in employee disputes: How and when will managers from China, Japan and the USA act differently? *Management and Organization Review*, 3(2), 183–204.

Brew, F. P. & Cairns, D. R. (2004). Do culture or situational constraints determine choice of direct or indirect styles in intercultural workplace conflicts? *International Journal of Intercultural Relations*, 5(28), 331–352.

Cai, D. & Fink, E. (2002). Conflict style differences between individualists and collectivists. *Communication Monographs*, 69(1), 67–87.

Casmir, F. L. (1993). Third-culture building: A paradigm shift for international and intercultural communication. *Communication Yearbook*, 16, 407–428.

Chan, K. B., Luk, V., & Wang, G. X. (2005). Conflict and innovation in international joint ventures: Toward a new Sinified corporate culture or 'alternative globalization' in China. *Asia Pacific Business Review*, 11(4), 461–482.

Chen, G. M. & Chung, J.(1994). The impact of Confucianism on organizational communication. *Communication Quarterly*, 42(2), 93–105.

Chen, C. C., Meindl, J. R., & Hunt, R. G. (1997). Testing the effects of vertical and horizontal collectivism a study of reward allocation preferences in China. *Journal of Cross-Cultural Psychology*, 28(1), 44–70.

Chen, G., Liu, C. & Tjosvold, D. (2005). Conflict management for effective top management teams and innovation in China. *Journal of Management Studies*, 42(2), 277–300.

Chen, G. M., Ryan, K., & Chen, C. (1999). The determinants of conflict management among Chinese and Americans. *Intercultural Communication Studies*, 9, 163–175.

Chen, G. M. & Starosta, W. J. (1997). Chinese conflict management and resolution: Overview and implications, *Intercultural Communication Studies*, 7, 1–16.

Chung, J. (1996). Avoiding a "Bull Moose" rebellion: Particularistic ties, seniority, and third-party mediation. *International and Intercultural Communication Annual*, 20, 166–185.

De Dreu, C. K. W. & Weingart, L. R. (2003). Task versus relationship conflict, team performance, and team member satisfaction: a meta-analysis. *Journal of Applied Psychology*, 88(4), 741–749.

Deng, Y. & Xu, K. (2014). Chinese employees negotiating differing conflict management expectations in a US-based multinational corporation subsidiary in Southwest China. *Management Communication Quarterly*, 28(4), 609–624.

Deutsch, M. (1949). An experimental study of the effects of cooperation and competition upon group process. *Human Relations*, 2(3), 199–231.

Deutsch, M. (1968). The effects of co-operation and competition upon group processes. In J. R. French, B. Raven, D. Cartwright, & A. Zander (Eds.), *Group Dynamics* (pp. 461–481). New York, NY: Harper & Row.

Deutsch, M. (1990). Sixty years of conflict. *International Journal of Conflict Management*, 1(3), 237–263.

Elsayed-EkJiouly, S. M. & Buda, R. (1996). Organizational conflict: A comparative analysis of conflict styles across cultures. *International Journal of Conflict Management*, 7(1), 71–81.

Friedman, R., Chi, S. C., & Liu, L. A. (2006). An expectancy model of Chinese–American differences in conflict-avoiding. *Journal of International Business Studies*, 37(1), 76–91.

Hall, E. T. (1973). *The silent language*. New York, NY: Anchor.

Hall, E. T. (1989). *Beyond culture*. New York, NY: Anchor Press.

Hall, J. (1969). *Conflict management survey*. Conroe, TX: Teleometrics.

Hofstede, G. (1980). *Culture's consequences*. Beverly Hills, CA: Sage.

Huang, L. L. (1999). *Interpersonal harmony and conflict: Indigenous theories and research*. Taipei, Taiwan: Gui Guan.

Hwang, K. K. (1998). Guanxi and mientze: Conflict resolution in Chinese society. *Intercultural Communication Studies*, 7, 17–42.

Hwang, K. K. (2000). Chinese relationalism: Theoretical construction and methodological considerations. *Journal for the Theory of Social Behavior*, 30(2), 155–178.

Jehn, K. A. (1997). Affective and cognitive conflict in work groups: Increasing performance through value-based intragroup conflict. In C. K. W. De Dreu & E. Van de Vliert (Eds.), *Using conflict in organizations* (pp. 87–100). London, UK: Sage.

Jia, W.(1998). Facework as a Chinese conflict-preventive mechanism: A cultural/discourse analysis. *Intercultural Communication Studies*, 7, 43–62.

Kilmann, R. H. & Thomas, K. W. (1978). Four perspectives on conflict management: An attributional framework for organizing descriptive and normative theory. *Academy of Management Review*, 3(1), 59–68.

Knutson, T. J., Hwang, J. C., & Deng, B. C.(2000). Perception and management of conflict: A comparison of Taiwanese and US business employees. *Intercultural Communication Studies*, 9(2), 1–32.

Koch, P. T. & Deng, Y. (2009). *Under harmony and cooperation: An interview study of conflict and competition in Hong Kong organizations*. Paper presented at the Midwest Academy of Management Meeting, Chicago, IL.

Lee, H. O. & Rogan, R. G. (1991). A cross-cultural comparison of organizational conflict management behaviors. *International Journal of Conflict Management*, 2(3), 181–199.

Leung, K. (1988). Some determinants of conflict avoidance. *Journal of Cross-Cultural Psychology*, 19(1), 125–136.

Leung, K., Bhagat, R. S., Buchan, N. R., Erez, M., & Gibson, C. B. (2005). Culture and international business: Recent advances and their implications for future research. *Journal of International Business Studies*, 36(4), 357–378.

Leung, K., Koch, P. T., & Lu, L. (2002). A dualistic model of harmony and its implications for conflict management in Asia. *Asia Pacific Journal of Management*, 19(2–3),201–220.

Leung, K. & Tjosvold, D. (1998). *Conflict management in the Asia Pacific: Assumptions and approaches in diverse cultures*. Singapore: John Wiley & Son Ltd.

Leung, K. & Wu, P. G. (1998). Harmony as a double-edge sword in management. In B. S. Cheng, K. L. Huang, & C.C. Kuo (Eds.), *Human resources management in Taiwan and China.* Taipei, Taiwan: Yuan Liou Publishing.

Lin, C. (2010). Studying Chinese culture and conflict: A research agenda. *International Journal of Conflict Management,* 21(1), 70–93.

Liu, S. & Chen, G. M. (2000). Assessing Chinese conflict management styles in joint ventures. *Intercultural Communication Studies,* 9(2), 71–90.

Liu, L. A., Friedman, R. A., & Chi, S. C. (2005). 'Ren Qing' versus the 'Big Five': The role of culturally sensitive measures of individual difference in distributive negotiations. *Management and Organization Review,* 1(2), 225–247.

Miyahara, A., Kim, M. S., Shin, H. C., & Yoon, K. (1998). Conflict resolution styles among collectivist cultures: A comparison between Japanese and Koreans. *International Journal of Intercultural Relations,* 22(4), 505–525.

Morris, M. W., Leung, K., Ames, D., & Lickel, B. (1999). Views from inside and outside: Integrating emic and etic insights about culture and justice judgment. *Academy of Management Review,* 24(4), 781–796.

Oetzel, J. G. (1998). The effects of self-construals and ethnicity on self-reported conflict styles. *Communication Reports,* 11(2), 133–144.

Oetzel, J. G. & Ting-Toomey, S. (2003). Face concerns in interpersonal conflict: A cross-cultural empirical test of the face negotiation theory. *Communication Research,* 30 (6), 599–624.

Oetzel, J. G., Ting-Toomey, S., Masumoto, T., Yokochi, Y., Pan, X., Takai, J., & Wilcox, R. (2001). Face and facework in conflict: A cross-cultural comparison of China, Germany, Japan, and the United States. *Communication Monographs,* 68(3), 235–258.

Pearson, V. M. & Stephan, W. G. (1998). Preferences for styles of negotiation: A comparison of Brazil and the US. *International Journal of Intercultural Relations,* 22(1), 67–83.

Peng, S., He, Z., & Zhu, J. H. (2000). Conflict management styles among employees of Sino-American, Sino-French, and state-owned enterprises in China. *Intercultural Communication Studies,* 9(2), 33–46.

Pruitt, D. G. (2013). *Negotiation behavior.* New York, NY: Academic Press.

Putnam, L. L. & Wilson, C. E. (1982). Communicative strategies in organizational conflicts: Reliability and validity of a measurement scale. *Communication Yearbook,* 6, 629–652.

Rahim, M. A. (1983). A measure of styles of handling interpersonal conflict. *Academy of Management Journal,* 26(2), 368–376.

Stahl, G. K. & Tung, R. L. (2015). Towards a more balanced treatment of culture in international business studies: The need for positive cross-cultural scholarship. *Journal of International Business Studies,* 46(4), 391–414.

Tajfel, H. & Turner, J. C. (2004). The Social Identity Theory of Intergroup Behavior. In J. T. Jost & J. Sidanius (Eds.), *Political Psychology* (pp. 276–293). New York, NY: Psychology Press.

Thomas, K. W. & Kilmann, R. H. (1978). Comparison of four instruments measuring conflict behavior. *Psychological Reports,* 42(3c), 1139–1145.

Ting-Toomey, S. (2005). The matrix of face: An updated face-negotiation theory. In W. B. Gudykunst (Ed.), *Theorizing about intercultural communication* (pp. 71–92). Thousand Oaks, CA: Sage.

Ting-Toomey, S. (1999). Constructive intercultural conflict management. In S. Ting-Toomey (Ed.), *Communicating across cultures* (pp. 195–227). New York, NY: The Guilford Press.

Ting-Toomey, S. (2010). Applying dimensional values in understanding intercultural communication. *Communication Monographs,* 77(2), 169–180.

Ting-Toomey, S., Gao, G., Trubisky, P., Yang, Z., Soo Kim, H., Lin, S. L., & Nishida, T. (1991). Culture, face maintenance, and styles of handling interpersonal conflict: A study in five cultures. *International Journal of Conflict Management*, 2(4), 275–296.

Ting-Toomey, S. & Kurogi, A. (1998). Facework competence in intercultural conflict: An updated face-negotiation theory. *International Journal of Intercultural Relations*, 22(2), 187–225.

Ting-Toomey, S., Yee-Jung, K. K., Shapiro, R. B., Garcia, W., Wright, T. J., & Oetzel, J. G. (2000). Ethnic/cultural identity salience and conflict styles in four US ethnic groups. *International Journal of Intercultural Relations*, 24(1), 47–81.

Tjosvold, D., Hui, C., & Law, K. S. (1998). Empowerment in the manager-employee relationship in Hong Kong: Interdependence and controversy. *The Journal of Social Psychology*, 138(5), 624–636.

Tjosvold, D., Hui, C., & Sun, H. (2004). Can Chinese discuss conflicts openly? Field and experimental studies of face dynamics in China. *Group Decision and Negotiation*, 13(4), 351–373.

Tjosvold, D., Nibler, R., & Wan, P. (2001). Motivation for conflict among Chinese university students: Effects of others' expertise and one's own confidence on engaging in conflict. *The Journal of Social Psychology*, 141(3), 353–363.

Tjosvold, D. & Sun, H. F. (2000). Social face in conflict: Effects of affronts to person and position in China. *Group Dynamics: Theory, Research, and Practice*, 4(3), 259–271.

Tjosvold, D. & Sun, H. F. (2001). Effects of influence tactics and social contexts in conflict: An experiment on relationships in China. *International Journal of Conflict Management*, 12(3), 239–258.

Tjosvold, D. & Sun, H. F. (2003). Openness among Chinese in conflict: Effects of direct discussion and warmth on integrative decision making. *Journal of Applied Social Psychology*, 33(9), 1878–1897.

Tjosvold, D. & Wong, A. S. (2004). Innovating across cultural boundaries: Applying conflict theory to develop a common approach. *International Negotiation*, 9(2), 291–313.

Triandis, H. C. (2001). Individualism-collectivism and personality. *Journal of Personality*, 69 (6), 907–924.

Trubisky, P., Ting-Toomey, S., & Lin, S. L. (1991). The influence of individualism-collectivism and self-monitoring on conflict styles. *International Journal of Intercultural Relations*, 15(1), 65–84.

Tse, D. K., Francis, J., & Walls, J. (1994). Cultural differences in conducting intra-and intercultural negotiations: A Sino-Canadian comparison. *Journal of International Business Studies*, 25(3), 537–555.

Tsui, A. S., Schoonhoven, C. B., Meyer, M. W., Lau, C. M., & Milkovich, G. T. (2004). Organization and management in the midst of societal transformation: The People's Republic of China. *Organization Science*, 15(2), 133–144.

Wang, C. L., Lin, X., Chan, A. K., & Shi, Y. (2005). Conflict handling styles in international joint ventures: A cross-cultural and cross-national comparison. *Management International Review*, 45(1), 3–21.

Wang, G., Jing, R., & Klossek, A. (2007). Antecedents and management of conflict: Resolution styles of Chinese top managers in multiple rounds of cognitive and affective conflict. *International Journal of Conflict Management*, 18(1), 74–97.

WallJr., J. A. (1990). Managers in the People's Republic of China. *The Executive*, 4(2), 19–32.

Westwood, R. I. & Chan, A. (1995). The transferability of leadership training in the East Asian context. *Asia Pacific Business Review*, 2(1), 68–92.

Yuan, W. (2010). Conflict management among American and Chinese employees in multinational organizations in China. *Cross Cultural Management: An International Journal*, 17(3), 299–311.

12

INTERCULTURAL COMPETENCE AND HARMONIOUS INTERCULTURAL RELATIONS

Interdisciplinary Perspectives and Insights

Helen Spencer-Oatey

Introduction

There is increasing awareness of the importance of intercultural competence and various rationales for its importance have been proposed. For instance, the 'global competence framework' produced by the OECD (2018) identifies four reasons as to why we need global (intercultural) competence:

- To live harmoniously in multicultural communities
- To thrive in a changing labour market
- To use media platforms effectively and responsibly
- To support the Sustainable Development Goals (of the United Nations).

This chapter focuses on the first one: living harmoniously in multicultural communities. The OECD (2018) explains the importance of this element as follows:

> Education for global competence can promote cultural awareness and respectful interactions in increasingly diverse societies. [...] Contemporary societies call for complex forms of belonging and citizenship where individuals must interact with distant regions, people and ideas while also deepening their understanding of their local environment and the diversity within their own communities. By appreciating the differences in the communities to which they belong—the nation, the region, the city, the neighbourhood, the school—young people can learn to live together as global citizens.
>
> *(pp. 4–5)*

This goal raises several questions, including: what does intercultural competence for harmonious interactions entail, how can it be fostered, and what criteria can/

DOI: 10.4324/9781003252955-14

should be used to judge whether or not it has been achieved? The OECD (2018) framework proposes four target dimensions that people need to apply in their lives in order to develop intercultural competence and one of these is particularly relevant to the goal of living harmoniously in multicultural communities. It is explained as follows:

> **Dimension 3: Engage in open, appropriate and effective interactions across cultures**.
>
> This dimension describes what globally competent individuals are able to do when they interact with people from different cultures. They understand the cultural norms, interactive styles and degrees of formality of intercultural contexts, and they can flexibly adapt their behaviour and communication to suit. This dimension addresses appreciation for respectful dialogue, desire to understand the other and efforts to include marginalised groups. It emphasises individuals' capacity to interact with others across differences in ways that are open, appropriate and effective. Open interactions mean relationships in which all participants demonstrate sensitivity towards, curiosity about and willingness to engage with others and their perspectives. Appropriate refers to interactions that respect the expected cultural norms of both parties. In effective communication, all participants are able to make themselves understood and understand the other.
>
> *(OECD, 2018, p. 10)*

In terms of competence, this framework identifies two core abilities: understanding of "the cultural norms, interactive styles and degrees of formality of intercultural contexts" and the ability to "flexibly adapt their behaviour and communication" (p. 10). Moreover, three criteria are identified for judging people's interaction: openness, appropriateness, and effectiveness. In reality, these are extremely challenging competence goals and criteria and it is important, therefore, to explore them in greater detail. In this chapter I argue that valuable insights can be gained from work in interpersonal pragmatics. First, though, I consider how intercultural competence as it pertains to interpersonal relations across cultures has been conceptualised in the intercultural literature.

Interpersonal Relations and Conceptualisations of Intercultural Competence

There are numerous conceptualisations of intercultural competence in the literature (e.g., for reviews, see Spencer-Oatey & Franklin, 2009; Spitzberg & Changnon, 2009). Many of these are compositional in approach (Spitzberg & Changnon, 2009) in that they aim to specify the components comprising intercultural competence. Table 12.1 summarises a number of key conceptualisations that have been proposed by various authors.

TABLE 12.1 Conceptualisations of the component constructs of intercultural competence according to different authors

Author(s)	Component Constructs
Brinkmann and van Weerdenburg (2014)	Intercultural sensitivity (cultural awareness & attention to signals); Intercultural communication (active listening & adapting communication style); Building commitment (building relationships & reconciling stakeholder needs); Managing uncertainty (openness to cultural diversity & exploring new approaches)
Byram (1997)	Attitudes; Knowledge; Skills of interpreting & relating; Skills of discovering & interacting; Critical cultural awareness/political education
Chen and Starosta (2005)	Personal attributes; Communication skills; Psychological adaptation; Cultural awareness
Deardorff (2006)	Attitudes; Knowledge & comprehension; Desired internal outcomes; Desired external outcomes
Gudykunst (2004)	Motivation; Knowledge; Skills
Mendenhall, Stevens, Bird, and Oddou (2010)	Perception management; Relationship management; Self management
Prechtl and Davidson Lund (2009)	Tolerance for ambiguity; Behavioural flexibility; Communicative awareness; Knowledge discovery; Respect for otherness; Empathy
Spencer-Oatey and Stadler (2009)	Knowledge & ideas; Communication; Relationships; Personal qualities and dispositions
Ting-Toomey (1999); Ting-Toomey and Dorjee (2019)	Mindfulness: Knowledge factors, Motivational factors (mindset and attitudes), Skill factors (communication)

As can be seen from Table 12.1, only three of the frameworks explicitly identify relationship management as a core component of intercultural competence. Of course, many of the attributes listed by others are also relevant, such as respect for otherness (Prechtl & Davidson Lund, 2009) and mindfulness (Ting-Toomey, 1999; Ting-Toomey & Dorjee, 2019). Communication, which is listed by almost all authors, is also of crucial importance for relationship management. Nevertheless, relational management needs to be identified more explicitly and this is something that Deardorff (2009) draws attention to. In her synthesis of the 13 chapters on conceptualising intercultural competence in her handbook, she argues that a stronger focus needs to be given to it, noting that it emerges as a theme in many of the chapters, especially in non-Western contexts.

It is important, therefore, to consider how competence in managing interpersonal relations in intercultural contexts can be conceptualised. Mendenhall et al. (2010) and Spencer-Oatey and Franklin (2009) each identify a number of component elements (see Table 12.2), but there is clearly a need for more work in this area, especially from a process perspective. One potential source of inspiration is work in interpersonal pragmatics on relations and relating, and I turn to that next.

TABLE 12.2 Intercultural relationship/rapport management competencies according to Mendenhall et al. (2010) and Spencer-Oatey and Franklin (2009)

Author(s)	Competency	Explanation
Relationship management global competencies according to Mendenhall et al. (2010, pp. 9–14)	Relationship interest	The extent to which people exhibit interest in, and awareness of, their social environment
	Interpersonal engagement	The degree to which people have a desire and willingness to initiate and maintain relationships with people from other cultures
	Emotional sensitivity	The extent to which people have an awareness of, and sensitivity to, the emotions and feelings of others
	Self awareness	The degree to which people are aware of: 1) their strengths and weaknesses in interpersonal skills, 2) their own philosophies and values, 3) how past experiences have helped shape them into who they are as a person, and 4) the impact their values and behavior have on relationships with others
	Social flexibility	The extent to which individuals present themselves to others in order to create a favourable impression and to facilitate relationship building
Rapport management intercultural competencies according to Spencer-Oatey and Franklin (2009, p. 102)	Contextual awareness	Sensitive to key features of the interaction, including participant relations (equality/inequality and distance/closeness), the rights and obligations of people's roles, and the nature of the communicative activity
	Interpersonal attentiveness	Pays focused attention to people's face sensitivities (e.g., their status, competence, social identity), behavioural expectations and interactional goals, and manages them effectively
	Social information gathering	Gathers information about the interactional context (e.g., people's roles and positions in a hierarchy) by asking relevant others or by careful observation
	Social attuning	Uses indirect signals such as paralanguage (e.g., intonation, speaking volume and speed, pausing) and non-verbal communication (e.g., eye contact and other elements of body language) to infer social meaning – how he/she is coming across to others (how his/her behaviour is being evaluated from a relational point of view) and what the emotional state (e.g. offended, annoyed) of the other person is
	Emotion regulation	Resilient – is able to handle criticism or embarrassment when things go wrong. Accepts and feels at ease with people who are different e.g., who hold different views or values
	Stylistic flexibility	Uses a range of strategies flexibly so that they are congruent with people's rapport sensitivities

Pragmatic Perspectives on Interpersonal Relations

A very important branch of pragmatics – (im)politeness theory – has focused on interpersonal relations for many years. Early scholars defined (im)politeness in those terms, as the following quotations indicate:

> [The role of the politeness principle is] to maintain the social equilibrium and the friendly relations which enable us to assume that our interlocutors are being cooperative in the first place.
>
> *Leech (1983, p. 82)*

> I define linguistic politeness as the language usage associated with smooth communication ...
>
> *Ide (1989, p. 225)*

> Politeness can be defined as a means of minimizing the risk of confrontation in discourse.
>
> *Lakoff (1989, p. 102)*

In other words, they drew attention to the role that language plays in maintaining harmonious relations and minimising confrontation. Over the years there have been numerous concepts and frameworks proposed, and recently there has been a particularly strong move towards the relational in interpersonal pragmatics. This has also involved an increasing emphasis on evaluation rather than just on what one should do or say. This means that it is important not only to understand what strategies can be used to manage smooth relations, but also to understand the evaluation process that underpins people's judgements of the appropriateness of behaviour. Despite Fraser and Nolan (1981, p. 96) arguing many years ago that words and phrases are not inherently polite or impolite, but rather are judged as such by participants, strangely there has been remarkably little research into this process since then. However, this has begun to change recently, with a number of papers reporting empirical studies of people's evaluative judgements. Moreover, there have also been a number of publications that have aimed at theorising the evaluation process.

Spencer-Oatey and Kádár (2021) provide a particularly detailed explication of the evaluation process and here I summarise the steps of the evaluation process. They take place in a flash, almost instantaneously, but can be seen as entailing four key elements, which for the sake of simplicity I refer to here as steps:

Step 1: Assessment of the 'normalcy' of the behaviour for the given context. If it is unexpected, then ...
Step 2: Evaluation of the behaviour and the agent, drawing on the evaluation warrant which comprises:
a   Interpersonal concerns: face + goals + rights and obligations
b   Social and moral orders

Step 3: Judgement of appropriateness (offensive – complimentary) of behaviour and agent

Step 4: Impact on interpersonal rapport.

Step 1: Contextually Based Normalcy Judgements

Behaviour always takes place in a situational context and our interpretation of this situational context is a very important aspect of the evaluation process. People build up background knowledge over time on a wide range of different types of situational context, holding schematic-type knowledge on what typically happens, who is present to say and do what, and so on. In other words, through socialisation in a range of social groups, people develop cultural schemas and cultural norms about situations and their participants, and these give rise to expectations as to what will and will not happen, as well as to what should or should not happen.

A very useful notion used in pragmatics for interpreting the context is that of communicative activity (also known as activity type). Allwood (2000, 2007) has developed this into a framework, specifying the key contextual parameters, as shown in Table 12.3.

Allwood explains that the type, purpose, or function of an activity gives it its rationale, and that procedures typically become established in order to facilitate the regular and smooth achievement of that purpose. Moreover, in order for the procedures to be carried out, there are standard activity roles with associated rights and obligations, which require an appropriate level of competence to fulfil them. Similarly, there are expected artifacts (e.g., a whiteboard and projector for a lecture) and features of the environment (e.g., rows of seats, possibly tiered, for a lecture).

People bring their socialisation/experience-based expectations to any communicative activity, and it is these expectations that give rise to evaluative moments. If a form of behaviour is completely expected, it will fall below the evaluation trigger threshold and so will typically not even be noticed. If it is perceived to be a deviation, but only a minor one, it will typically be ignored, and the evaluation process

TABLE 12.3 Allwood's communicative activity contextual parameters

Parameter	Explanation
Purpose	The reason for the activity taking place (i.e., its function and purpose), along with the associated procedures for achieving it.
Roles	The expectations (and sometimes formal requirements) associated with the activity, especially the rights, obligations, and skills needed to perform the given roles of the participants of the activity.
Artifacts	The instruments, tools, media, and other resources used in the process of carrying out the activity.
Environment	The environment the activity occurs in – both the physical environment (e.g., sound, temperature, and furniture) and the social environment (macro factors such as social institution, socio-linguistic context).

stops here on this occasion. In other words, instances of behaviour that a participant regards as not deviating or only deviating to a minor degree from their expectations, remain below the evaluation trigger threshold and are probably barely noticed.

When the divergence from expectations is greater and exceeds a person's subjective trigger threshold (i.e., it is marked in some way), this is when the (im) politeness evaluation process really gets started. It is important to note that the trigger threshold can be exceeded in both positive and negative senses.

Step 2: Evaluation of Behaviour and Agent

Once evaluation has been activated, both the behaviour itself and the person performing the behaviour are subject to evaluation. People draw on the evaluation warrant when making their evaluations. As indicated in the list of steps above, the evaluation warrant comprises two elements: interpersonal sensitivities (face, goals, and rights and obligations) and the socio-moral warrant. The interpersonal sensitivities (Step 2a) refer to Spencer-Oatey's (2008, 2015) bases of rapport, which she explains as follows:

> *Face*: It is concerned with people's sense of worth, dignity, and identity, and is associated with issues such as respect, honour, status, reputation, and competence. People have a fundamental desire for others to evaluate them positively and *not* to evaluate them negatively. When others fail to do this, it can cause upset and disturb rapport.
>
> *Goals*: People often (although not always) have specific goals when they interact with others. These can be relational as well as transactional (i.e., task-focused) in nature. These 'wants' can significantly affect their perceptions of rapport because any failure to achieve them can cause frustration and annoyance and hence disturb rapport.
>
> *Rights and obligations*: People regard themselves as having a range of sociality rights and obligations in relation to other people. People develop behavioural expectations in relation to their perceived sociality rights and obligations, and if these are not fulfilled, interpersonal rapport can be negatively affected.
>
> *(Spencer-Oatey 2008, pp. 14, 17, 15)*

When people make evaluations based on these interpersonal sensitivities, they often add comments to justify their appraisal; for instance, someone may say "I was really embarrassed by what he said" (face threat), or "She had no right to treat me like that" (infringement of sociality rights). However, sometimes people appeal to a 'deeper reason', arguing that something is 'unethical' or simply 'wrong'. In other words, they are using a moral criterion. Several theorists within politeness theory (e.g., Haugh, 2013a; Kádár & Haugh, 2013) have drawn attention to this, arguing that people implicitly subject behaviour to moral evaluations. However, these authors do not unpack the concept further, and so it is useful to refer to work in moral psychology for more insights. A particularly well-known framework is that developed by Haidt and his colleagues (e.g., Graham et al., 2018; Haidt & Kesebir,

2010): the Moral Foundations Theory. Their core theory identifies five moral foundations:

- *Care/harm*: Upholding of the virtues of care and compassion; disapproval of harm or neglect of others.
- *Fairness/cheating*: Upholding of the notions of justice and rights; disapproval of unfair treatment and cheating.
- *Loyalty/betrayal*: Upholding the obligations of group membership, including qualities such as loyalty, self-sacrifice; disapproval of betrayal.
- *Authority/subversion*: Upholding of the obligations of hierarchical relationships, such as obedience and respect for those in authority; disapproval of subversion and failure to fulfil role-based duties
- *Purity/degradation*: Upholding of the virtues of chastity and wholesomeness; disapproval of failure to control desires or degrade spiritual values.

People often appeal (frequently implicitly, but sometimes explicitly) to the fundamental values shown in their framework; for instance, they may appeal to the need to show care for others, to act fairly and honestly, to be loyal, to respect authority, and to show moral uprightness.

Spencer-Oatey and Kádár (2021) label these concerns the socio-moral warrant. In interpersonal pragmatics, authors such as Haugh (2013a) and Kádár and Haugh (2013) argue that people's (im)politeness judgements (implicitly) appeal to a moral order. In moral psychology, however, a distinction is widely made between social proscriptions/prescriptions and moral proscriptions/prescriptions (e.g., Huebner, Lee, & Hauser, 2010; Turiel, 1983). Similarly, some pragmaticists (e.g., Culpeper, 2011) have distinguished between 'social oughts' and 'moral oughts'. The basic idea is that some behavioural conventions seem to be just a matter of convention – they are local protocols and simply facilitate social interaction through a shared understanding of group etiquette. There does not seem to be a strong moral underpinning to them. These are known as social rules or 'social oughts'. In contrast, moral rules seem to proscribe behaviour that is more wrong and more punishable, with the wrongness being more authority independent. So, for example, if a child fails to raise his or her hand in class (when that is what the teacher requires them to do), most adults would interpret this as less 'bad' than someone physically hitting another child so hard that the latter is injured. Hand raising would be regarded as a social rule or social convention while avoiding physical or emotional harm to others would be regarded as a moral rule. In psychology, many theorists (e.g., Huebner et al., 2010) (but not all) consider there to be a continuum between social orders and moral orders, and the name 'socio-moral' warrant is an attempt to indicate this. However, breaches on all parts of the spectrum can affect interpersonal relations. There is likely to be greater cultural variation towards the social order end of the spectrum and so acquiring intercultural competence in upholding the social order is likely to be particularly challenging.

Steps 3 and 4: Judgement of Behaviour and Agent and the Impact on Rapport

The final two steps in the evaluation process are the judgement itself and its relational consequences. The judgement can be positive (i.e., complimentary) or negative (i.e., offensive) and frequently it is applied to both the behaviour and the agent (i.e., the person performing the behaviour). In fact, people often make no conscious distinction between the two and simply focus on the agent. This can have very important consequences for the degree of rapport between the participants concerned, enhancing it or undermining it. When the judgement is positive, it is likely to enhance interpersonal relations. When the judgement is negative, it is likely to have a negative impact on interpersonal relations, undermining rapport, unless other steps are taken (such as an apology) to mitigate it.

Intercultural Competence and Harmonious Relations

How then can these pragmatic perspectives inform our understanding of intercultural competence? I explore the question in relation to two of the statements made by the OECD (2018):

> They [globally competent individuals] understand the cultural norms, interactive styles and degrees of formality of intercultural contexts, and they can flexibly adapt their behaviour and communication to suit.
>
> *(OECD, 2018, p. 10)*

> It [intercultural competence] emphasises individuals' capacity to interact with others across differences in ways that are open, appropriate and effective. [...] Appropriate refers to interactions that respect the expected cultural norms of both parties.
>
> *(OECD, 2018, p. 10)*

Understanding Cultural Norms

The word 'norm' has several different meanings; for example, Cialdini (e.g., 2007, 2012) distinguishes between descriptive norms (what is typically/usually said or done) and injunctive norms (what people believe ought to be said or done, or what ought to be avoided). Both are important from an intercultural competence point of view, although injunctive norms are likely to have a greater impact on rapport if breached. Both are highly context dependent. This raises a very fundamental question: how feasible is it for anyone to understand the cultural norms for all social groups and in all contexts? I would argue that this is an impossible task for anyone. The goal should not be for people to understand (in advance) what norms will be operating in innumerable unspecified situations, but rather to have the ability to perceive norms, whatever context they find themselves in. This is in line with the well-known saying, "Give a man a fish (i.e., explain specific patterns of behaviour), and you feed him for a day. Teach a man to fish (i.e., give him the tools to identify the patterns operating in the specific context they are in), and you feed him for a lifetime."

To help achieve this, I would suggest the following approach, at least as a starting point: that people are helped to understand the key parameters for interpreting (a) unfamiliar contexts and (b) interactional styles. In terms of the former, Allwood's (2000, 2007) explication of communicative activities (outlined above) provides an extremely useful framework for considering key features of the context. This then needs to be supplemented with sensitivity to/mindfulness towards interactional styles. There is still debate over the conceptualisation of styles, although the notion of relational dialectics offers a potential way forward. For example, Baxter and Montgomery (1996) identify three main dialectics that are pertinent to interpersonal relations: connection–separation, openness–closedness, and certainty–uncertainty, each with multivocal constellations.

An example may be helpful here to illustrate the importance of these two issues. The data comes from a study by Wang (2013) in which she collected recordings and reflections on the experiences of a group of Chinese officials who visited their counterparts in the USA (see also Spencer-Oatey & Wang, 2019; Wang & Spencer-Oatey, 2015). The example presented here concerns the degree to which people display emotion or show restraint (identified by Spencer-Oatey, 2013, as a multivocal variant of openness–closedness), and the associated evaluation judgements.

On one occasion, the delegation was attending a meeting in a very grand, majestic building in a certain US city. They were greatly struck by the grandeur of the building and very enthusiastically took photos for five minutes, while the American host who was receiving them stood waiting patiently for them. In the evening, at an internal delegation meeting, the Head of Delegation reprimanded the Chinese delegates as shown below:

HEAD: I could understand the awe that everyone experienced [...] but taking photos continuously before the meeting was not polite and lost part of our face. Fortunately, the research director was patient enough to look at us taking photos for 5 minutes. I did not stop you because we had the interpreter employed by the Americans who could understand Chinese. I didn't want to make you lose face and moreover I didn't want to lose our delegation's face. Such behaviour was detrimental to our delegation's image. If we were in a scenic spot, just do it, but we were in a formal setting dealing with American counterparts and we must consider our image. Everyone's behaviour will impact our group's image.

(Wang & Spencer-Oatey, 2015, p. 58)

In other words, the Head of Delegation wanted his delegation members to show emotional restraint in their behaviour, and when they did not, he regarded it as a loss of face for the delegation. However, on another occasion he took the opposite position. Towards the end of the delegation's visit to the USA, the members attended a farewell banquet organised by their American hosts. In the evening, at their internal delegation meeting, the Head and Deputy Head of Delegation, expressed regret at the restrained atmosphere during the event:

HEAD: The problem was that the farewell lunch was too short and too quiet – too short to develop deeper personal relationships, and too quiet for a farewell lunch of an official delegation trip.

DEPUTY HEAD: I also felt that the farewell lunch lacked the due atmosphere of a successful completion of a visit. It should be a jolly, warm and exciting event where people talk animatedly, emphasise how successful the trip has been, indicate the possibility for future cooperation and exchange visits, and show greater care for each other's work and life, and so on. Most of our expectations fell short. No liquor and no animated talk. It was too formal and too quiet for a farewell lunch and it was a little bit disappointing.

(Wang, 2013, p. 180)

On this occasion, both the Head and the Deputy Head of the delegation were disappointed that little emotion was shown – that everything was so quiet, with no animated discussion and no spirits for toasting, and that it therefore did not suitably reflect the success of the trip.

What emerges very clearly from these comments from the Head and Deputy Head is the vital impact of context on what counts as an 'appropriate' interactional style. The communicative activity of 'farewell banquet' was treated as significantly different from the early stages of a formal meeting. In applying Allwood's (2000, 2007) framework, we can note the impact of all elements (purpose, roles, artifacts, environment) on the expected level of emotional display–restraint. As a result, in one context, conveying enthusiasm was criticised, while in another context lack of animation was criticised. The Chinese delegation clearly had normative expectations as to what 'should' and 'should not' happen in each context and made evaluative judgements of 'successfulness' and 'appropriateness' accordingly.

In terms of developing intercultural competence in 'understanding cultural norms', it is possible that with experience people may be able to build up their understanding of norms in given contexts with certain types of participants. However, it must always be remembered that if the participants change (e.g., university academics rather than government officials, even when the nationalities are kept constant) and/or if the communicative activity changes, the norms and associated expectations will change too. As a result, it can be dangerous to predict how people of a given nationality will behave; rather, if people are familiar with the key parameters that can lead to different (normative) behaviour and can develop skills in 'reading the situation' and being sensitive to prevalent interactional styles, this is likely to be more useful in the long run.

People are likely to need help in learning about these parameters, but they also need more than that. Spencer-Oatey, Franklin, and Lazidou (2022) propose the notion of the 'Global Fitness Development Cycle'. Referring to intercultural competence as 'global fitness' (to try and make the concept more accessible to non-specialists), they argue that, as with physical fitness, 'global fitness' needs to be developed on an ongoing basis and entails three main aspects: the 'global fitness environment' (cf. the gym), 'global fitness engagement' (cf. exercises), and 'global fitness in practice' (cf. physical fitness). These three elements of the Global Fitness Development Cycle all support each other in an interactive manner, helping foster a person's ongoing journey of building global fitness (i.e., developing intercultural competence).

The notion of 'global fitness engagement' builds on the concept of transformative learning (Mezirow, 2000; Taylor, 1994). According to this theory of learning, two key elements are particularly important for personal development: an unexpected or challenging experience followed by reflection. Spencer-Oatey et al. (2022) argue that this process is particularly valuable for individuals who wish to develop 'global fitness' and demonstrate it in practice. People need to move outside their comfort zones and engage with difference; in other words, they need to embrace the unfamiliar so that new thinking is stimulated. Importantly, though, this is not enough on its own; two further steps are necessary. They need to reflect on their experiences, thinking them through from different perspectives; in other words, they need to reflect mindfully. They need to try out new ways of doing things, making further adjustments in accordance with feedback.

Appropriateness as a Criterion of Competence

Several competence criteria have been proposed by theorists, most notably effectiveness and appropriateness. Ting-Toomey and Dorjee (2019) also identify adaptability, while Dai and Chen (2015) refer to the moral dimension. In relation to interpersonal harmony, the criterion of appropriateness is very widely mentioned. Ting-Toomey and Dorjee (2019, p. 139) define it as follows:

> Communication appropriateness refers to the degree to which the exchanged behaviors are regarded as proper and match the expectations generated by the culture's insiders.

Yet Spencer-Oatey and Franklin (2009) explain that the criterion poses several challenges: it is a subjective judgement and it is always context dependent. They also argue that it is the issue of 'whose appropriateness' that needs engaging with more thoroughly:

> A shortcoming of the appropriateness criterion as commonly conceptualized is that it is often interpreted as the creation of *cultural* appropriateness with respect to the other *interactant(s)* rather than *communicative* appropriateness with respect to the *communication situation* in which the interactants find themselves. There is often an implicit assumption that the interaction of the parties to the communication must be modified primarily to take account of cultural

differences between the interactants, for example, in communication style. Another implicit assumption is that the other interactant is a prototypical member of the other or 'host' culture towards whose culturally based expectations the first interactant has to adjust, rather than a person possessing intercultural experience and/or competence *also* able to adjust in order to create interactional appropriateness.

(pp. 54–55, emphasis in original)

The pragmatic perspective on the evaluation process, explained above, offers a way of exploring the issue of appropriateness in greater depth. First, interlocutors need to pay attention to the interpersonal sensitivities of face, goals, and rights and obligations. In fact, it should be possible to be sensitive to all participants' face concerns and to gain insights into their respective goals, if all are mindful as they interact. However, rights and obligations are more challenging because they are particularly subject to cultural variation. On the one hand, they are highly context specific; on the other, people's rights and obligation claims are affected by their sense of the socio-moral warrant. Appeals to the more social aspects of the warrant are particularly subject to cultural variation, while for more serious violations, the various components of Haidt's (e.g., Graham et al., 2018; Haidt & Kesebir, 2010) Moral Foundations Theory can offer helpful insights.

Dai and Chen (2015, pp. 107–108) identify the moral dimension as important for harmonious relationships and depict it as underpinning the other facets of intercultural competence. Dai (2019) has also rightly pointed out that the moral dimension has been omitted from most (if not all) Western conceptions of intercultural competence. Clearly, given the importance of the socio-moral order in interpersonal pragmatics, along with its recognition within some Chinese conceptions of intercultural competence, there is a definite need for it to be incorporated more centrally within intercultural competence frameworks. Yet more work needs to be done on what it entails; for example, how do Dai and Chen's (2015) moral dimension components relate to those of Haidt's (Graham et al., 2018; Haidt & Kesebir, 2010) Moral Foundations Theory, and to those in other frameworks such as in Janoff-Bulman and Carnes' (2018) Moral Motives Model? It seems clear that the moral criterion operates at a deep level, yet is also extremely important, warranting further attention, particularly with respect to interpersonal relations.

Conclusion

Harmonious interpersonal relations are vitally important for individuals, social groups, and whole nations. They are never easy to achieve but can be particularly challenging in intercultural contexts. They are, therefore, an extremely important facet of intercultural competence, yet strangely there has been little unpacking of what this means both conceptually and practically. This chapter has explored the insights that can be offered from work in interpersonal pragmatics and has argued that achieving 'understanding of norms' is particularly challenging, while appropriateness is a complex concept that raises the question of 'appropriate for whom'? There are no quick and easy solutions to these issues, but it seems that further research into the evaluation process and the criteria that people use for making their judgements could be highly beneficial. Graham et al. (2018, p. 213) acknowledge that "there likely are many other moral foundations" and Spencer-Oatey and Xing (2019) found that neither the Moral Foundations Theory (e.g., Graham et al., 2018; Haidt & Kesebir, 2010) nor the Moral Motives Model (e.g., Janoff-Bulman & Carnes, 2018) is fully satisfactory for explaining data. So perhaps a useful way forward would be to combine work within moral psychology with Chinese perspectives on the moral dimension of intercultural competence (Dai & Chen, 2015) and thereby to achieve synergistic new insights.

References

Allwood, J. (2000). An activity approach to pragmatics. In H. Bunt & W. Black (Eds.), *Abduction, belief and context in dialogue: Studies in computational pragmatics* (pp. 47–80). Berlin: John Benjamins.

Allwood, J. (2007). Activity based studies of linguistic interaction. *Gothenburg Papers in Theoretical Linguistics*. Available at: https://halshs.archives-ouvertes.fr/hprints-00460511/document (accessed 23 May 2018).

Baxter, L. A. & Montgomery, B. M. (1996). *Relating: dialogues and dialectics*. New York: Guilford Press.

Brinkmann, U. & van Weerdenburg, O. (2014). *Intercultural readiness: Four competences for working across cultures*. Basingstoke: Palgrave Macmillan.

Byram, M. (1997). *Teaching and assessing intercultural communicative competence*. Clevedon, OH: Multilingual Matters.

Chang, W.-L. M. & Haugh, M. (2011). Evaluations of im/politeness of an intercultural apology. *Intercultural Pragmatics*, 8(3), 411–442. DOI:10.1515/iprg.2011.019.

Chen, G. M. & Starosta, W. J. (2005). *Foundations of intercultural communication* (2nd ed.). Lanham, MD: University Press of America.

Cialdini, R. B. (2007). Descriptive social norms as underappreciated sources of social control. *Psychometrika*, 72(2), 263–268.

Cialdini, R. B. (2012). The focus theory of normative conduct. In P. A. M. Van Lange, A. W. Kruglanski, & E. T. Higgins (Eds.), *Handbook of theories of social psychology, Vol 2* (pp. 295–312). London: Sage.

Culpeper, J. (2011). *Impoliteness: Using language to cause offence*. Cambridge: Cambridge University Press.

Dai, X. D. (2019). *Intercultural competence theory building in China: A thirty years' review*. Paper presented at the International Academy for Intercultural Research (IAIR)/China Association for Intercultural Communication (CAFIC) Conference, Shanghai, China,7–10 July 2019.

Dai, X. D. & Chen, G. M. (2015). On interculturality and intercultural communication competence. *China Media Research*, 11(3), 100–113.

Davies, B. L. (2018). Evaluating evaluations: What different types of metapragmatic behaviour can tell us about participants' understandings of the moral order. *Journal of Politeness Research*, 14(1), 121–151. https://doi.org/110.1515/pr-2017-0037.

Deardorff, D. K. (2006). Identification and assessment of intercultural competence as a student outcome of internationalization. *Journal of Studies in International Education*, 10(3), 241–266.

Deardorff, D. K. (2009). Synthesizing conceptualizations of intercultural competence. In D. K. Deardorff (Ed.), *The Sage handbook of intercultural competence* (pp. 264–269). Los Angeles, CA: Sage.

Economidou-Kogetsidis, M. (2016). Variation in evaluations of the (im)politeness of emails from L2 learners and perceptions of the personality of their senders. *Journal of Pragmatics*, 106, 1–19. http://dx.doi.org/10.1016/j.pragma.2016.1010.1001.

Fraser, B. & Nolan, W. (1981). The association of deference with linguistic form. In J. Walters (Ed.), *The sociolinguistics of deference & politeness* (pp. 93–111). Special issue (127) of the *International Journal of the Sociology of Language*. The Hague: Mouton.

Fukushima, S. (2013). Evaluation of (im)politeness: A comparative study among Japanese students, Japanese parents and American students on evaluation of attentiveness. *Pragmatics*, 23(2), 275–299. https://doi.org/210.1075/prag.1023.1072.1004fuk.

Graham, J., Haidt, J., Motyl, M., Meindl, P., Iskiwitch, C., & Mooijman, M. (2018). Moral foundations theory. In K. Gray & J. Graham (Eds.), *Atlas of moral psychology* (pp. 211–222). New York, NY: The Guilford Press.

Gudykunst, W. B. (2004). *Bridging differences: Effective intergroup communication* (4th ed.). London: Sage.

Haidt, J. & Kesebir, S. (2010). Morality. In S. Fiske, D. Gilbert, & G. Lindzey (Eds.), *Handbook of social psychology* (5th ed., pp. 797–852). Hoboken, NJ: John Wiley.

Haugh, M. (2013a). Im/politeness, social practice and the participation order. *Journal of Pragmatics*, 58, 52–72. https://doi.org/10.1016/j.pragma.2013.07.003.

Haugh, M. (2013b). Speaker meaning and accountability in interaction. *Journal of Pragmatics*, 48(1), 41–56. http://dx.doi.org/10.1016/j.pragma.2012.1011.1009.

Haugh, M. & Chang, W.-l. M. (2019). "The apology seemed (in)sincere": Variations in the perceptions of (im)politeness. *Journal of Pragmatics*, 142, 207–222. https://doi.org/10.1016/j.pragma.2018.11.022.

Haugh, M., Kádár, D. Z., & Mills, S. (2013). Interpersonal pragmatics: Issues and debates. *Journal of Pragmatics*, 58, 1–11. https://doi.org/10.1016/j.pragma.2013.09.009.

Huebner, B., Lee, J. J., & Hauser, M. D. (2010). The moral-conventional distinction in mature moral competence. *Journal of Cognition and Culture*, 10(1), 1–26. doi:10.1163/156853710X156497149.

Ide, S. (1989). Formal forms and discernment: Two neglected aspects of universals of linguistic politeness. *Multilingua*, 8(2/3), 223–248.

Janoff-Bulman, R., & Carnes, N. C. (2018). The model of moral motives. A map of the moral domain. In K. Gray & J. Graham (Eds.), *Atlas of moral psychology* (pp. 223–230). New York, NY: The Guilford Press.

Kádár, D. Z. & Haugh, M. (2013). *Understanding politeness*. Cambridge, UK: Cambridge University Press.

Kádár, D. Z. & Márquez-Reiter, R. (2015). (Im)politeness and (im)morality: Insights from intervention. *Journal of Politeness Research*, 11(2), 239–260. doi:210.1515/pr-2015-0010.

Lakoff, R. (1989). The limits of politeness: Therapeutic and courtroom discourse. *Multilingua*, 8(2/3), 101–129.

Leech, G. (1983). *Principles of pragmatics*. London: Longman.

Locher, M. A. & Graham, S. L. (Eds.). (2010). *Interpersonal pragmatics*. Berlin: Mouton de Gruyter.

Mendenhall, M. E., Stevens, M. J., Bird, A., & Oddou, G. R. (2010). Specification of the content domain of the Global Competencies Inventory (GCI). *Kozai Working Paper Series*, 1(1), 1–40. Retrieved from https://intercultural.org/wp-content/uploads/2018/2005/GCITechReport.pdf and http://files2017.webydo.com/2091/9185608/UploadedFiles/

9185606A9185600FAC9185632-9185684CB-A9185604EC-9185630AC-A9118937CE9 186150.pdf.

Mezirow, J. (Ed.) (2000). *Learning as transformation: Critical perspectives on a theory in progress.* San Francisco, CA: Jossey-Bass.

Montgomery, B. M. & Baxter, L. A. (Eds.). (1998). *Dialectical approaches to studying personal relationships.* New York, NY: Psychology Press.

O'Driscoll, J. (2013). The role of language in interpersonal pragmatics. *Journal of Pragmatics,* 58, 170–181.

OECD. (2018). Preparing our youth for an inclusive and sustainable world. The OECD PISA global competence framework. Retrieved from https://www.oecd.org/education/Global-competency-for-an-inclusive-world.pdf (accessed 1 October 2019).

Prechtl, E. & Davidson Lund, A. (2009). Intercultural competence and assessment: Perspectives from the INCA project. In H. Kotthoff & H. Spencer-Oatey (Eds.), *Handbook of intercultural communication* (pp. 467–490). Berlin: Mouton de Gruyter.

Spencer-Oatey, H. (2008). Face, (im)politeness and rapport. In H. Spencer-Oatey (Ed.), *Culturally speaking: Culture, communication and politeness theory* (pp. 11–47). London: Continuum.

Spencer-Oatey, H. (2013). Relating at work: Facets, dialectics and face. *Journal of Pragmatics,* 58, 121–137.

Spencer-Oatey, H. (2015). Rapport management model. In K. Tracy, C. Ilie, & T. Sandel (Eds.), *The international encyclopedia of language and social interaction, Vol. 3* (pp. 1286–1291). London: John Wiley.

Spencer-Oatey, H. & Franklin, P. (2009). *Intercultural interaction: A multidisciplinary approach to intercultural communication.* Basingstoke: Palgrave Macmillan.

Spencer-Oatey, H., Franklin, P., & Lazidou, D. (2022). *Global fitness for global people: How to manage and leverage cultural diversity at work.* Melbourne: Castledown.

Spencer-Oatey, H., & Kádár, D. Z. (2016). The bases of (im)politeness evaluations: Culture, the moral order and the East-West debate. *East Asian Pragmatics,* 1(1), 73–106. doi:110.1558/eap.v155li1551.29084.

Spencer-Oatey, H. & Kádár, D. Z. (2021). *Intercultural politeness: Managing relations across cultures.* Cambridge, UK: Cambridge University Press.

Spencer-Oatey, H. & Stadler, S. A. (2009). *The Global People Competency Framework. Competencies for Effective Intercultural Interaction.* Warwick Occasional Papers in Applied Linguistics. https://warwick.ac.uk/fac/cross_fac/globalpeople2/knowledgeexchange/papers/workingpapers/gppublications/gp_competency_frmwk_v2.pdf.

Spencer-Oatey, H. & Wang, J. (2019). Culture, context, and concerns about face: Synergistic insights from pragmatics and social psychology. *Journal of Language and Social Psychology,* 38(4), 423–440.

Spencer-Oatey, H. & Xing, J. (2019). Interdisciplinary perspectives on interpersonal relations and the evaluation process: Culture, norms and the moral order. *Journal of Pragmatics,* 151, 141–154. https://doi.org/110.1016/j.pragma.2019.1002.1015.

Spitzberg, B. H. & Changnon, G. (2009). Conceptualizing intercultural competence. In D. K. Deardorff (Ed.), *Sage handbook of intercultural competence* (pp. 2–52). Thousand Oaks, CA: Sage.

Taylor, E. W. (1994). Intercultural competency: A transformative learning process. *Adult Education Quarterly,* 44(3), 154–174.

Ting-Toomey, S. (1999). *Communicating across cultures.* New York, NY: The Guilford Press.

Ting-Toomey, S. & Chung, L. C. (2005). *Understanding intercultural communication.* Los Angeles: Roxbury Publishing Company.

Ting-Toomey, S. & Dorjee, T. (2019). *Communicating across cultures* (2nd ed.). New York, NY: The Guilford Press.

Turiel, E. (1983). *The development of social knowledge. Morality and convention.* Cambridge, UK: Cambridge University Press.

Wang, J. (2013). Relational management in professional intercultural interaction: Chinese officials' encounters with American and British professionals. Unpublished PhD thesis, University of Warwick.

Wang, J. & Spencer-Oatey, H. (2015). The gains and losses of face in ongoing intercultural interaction: A case study of Chinese participant perspectives. *Journal of Pragmatics*, 89, 50–65. https://doi.org/10.1016/j.pragma.2015.09.007.

Section Two

Intercultural Conflict Management and Harmony Building in Contexts

13

THE DISCURSIVE CONSTRUCTION OF IDENTITIES AND CONFLICT MANAGEMENT STRATEGIES IN PARENT-CHILD CONFLICT NARRATIVES WRITTEN BY CHINESE UNIVERSITY STUDENTS[1]

Xuan Zheng and Yihong Gao

Introduction

Background

The parent-child relationship is one of the most difficult yet intriguing areas of study for researchers from different fields, including communication, sociolinguistics, psychology, and sociology. One of the greatest difficulties for the parent-child relationship is managing the balance between the need for autonomy and the need for interdependence. University students, most of whom have just started to learn to live on their own for the first time, face major challenges in balancing autonomy and interdependence with their parents. Conflicts are unavoidable in families that have children at this stage of their life, and these conflicts actually play a central role in their socialization process as they move towards adulthood (Briggs, 1996; Erikson, 1959). Whether culture plays a role in how university students around the globe manage parent-child conflicts still needs a closer scrutiny. Due to the rapid development of globalization, young people nowadays experience conflicts in different cultures more often than ever before. It is therefore critical to further explore the nature of identity in both local and global contexts (Arnett, 2002). It is especially interesting to examine how young people deal with conflicts with their parents in China, where traditional values are changing very quickly. This chapter attempts to examine the discursive construction of identities and conflict management strategies in parent-child conflict narratives written by Chinese university students.

Students' written narratives are used as data source in this study. As recountings of personal experiences, written narratives contribute to constructing and displaying our sense of who we are and our relationship with others (Connelly & Clandinin,

DOI: 10.4324/9781003252955-16

1990). Scholars have been debating the transformative function of narratives for years. For example, Bruner (1987) argued that "in the end, we become the autographical narratives by which we 'tell about' our lives" (p. 15). Although narratives have been widely studied in the field of linguistics, few scholars have analyzed stories of parent-child conflict told by children during the period in which their personal and social identities are being formed. Moreover, studying the linguistic details of the narratives written by university students may go beyond what mere content analyses can provide.

Literature Review

There are many different definitions of the term "conflict." Most of them present conflict in terms of goals, interests, or resources (e.g. Putnam, 2006), but these definitions do not fit well with the parent-child conflict situation. Parents and children may have the same goals or interests, but the incompatibilities between them lie in the way they choose to reach these goals or engage these interests—and this involves both communication styles and value systems. Therefore, an individual's gain may not mean another's loss in the parent-child relationship. In this chapter, we employ Folger, Poole, and Stutman's (2013) definition that conflict is "the interaction of interdependent people who perceive incompatibility and the possibility of interference from others as a result of this incompatibility" (p. 4).

Research on conflict management has explored a wide range of relationships (e.g. teacher-student, supervisor-employee and co-worker) and has categorized conflict management strategies based on cultural contexts types (e.g. Chen, Ryan, & Chen, 2000; Nguyen & Yang, 2012; Ting-Toomey, 2009). In a collectivistic culture, the needs of groups are given priority over those of individuals, and conflict tends to be viewed as destructive and harmful for relationships (Ting-Toomey & Takai, 2006). Jackson (2014) pointed out that "to preserve relational harmony and one's public face, pacifism is generally favored, that is individuals strive to avoid conflict situations" and "if conflicts arise, people tend to restrain their emotions and try to manage disputes indirectly" (p. 259). Besides, cross-cultural comparisons also found that the Chinese prefer negotiated and mediated strategies while Americans prefer direct confrontation, although strategies also depend on other variables such as conflict situation type, power relations, gender, and age (e.g. Chen et al., 2000; Dixon, Graber, & Brooks-Gunn, 2008; Nguyen & Yang, 2012; Ting-Toomey, 2009). Some of the central cultural values of the Chinese are the Confucian values of family, filial piety, respect for one's elders, group over the individual, and gender-based divisions of family. These traditional values in China were also found to be changing (Sandel, Lowe, & Chao, 2012). Other researchers have recently identified generational differences in people's perceptions of conflict. For example, Zhang, Harwood, and Hummert (2005) found that young people in modern China increasingly prefer collaborative style to resolve disputes, whereas their elders still favor the avoidance style. The gap between traditional and contemporary value orientations in conflict management calls for further research.

Among the different taxonomies developed to categorize conflict management strategies, the dual concern theory has been widely used by intercultural communication scholars and proved to be useful (e.g. Yuan, 2010). Based on disputants' two basic concerns—namely, their own needs, goals, and feelings, and other parties' needs, goals, and feelings—five conflict management strategies were identified: dominating, integrating, compromising, obliging, and avoiding (Rahim & Bonoma, 1979). The *dominating* strategy is usually interpreted as a win-lose strategy, *integrating* a win-win strategy, *compromising* a no-win no-lose strategy, *obliging* a lose-win strategy, and *avoiding* a lose-lose strategy. Nevertheless, some researchers have pointed out that the interpretation of conflict management styles differs across cultures. For example, Yuan (2010) indicated that *avoiding* was functional and contributed to relationship maintenance, and that it was therefore a win-win strategy, in which participants showed a high concern for both self and other.

Although studies on conflict management have been fruitful, the level of analysis mostly remains at the content level of reported data. The research focus of conflict management has not yet been on the linguistic details of how the participants manage conflicts and discursively construct themselves. However, some linguists and discourse analysts have explored conflict episodes in families. For instance, narrative analyses of stories told by a Jewish mother about her daughter's dating choices revealed that the metaphor used in the mother's story evaluation displayed her unsupportive attitude toward her daughter, which was in sharp contrast with her neutral and tolerant stance in the story world (Schiffrin, 1996). Through the linguistic strategy of indirectness, the mother in the study created a mother-daughter relationship that balanced "closeness with distance, autonomy with control" (p. 198). Similarly, the analysis of the language of stories written by university students may also reveal how they construct positions in their family and their identities as adults.

This chapter aims to investigate conflict management strategies and discursive identity construction in parent-child conflict narratives written by Chinese university students. Three research questions are proposed as follows:

RQ1: What conflict management strategies do the students use, as narrated in their writing?
RQ2: How are these narrated strategies characterized by their linguistic features?
RQ3: What value orientations or identities do these strategies suggest?

Methods

Participants and Data Collection

The participants were 41 undergraduates enrolled in a course entitled "Language, Culture and Communication" at a top-tier university in Beijing. The demographic information of participants is shown in Table 13.1. The course is one of the content-based English classes offered by the university for interested undergraduates from all majors.

TABLE 13.1 Demographic information of participants

Variable	Range	Number	Percentage
Gender	Male	18	44%
	Female	23	56%
Year in college	Freshman	5	12%
	Sophomore	19	46%
	Junior	9	22%
	Senior	8	20%
Major	Humanities	5	12%
	Social sciences	21	51%
	Natural sciences	13	32%
	Interdisciplinary	2	5%

The instructor, one of the authors of this chapter, assigned a writing exercise to elicit students' past conflict stories. Participants were invited to write in English about a recent conflict they had had with their parents. The writing assignment was worded as follows:

Tell us about a recent conflict story between you and your parents.

- How did it happen and why?
- How did you deal with the conflict?
- Do you think there are better ways to deal with the conflict? How and why?

Students were given extra credits for writing this paper (0–5 points), which was evaluated based on a grading rubric developed by the instructor (i.e., details of the story, depth of reflection, and the appropriateness of language use). Before assigning the paper, the instructor briefly introduced the topic of intercultural conflict and taught the participants about cross-cultural comparisons in conflict management styles.

Data Analysis

Categorization of Conflict Strategies

The dual concern theory was used as the framework for the analysis of conflict strategies (Pruitt & Rubin, 1986; Ruble & Thomas, 1976). Five conflict management strategies proposed by the dual concern theory— namely, dominating, integrating, compromising, obliging, and avoiding—were used as a starting point for categorization in this study (Rahim & Bonoma, 1979). The authors each independently coded the types of strategies used in the students' narratives, discussed coding difficulties together, and then moved on to the next round of independent coding. Not until the inter-rater reliability reached 0.83 did we code the papers separately. New categories of strategies that emerged from the analyses were reported.

In calculating the occurrences of the strategies, we first listed all the types of strategies in order. Then the percentage of each strategy was calculated by totalizing the number of occurrences of this strategy in all the students' essays and dividing it by the total number of strategies. Actual strategies (their answers to question 2 in the assignment) and proposed strategies (their answers to questions 3) from the data were also separated.

Categorization of Transitivity Processes of the Strategy-Related Verbs

Using the tool (i.e., transitivity system) provided by Systematic Functional Grammar (SFG) (Halliday, 1985), we analyzed the verb processes students used in managing conflicts. We only coded the verbs that described the students, rather than their parents, as agents of conflict management. When faced with complex verb phrases which may suggest different processes (e.g. "settled with my bad-temper"), we coded the main verb first (i.e. "settle" is a material process), rather than coding it by its meaning (i.e. "settled with my bad-temper" is a mental process). Then we noted and categorized what came after the material process (e.g. mental as in "settled with my bad-temper" or verbal as in "initiated a quarrel"). We each coded the verbs in the conflict management section in all essays and invited a third coder trained in SFG to help resolve the disputes we had.[2] We strove for consistency in our coding and arrived at a consensus.

Results and Discussion

A total of 41 papers were collected, 18 written by males and 23 written by females. Among these, five were about conflicts between mother and son, one was between father and son, 12 were between "parents" and son, 10 were between mother and daughter, three were between father and daughter, and 10 were between "parents" and daughter. Conflicts between children and their mothers seemed to be more salient.

Triggering Events

There were 43 conflict narratives in total because one student wrote three different conflict episodes. In the students' narratives, there were different triggering events that led to the conflict (see Table 13.2). Most of the triggering events had to do with making major life decisions, such as choosing a career path, a university, or a boyfriend. Another type of the triggering event had to do with various aspects of the students' college life, ranging from making holiday plans to starting a business. Domestic issues such as cleaning rooms or eating habits were also major types of triggering events. These stories often involved a nagging parent whose control of daily family chores irritated the child. This corresponded to the previous finding that nagging was a main source of conflict in the family arena (Boxer, 2002).

TABLE 13.2 Triggering event of conflict

Theme	Total occurrences	Percentage	Details		
Making major life decisions	18	42%	Choosing major for college		8
			Choosing career after college		8
			Choosing boyfriend		2
College life	13	30%	Holiday plans		4
			Internship		3
			Studying abroad		2
			Time management		1
			Joining club		1
			Joining the Communist Party		1
			Starting a business		1
Domestic issues	12	28%	Nagging about ...	Cleaning room	3
				Eating habits	2
				Wearing skirt	1
				Homework	1
			Laundry		1
			Watching TV		1
			House renovation		1
			Parents' conflict		1
			Asking for a sibling		1

Conflict Management Strategies

In categorizing the conflict management strategies provided by students' essays, the five major conflict management strategies (i.e. dominating, integrating, compromising, obliging, and avoiding) previously identified by scholars were all found in the data. In addition, we found a strategy that could not be categorized based on the dual concern theory. This strategy was labeled "articulating." The meaning of each strategy is illustrated below.

Dominating

This strategy in our study suggested verbal or nonverbal confrontation with expressed emotion. It usually involved forceful behaviors and ignoring the needs of others. Examples were:

1. Shouting back was what I did.
2. I appeared upset and not interested in anything for a whole day … I turned them down.

3. I left the dining room with half of the rice left in my bowl … locked myself in my room without talking to my dad the whole day through.

Integrating

This strategy showed a high concern for both self and others. The student collaborated with their parents to reach a mutually acceptable solution. In the actual strategies students employed, examples of integrating were:

1. Both of us can stand on each other's point, trying to be considerate to avoid conflicts hurting others.
2. So we finally agree on that; I promise I would take care for myself and never carry more loads beyond my reach.

In proposed strategy, examples were:

1. If I had told them earlier, maybe we could work out with a better plan suited every side.
2. I should also try to figure out a plan together with my parents to find out a win–win approach for how I arrange my room.

Compromising

This was a give-and-take situation, in which both sides gave up something in order to reach a consensus:

1. I finally insisted on my choice and made a concession by signing a three-month contract, which ended at the beginning of summer when I can meet choices again.
2. I compromised after a heated argument. I promised that if my father really wanted me to read Korean I would read for him but not speak Korean at all times.
3. My dad and I have come to a consensus not to talk about my eating habits any more.

Obliging

In this strategy, the student attempted to satisfy their parents and reach an agreement. It usually indicated low concern for self and high concern for others.

1. I had no choice but to rush into my room; I stuffed clothes into a suitcase and then bundled clutter from my desk into the drawers.
2. However, when she is in a bad mood, I'd better do exactly what she tells me to do at once and avoid making things worse.

Interestingly, sometimes the obliging strategy was *obliging on the surface*, which meant that the student attempted to satisfy their parents and reach an agreement on the surface while choosing in private to remain uncooperative. This strategy suggested high concern for both self and others:

1. I tried to pretend to balance my life in the way they hoped while actually dealing with the course stress according to my own understanding.
2. ... though I won't actually do it, I will reply with a good temper saying "OK, I'll do it right now."

Avoiding

In this strategy, there was a tendency for the student to withdraw from or otherwise avoid conflict:

1. I even missed their calls on purpose.
2. ... didn't call them for several days.
3. And then they became angry too, and stopped talking to me. The silence lasted for two days before we both thought it was time to let it go. So we went back to normal, and no one ever brought it up again.

In limited cases, the students did not provide a strategy, but described the difficulties in arriving at a solution instead. Such cases were categorized "no strategy." In strategy distribution calculation, these cases were merged with avoiding.

Articulating

In addition to the major strategies, a new strategy, namely "articulating", was found. In this strategy, the university students directly articulated their needs and wants or, in their words, "talk things out" with their parents face to face. In articulating, students often used several persuasion techniques, such as showing evidence or showing empathy. Sometimes they invited a third party, such as their parents' friends or other relatives, to back them up. In contrast to the dominating strategy, the students did not confront their parents with strong and often negative emotions, but showed both high concern for self and others in this strategy. It also differed from integrating in that the students were not immediately satisfied with collaborating with their parents. The students knew what worked in their situation; therefore, they tried to explain why that was the case to their parents. This statement showed the students' assumption, "I win and you will eventually win in the future too." Examples of actual strategies in this category were as follows:

1. I finally chose to work up enough patience to explain why I would ignore some of their suggestions and how my life was different from their thoughts.

2.   Firstly, I clarified that Ph.D. and Master's degrees were two totally different
     things. One concentrated on academic research and the other focused more
     on practical use. After that I told them my current thoughts and self-
     exploration about what suited me more. … What's more, I have also shown
     them the outline of Princeton's program and told them that I was the only
     student from mainland China to be admitted this year.

Articulating was also the top proposed strategy. Examples were:

1.   I should also communicate in a timely manner with my parents. Don't
     quarrel, just say what I think.
2.   … the only thing I can do better is to stay calm and explain my excuses
     patiently.
3.   I will try to deal with the problem in a new way by telling my father why I would
     like to watch the movie and ask him why he would love to watch the news.

Overall Strategy Distribution

As illustrated in Figure 13.1, among actual strategies used, *dominating* ranked first and
was followed by the new strategy: *articulating*, and then *avoiding*. The chi-square test
result was $X^2 = 28.82$ (df = 5), greater than the table value 11.11 at the p < 0.05
significance level. This showed a significant difference in the frequency distribution
across strategy categories.

The strategies the students would like to use in future conflict situations (which we
named "proposal strategies") also consisted of six different strategies, but the majority
of them belonged to the *articulating* and *integrating* categories (see Figure 13.2). For

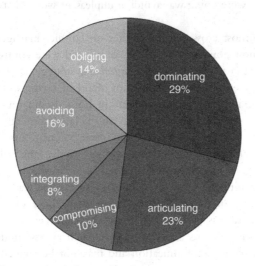

FIGURE 13.1 Distribution of actual strategies

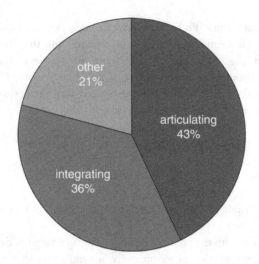

FIGURE 13.2 Distribution of proposed strategies

proposed strategies, $X^2 = 0.27$ (df = 2), smaller than the table value 5.99 at the p < 0.05 significance level. This showed that there was no significant difference in the frequency distribution across the three major categories: articulating, integrating, and other categories,

To sum up, similar to the findings of previous studies, *avoiding* was one of the major conflict management strategies and "conflict avoidance" was often a stated goal of the students. Also similar to what most scholars have found in Asian contexts (e.g. Yuan, 2010), *avoiding* was not necessarily a negative strategy. It may show great concern for both the self and the other: as the students said in their papers, what they were doing was avoiding unpleasant words that would hurt their parents.

In contrast to most cross-cultural studies on conflict management, this study found that the most popular strategies students used were confrontational (dominating) and direct (articulating). In the *articulating* strategy, students were capable of managing their emotions and were not afraid of saying out loud what they truly felt and thought. Although students in both dominating and articulating showed great concern for their own needs, in the latter students were not making themselves "win" and the other party (i.e. their parents) "lose," but presenting their ideas in a clear and convincing manner so that the other party would understand and give them support. In this sense, it was a win–win situation. However, it also differed from integrating in that what was addressed was the desire of one party (i.e. the student), rather than those of both parties. The underlying assumption is perhaps that there is no ultimate conflict in the needs and interests of the students and the parents. Such an assumption is admittedly specific to parent-child communication and may not be applied indiscriminately to other conflict situations.

Linguistic Features of Narrated Strategies: Transitivity Processes

Overall Occurrences of Transitivity Processes

Linguistic features, including verbal transitivity processes, were scrutinized to further examine distinct features of the conflict strategies shown in the students' papers. In SFG, grammar is considered a resource for creating meaning in the form of wordings (Halliday, 1985, 1994, 2004). It regards language as presenting three meta-functions in social contexts: ideational, interpersonal, and textual. The ideational meta-function is concerned with "ideation"—the grammatical resources for the function of representing, reflecting, or construing the world (Halliday, 1985, 1994, 2004). This meta-function is realized largely through the transitivity system of language. The transitivity system views language in terms of processes (material, mental, verbal, behavioral, existential, relational) which are realized by verbal groups and reflect doing, sensing, saying, behaving, the existence of things, and the relationship between participants. Table 13.3 shows several examples of these processes.

Based on the transitivity system, we coded the verbs used in the strategies. Tables 13.4 and 13.5 show the occurrences of these processes:

TABLE 13.3 Transitivity system

Processes	Explanation	Examples
Material process	A process of doing	build, break, create, make
Mental process	A process of sensing: perception; reaction; cognition	see, like, know, believe
Verbal process	A process of saying	say, tell, describe, ask
Behavioral process	A process of behaving	breathe, cough, laugh, cry
Existential process	A process of existing	be, exist, arise
Relational process	A process of being: attribute; identifying	be, become, add up to, mean, represent

TABLE 13.4 Occurrences of transitivity processes in actual strategies

	Dominating	Articulating	Integrating	Compromising	Obliging	Avoiding
Material	34	26	11	17	20	13
Mental	10	6	3	0	1	11
Verbal	21	28	10	5	8	7
Behavioral	1	0	2	1	1	2
Existential	0	0	0	0	0	0
Relational	6	14	0	0	1	0

TABLE 13.5 Occurrences of transitivity processes in proposed strategies

	Articulating	Integrating	Compromising	Obliging	Avoiding (including no strategy)
Material	23	30	4	10	3
Mental	4	15	1	1	4
Verbal	20	8	0	0	0
Behavioral	1	1	0	0	1
Existential	1	0	0	0	1
Relational	4	8	1	2	0

We found that the transitivity system is a useful analytical tool because there was a clear distinction in the verbs that students used in different types of conflict management strategies. While applying the transitivity system in coding the verbs, it became clear that it was not only the types of verbs that varied in these strategies, but also the combination of these verb processes. This linguistic evidence has further supported our categorization—especially among dominating, articulating, and integrating strategies.

Transitivity Processes in Dominating, Articulating, and Integrating

Table 13.6 shows the comparison in transitivity processes among dominating, articulating and integrating strategies.

TABLE 13.6 Percentage of transitivity processes in *dominating, articulating* and *integrating*

		Dominating	Articulating	Integrating
Actual	Material	47%	35%	42%
	Mental	14%	8%	12%
	Verbal	29%	38%	38%
	Behavioral	2%	0%	8%
	Existential	0%	0%	0%
	Relational	8%	19%	0%
Proposed	Material	0%	43%	48%
	Mental	0%	8%	24%
	Verbal	0%	38%	13%
	Behavioral	0%	2%	2%
	Existential	0%	2%	0%
	Relational	0%	7%	13%

Dominating

In examples of *dominating*, however, what came after the verbal process was often not the true thoughts and needs of the students, but direct accusations that their parents did not understand them. This was frequently shown in the form of direct quotes, with their parents being referred to directly as "you."

1. I didn't know how I plucked up my courage and *said,* "You have no idea of what true love is and you know nothing about me."
2. I once *said*: "If you really value the university so much, how about you give me the money that was meant for college and pretend you never had such a daughter?"
3. "I'll choose whatever I want! This is none of your business!" I *shouted* and shut the door of my bedroom.

Moreover, the percentage of material processes (in **bold**) in *dominating* ranked top among verbs in all strategies. A detailed analysis revealed that such material processes were often tantamount to the behavioral acting out of antagonistic feelings. For example:

1. I **left** the dining room with half of the rice left in my bowl ... **locked** myself in my room without talking to my dad the whole day through.
2. I **stopped** talking to my father, **went** back to my room, and **started** the movie on my laptop as a protest.

Furthermore, the types of verbs in the *dominating* strategy also differed from those in other strategies, where students simply and calmly "said" or "told." In *dominating* the verbal verbs suggested the presence of an intense argument with explosive sound: "yell, shout, debate, quarrel, bicker;" or sometimes came up in the form of a "cold war": "not (stop/without) talking." The material verbs were also full of destructive power: "shut (the door), break (into blame), subdue (my fury)." Sometimes they were failed attempts at managing negative emotions: "failed to subdue my fury," "(cannot) keep calm." Even a behavioral one, "burst out," entailed a strong and sudden negative energy. Lastly, the mental processes were mostly negative in that the mental verbs often came with negation:

1. I didn't <u>want</u> to hurt her feeling but I can't agree with her.
2. I didn't <u>know</u> how I plucked up my courage and said, "You have no idea of what true love is and you know nothing about me."
3. "I don't <u>miss</u> them," I answered coldly.
4. I act as still caring about this and didn't <u>want</u> to reach a compromise.

The negations suggested a denial of mental processes (especially a strong and negative emotion) the students were actually experiencing. To sum up, in *dominating* students did not yet know how to manage their intense emotions properly when their needs were refused by their parents. They either gave vent their anger and frustration through bitter words, or suppressed/denied their emotions and acted out their protest.

Articulating

What stood out as significant was the combination of verbal and mental processes in the *articulating* strategy: the verb in the main sentence (used in the context of the student conflict management) was a verbal process, while the subordinate clause that came after the main verb involved a mental process. In the following sentences used to exemplify this finding, the verbal verbs are in *italics*, while the mental verbs are underlined. This finding suggested that in *articulating* students were verbalizing their true thoughts, needs, wants, interests, and preferences. In dealing with the conflict, they explained verbally what they preferred, what their thoughts were, and why they preferred their own way. This feature was not found in other strategies.

1. After that I *told* them my current thoughts and self-exploration about what suited me more.
2. My mother and I both *elaborated* on our thoughts and added some supportive evidence, like why she cared about the family background of my boyfriend and why I thought vagueness was terrible in dealing with such relationship.
3. At first, I firmly held my decision and *told* them that I wanted to choose what I liked.
4. I finally chose to work up enough patience to *explain* why I would ignore some of their suggestions and how my life was different from their thoughts.

This was also the case in the proposed *articulating* strategy:

1. I will try to deal with the problem in a new way by *telling* my father why I would like to watch the movie and *ask* him why he would love to watch the news.
2. … need to *tell* them patiently and sincerely that I like computer science and have confidence in learning it well.

Before directly telling their parents what they preferred, some students were able to successfully handle their emotions, so that they could approach their parents in a calm manner. This was shown by material verbs (in **bold**) followed by a noun (in parentheses) that indicated emotion:

1. 1. I finally **chose** to **work up** enough (patience) to *explain* why I would ignore some of their suggestions and how my life was different from their thoughts.

Integrating

In *integrating*, the mental,*verbal*,**material** and [behavioral] verbs all suggested a willingness and a gesture from the students' side in listening, understanding, discussing, and collaborating with their parents.

1. So we **sat** together and *talked* on it, **trying** to **smooth** it away … I <u>understood</u> her. She understood me too … so we finally *agreed* on that, I *promised* I would **take** care for myself, and never **carry** more loads beyond my reach.
2. I [listened] to my father's suggestions and *discussed* with him … Finally, I <u>decided</u> to **take** their advice and **stick** to my current major for a master's degree in the U.S.A.

In the proposed strategy, there were a large number of mental processes, more than those used in articulating or avoiding. Unlike those in the *articulating* strategy, these mental processes did not come after verbal processes, but showed up alone. Below there are examples with the mental verbs underlined:

1. While I do not <u>want</u> to bring financial burden to them, I <u>want</u> to take as much as I can to ease the financial burden I brought to them. I <u>think</u> both of us are with good intensions at the beginning, but are too emotional and irrational when we express our opinions.
2. I would <u>prefer</u> to firstly think from others' prospective and then have a mild touch rather than be irritated and ignored.

These examples suggested that in *integrating* the students had undergone a complex mental process in which they were considering both sides' concerns and feelings. This complex thinking process, however, had not yet been made verbally accessible to their parents, and this could be because *integrating* showed up most often in the proposed strategies, which were hypothetical situations where students were contemplating the best strategies to use.

Lastly, in *integrating* the students were concerned about their parents' feelings. They apologized for their disrespect and thought that they should have listened to their parents with patience and even applied verbal strategies to soothe their parents' emotions.

1. I *apologized* for my ignorance and disrespect of their opinions.
2. I should have *told* her more information and **used** more warm words to **make** her feel at ease but not **let out** my anger.
3. I should also have [listened] to her patiently and *told* her that I understood before *voicing* my own opinion.

To sum up, the different types and combinations of verbs marked the distinction between the *dominating, articulating,* and *integrating* strategies.

Value Orientations and Identities

The students' papers have demonstrated value orientations that leaned toward low power distance, individualism, and assertiveness based on the descriptions of the "cultural dimensions" identified by cultural theorists (e.g. Hofstede, 1984). These orientations were best exemplified in the *articulating* strategy, where students attached importance to their own needs and wants and directly communicated these to their parents by using different persuasion techniques. In this strategy, the students were constructing an "equal" self in relation to their parents, who were capable of making important life decisions and taking on the responsibilities thereof.

In the *dominating* strategy, students constructed a paradoxically dependent and independent self. On the one hand, they strived to have their own thoughts, exercise control over their own futures, and be adults; on the other hand, they were still reliant on their parents like children. For instance, the reason that one student came into conflict with his parents was because he wanted to go back home during the holidays, but his parents did not allow him to. The linguistic features of the verbs used in this strategy, characterized by a verbal attack and physical (material) "acting out," also showed that the students often had strong negative emotions and did not know how to handle them properly. Although they were upset by their parents' words or decisions, who did not seem to grant them freedom to be grown adults, they did not yet know how to communicate their true thoughts to their parents and carry out their choices.

It is worth noting that the narratives also demonstrated a considerable amount of deep care, concern, love, and understanding on the part of the students toward their parents. They understood perfectly well the other side of the conflict, even when it was different from their own (e.g. their parents' life experiences, values, what they considered was right, the way they showed their love). Students often regretted their immaturity in using the *dominating* style in dealing with conflict because they knew their parents loved them.

Although these students' conflict management strategies may reflect value orientations and parent-child relations in contemporary Chinese families, it is important to remember that these papers were collected from a specific English class, which emphasized effective communication skills. In this class, articulating strategies, which were often taught as a "Western" communication style, were valued and seen as positive, while avoiding, which was often categorized as a typical "Chinese" style, may have been regarded as negative, less competent, or backward. It is likely that in this "extra credit" writing situation, students were actively constructing an identity as a competent, successful student, who could confront a conflict situation effectively and manage their emotions properly.

Conclusion

In sum, in this study we have identified six management strategies that students used in dealing with parent-child conflicts: dominating, articulating, integrating, compromising, obliging, and avoiding. While avoiding was still one of the most popular strategies, the *dominating* and *articulating* strategies were favored more by these students. The d*ominating* strategy revealed a paradoxically independent and dependent self, whereas in the *articulating* strategy students were constructed as equal and capable communicators in handling conflicts with their parents.

Linguistic analyses, specifically transitivity analysis carried out from the perspective of SFG, provided strong supporting evidence for the categories generated in content analyses in this study. Analyses of the verbs used in the students' narratives suggested that there was a clear distinction between the dominating, articulating, and integrating strategies. In dominating, verbal process often entailed a direct quote addressed to the parents that was loaded with negative emotions. The verbal verbs in dominating often suggested an intense argument with explosive sound. The mental processes in dominating often came with negations, thereby indicating a denial of the cognitive and emotional processes that the students were actually experiencing. In *integrating*, the verbs showed a strong willingness on the part of the students to listen, understand, and collaborate with their parents. A great number of mental verbs suggested that students experienced an active thinking process in considering both sides' concerns. In *articulating*, the verbal process was often followed by a subordinate clause that contained a mental process, which suggested that the students were verbalizing their own needs, wants, and preferences. Transitivity analysis only serves as one aspect of linguistic analysis, as the use of voice, pronouns, and metaphors may also explain how students position and construct themselves in their narratives.

Compared to previous studies on cross-cultural comparisons in conflict and conflict management (e.g. Chen et al., 2000; Nguyen & Yang, 2012; Ting-Toomey, 2009), the narrated strategies in this study have suggested a reduced power distance, as well as individualistic and assertive value orientations, which seem to deviate from previous findings that collectivist cultures (including the Chinese culture) prefer to adopt an avoidance strategy in order to deal with conflict. This may indicate a change in value orientations in the young generation (i.e. those born after 1995) in contemporary China. This generational difference has been noticed and reported by others. For example, Zhang et al. (2005) found that young people in modern China differ from the older generations in their ways of resolving disputes. The younger generation prefers to solve disputes collaboratively, while the older generations still prefer to avoid conflict situations. As the strategies examined here were narratives written by students, and as the narratives may be influenced by what the students were taught in class, further investigation of real conflict situations is needed to substantiate this claim of generational change.

Despite the fact that this study has demonstrated that the students tend to directly articulate their needs and wants, there is still a need to explore parents' perspectives because the communication scenarios always involved both sides and identities are co-constructed. Although verbalizing one's true needs, wants, and feelings to one's parents in conflict situations may be an ideal strategy for children, it may not work if the verbalization of their mental processes is repeatedly rejected by their parents. Future studies should approach parent–child conflict management from the perspectives of both sides.

Notes

1 We would like to thank our colleague Jianqiu Tian, an expert in Systemic Functional Grammar, for helping with the coding of the transitivity processes of the verbs in the data. We are also very grateful to Xiaodong Dai and Guo-Ming Chen for their helpful comments and careful editing of the manuscript.
2 For a very limited number of verbs that can be coded as different processes, we coded them based on what they meant in the context (e.g. "agree" was a mental process in "I didn't want to hurt her feelings, but I can't agree with her," but a verbal process in "we finally agreed on that").

References

Arnett, J. J. (2002). The psychology of globalization. *American Psychologist*, 57(10), 774–783.

Boxer, D. (2002). Nagging: The familial conflict arena. *Journal of Pragmatics*, 34(1), 49–61.

Briggs, C. L. (Ed.). (1996). *Disorderly discourse: Narrative, conflict, & inequality*. New York, NY: Oxford University Press.

Bruner, J. (1987). Life as narrative. *Social Research*, 54(1), 11–32.

Chen, G. M., Ryan, K., & Chen, C. (2000). The determinants of conflict management among Chinese and Americans. *Intercultural Communication Studies*, 9(2), 163–175.

Connelly, F. M. & Clandinin, D. J. (1990). Stories of experience and narrative inquiry. *Educational Researcher*, 19(5), 2–14.

Dixon, S. V., Graber, J. A., & Brooks-Gunn, J. (2008). The roles of respect for parental authority and parenting practices in parent–child conflict among African American, Latino, and European American families. *Journal of Family Psychology*, 22(1), 1–10.

Erikson, E. H. (1959). *Identity and the life cycle*. New York, NY: International Universities Press.

Folger, J. P., Poole, M. S., & Stutman, R. K. (2013). *Working through conflict: Strategies for relationships, groups, and organizations* (7th ed.). Boston, MA: Pearson.

Halliday, M. A. K. (1985/1994/2004). *Introduction to functional grammar*. London, UK: Arnold.

Hofstede, G. (1984). *Culture's consequences: International differences in work-related values*, Vol. 5. Newbury Park, CA: Sage.

Jackson, J. (2014). *Introducing language and intercultural communication*. London, UK: Routledge.

Nguyen, H.-H. D. & Yang, J. (2012). Chinese employees' interpersonal conflict management strategies. *International Journal of Conflict Management*, 23(4), 382–412.

Pruitt, D. G. & Rubin, J. Z. (1986). *Social conflict: Escalation, impasse, and resolution*. Reading, MA: Addison-Wesley.

Putnam, L. L. (2006). Definitions and approaches to conflict and communication. In J. G. Oetzel & S. Ting-Toomey (Eds.), *The Sage handbook of conflict communication: Integrating theory, research, and practice* (pp. 1–32). Thousand Oaks, CA: Sage.

Rahim, A. & Bonoma, T. V. (1979). Managing organizational conflict: A model for diagnosis and intervention. *Psychological Reports*, 44(3), 1323–1344.

Ruble, T. L. & Thomas, K. W. (1976). Support for a two-dimensional model of conflict behavior. *Organizational Behavior and Human Performance*, 16(1), 143–155.

Sandel, T. L., Lowe, A. W., & Chao, W.-Y. (2012). What does it mean to be "Chinese"? Studying values as perceived by Chinese immigrants to the United States and by their children. In S. J. Kulich, M. H. Prosser, & L.-P. Weng (Eds.), *Value frameworks at the theoretical crossroads of culture* (pp. 529–558). Shanghai, China: Shanghai Foreign Language Education Press.

Schiffrin, D. (1996). Narrative as self-portrait: Sociolinguistic constructions of identity. *Language in Society*, 25(2), 167–203.

Ting-Toomey, S. (2009). Intercultural conflict competence as a facet of intercultural competence development. In D. Deardoff (Ed.), *The Sage handbook of intercultural competence* (pp. 100–120). Thousand Oaks, CA: Sage.

Ting-Toomey, S. & Takai, J. (2006). Explaining intercultural conflict: Promising approaches and directions. In J.G. Oetzel & S. Ting-Toomey (Eds.), *The Sage handbook of conflict communication: Integrating theory, research, and practice* (pp. 691–723). Thousand Oaks, CA: Sage.

Yuan, W.-L. (2010). Conflict management among American and Chinese employees in multinational organizations in China. *Cross-Cultural Management*, 17(3), 299–311.

Zhang, Y. B., Harwood, J., & Hummert, M. L. (2005). Perceptions of conflict management styles in Chinese intergenerational dyads. *Communication Monographs*, 72(1), 71–91.

14

NO INTERGENERATIONAL CONFLICT

Older Adults' Reports of Communication Characteristics in American Family and Nonfamily Intergenerational Relationships

Yan Bing Zhang and Weston T. Wiebe

Communication accommodation theory (CAT) explains the processes by which individuals adjust their communication behaviors based on perceptions of communication competence, conversational and emotional needs, and/or role relations between conversational partners to manage their social, relational, and communicative distance and goals (Coupland et al., 1988; Giles, 2008). In a broad picture, CAT specifies two communication strategies in explaining the motivations behind and consequences of interpersonal and intergroup interactions (Zhang & Pitts, 2019). The first strategy is *accommodation*: the perceived communicative adjustment in an interaction that enhances effective communication, relational solidarity, and identification (Gasiorek, 2017). Accommodative behaviors such as socioemotional support, mutuality, and positive emotional expression (Hummert, 2019; Williams & Giles, 1996) can enhance interpersonal similarity or reinforce self-identity in order to reduce uncertainty and improve communication. They can also bridge distance between and build solidarity with outgroup members (Giles, 2008).

The second major strategy that CAT specifies is *nonaccommodation*, which contains major sub-strategies of *overaccommodation* and *underaccomodation* (Coupland, Giles, & Henwood, 1988; Giles, 2008). *Nonaccommodation* refers to how individuals adjust their "communication in ways that hinder effective communication, enhance intergroup differentiation, and/or increase social distance" (Gasiorek, 2017, p. 2). *Overaccommodation* occurs when speakers adjust their communication more than what is perceived as necessary, while *underaccommodation* occurs when speakers do not adjust their communication sufficiently for a listener's needs or desires (Coupland et al., 1988; Giles, 2008; Soliz & Giles, 2014; Zhang & Giles, 2018). Essentially, CAT suggests that social identities and stereotypes influence the behaviors of individuals in communicative interactions. CAT helps us understand some of the psychological forces (e.g., liking, social identity) that may affect shifts in language and communication (e.g., word choice, accent, and tone of voice), and

DOI: 10.4324/9781003252955-17

how such communication adjustments "enhance perceptions of affiliation" or "increase perceptions of difference" (Zhang & Pitts, 2019, p. 192).

In nearly four decades since its inception, CAT has become "one of the most influential behavioral theories of communication" (Littlejohn & Foss, 2005, p. 147) that can explain both interpersonal and intergroup encounters. Due to its theoretical scope and unique interpersonal and intergroup features, CAT has provided a major framework for much of the research in communication between individuals from different age groups (Hummert, 2019). Prior research acknowledges that accommodation (Harwood, 1998; Harwood, McKee, & Lin, 2000; Williams & Giles, 1996) and nonaccommodation (Giles & Williams, 1994; Kemper, 1994; Williams & Giles, 1996) are important strategies to consider when examining intergenerational communication between older and younger individuals.

However, there are a few gaps in this line of literature. First, although some positive stereotypes exist, negative age stereotypes are prevalent (Hummert, 1994). Hence, most of the intergenerational communication literature has examined nonaccommodation and its negative correlates (Coupland et al., 1988; Harwood et al., 2000; Zhang & Lin, 2009). This is especially true for those research streams that are linked to the Communicative Predicament Model of Aging (Ryan et al., 1986; Zhang, 2004; Zhang & Lin, 2009). Further, this line of research has also focused on stranger, acquaintance, or institutional relationships, even though most intergenerational communication occurs between grandparents and grandchildren (Harwood et al., 2005; Ng et al., 1997; Zhang et al., 2018). Lastly, most of the foundational research on intergenerational communication has been conducted from perspective of young adults. Thus, considering CAT and given these gaps in prior literature, the current study examined characteristics of family and nonfamily intergenerational relationships that are marked by a lack of conflict from older adults' (i.e., those who are 65 and above) perspective.

Prior research examined conversations between young and older adults in primarily nonfamily intergenerational relationships from the perspective of young adults and revealed some accommodative characteristics in intergenerational communication (Williams & Giles, 1996). The characteristics that facilitated intergenerational conversations include socioemotional support provided to the other, narratives told by the young (e.g., career plans and school) and older adult (e.g., interesting stories), astereotypical of and positively expressive older adult, mutuality (i.e., shared respect, understanding, and conversational goals), and elder accommodation (i.e., treating the young adult as an equal). These positive intergenerational communication behaviors could be broadly classified along the CAT dimensions such as approximation, interpretability, interpersonal control, discourse management, and emotional expression (Zhang & Pitts, 2019). Research supports these findings (Harwood, Mckee, & Lin, 2000) and acknowledges that family relationships add alternative accommodative characteristics (e.g., interpersonal boundaries; Fowler, Fisher, & Pitts, 2013) due to the interpersonal and intergroup nature of family intergenerational relationships. Although scholars have examined appropriate and inappropriate intergenerational accommodation (Harwood, 1998; Harwood et al., 2006; Wiebe & Zhang, 2017; Williams & Giles, 1996; Zhang &

Lin, 2009), scholars have not developed a comprehensive list of communication characteristics from older adults' perspective in intergenerational relationships that are marked by a lack of conflict. Conflict is an inevitable part of all relationships (Zhang, 2004), however, some intergenerational relationships might be more conflictual than others. As the absence of conflict does not mean presence of positive or beneficial communication, or relational satisfaction, we hope to identify unique accommodative characteristics of intergenerational relationships that are marked by a lack of conflict. Hence, the following research question is proposed.

RQ1: To what communication characteristics do older adults attribute a lack of intergenerational conflict with family and nonfamily young adults?

An Intergroup Perspective on Intergenerational Communication

One of the theoretical foci that comes into play when dealing with intergenerational communication between young and older adults is the juxtaposition of age and family. An intergroup perspective highlights the notion that intergenerational relationships may be characterized by both an ingroup membership in shared family identity and an outgroup membership in age. Social identity theory (SIT; Tajfel & Turner, 1986) and the Common Ingroup Identity Model (CIIM; Gaertner & Dovidio, 2000) help describe these dynamics.

Social Identity Theory

SIT was developed in order to explain how psychological and sociological processes interact to produce micro and macro intergroup dynamics (Tajfel & Turner, 1986). Subsequently scholars have studied the intergroup prospective and applied it to communication. Intergroup communication occurs when either party in a social interaction defines the self or the other in terms of group memberships (Harwood, Giles, & Palomares, 2005). SIT states that individuals have both a personal and a social identity (Tajfel & Turner, 1986). Personal identity refers to the perception of self as a unique individual with traits and preferences, while social identity refers to the perception of self as a member of particular groups, along with the cognitive, affective, and behavioral associations appropriate to those groups (Harwood et al., 2005). To maintain a positive social identity, individuals must recognize their positive distinctiveness in comparison with outgroups. Group memberships affect the way that people interact with each other. Not all the individuals involved in an interaction have to be aware of the intergroup communication in order for it to occur (Harwood et al., 2005). They also argue that self- and other-categorizations are linked. For example, when a young person categorizes someone as an older person, they invoke an implicit self-categorization as not an older person. This categorization then becomes relevant to both parties in a particular communication situation. Hence, when intergroup communication occurs, self- and other-categorization are inherent. One important group membership that links the grandparent-grandchild (GP-GC) dyad is shared family identity. However, the GP-GC dyad is unique because there is a difference in age-group membership. This makes the GP-GC dyad more complex than nonfamily encounters because there are multiple salient group memberships (Soliz & Harwood, 2006). One of the goals of the current study is to compare the accommodative behaviors that occur in familial vs. nonfamilial intergenerational relationships.

Common Ingroup Identity Model

If members of different age groups (i.e., grandchildren and grandparents) think of each other in terms of the ingroup membership they share (i.e., family), their communication can be mutually satisfying, leading to better intergenerational relationships. A useful theoretical framework for highlighting the complexity of family relationships is Gaertner and Dovidio's (2000) CIIM. This model stipulates that if members of different groups can think of themselves within a single group rather than as separate groups, attitudes toward former outgroup members will become more positive through the cognitive and motivational processes involving pro-ingroup bias (Gaertner & Dovidio, 2000). If one can identify with an outgroup enough to acknowledge a broader categorization, then there can be more positive thoughts, feelings, and behaviors toward that individual.

Interactions in which the individuals involved do not have family as a common ingroup will provide a baseline for comparing the differences CIIM might have on accommodative communication in intergenerational relationships. Further, the family provides a context where it is relatively easy to establish a common ingroup identity (Banker & Gaertner, 1998), and shared family identity has been conceptualized as a common ingroup identity (Zhang, 2004; Soliz & Harwood, 2006; Song & Zhang, 2012). If grandparents can see the grandchild as part of the same group (i.e., family), then this can influence the way that they communicate. As such, extending prior literature, the current study examines intergenerational communication exchanges and dynamics between young and older adults in family and nonfamily relationships from the older adults' perspective by focusing on their accounts of communication characteristics in the intergenerational relationship with the grandchild or nonfamily young adult. Considering SIT/CIIM and prior literature, the following research question is proposed.

RQ2: How do the communicative characteristics to which older adults attribute a lack of intergenerational conflict differ in family and nonfamily contexts?

Method

Participants: Background Information

The current study was part of a larger project the objective of which was to examine intergenerational communication themes in conflict situations from older adults' perspective in the United States. We recruited 427 older participants (i.e., 65 years old or above) initially. Specifically, we randomly asked the participants to think about an intergenerational relationship with a college age grandchild (the most frequently contacted grandchild) or with a college age nonfamilial young adult (the most frequently contacted nonfamily young adult). We then asked the participants to report a specific intergenerational conflict in the intergenerational relationship they had experienced or were experiencing. Among the 427 older participants recruited, 57.6 percent of them (i.e., 246) indicated that there was no conflict in the intergenerational relationship (126 in the family context and 120 in the nonfamily context). We then asked them to explain why they did not have conflict by focusing on describing communication characteristics in the intergenerational relationship with the grandchild or the nonfamily young adult respectively. In other words, this study examined the 246 older adults' (M age = 73.64, SD = 5.88, age range = 60–89; 174 females) written accounts about communication characteristics they attributed to a lack of conflict in the intergenerational relationships with the grandchild (i.e., 126) or the nonfamily young adult (i.e., 120).

Participants and Procedures

The current study recruited participants through a local Osher Lifetime Learning Institute and grandparent referrals. In 2018, an Osher Lifelong Learning Institute at a Midwestern university, which provides educational programs for older adults, agreed to send out an email to a group of their students to make them aware of the study. After Internal Review Board (IRB) approval, those who were interested in participating emailed their contact information to the researcher. In terms of grandparent referrals, we specifically asked student volunteers from a large Midwestern university and a small Midwestern private college to provide information about a grandparent who might be interested in participating in a study on intergenerational communication. Students received class credits for their referral.

The researchers gathered the older adults' contact information and sent them a survey with a self-addressed stamped return envelope. They were informed that their participation was voluntary, their name would not be associated in any way with the research findings, and that no one other than the researchers would have access to their responses in this study.

The older adults were primarily European-American/Caucasian/White (n = 224; 91.1 percent) with a small number of other ethnicities (i.e., 10 Asian Americans, 3 African- Americans, 4 Native Americans, and 2 other). They were randomly assigned one of the two survey conditions, asking them to think of an intergenerational relationship with a nonfamily young adult (approximately 18–25 years old) or a grandchild (approximately 18–25 years old) with whom they had the most frequent contact. The older adults then described the communication characteristics in the relationship they attributed to a lack of conflict. Of the participants 126 reported communication characteristics with the grandchild and 120 older adults reported communication characteristics with the nonfamily young adults. Following that, participants answered questions on the grandchild or the nonfamily young adult and questions about their own demographic information.

The grandchildren (*M* age = 20.39, *SD* = 2.59, age range = 18–31) reported in the intergenerational relationships were 42.1 percent female (*n* = 53) and 68 percent male (*n* = 73). The majority of the participants had never been the caretaker of the grandchild they reported on (*n* = 97; 76.9 percent), but a minority had (*n* = 29; 23 percent). The participants were related to the grandchildren both paternally (*n* = 45; 35.7%) and maternally (*n* = 80; 64.5 percent). Ninety-seven percent of grandchildren were full-grandchildren (*n* = 123), while two were step-grand-children, and in one case the relationship was not specified. Overall, the reported grandchildren were 91.3 percent European-American/Caucasian/White (*n* = 115) with a small number of other ethnicities (2 African-Americans, 4 Asian-Americans, 2 Native Americans and 1 other).

The nonfamily young adults (*M* age = 22.31, *SD* = 3.87, age range = 17–34) were 51 percent female (*n* = 61) and 49 percent male (*n* = 59). They were primarily European-American/Caucasian/White (*n* = 109; 90.8 percent) with a small number of other ethnicities (1 African-American, 6 Asian-Americans, 2 Native Americans, and 2 other). Overall, participants reported the young adults as co-workers (*n* = 6; 5 percent), neighbors (*n* = 22; 18.3 percent), acquaintances (*n* = 30; 25 percent), friends (*n* = 31; 25.8 percent), and other (*n* = 31; 25.8 percent). The length of the relationship ranged from zero years to thirty years (*M* = 8.09, *SD* = 7.97).

Development of the Coding Scheme

The older participants' written accounts typically ranged from a couple of sentences to one paragraph (about 100 words) with a few who wrote just a few words. A coding scheme, which consisted of refined categories from the literature and novel codes from the data, was developed to describe communication characteristics older adults attributed to a lack of conflict in family and nonfamily intergenerational relationships (see Table 14.1). Scholars have reported characteristics in satisfactory and unsatisfactory intergenerational communication (Harwood, 1998; Williams & Giles, 1996), including conflict situations (Wiebe & Zhang, 2017; Zhang & Lin, 2009). The coders first developed an a priori coding list (Table 14.1) based on these studies (see Hummert, 2019 for a review). Two coders familiarized themselves with prior literature on accommodative intergenerational communication such as mutual support/helping and understanding as a reference point for potential categories for the characteristics of intergenerational relationships reported by the participants in this study (Harwood, 1998; Harwood, McKee, & Lin, 2000; Williams & Giles, 1996). Older adults' reports with both grandchildren and nonfamily young adults were analyzed. A single, dominant code or characteristic was assigned to each narrative/scenario. A characteristic that appeared across several scenarios was considered to be a category. In the course of the process, new codes were added to the refined a priori list. Hence, the final coding scheme consisted of a mix of emergent codes/categories and manifest categories (a priori from the literature).

TABLE 14.1 Communicative characteristics attributed to the lack of conflict in intergenerational relationships as reported by older adults

Respect:* The older adult attributes the lack of conflict to the young adult's respect for them. Respondents often believe this was the result of how the young adult was raised. This respect can be mutual.
Example 1"We do our best to respect each other." (Grandchild)
Example 2"Mutual respect." (Nonfamily young adult)
Example 3"We have wonderful grandchildren and believe they were raised to respect us." (Grandchild)
Example 4"We have a relationship that respects one another's opinions." (Grandchild)
Example 5"She is extremely polite and respectful, and I can't imagine us having a conflict." (Grandchild)
Example 6"They love and respect me." (Grandchild)
Example 7"They have been taught and understand love and respect." (Grandchild)
Example 8"Parents raised the grandchildren to be polite and mind their manners." (Grandchild)
Example 9"My grandchildren were taught to respect their elders." (Grandchild)

Relational Closeness: The older adult attributes the lack of conflict to the high level of relational closeness with the young adult. These relationships seem enjoyable for both parties.
Example 1"I feel a closeness with young adults and enjoy talking to them." (Nonfamily young adult)
Example 2"We've always been close and had a good relationship since he was a young child." (Nonfamily young adult)
Example 3"My grandchildren and I have had an integral, loving, reciprocal relationship throughout their lives." (Grandchild)
Example 4"My grandchildren and I are very close." (Grandchild)
Example 5"I think I have a very good relationship with my grandchildren." (Grandchild)

Understanding:* The older adult attributes the lack of conflict to their general understanding of the young adult or mutual understanding of each other, which typically includes generational understanding.
Example 1"If I do run into a situation with a young non-family youth, I try to understand what they are looking for before I react." (Nonfamily young adult)
Example 2"I try to relate to young people, we were all young once. Human nature hasn't changed much." (Nonfamily young adult)

Lack of Interaction: The older adult attributes the lack of conflict to low levels of involvement, communication, or contact with the young adult.
Example 1"Not around them very much." (Grandchild)
Example 2"My exposure to this age group is minimal." (Nonfamily young adult)
Example 3"I am not around other young people that are not my family often enough to encounter a conflict." (Nonfamily young adult)
Example 4"Don't know them well enough to get into that situation." (Nonfamily young adult)

Attentive Communication and Listening:* The older adult attributes the lack of conflict to active listening and awareness while communicating with the young adult. This often included careful, strategic, and/or open communication between the parties.
Example 1"Good listening goes a long way toward a solution." (Grandchild)
Example 2"I listen. Give no advice." (Nonfamily young adult)
Example 3"I listen well and don't give unsolicited advice." (Nonfamily young adult)
Example 4"I try to listen first and respond sensitively." (Nonfamily young adult)
Example 5"We talk things through." (Grandchild)
Example 6"We have a very good line of communication with our grandchildren. We don't always agree, but we listen to each other." (Grandchild)

Respect of Interpersonal Boundaries:* The older adult attributes the lack of conflict to their attention to interpersonal boundaries and autonomy of the other individual. Some of the boundaries lead older adults to practice conflict avoidant and non-confrontational tendencies. Further, they believe interjecting opinions on difficult matters with the young adult would be inappropriate based on the older adult's role in some cases.

Example 1"I don't feel it is my place to interject myself into these situations." (Nonfamily young adult)

Example 2"It is not my business to express my opinions that might disagree with other young adults." (Nonfamily young adult)

Example 3"I don't always agree with the actions of the young adults of today, but I have never been in a position where it was my place to become involved with them." (Nonfamily young adult)

Example 4"Because if they are not my family I feel as though I should not butt in." (Nonfamily young adult)

Topics of Interest:* The older adult attributes the lack of conflict to pursuing commonalities with the young adult. The individuals usually focus on behaviors, opinions, and attitudes that are similar.

Example 1"These topics are ones that are not brought up with this young adult." (Nonfamily young adult)

Example 2"We avoid subjects of any depth and focus on just light talk and visits." (Grandchild)

---

* Characteristics that are accommodative in nature based on prior literature (see Hummert, 2019).

In the coder training process, the two coders coded the communication characteristics in intergenerational relationships with grandchildren ($n = 40$) and nonfamily young adults ($n = 40$). If there were any disagreements, the coders discussed the scenario together in more detail until an agreement was reached. Throughout the coder training process, adjustments were made to clarify the operational definitions of the communication characteristics attributed to a lack of conflict in their intergenerational relationships. When the list of communicative characteristics (Table 14.1) became exhaustive or saturated, the scenarios used for coder training were returned to the larger pool for coding later but were not included in the subsequent reliability check.

Coding and Reliability Check

Each of the two coders individually analyzed 60 responses (24.39 percent; 20 at the beginning, in the middle of the coding, and at the end, respectively). If a response had a characteristic that did not fall into any category on the list, it was coded into the "other" category. The overall intercoder reliability for the characteristics was measured using both percent agreement (0.97) and Scott's Pi (0.95), which was satisfactory. The remaining 186 responses were split up and individually coded by each coder. Six characteristics (i.e., 2.43 percent) were placed in the "other" category (e.g., "I like to get along with people" or "I'm a peaceful person"). Two of these characteristics involved a third party, usually a parent of the young adult, who protected the relationship from potentially problematic issues that could lead to conflict and two cases simply did not provide enough information to code (e.g., repeated that they did not have any conflict).

Results

Research Question 1 examined older adults' report of communication characteristics attributed to a lack of conflict in intergenerational relationships with young adults. Seven characteristics were identified through content analysis (i.e., respect, relational closeness, understanding, lack of interaction, attentive communication and listening, interpersonal boundaries, and topics of interest; see Table 14.1 for examples).

Table 14.2 presents the frequencies of the seven communicative characteristics explaining why older adults did not have intergenerational conflict with young adults. A one-way chi-square test indicated a significant difference in the frequency distributions of these characteristics, overall χ^2 (6) = 77.80, p <0.001. Follow-up pairwise comparisons evaluated the differences among these proportions (Green &

TABLE 14.2 Characteristics attributed to the lack of conflict in family and nonfamily intergenerational relationships as reported by older adults

Intergenerational Relationship Type				
Factors	Frequency	Family (%)	Nonfamily (%)	Adjusted Residual
Respect †	57[a]	46 (36.5%)	11 (9.2%)	5.1***
Relational Closeness	16[b]	15 (11.9%)	1 (0.8%)	3.5**
Understanding †	20[b]	5 (4.0%)	15 (12.5%)	2.4*
Lack of Interaction	65[a]	22 (17.5%)	43 (35.8%)	3.3***
Attentive Communication and Listening †	17[b]	11 (8.7%)	6 (5.0%)	1.2
Respect Interpersonal Boundaries †	46[a]	14 (11.1%)	32 (26.7%)	3.1**
Topics of Mutual Interest †	19[b]	11 (8.7%)	8 (6.7%)	0.6
Other	6	2 (1.6%)	4 (3.3%)	–
Total Count	246	126	120	–
Percentages	100	100	100	–

Note. Different superscripts in frequency column indicate significant differences according to Chi-square analyses. Overall χ^2(7) = 55.07, p <0.01.
*p <0.05 if adjusted residual >1.96; **p <0.01 if adjusted residual >2.58; *** p <0.001 if adjusted residual >3.20.
†Characteristics that are accommodative in nature based on prior literature.

Salkind, 2011; see Table 14.2). The results indicated that lack of interaction (n = 65; 26.42 percent), respect (n = 57; 23.17 percent), and interpersonal boundaries (n = 46; 18.70 percent) were the most frequently reported characteristics (no significant difference between the frequency distributions of the three characteristics). The results also indicated that relational closeness (n = 16; 6.50 percent), understanding of the other's perspective (n = 20; 8.13 percent), attentive communication and listening (n = 17; 6.91 percent), and topics of interests (n = 19; 7.72 percent) were less frequently reported characteristics (no significant difference between the four characteristics). In line with prior literature, respect, interpersonal boundaries, attentive communication, and topics of mutual interests were deemed accommodative (Hummert, 2019).

Research Question 2 examined how the characteristics varied based on family and nonfamily intergenerational relationships. A two-way contingency table analysis was conducted to evaluate whether there was a significant difference in the frequency distribution of the communication characteristics between family and nonfamily relationships. The type of relationship and the communicative characteristics were found to be significantly related, Pearson χ^2 (6,, n = 240) = 54.31, p <0.001, Cramér's V = 0.47. First, respect (adjusted residual = 5.1, p <0.001) and relational closeness (adjusted residual = 3.5, p <0.001) were reported more frequently as characteristics in family intergenerational relationships than in nonfamily intergenerational relationships. Second, understanding (adjusted residual = 2.4, p <0.05), lack of interaction (adjusted residual = 3.3, p <0.01), and interpersonal boundaries (adjusted residual = 3.1, p <0.01) were all reported more frequently as characteristics in nonfamily intergenerational relationships than in family intergenerational relationships (see Table 14.2).

Discussion

The accommodative characteristics that emerged from the older participants' written accounts describing their intergenerational relationships with young adults add a significant new perspective to intergenerational communication research. The results not only expand prior communication accommodation literature, they also provide new ground for future research. Based on communication accommodation theory (CAT) and the CIIM, this study contributes to prior literature in both communication accommodation and family and nonfamily intergenerational communication in several meaningful ways.

It is important to note that out of the total number of participants in the larger study with 427 participants, conflict was reported in less than 43 percent (n = 181) of the relationships. This study seems to show that intergenerational conflict may not be as prevalent as prior literature from the young adults' perspective suggests. The participants who reported that there was no conflict in their intergenerational relationships with young adults provide a fruitful insight into intergenerational communication. Most frequently in these cases, individuals show respect for one another, show respect for interpersonal boundaries, or lack interaction to experience conflict. Older adults also report relational closeness, an understanding of the other's perspective, attentive communication and listening, and discussing topics of interest as characteristics of intergenerational relationships that explain why they did not have intergenerational conflict.

Five of these characteristics (i.e., respect, attentive communication and listening, interpersonal boundaries, understanding, and topics of interest) reflect the findings of prior literature on intergenerational accommodation in satisfactory interactions (Harwood et al., 2000; Williams & Giles, 1996; Zhang & Hummert, 2001). The current study supports those claims by revealing the same reasons given by older adults to explain why they did not have conflict in their intergenerational relationships with young adults.

Contributions to CAT and Practical Implications

CAT is a theory that accounts for interpersonal and intergroup accommodation and nonaccommodation and thus provides a theoretical base and knowledge for the promotion of accommodative communication. Accommodative behaviors bridge the psychological distance between group members and provide a conducive environment for satisfying communication. Although most of the prior intergenerational research on CAT focuses on nonaccommodative communication, literature focusing on accommodative communication does exist (Harwood, 1998; Williams & Giles, 1996). The current study contributes to this body of research by showing that accommodative communication not only takes place in satisfactory intergenerational interactions (e.g., Williams & Giles, 1996), but also has specific attributes that contribute to an environment in which intergenerational conflict is not experienced.

Older adults report respect, interpersonal boundaries, and the lack of interaction as the most common characteristics explaining why there was no conflict in intergenerational relationships. The two most reported characteristics (i.e., respect and interpersonal boundaries) support prior literature on accommodative communication in intergenerational relationships. Young and older adults believe that respect is accommodative (Harwood et al., 2000) and young adults specifically report that respect from the older adults leads to satisfactory interactions (Williams & Giles, 1996). Further, respecting the autonomy of young adults and interpersonal boundaries is accommodative by nature (Fowler et al., 2013; Zhang & Hummert, 2001). This study adds to the literature by highlighting the two accommodative characteristics that exist in intergenerational relationships that are marked by a lack of conflict: a general respect for one another and interpersonal boundaries. Moreover, older adults attributed their low levels of contact and communication with young adults as a major reason why they had not experienced any recent conflict (i.e., lack of interaction), demonstrating that the absence of conflict does not mean presence of positive or beneficial communication (especially in relation to "lack of interaction").

The current study also demonstrates that understanding, attentive communication and listening, and topics of mutual interest (Williams & Giles, 1996) exist in intergenerational relationships that are marked by a lack of conflict. These findings provide fruitful ground for future research as well as practical takeaways for intergenerational relationships. The positive themes uncovered in the current study highlight the benefits of certain specific accommodative moves that may sustain positive intergenerational relationships for older adults. According to Abrams, Eller, & Bryant. (2006), adults who have had positive experiences with intergenerational communication were less likely to exhibit stereotypical behavior and performed much better on cognitive tasks than their counterparts who have had negative experiences with intergenerational contact. Hence, the accommodative characteristics not only add to CAT, they also provide fruitful grounds for future intervention research that could give individuals practical instruction on how to manage and reduce conflict in intergenerational relationships.

Family and Nonfamily Differences

CIIM provides a theoretical lens through which to view the conflict reports from the older adults. Shared family identity is relatively easy to establish (Banker & Gaertner, 1998) and can lead to more positive interactions (Gaertne & Dovidio, 2000). Additionally, family elders have been shown to be more supportive of young people than nonfamily elders (Giles et al., 2003; Ng et al., 1997). Therefore, shared family identity could enhance intergenerational communication in general.

Considering CIIM and previous supporting research on the influence of relationship type on intergenerational communication, the current study confirms that intergenerational communication differs in family and nonfamily contexts. Family relationships are characterized by respect and relational closeness, hence, older adults attributed the lack of conflict in intergenerational family relationships to respect and relational closeness more often than nonfamily relationships. Older participants who wrote about their communication with a grandchild in the current study often believed this was the result of the young adult's upbringing, which is most likely fostered by the grandparents' sense of pride in their own children's parenting capabilities. On the other hand, in these relationships characterized by relational closeness, older adults also attributed the lack of conflict to the level of relational closeness with young adults. These relationships seemed to be pleasing to both parties and reflect an ideal GP-GC relationship.

Moreover, older adults reported understanding, lack of interaction, and respecting interpersonal boundaries as reasons for lack of conflict more frequently in nonfamily intergenerational relationships than in family contexts. Understanding refers to the lack of conflict due to the older adult's general understanding of the young adult or mutual understanding of each other. Lack of interaction refers to the low level of involvement, communication, or contact with the young adult or vice versa, contributing to the absence of intergenerational conflict. Finally, interpersonal boundaries denote respect for limits and the autonomy of the other individual as an explanation for not having intergenerational conflict. Respect for boundaries is associated with older adults' practice of conflict avoidant and non-confrontational tendencies.

It is interesting to note that interpersonal boundaries are more likely to be acknowledged by nonfamily older adults as a characteristic of relationships that lack conflict. As discussed above, family elders may feel a heightened sense of obligation to their grandchildren and therefore may impose their own opinions and desires on young adult relatives (Zhang & Lin, 2009). Perhaps it is more that the shared family identity of grandparents and grandchildren loosens the interpersonal boundaries, which is consistent with findings in prior literature about the "grandparents' right to interfere." Grandparents are less likely to recognize or be willing to respect the interpersonal boundaries of their grandchildren. However, the failure to recognize or respect the interpersonal boundaries of their grandchildren has the potential to lead to conflict (Wiebe & Zhang, 2017; Zhang & Lin, 2009). The current study provides evidence that older adults believe interjecting opinions on difficult matters with a nonfamily young adult would be inappropriate, based on their role. However, the shared ingroup identity (i.e., shared family identity) seems to justify the grandparents' right to interfere.

Problematic Side of Intergenerational Communication

The objective and reason for the contact hypothesis and its subsequent development of intergroup contact theory was to reduce intergroup conflict, disconfirm stereotypes, and develop meaningful interpersonal relationships across groups in the hope of improving intergroup relations. Intergroup contact theory has specifically emphasized the importance of individual-level contact with outgroup members in improving group-level attitudes (Allport, 1954; Brown & Hewstone, 2005; Gaertner & Dovidio, 2000). This line of research has explored the relationship between contact and intergroup attitudes in both family and nonfamily intergenerational relationships (Harwood et al., 2005; Zhang et al., 2018). As such, these previous studies collectively explain how intergroup conflict, prejudice, and stereotypes can be managed, mitigated, and reduced through various contact modes (e.g., the quantity, quality, and type of contact) and intervening variables (e.g., anxiety, relational solidarity, and common ingroup identification).

From an intergroup perspective, when frequency of contact is low, intergenerational relationships might be less interpersonal and are more likely to be influenced by stereotypes. It is important to note that older adults attributed the lack of conflict to their low-level of contact and communication with young adults (i.e. lack of interaction) in the intergenerational relationships. Although older adults reported that there was no conflict in these relationships, it does not mean that these relationships did not have any problems. This lack of intergenerational contact has serious intergroup implications for individuals who battle against ageism. The contact hypothesis adds a theoretical perspective from which to further examine this phenomenon.

Limitations and Future Research

This study analyzed intergenerational communication based on older adults' accounts that were written retrospectively. This method provided valuable insights into accommodation within intergenerational relationships. More specifically, the written responses provided a qualitative data set in which communicative acts and moves from both the young and older adult within the relationship could be ana-lyzed. However, it is important to discuss other possible reasons why older adults did not report conflict. There are a few theoretical frameworks that could help understand these ideas. In one line of thinking, social desirability bias (Edwards, 1957) or politeness theory (Brown & Levinson, 1987) explains how participants might have the tendency to answer questions in a way that would be viewed more favorably by others. Thus, unlike young adults, older participants might not report conflict because they view it as negative and destructive. This view of conflict might lead them to feel that others might look down on them or think less of them if conflict existed within their relationships with young adults. Alternatively, older adults have been shown to report low conflict frequency in their relationships with young adults because of their social maturity and emotional control (Sillars & Zietlow, 1993). This perspective matches the aforementioned positivity effect that has been well-documented throughout intergenerational research (Isaacowitz & Blanchard-Fields, 2012; Scheibe & Carstensen, 2010). Scholars should examine these ideas more closely in future.

Second, when considering participants written accounts, it is important to remember that the responses were recalled and documented from memory. Fur-ther, the scenarios may not be representative of typical situations experienced by older adults. Rather, the scenarios might have been the ones that were most salient in older adults' minds for a multitude of reasons. The scope of this study does not provide a comprehensive answer for why each participant reported on communication in the intergenerational relationship in the way they did. However, future research should use different methodologies to examine intergenerational accommodation.

Overall, the findings in this study have provided further evidence to demonstrate the theoretical utility of CAT in research examining communication in intergenerational relationships. The wide range of characteristics reported in intergenerational relation-ships that are marked by a lack of conflict demonstrate the complex nature of the interplay between shared family identity, accommodation, and type of relationship in shaping intergenerational communication. Overall, it is important to note that certain intergenerational characteristics (e.g., lack of interaction) have intergroup implications that should not be ignored and deserve further attention.

References

Abrams, D., Eller, A., & Bryant, J. (2006). An age apart: The effects of intergenerational contact and stereotype threat on performance and intergroup bias. *Psychology and Aging*, 4, 691–702. doi:10.1037/0882-7974.21.4.691.

Allport, G. W. (1954). *The nature of prejudice*. London: Addison-Wesley.

Banker, B. S. & Gaertner, S. L. (1998). Achieving stepfamily harmony: An intergroup-relations approach. *Journal of Family Psychology*, 12, 310–325. doi:10.1037/0893-3200.12.3.310.

Brown, P. & Levinson, S. (1987). *Politeness: Some universals in language usage.* New York, NY: Cambridge University Press.

Brown, R. & Hewstone, M. (2005). An integrative theory of intergroup contact. In M. P. Zanna (Ed.), *Advances in experimental social psychology* (Vol. 37; pp. 255–343). Elsevier Academic Press. doi:10.1016/S0065-2601(05)37005-5.

Coupland, N., Coupland, J., Giles, H., & Henwood, K. (1988). Accommodating the elderly: Invoking and extending a theory. *Language and Society*, 17, 1–41. doi:10.1017/s0047404500012574.

Edwards, A. (1957). *The social desirability variable in personality assessment and research.* New York, NY: The Dryden Press.

Fowler, C., Fisher, C. L., & Pitts, M. J. (2013). Older adults' evaluations of middle-aged children's attempts to initiate discussion of care needs. *Health Communication*, 29, 717–727. doi:10.1080/10410236.2013.786278.

Gaertner, S. L. & Dovidio, J. F. (2000). *Reducing intergroup bias: The common ingroup identity model.* New York, NY: Psychology Press. doi:10.4324/9781315804576.

Gasiorek, J. (2017). Nonaccommodation. In H. Giles & J. Harwood (Eds.), *Oxford encyclopedia of intergroup communication* (pp. 179–192). New York: Oxford University Press. doi:10.1093/acrefore/9780190228613.013.440.

Giles, H. (2008). Communication Accommodation Theory. In L. A. Baxter & D. O. Braithwaite (Eds.), *Engaging theories in interpersonal communication: Multiple perspectives* (pp. 1–22). Thousand Oaks, CA: Sage.

Giles, H. Noels, K., Williams, A., Lim, T.-S., Ng, S.-H., Ryan, E. *et al.* (2003). Intergenerational communication across cultures: Young people's perceptions of conversations with family elders, nonfamily elders, and same age peers. *Journal of Cross-Cultural Gerontology*, 18, 1–30. doi:10.1023/a:1024854211638.

Giles, H. & Williams, A. (1994). Patronizing the young: Forms and evaluations. *International Journal of Aging and Human Development*, 39, 33–53. doi:10.2190/0LUC-NWMA- K5LX-NUVW.

Green, S. & Salkind, N. (2011) *Using SPSS for Windows and Macintosh: Analyzing and understanding data.* Boston: Prentice Hall.

Harwood, J. (1998). Young adults' cognitive representations of intergenerational conversations. *Journal of Applied Communication Research*, 26, 13–31. doi:10.1080/00909889809365489.

Harwood, J., Giles, H., & Palomares, N. A. (2005). Intergroup theory and communication processes. In J. Harwood & H. Giles (Eds.), *Intergroup communication: Multiple perspectives* (pp. 1–18). New York, NY: Peter Lang.

Harwood, J. & Lin, M-C. (2000). Affiliation, pride, exchange and distance in grandparents' accounts of relationships with their college-age grandchildren. *Journal of Communication*, 50, 31–47. doi:10.1111/j.1460-2466.2000.tb02851.x.

Harwood, J., McKee, J., & Lin, M.-C. (2000). Younger and older adults' schematic representations of intergenerational communication. *Communication Monographs*, 67, 20–41. doi:10.1080/03637750009376493.

Harwood, J. Raman, P., & Hewstone, M. (2006). Communicative predictors of group salience in the intergenerational setting. *Journal of Family Communication*, 6, 181–200. doi:10.1207/s15327698jfc0603_2.

Hummert, M. L. (1994). *Stereotypes of the elderly and patronizing speech.* In M. L. Hummert, J. M. Weimann, & J. F. Nussbaum (Eds.), *Interpersonal communication in adulthood* (pp. 162–184). Newbury Park, CA: Sage.

Hummert, M. L. (2019). Intergenerational communication. In J. Harwood, J. Gasiorek, H. Pierson, J. F. Nussbaum, & C. Gallois (Eds.), *Language, communication, and intergroup relations: A celebration of the scholarship of Howard Giles* (pp. 130–161). New York, NY: Routledge.

Isaacowitz, D. M. & Blanchard-Fields, F. (2012). Linking process and outcome in the study of emotion and aging. *Perspectives on Psychological Science*, 7, 3–16. doi:10.1177/1745691611424750.

Kemper, S. (1994). "Elderspeak": Speech accommodations to older adults. *Aging and Cognition*, 1, 17–28. doi:10.1080/09289919408251447.

Littlejohn, S. W. & Foss, A. F. (2005). *Theories of human communication*. Belmont, CA: Thomson and Wadsworth.

Ng, S. H, Liu, J. H., Weatherall, A., & Loong, C. F. (1997). Younger adults' communication experiences and contact with elders and peers. *Human Communication Research*, 24, 82–108. doi:10.1111/j.1468-2958.1997.tb00588.x.

Pitts, M. & Harwood, J. (2015). Communication accommodation competence: The nature and nurture of accommodative resources across the lifespan. *Language and Communication*, 41, 89–99. doi:10.1016/j.langcom.2014.10.002.

Ryan, E. B., Giles, H., Bartolucci, G., & Henwood, K. (1986). Psycholinguistic and social psychological components of communication by and with the elderly. *Language and Communication*, 6, 1–24. doi:10.1016/0271-5309(86)90002–90009.

Scheibe, S. & Carstensen, L. L. (2010). Emotional aging: Current and future trends. *Journal of Gerontology*, 65, 133–144. https://doi.org/10.1093/geronb/gbp132.

Sillars, A. & Zietlow, P. H. (1993). Investigations of martial communication and lifespan development. In N. Coupland & J. F. Nussbaum (Eds.), *Discourse and lifespan identity* (pp. 237–261). Newbury Park, CA: Sage.

Soliz, G. & Giles, H. (2014). Relational and identity processes in communication: A contextual and meta-analytical review of communication accommodation theory. In E. Cohen (Ed.), *Communication yearbook 38* (pp. 106–143). New York, NY: Routledge.

Soliz, J. & Harwood, J. (2006). Shared family identity, age salience, and intergroup contact: Investigation of the grandparent-grandchild relationship. *Communication Monographs*, 73, 2006. doi:10.1080/03637750500534388.

Song, Y. & Zhang, Y. B. (2012). Husbands' conflict styles in Chinese mother/daughter-in-law conflicts: Daughters-in-law's perspectives. *Journal of Family Communication*, 12, 57–74. doi:10.1080/15267431.2011.629968.

Tajfel, H. & Turner, J. C. (1986). The social identity theory of intergroup behavior. In S. Worchel & W. Austin (Eds.), *Psychology of intergroup relations* (pp. 7–24). Chicago: Nelson-Hall.

Wiebe W. T. & Zhang, Y. B. (2017). Conflict initiating factors and management styles in family and nonfamily integrational relationships: Young adults' retrospective written accounts. *Journal of Language and Social Psychology*, 36, 368–379. doi:10.1177/0261927X16660829.

Williams, A. & Giles, H. (1996). Intergenerational conversations: Young adults' retrospective accounts. *Human Communication Research*, 23, 220–250. doi:10.1111/j.1468- 2958.1996.tb00393.x.

Zhang, Y. B. (2004). Initiating factors of Chinese intergenerational conflict: Young adults' written accounts. *Journal of Cross-Cultural Gerontology*, 19, 299–319. doi:10.1023/B:JCCG.0000044686.61485.94.

Zhang, Y. B. & Giles, H. (2018). Communication accommodation theory. In Y. Y. Kim (Ed.), *The international encyclopedia of intercultural communication* (pp. 95–108). Hoboken, NJ: Wiley. doi:10.1002/9781118783665.ieicc0156.

Zhang, Y. B. & Hummert, M. L. (2001). Harmonies and tensions in Chinese intergenerational communication. *Journal of Asian Pacific Communication*, 11, 203–230. doi:10.1075/japc.11.2.06zha.

Zhang, Y. B. & Imamura, M. (2018). Communication accommodation theory and intergroup communication. In H. Giles & J. Harwood (Eds.), *Oxford encyclopedia of intergroup communication* (Vol. 1, pp. 133–150). New York, NY: Oxford University Press. doi:10.1093/acrefore/9780190228613.013.484.

Zhang, Y. B. & Lin, M.-C. (2009). Conflict initiating factors in intergenerational relationships. *Journal of Language and Social Psychology*, 28, 343–363. doi:10.1177/0261927X09341836.

Zhang, Y. B., Paik, S., Xing, C., & Harwood, J. (2018). Young adults' contact experiences and attitudes toward aging: Age salience and intergroup anxiety in South Korea. *Asian Journal of Communication*, 28, 468–489. doi:10.1080/01292986.2018.1453848.

Zhang, Y. B. & Pitts, M. J. (2019). Interpersonal accommodation. In J. Harwood, J. Gasiorek, H. Pierson, J. F. Nussbaum, & C. Gallois (Eds.), *Language, communication, and intergroup relations: A celebration of the scholarship of Howard Giles* (pp. 192–216). New York, NY: Routledge.

15

INTERCULTURAL COMMUNICATION MANAGEMENT PROFESSIONALS IN THE JAPANESE LINGUISTIC AND CULTURAL ENVIRONMENT

Yuko Takeshita

Introduction

Having had the Tokyo Olympic Games in 2020, the inscriptions of Mt. Fuji (2013) and Tomioka Silk Mill (2014) on the UNESCO World Heritage List, and the addition of *washoku*, or traditional Japanese cuisine (2013), and *washi*, or traditional Japanese handmade paper (2014), to the list of the UNESCO Intangible Cultural Heritage, Japanese people have never been so enthusiastic about globalization and internationalization as they are today. At the same time, in a country where the nationals can meet almost all of their basic needs in the Japanese language, opportunities are still scarce for actual practices of international and intercultural communication. Looking for ways to fill the gap is a serious challenge for Japanese society.

Ever since the Japanese government started a campaign called Visit Japan, the number of foreign tourists has been increasing (see Figure 15.1), and it is expected to rise even more in the future, especially in the metropolitan area that surrounds the Olympic venues. Therefore, the country needs to be prepared for an unprecedented international environment on the archipelago.

In many attempts to promote international communication competence for Japanese citizens, English education has been the focus of attention. English teaching was recently introduced in primary school classrooms, involving pupils and their parents, teachers and educators and even preschoolers and their pushy mothers to discuss formal and informal English education. English language schools for children as well as adults are flourishing in towns and cities throughout the country, and companies are asking their employees and job-hunters for higher English proficiency test scores. However, people also acknowledge that English skills do not necessarily guarantee the acquisition of intercultural communication competency.

DOI: 10.4324/9781003252955-18

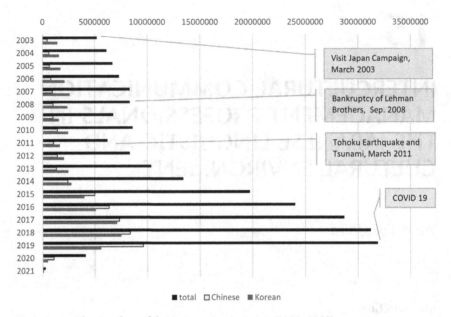

FIGURE 15.1 The number of foreign tourists in Japan (2003–2022)

In such a situation, there have new attempts to provide better learning and enlightening opportunities. One example is a Tokyo-based non-profit organization that started in 2013 to issue certificates of International Communication Management Professionals. These are given to those who have successfully finished an e-learning program that provides learners with opportunities to study different aspects of international communication and to solve problems and manage conflicts in international and intercultural situations with different kinds of knowledge and skills.

In this chapter, I will addresses questions regarding why Japanese society needs communication professionals; what their roles and contributions might be for Japanese institutions and organizations that have previously been solely domestically oriented; and what new opportunities they could create in various business fields by improving the international competence of corporate enterprises, government bodies and other organizations that are in dire need of multinational business dealings and intercultural activities. All these viewpoints give a clearer picture of how the professionals could help their follow citizens avoid intercultural conflicts both at home and abroad.

The significance of internationalizing Japanese citizens can be illustrated by numerous cases of intercultural conflicts. An example in September 2013 created much discussion and helped raise awareness among Japanese people as to how we can face people with different thoughts and ideas as well as appearance. The fact that no conclusion has been reached, however, indicates how difficult it may be for Japanese to become familiar with things that have not been in their cultural and historical heritage. The conflict arose because a Maori woman was refused entry to a public bath in Hokkaido, the farthest north island of the archipelago (Agence

France-Press, 2013). This woman had facial *ta moko* tattoos, which are traditionally worn by members of various indigenous groups in New Zealand. Many Japanese public institutions, especially bathing facilities, deny entry to people with tattoos because they are associated with members of Japan's organized crime syndicates, many of whom have tattoos on their bodies. While the Maori woman and her supporters considered this to be discrimination, the official of the facility said that it was not possible for Japanese people to understand the reason for the Maori woman's tattoos even if they were part and parcel of her traditional, indigenous culture.

While the episode shows that it may take more time and effort for Japanese facilities to decide whether to modify their attitude toward cases involving different cultural traditions, the food business seems to take advantage of the culinary traditions that have come into Japan via foreign tourists. With the increase in the number of tourists from Islamic countries, more restaurants in Japan put signs saying that they serve Halal food. Nevertheless, this change has resulted in upsetting some Muslims because many Japanese still lack a great deal of knowledge when it comes to their local food cultures, an example of which is the fact that alcoholic beverages are often served in abundance in Halal restaurants.

International communication management professionals in Japan described in this chapter are trained to make contributions in various ways. For instance, they can work as preventers of cultural conflicts, advisors to people trying to become culturally and socially tolerant and flexible and mediators in situations where there are disagreements as a result of different cultural values and behaviors.

Linguistic Auditing Plus in the Japanese Situation

When we as researchers started discussing ways to promote international and intercultural communication competence for Japanese people, we focused on language auditing because English proficiency was (and still is) necessary in many international situations. According to Koster (2004), linguistic or language auditing is "an investigation of the language needs of a particular organization," and its findings provide "the basis of a report outlining what action the organization needs to undertake in order to increase the language competence of its employees and thereby improving contacts with foreign clients" (p. 5). Koster (2004) clarified the two main purposes of a language audit: (1) to help an organization develop and implement a foreign-language policy; and (2) to collect data that enable a language school or language trainer to develop a customized course for individual employees and/or for specified groups of employees.

Reeves and Wright (1996) explained the objective of a language audit from another perspective. It is "to help the management of a firm identify the strengths and weaknesses of their organization in terms of communication in foreign languages," so that it can "map the current capability of departments, functions and people against the identified need and establish that need at the strategic level, at the process ... level and at that of the individual postholders" (p. 5).

Thus, we concluded that Japan needs a language auditing program for business and government bodies as well as individual employers and employees. The

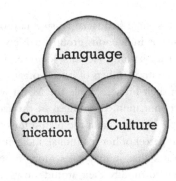

FIGURE 15.2 Three important factors of Japanese people's awareness for internationalization

responsibility of a language auditor is to make an accurate assessment of the international language environment and to deal with the situations that may arise therein (Honna, Saruhashi, & Takeshita, 2011). By assessing linguistic abilities for international communication and writing training plans, and by a having a clear foreign-language plan, Japanese organizational bodies can better identify their strategic needs and increase their business opportunities. As for international communication with a focus on languages, linguistic auditing is likely to be a key to improving the communication competence of Japanese people.

However people's experiences in international situations make it evident that trying to overcome the weaknesses of Japanese organizations and increase their intercultural/national communication capabilities—by training employees in language skills—will not solve the problem. It is difficult for Japanese people with a high-context culture and a distinguished national language to engage and accept different cultures and communication styles. In other words, the solution we are looking for needs not only to pay attention to foreign language learning and training but to culture and communication. That is, companies and organizations should have a linguistic as well as a cultural and communication audit that is followed and supported by a systematic attempt to increase people's awareness of the importance of obtaining language as well as cultural sensitivity and communication skills. They need to be made aware that these skills will make them more competent and feel more at ease in international and intercultural communication (see Figure 15.2).

International Communication Management Professionals

Foreign languages such as English are taught at different levels of education in Japan with notable differences in rigor, enthusiasm and proficiency. However, opportunities for students to learn about various cultures and to interact with people from different cultures are very limited, especially in a classroom situation. This has produced learners who may have some basic language ability, but who do not have any cultural knowledge and experience in real communication situations. Training students to become capable auditors in language, culture and communication has not been successful in Japanese schools.

In order to tackle this problem, when organizing a study course for linguistic, cultural and communication auditors, we introduced the instructor as an International Communication Management Professional (ICMP), who was engaged in International Communication Management (ICM). Although the course aimed to train people to become an ICMP, we also developed a beginner's course wherein people could train to be an International Communication Associate Professional (ICM-AP), so that the training could proceed from the introductory to the professional level.

The responsibility of an ICMP is to identify the international linguistic, cultural and communication environment and develop strategic plans according to the situation. In relation to professionals in business, they are expected to respond competently to various issues in conflict and crisis management to create new business opportunities.

In the training the differences between ICM-AP and ICMP are clarified, so that the learners can set specific goals for their learning activities and envisage business possibilities. Thus, an ICM-AP is a person who:

- understands the basics of English as an international language, intercultural communication and international communication management;
- is capable of putting the knowledge in to practice.

An ICMP is a person who:

- has a good command of international languages, cultures and communication strategies that are required in global business;
- has a sufficient understanding of the theory of international communication management;
- knows how to cope with language use and develop international communication strategies in her/his company.

More precisely, Figure 15.3 shows a can-do list for an ICM-AP and an ICMP.

ICM-AP	ICMP
• can acknowledge the importance of communication in daily business activities. • can know how to communicate without depending on "*sasshi*" or tacit understanding. • can understand international communication management and devise ways of communicating interculturally. • can understand what it means for English to be an international language. • can actively use English as an international language.	• can understand how to practically develop international cooperative communication. • can analyze needs for business skills and languages required in international business situations, and make a general plan containing measures that correspond to various needs. • can understand how to develop international communication strategies and programs for developing global human resources. • can specifically understand the importance of intercultural communication and how to manage it.

FIGURE 15.3 A can-do list for the ICM-AP and the ICMP

It is desirable for every governmental or private organization to have at least one full-time ICMP. However, taking advantage of outsourced professionals is also beneficial because of the large amount of time and the cost of training one's own employees. In order to provide qualified ICMPs for people and organizations engaging in international business within and outside Japan, the training program offered its students the following services:

1.   A book published by an educational publisher in Tokyo on international communication management is used as a textbook for the learners of ICMP and ICM-AP.
2.   An e-learning program for ICMPs and ICM-APs. e-Learning content is provided by a university-related private educational company, and the ICMP office is located in a private language school.
3.   Certificates of qualification for ICMPs and ICM-AP are issued by a non-profit organization.

The provider of e-learning courses, the ICMP office, the publisher and the non-profit organization are all independent from one another, but they may cooperate and work together to help train ICM-APs and ICMPs.

The Book

The title of the 245-page book on ICMP can be translated as *How Enterprises and Universities Can Cultivate People for Global Communities: A Recommendation of International Communication Management* (*kigyo daigaku wa gurobaru jinzai wo dou sodateruka: kokusai komyunikeshion manejimento no susume*). The book is used for general readers and learners in ICM-AP and ICMP programs. The table of contents of this supplemental textbook demonstrates the knowledge we expect learners to acquire in e-learning programs.

Chapters 1–3 contain introductory and theoretical information that serves as required reading for CM-AP learners. Chapters 5, 10, 11, 15, 16, 17 and 20 are for ICMP learners and focus on real-life situations and offer pragmatic instructions. However, learners at both levels are referred to any of these chapters whenever their tasks in the programs demand it.

The e-Learning Programs and Qualifications for ICMP and ICM-AP

The procurement of the ICM-AP is a prerequisite for the ICMP. It is intended for undergraduate and graduate students who wish to work for global enterprises, company recruits, young employees, communication and human resource professionals and those facing multi-cultural communication issues in the workplace. The length of this course is three months, during which time learners are asked to complete three written assignments, with each assignment corresponding to one of the introductory chapters of the textbook.

kigyo daigaku wa gurobaru jinzai wo dou sodateruka: *kokusai komyunikeshion manejimento no susume*	
Part 1:	**Why We Need International Languages, Cultures and Communication Today**
Chapter 1	International Cooperative Communication: Beyond the Culture of *sasshi*, or Tacit Understanding
Chapter 2	What It Means That English is an International Language
Chapter 3	What is International Communication Management?
Part 2:	**How Organizations Deal with Languages**
Chapter 4	In-house English Education and Cultivating Global-Minded Employees
Chapter 5	Enhancement of English for Specific Purposes
Chapter 6	Assessment of Employees' English Proficiency
Chapter 7	Japanese English and Its Assessment
Chapter 8	Enterprises and Languages Other Than English
Chapter 9	Enterprises and Communication in Sign Language: In View of Language Rights for Minorities
Chapter 10	Japanese as a Foreign Language
Chapter 11	Plain Japanese: Enhancement of Communication with Consumers
Chapter 12	Plain English: For Sending Out Information Effectively from Japan
Chapter 13	Teaching English as an International Language: Possibilities for Cultivating Global Citizens in Universities
Chapter 14	Common Target Level for Language Learning: Significance and Application of CEFR
Part 3:	**Intercultural Communication and Multicultural Management**
Chapter 15	Communication and Cultural Understanding
Chapter 16	Multiculturalization of English and Intercultural Literacy
Chapter 17	Communication and Humor
Chapter 18	Communication That Does Not Depend on Languages: The Bright and Dark Sides of Non-Verbal Communication
Chapter 19	Presentation in English as an International Language and Its Training
Chapter 20	Global Business Mind and Communication
Part 4:	**Toward the Practice of International Communication Management**
Chapter 21	Multicultural Management Organization and Business Management
Chapter 22	Linguistic Needs Analysis and Measures in Enterprises
Chapter 23	Planning, Monitoring and Assessing Training Programs

FIGURE 15.4 The table of contents

The ICMP is also intended for those in charge of human resources development and those working in overseas businesses or solving multi-cultural issues in enterprises and public administration. This course can extend to six months, and learners are then expected to submit seven written assignments in the program.

In the training program, finishing the course and applying for a certificate are two separate issues. If a company, for example, treats the learning program as part

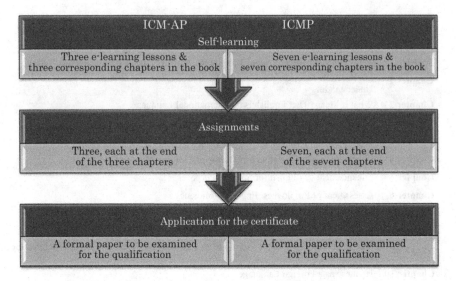

FIGURE 15.5 The flow for the qualifications of the ICM-AP and the ICMP

of its in-house education, learners may receive a certificate of completion of the course. Learners may satisfactorily complete an extra paper on a specified theme to become a qualified ICM-AP or ICMP.

The learning is carried out in an educational environment, although it is a self-supported process. In this process learners submit mini-reports at the end of each lesson and receive feedbacks from instructors. If learners fail at the final qualification stage, they will receive the evaluator's advice, so that they can redo the paper and submit it for a second time. Generally, a learner starts the program at the ICM-AP level and then proceeds to the ICMP level. Learners with international work and /or study experience or who have previously participated in an international communication management program are eligible for an exemption from the ICM-AP program and can begin their training at the ICMP level. College students are usually not eligible for this exemption because they often have not previously worked in an international environment or taken part in an international communication program.

Some Specific Situations Where International Communication Management is Needed

There are both immediate and potential needs for ICMPs in Japan. Despite the beautiful network of trains, buses and subways, convenience stores and vending machines at every street corner, numerous TV channels in hotel rooms, several large-scale national newspapers and police officers who can act as a guide and provide directions, foreign tourists in Tokyo will almost immediately find that getting around in the city is not easy unless they can read Japanese.

In 2014 there was a move toward a more internationally friendly environment is the rewording of street signs. In August 2014 the Ministry of Land, Infrastructure, Transport and Tourism, in collaboration with the Tokyo Metropolitan Government, started to rewrite some street signs in Tokyo, so that the signs could be more easily understood by foreigners. For example, the sign at the traffic intersection nearest to the national diet, or *kokkai*), used to read as 国会前 and *Kokkai* in the Latin alphabet (see Figure 15.6) indicating how the Japanese word for the national diet is pronounced. However, it now reads as 国会前 and The National Diet (see Figure 15.6). Non-Japanese readers may no longer know how The National Diet is pronounced in Japanese, but they do know where they are. The example shows three things that an ICMP should be aware of and act upon in in this scenario. They should (1) be able to recognize that *Kokkai* may not mean anything to non-Japanese readers; (2) know that the English translation of *kokkai* is The National Diet; and (3) persuade the authorities to replace the Japanese pronunciation with the translation of the term.

International communication management is significant in the information age, in which the Internet is a key medium for international business. As Honna, Takeshita, Miyake, and Mase (2012) observed, "While much is disseminated in Japanese for domestic consumption, little is prepared in English for international audiences" (p. 74). As a result, those "abroad who attempt access to English language websites of Japanese government offices and companies have more often than not been largely disappointed at not finding what they wish to obtain" (p. 74). This is a reason why Japan is seen as an "invisible" country, which may lead to misunderstanding and distrust. To welcome more foreign tourists, Japan should improve this situation by building a more internationally friendly environment both online and on the ground.

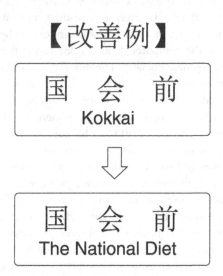

FIGURE 15.6 The internationalization of street signs in Tokyo

Therefore, governmental and private organizations in Japan urgently need an effective international communication management strategy. While the services they require in this regard are to benefit foreigners, it could also help Japanese people become more internationally oriented. Moreover, the ICM approach can create new business opportunities for companies in the international arena. Honna, Takeshita and D'Angelo (2012) gave three specific examples of Japanese companies finding a way to survive in difficult times. The first is businesses making small parts that were abandoned by automobile manufacturers in the economic depression. Those small businesses that were able to advertise the quality of their products through their English websites not only survived but also proved to be more prosperous by selling their products to international customers.

A similar success story applies to local Japanese *sake* breweries that lost their business in Japan, but were able to find international customers through the promotion of Japanese food culture overseas. The last example is domestic Japanese-style inns that lost domestic customers due to the preference for more modern and convenient western-style hotels. Those inns are now flourishing with foreign tourists who want like to stay there to enjoy the Japanese atmosphere. International business opportunities are abundant domestically and internationally. It is the responsibility of the ICMP to help people become aware of such needs, locate where the needs are and provide appropriate information in such a way that recipients can benefit from it.

Conclusion

It is a huge challenge, to say the least, for a learning program to be able to help learners successfully acquire languages, cultures and communication skills so that they are able to apply them effectively in real-time international environments. This is due, in part, to the fact that real-life situations cannot be precisely mimicked in the classroom or on the computer. It is also due to the fact that such situations are not common in Japanese society. Though the e-learning content discussed above tends to be theoretical rather than practical, it does help to raise people's awareness of issues and problems in international situations and of the needs for effective ways to manage international communication. In addition, the programs described in this chapter provide a DVD as a backup s to avoid technical problems learners may encounter in the e-learning system, and the learning materials are constantly updated to reflect social trends and meet changing demands.

Finally, the increase in foreign tourists visiting Japan, which causes a demand for a more international environment in Japan, is the catalyst for the design of the program discussed in this chapter. In addition to the situations described above, the working environment for non-Japanese employees also deserves to be mentioned. There are many foreign employees in Japan, and their linguistic and cultural differences may cause misunderstanding and conflict in the workplace. As the ICMP program increases cultural and linguistic diversity it can reduce the likelihood of potential conflict that could result from linguistic and cultural misunderstandings in the process of intercultural and international communication.

References

Agence France-Presse. (2013, September 13). Tattooed Maori woman barred from Japanese public bath. *ABC News*. Retrieved from www.abc.net.au/news/2013-09-13/tattooed-ma ori-woman-barred-from-japanese-public-bath/4957234.

Honna, N., Saruhashi, J., & Takeshita, Y. (2011). *Practicing effective international language management in business context*. Tokyo, Japan: ALC.

Honna, N., Takeshita, Y., & D'Angelo, J. (2012). *Understanding English across cultures*. Tokyo, Japan: Kinseido Publishing Company, Ltd.

Honna, N., Takeshita, Y., Miyake, H., & Mase, Y. (Eds.). (2012). *How enterprises and universities can cultivate people for global communities: A recommendation of international communication management*. Tokyo, Japan: ASK.

Koster, C. (2004). Language auditing: An introduction. In C. Loster (Ed.), *A handbook on language auditing* (pp. 5–13). Amsterdam, The Netherlands: Editions De Werelt.

Reeves, N. & Wright, C. (1996). *Linguistic auditing: A guide to identifying foreign language communication needs in corporations*. Clevedon, UK: Multilingual Matters.

16

CONFLICTS IN AN INTERNATIONAL BUSINESS CONTEXT

A Theoretical Analysis of Interpersonal (Pseudo) Conflicts

Michael B. Hinner

Introduction

While competition is a key component of any market driven economy, business relationships are generally conducted in good faith. These relationships revolve around cooperation and trust for the mutual benefit of both business partners (Friman, Gärling, Mattsson, & Johnston, 2002; Walter, Ritter, & Gemünden, 2001). However, misunderstandings and misperceptions are possible even in the best relationships (Adler, Rodman, & du Pré, 2020; DeVito, 2015; Gamble & Gamble, 20212). While misunderstandings are not deliberately designed to confuse or irritate one's business partner, they do have the potential for conflict. In fact, often well intended messages or gestures may be misconstrued and, thus, unintentionally result in a conflict that no one wanted (Adler et al, 2020; DeVito, 2015; Gamble & Gamble, 2012). Over the past decades, English has become the *lingua franca* of the global business world (Seidelhofer, 2005). While this may seem to have simplified communication, that is not always the case because if the interlocutors use English as the language of communication, this may further complicate matters. After all, people tend to transfer the meaning of words from their own native language to English. If one or both interlocutors are non-native speakers of English, then even the denotative meaning may not be shared (Klopf, 1998). Yet people often tend to assume that others share their meaning; even when that may not actually be the case (Ruhly, 1982). Such a misunderstanding can compound matters when people assume they share meaning, but in fact do not, and later discover that they had not shared meaning (Dougherty, Mobley, & Smith, 2010). Then such disconfirmed expectations can create disappointment which could result in conflict. On the other hand, using English as a second language may make people more aware of potential misunderstandings because people tend to be more circumspect when communicating in a language in which they are not very fluent (Keysar, Hayakawa, & An, 2012).

DOI: 10.4324/9781003252955-19

In order to understand how and why people communicate the way they do with other people, it is necessary to understand what factors influence communication at the individual, the interpersonal, and the (inter)cultural levels (Doise, 1986).[1] That is why this chapter will examine how identity, culture, perception, self-disclosure, and trust influence interpersonal communication and relationships. These factors can provide clues as to how and why misunderstandings and misperceptions can arise which can culminate in conflict. With a better understanding of the causes of interpersonal conflicts due to misunderstandings and misperceptions, it is possible to consider the means of overcoming such conflicts. Social metacognition can be helpful in identifying the probable cause(s) of conflicts that are the result of misunderstandings and misperceptions. Conflict management is fairly complex and requires considerable cognitive input and multiple strategies to successfully manage and resolve interpersonal conflicts (Canary & Lakey, 2006; Canary & Spitzberg, 1987; Canary & Spitzberg, 1989; Caughlin & Vangelisti, 2006; Roloff & Ifert, 2000; Roloff & Wright, 2013; Sillars, 2010; Sillars, Roberts, Leonard, & Dun, 2000; Sillars & Weisberg, 1987).

Identity

To understand conflicts at the individual level, it is necessary to understand identity. Identity refers to how individuals perceive themselves, i.e. self-concept, as well as the relationship and interaction of the self with others, i.e. cultural identity (Doise, 1986). Self-concept, in turn, consists of self-awareness, self-image, and self-esteem (Adler et al., 2020; Gamble & Gamble, 2012).

Self-awareness refers to the ability to recognize oneself as an individual separate from the environment and other individuals, i.e. consciousness (Duval & Wicklund, 1972). Rochat (2003) has identified five levels of self-awareness ranging from no self-awareness, which is classified as *Level 0: Confusion*, all the way to *Level 5: Self-consciousness or "Meta" Self-awareness*. At Level 5, a person sees him/herself not only from his/her own perspective, but is also aware that others see one as well and this perception could be different from one's own self-perception (Rochat, 2003). Rochat points out that while humans move from one level of awareness to the next, not everyone actually reaches Level 5. In other words, not everyone may actually be able to consider that other people may perceive oneself differently than one sees oneself. As was pointed out above, this may play a crucial role in conflict management.

Self-image refers to how a person sees him/herself and how that person thinks others see him/her which is based on his/her interaction with others. Self-image essentially refers to how one defines oneself. Once established, it is fairly resistant to change. A positive self-image means that individuals have high self-worth, are open-minded, and have a positive other evaluation. Those who have a negative self-image are more likely to have poor self-worth, be susceptible to stereotypes and prejudices, and have a negative other-evaluation (Adler et al., 2020, Gamble & Gamble, 2012).

Self-esteem influences the self-image with a predominantly positive or negative concept (Adler et al., 2020). Hence, if someone has a generally positive self-image, then that person will probably have high self-esteem. Someone with high self-esteem is more willing to communicate than someone with low self-esteem (Adler et al., 2020; Hamacheck, 1992). They are also more likely to think highly of others and expect to be accepted by others. People with high self-esteem are not afraid of the reactions of others and perform well when others watch them. When confronted with criticism, they are comfortable defending themselves. In contrast, someone with a negative self-image will probably have low self-esteem. People with low self-esteem are likely to be critical of others and expect rejection from them (Adler et al., 2020; Hamacheck, 1992). They are also critical of their own performance and are sensitive to the possible disapproval of others and perform poorly when watched. People with low self-esteem feel threatened by others they perceive as superior and have difficulty in defending themselves against the negative comments of others. Clearly these differences in a person's identity can have a considerable impact on how that person relates to and communicates with others, which, in turn, has an impact on conflict management.

In this context, it is also necessary to briefly discuss the Dunning-Kruger effect. This refers to a cognitive bias people have which prevents them from properly evaluating their own competence and that of others due to a low level of self-awareness. This is coupled with a low cognitive ability which results in those people overestimating their own abilities which, in turn, means that they are incapable of accurately assessing their own knowledge. These people consider themselves to be better and more cognizant than others, fail to recognize their own failings, and cannot properly evaluate the abilities of others. Here again, it is quite obvious that this could have an impact on conflict management because a proper assessment of one's own abilities and those of others is not possible, which could create disagreement over how well or poorly one has performed. Research has shown that metacognitive training can help overcome the Dunning-Kruger effect (Kruger & Dunning, 1999).

Culture

Another important influencing factor of identity is culture (Doise, 1986; Servaes, 1989). Cultural preferences can have a considerable impact on whether one is expected to conform to such cultural norms (Markus & Kitayama, 1991; Swann, Jetten, Gomez, Whitehouse, & Bastina, 2012).[2] According to Piaget (1954), construction of the self occurs as a person acts on his/her environment and figures out what one can and cannot do. Identity is, thus, a social construct that is created over time and is subjective rather than fixed and objective (Yep, 1998), i.e. a social construct that is given meaning through interaction and communication with others (Collier & Thomas, 1988; Combs & Snygg, 1959).

That is why culture also plays an important role in determining the rules and regulations as well as the norms of interaction within a larger social context. After all, people are not only reared to learn a language, but also taught how to behave and interact with other people in specific contexts. Even if one does not identify oneself with all aspects of a culture, one might still know the *expected* behavior and communication for a given context. For example, one learns the expected answer to an assignment or test in order to get a good grade, even though one may think that the expected answer is misguided. This permits people to interact successfully with other members of society because the other members of that society learned the same rules, regulations, and norms. Sharing this information facilitates the interaction and communication within that culture. One typically only becomes aware that other norms might exist when interacting with members from other cultures (Chen & Starosta, 1998; Klopf, 1998; Lustig & Koester, 2013; Oetzel, 2009; Samovar, Porter, McDaniel, & Roy, 2017). That is why it is important to understand how culture influences human identity and communication.

Culture refers to the beliefs, values, rules, norms, customs, rituals, etc. that socially define a group of people and provide guidelines for the preferred mode of interaction and communication (verbal and nonverbal) with other members of that group (Chen & Starosta, 1998; Klopf, 1998; Oetzel, 2009; Samovar et al., 2017). In addition to influencing communication (Hall, 1976), behavior, and identity (Collier & Thomas, 1988; Combs & Snygg, 1959; Yep, 1998), culture also influences perception (Brekhus, 2015; Cole & Scribner, 1974; Fisher, 1997; Nisbett & Miyamoto, 2005; Pick & Pick, 1978). The emphasis here is on "influences" because culture does *not* determine human behavior and communication. Culture provides guidance as to what is the preferred style and behavior for its members (Doise, 1986). Individual deviation from preferred norms can and does exist even in collectivistic cultures. Cultural norms and frames serve as guidelines for communicating within specific contexts and with specific individuals. In order for people to be able to interact successfully, they will need to be able to communicate in the appropriate manner. Culture can influence what is considered appropriate for a given context.

Perception

Perception refers to the identification, organization, interpretation, and evaluation of sensory stimuli humans are exposed to (Adler et al., 2020; DeVito, 2015; Gamble & Gamble, 2012; Klopf, 1998). As a person grows up, interacts with other people, and experiences the world around him/her, that individual learns to associate specific meaning(s) with specific behavior and messages in specific contexts and categories. People learn to respond to those contexts and categories as they experienced them and as their culture instructs them. Thus, perception and culture are often interrelated (Brekhus, 2015; Cole & Scribner, 1974; Fisher, 1997; Nisbett & Miyamoto, 2005; Pick & Pick, 1978). Obviously, individual divergence exists as noted above, but some broad denotative meanings are shared, to a larger or lesser degree, among the members of a particular culture. After all, it is this shared denotative meaning that permits constructive interaction among members of that culture (Cole & Scribner, 1974; Fisher, 1997; Klopf, 1998; Lustig & Koester, 2013; Nisbett & Miyamoto, 2005; Oetzel, 2009; Pick & Pick, 1978).

People interpret what they perceive. Interpretation is important because it attaches meaning to what people perceive (Adler et al., 2020; DeVito, 2015; Gamble & Gamble, 2012; Klopf, 1998; Samovar et al., 2017). Interpretation is based on past experiences, expectations, needs, values, and beliefs as well as physical and emotional states (DeVito, 2015; Klopf, 1998; Samovar et al., 2017). With selective interpretation, people decode ambiguous or contradictory information in such a way that it is consistent with their established beliefs; thus, creating cognitive consistency (West & Turner, 2007). According to Goffman (1974), frames help people interpret information because they act as schemata of interpretation. In other words, people have specific templates for interpreting the sensory stimuli in a particular way. That is why two people exposed to the same situation can interpret it differently. But that is also why people growing up within the same cultural context and sharing the same cultural values, beliefs, and having made similar experiences due to regular interaction with other members of that culture in specific contexts which reinforce those values, beliefs, etc. can also share denotative meaning as to what the perceived event or message may mean. In other words, cultural frames create similar, but not identical, interpretations which facilitates interpersonal communication because it increases convergence in the denotative meaning.

Three factors influence interpretation: Disconfirmed expectations, predisposition, and attribution (DeVito, 2015; Klopf, 1998). Disconfirmed expectation refers to the phenomenon that people often anticipate that something will happen in a certain way. People expect it to happen that way because that is the way it happened to them before, or it happened to people they know, or it happened in accounts they read, saw, or heard about (Adler et al., 2020; DeVito, 2015; Gamble & Gamble, 2012; Klopf, 1998). If people's expectations are not met in the way that was anticipated, their expectations are disconfirmed. The result can be frustration (Adler et al., 2020; DeVito, 2015; Gamble & Gamble, 2012; Klopf, 1998; Samovar et al., 2017). For example, managers attending a business negotiation may have certain expectations of what they are going to encounter during the upcoming negotiation. During the meeting, however, conditions might be different from what the managers had expected. Their expectations are disconfirmed and frustration can set in.

Predisposition refers to the phenomenon that people tend to be predisposed to behave in certain ways. Needs, emotional states, values, beliefs, and attitudes constitute those predispositions which help people decide what is good or bad, right or wrong, important or unimportant in what they perceive. These factors play an important role in the meanings people assign to the stimuli they sense and explains why different people interpret the same phenomenon differently (Adler et al., 2020; DeVito, 2015; Gamble & Gamble, 2012; Klopf, 1998).

Attribution refers to the process of seeking explanations for the observed behavior of others (Adler et al., 2020; DeVito, 2015; Gamble & Gamble, 2012; Klopf,

1998). People try to make sense of the behavior of others and in doing so people attribute causes to that behavior. Even though one may not know why another person behaved the way he/she did, one assigns a probable cause to that behavior which is based on how one would have behaved in that situation. Yet most of the time, people are actually guessing (Adler et al., 2020; DeVito, 2015; Gamble & Gamble, 2012; Klopf, 1998). People use attribution to reduce uncertainty in an attempt to make the behavior of others more predictable (Berger & Calabrese, 1975).

The strength of the relationship between the interlocutors plays a crucial role in interpreting the perceived message (Adler et al., 2020; DeVito, 2015; Gamble & Gamble, 2012). The interlocutors often come to a particular conclusion as to what meaning a message has. People tend to interpret the message in ways that are consistent with their own interests; i.e. cognitive consistency. Such self-serving bias influences not only the interpretation of the message, but also the subsequent action of the interlocutors. Consequently, it is actually the perceived message which influences the subsequent behavior and communication of the interlocutors and not the actual, intended message of the sender. Interestingly, this divergence in meaning need not have a negative impact on the relationship of the interlocutors because misunderstandings may be remedied by rationalization (Adler et al., 2020; DeVito, 2015; Gamble & Gamble, 2012).

Rationalization refers to the efforts undertaken by the interlocutors to under-stand the perceived message (Adler et al., 2020; DeVito, 2015; Gamble & Gamble, 2012). If one of the interlocutors appears to behave in a manner contrary to the perceived meaning of the message, then the degree of deviation influences the rationalization. Thus, if the degree of deviation is considered to be irrelevant for the context of the message, then it will be ignored. For example, if the encoded message contains a few minor grammatical mistakes, or the nonverbal behavior contains a few unusual gestures, then people tend to ignore them. If, however, the degree of divergence is large, then the message might be misunderstood in part or entirely. So the more familiar one is with a particular individual and culture, the easier it will be to accurately anticipate and decode messages in a particular context with a specific individual and, thus, achieve greater convergence in meaning (Adler et al., 2020; DeVito, 2015; Gamble & Gamble, 2012). Hence, a person will probably expect to receive a particular message from a specific individual at, for example, a certain anniversary because similar messages were transmitted on similar, previous occasions by that same individual. People always seek information that reinforces their current perception of the environment. Hence, people are more likely to filter out undesirable information if it is inconsistent with the expectation of the message content. This is due to the need for cognitive consistency (Adler et al., 2020; DeVito, 2015; Gamble & Gamble, 2012) as noted above. In an inter-cultural context, the exchange of meanings is complex because consistency is not always guaranteed (Chen & Starosta, 1998; Klopf, 1998; Oetzel, 2009). That is why it is important to familiarize oneself with the other culture, i.e. become more cognizant of the culture and its preferences, if one wishes to communicate effectively in that cultural context (Chen & Starosta, 1998; Klopf, 1998; Oetzel, 2009; Samovar et al., 2017).

Relationships

Successful business relationships revolve around interpersonal relationships because it is people who conduct business (Friman et al., 2002; Walter et al., 2001; Yeung & Tung, 1996). And it is people who build and maintain those relationships. That is why it is important to also take a brief look at relationships and how they might influence misunderstandings and misperceptions.

The *Communication Accommodation Theory* (Giles, Coupland, & Coupland, 1991) explains interpersonal relationship development. The theory is based on three primary concepts: Convergence, divergence, and maintenance. Convergence refers to the change of one's language, vocabulary, speech style, speech rate, or tone of voice to become similar to the interactional partner. It functions to show solidarity, enhance understanding, or seek approval. In contrast, divergence refers to the emphasis of speech differences between the interactors. Maintenance refers to the continuing use of one's speech style in interaction with or without reference to the other's style. During interpersonal interactions, convergence tends to increase attraction between the interactors and divergence tends to inhibit it.[3] The theory proposes that the initial orientation of interpersonal encounters is strongly affected by one's personal and social identity which tends to let one view interactions in a particular way (Giles et al., 1991). But the situational constraints, such as the norms, topics, and competitiveness, of each interaction are likely to change the initial orientation of the interactors. Clearly convergence can help reduce potential conflicts while divergence could fuel them.

In some situations, people are consciously aware of how they interact with others, e. g. during a job interview (Adler et al., 2020). At other times, people react unconsciously to their counterpart; especially with nonverbal communication, e.g. when they are angry. Abelson (1981) postulates that people use scripts for many routine situations which do not require complete conscious awareness to facilitate an uninterrupted flow of communication. Some people are much more aware of their behavior than others (Gamble & Gamble, 2012). These people are called high self-monitors who have the ability to pay attention to their own behavior and others' reactions, adjusting their communication to create the desired impression, i.e. Rochat's Level 5, meta self-awareness. Low self-monitors express what they are thinking and feeling without much attention to the impression their behavior creates in others. People differ in their degree of identity management (Adler et al., 2020). For example, one might only select the information that confirms one's own self-concept and ignore the rest, i.e. selective perception. Self-awareness, thus, has a considerable impact on how one monitors one's own behavior and communication and that of others as noted above which, in turn, has an impact on conflict management.

To understand others, one must understand how they look at the world and other people. Self-awareness and how others perceive one can be explored through a psychological testing device known as the Johari Window created by Joseph Luft and Harrington Ingham (1955). The Johari Window consists of four quadrants; namely, the open, blind, hidden, and unknown "panes" (Adler et al., 2020; Gamble & Gamble, 2012). The open pane refers to information about oneself that is known to oneself and others (Adler et al., 2020; Gamble & Gamble, 2012). The size of this quadrant varies from one relationship to another and depends on the degree of closeness and trust one shares with another person. The blind pane contains information about a person that others are aware of, but that person is not aware of (Adler et al., 2020; Gamble & Gamble, 2012). Some people have a very large blind area and are unaware of their own faults and virtues. The hidden pane represents one's hidden self (Adler et al., 2020; Gamble & Gamble, 2012). It contains information one knows about oneself but does not want others to know for fear of being rejected. As one moves from the hidden pane to the open pane, one is engaged in self-disclosure. Self-disclosure occurs when one deliberately reveals to others information about oneself that the other person would otherwise not know (Adler et al., 2020; Gamble & Gamble, 2012).[4] And finally, the unknown pane contains information about a person which neither that person nor others are aware of (Adler et al., 2020; Gamble & Gamble, 2012).

People typically develop a style that is a consistent and preferred way of behaving toward others. Some people are very open. Their relationships with others are characterized by candor, openness, and sensitivity to the needs and insights of others. Others have a large hidden area. They desire relationships but also greatly fear exposure and generally mistrust others. And if the blind area dominates, then such persons are overly confident of their own opinions and painfully unaware of how they affect others or are perceived by others. People who are dominated by the unknown area adopt a fairly impersonal approach to personal relationships. They usually withdraw from contact, avoid personal disclosure or involvement, and project an image that is rigid, aloof, and uncommunicative (Adler et al., 2020; Gamble & Gamble, 2012). Here too, the preferred communicative style can affect the handling of a conflict.

Relationships are dynamic and influenced by communication with others. Relationships are hierarchical and include strangers, acquaintances, and intimate friends. Different levels of relationship call for different degrees of involvement. Relationships are reciprocal and exist when members in relationship networks satisfy each other's needs (DeVito, 2015). Prolonged reciprocal incompatibility usually results in a breakdown of the relationship. The Social Exchange Theory (Thibaut & Kelley, 1959) postulates that people will only work to maintain a relationship as long as the perceived benefits outweigh the costs. The benefits can include self-worth, sense of personal growth, greater sense of security, increased ability to cope with problems, and additional resources.[5] Costs can include the time spent trying to make the relationship work, psychological and physical stress, and damaged self-image. People enter a relationship with a comparison level in mind (DeVito, 2015). People have a general idea, standard, or expectation of the kinds of rewards and profits they believe they ought to get out of the relationship. When the rewards equal or surpass the comparison level, people feel satisfied about the relationship. People also have a comparison level for alternatives (Thibaut & Kelley, 1959). People compare the rewards they get from a current relationship with those they think they can get from an alternative relationship. If it is assumed the present relationship rewards are below those they could get from an alternative one, then they might exit the present relationship. People use communication to explore a relationship in order to determine if they wish to maintain the relationship or not (DeVito, 2015). The same applies to conflict management because individuals weigh the options of continuing a conflict or attempting to deescalate it.

The Uncertainty Reduction Theory (Berger & Calabrese, 1975) examines how people come to know each other in the initial stage of relationship development. Uncertainty refers to the cognitive inability to explain one's own or another's feelings and behaviors in interactions because an ambiguous situation evokes anxiety. The theory proposes that interpersonal relationships develop and progress when people are able to reduce the uncertainty about each other. That is why people seek to reduce uncertainty by exchanging information in the process of relationship development and while building trust.

Trust is an outgrowth of interpersonal communication and very important for interpersonal relationships (DeVito, 2015; Gamble & Gamble, 2012). Trust is a reflection of how secure one is that other people will act in a predicted and desired way. When one trusts other people, one is confident that they will behave as one expects them to and that they will not use whatever personal information one has revealed to them to harm one. The degree of trust one has in others depends on whether prior relationships reinforced trusting behavior or consolidated fears about the risks of exhibiting trusting behavior (DeVito, 2015; Gamble & Gamble, 2012). Trust is built by developing a positive communication climate that recognizes and acknowledges the other person's ideas and messages in a positive manner. Disconfirming responses, i.e. messages that deny the value of the other person's ideas, can prevent the establishment of trusting relationships (Adler et al., 2020). This does not mean, though, that one cannot disagree with the other person's opinion. What is important is how one communicates such disagreement. In other words, one needs to avoid personal attacks and/or messages that can be construed as being hurtful (Adler et al., 2020). In an intercultural context, though, verbal and nonverbal messages can be perceived very differently from their intended meaning due to different schemata, scripts, and frames as noted above. Consequently, a person's communication may be perceived as being disconfirming when that may not be the intention.

To summarize, people learn from past interaction how to identify, interpret, and evaluate specific social situations. These past experiences become mental templates, i.e. schemata, which are associated with specific scripts and frames that allow people to organize interactions into manageable categories. The scripts and frames include the respective roles of the interlocutors and the verbal and nonverbal messages that typically accompany such roles in specific contexts. This provides guidance on how a scene is to play out. This predictability reduces uncertainty.

These schemata, scripts, and frames are often acquired in a specific cultural context through interaction with others and include the respective roles and dialogues typically associated with those contexts. Previous personal experience influences how they are defined and played out. Most people use a specific role and script when they find themselves in what they perceive to be a specific known situation (Adler et al., 2020; DeVito, 2015) – this also applies to conflicts.

Conflicts

Conflicts are perceived disagreements and goal interference. They involve cognition and how the interlocutors define the context within which the conflict occurs (Roloff & Wright, 2013). According to Rahim (2002), a conflict is "an interactive process manifested in incompatibility, disagreement, or dissonance within or between social entities (i.e., individual, group, organization, etc.)" (p. 207). In other words, "a conflict can relate to incompatibilities, preferences, goals, and not just activities" (Rahim, 2002, p. 207). Such preferences can include the preferred style of communication and how those communication styles are perceived. After all, many forms of verbal and, in particular, nonverbal communication are due to cultural preferences. According to Imahori (2010), most of the problems that arise between American and Japanese business people are due to low vs. high context communication styles. Ting-Toomey and Oetzel (2007) point out that monochronic vs. polychronic behavior can also create conflict situations since both prefer a different conflict management style. So cultural differences can result in misperceptions and misunderstandings because members of different cultures have internalized different communication styles that are preferred in their respective cultures and such differences might create conflicting messages.

Not surprisingly, a particular category of conflicts are pseudo-conflicts which are not really conflicts, but have the appearance of a conflict. They often revolve around false either-or judgments or around simple misunderstandings or misperceptions (Bruner & Tagiuri, 1954; Cook, 1973; Darley & Oleson, 1993; Hartley, 1965; Krippendorff & Bermejo, 2009). Pseudo-conflicts are resolved when people realize that no conflict actually exists (Gamble & Gamble, 2012). Unless something was said or done in the meantime that might escalate the original misunderstanding or misperception into a real conflict.

Research has shown that conflicts are fairly complex (Canary & Lakey, 2006; Caughlin & Vangelisti, 2006; Roloff & Wright, 2013; Sillars, 2010; Sillars & Weisberg, 1987) even without adding the element of culture. The reason for this complexity is that many factors converge during conflicts. Conflicts often involve, for example, a variety of goals and goal incompatibility, incoherent and paradoxical action, escalating arguments and topic shifts, perceptual differences, cognitive biases; thus, creating a very demanding cognitive environment for the interlocutors. As conflicts escalate, new issues can arise which together with existing issues can make the conflict even more complex, diffuse, and abstract. At the same time, the different frames of the conflict parties create fragmented communication that ignores the concerns of one's counterpart. That is why the coordination of meanings is a particular problem in interpersonal conflicts (Roloff & Wright, 2013; Sillars, 2010). So it is not surprising that misunderstandings and misperceptions often play a significant role in most interpersonal conflicts. According to Sillars et al. (2000), people rarely attempt to take the other's perspective, but quickly infer what the intentions and actions mean without any real knowledge, i.e. faulty attribution. If conflicts are not deescalated, negative attitudes can quickly lead to dissatisfaction and termination of the relationship (Caughlin & Vangelisti, 2006).

Framing plays a critical role in how the conflict parties view one another, and how they view their relationship and the conflict task. Framing directs the attention of the parties and steers their focus to what is at stake in a conflict. Framing is a cognitive bias that people develop over time (Plous, 1993). Frames help people focus on specific information while filtering out other sensory stimuli they consider irrelevant for the situation as part of their perception. Frames define problems, analyze their causes, evaluate the situation, and offer solutions (Kuypers, 2009). As noted above, frames are the schemata of interpretation (Goffman, 1974). In other words, frames permit people to understand and respond to specific situations in a particular way because people experienced perceived similar events and learned or had been taught to respond to those events in a particular preferred manner. Culture includes a preferred means of handling specific situations and responding to those situations in a particular way that is deemed more desirable than other means (Chen & Starosta, 1998; Klopf, 1998; Lustig & Koester, 2013; Oetzel, 2009; Samovar et al., 2017). That is why Goffman (1974) postulates that the meanings of frames are to be found in culture.

People are more willing to accept a particular interpretation if they have existing schemata and frames for a specific situation. According to Entman (1993), frames highlight certain information to make the situation more understandable for the perceiver by selecting a specific problem definition, speculating about a particular probable cause, coming to a certain evaluation, and stimulating a specific reaction. People, thus, have particular biases toward interpreting, evaluating, and reacting to specific situations that reflect both personal experiences and also more general cultural preferences for the perceived situation; and scripts determine how people communicate in that situation. Drake and Donohue (1996) found that if the interlocutors can manage to achieve convergence of their individual frames, then this, not surprisingly, increases the frequency of agreement, i.e. convergence in meaning. That is why Lee (2014) can postulate that shared values could provide a means of overcoming differences. Drake and Donohue (1996) also discovered that frame convergence increases the focus, control, positive social attribution, and integrativeness of the interlocutors.

In line with the Social Exchange Theory, the interlocutors may consider the business relationship to be more important than maintaining or even escalating a conflict. In that case, people would probably attempt to deescalate the conflict. That is why it is so important to establish strong relationships that are based on mutual trust because then the interlocutors might realize that misunderstandings and misperceptions exist because they communicate openly about the conflict since they have established a degree of trust that permits them, or encourages them, to talk also about topics that would otherwise be difficult to address. After all, people usually feel more comfortable in the presence of someone they are familiar with and can trust than they do in the presence of someone they do not know and do not trust. The perceived benefits of such a mutually beneficial/profitable relationship outweigh the perceived costs of trustful relationships because even if one does not expect to get immediate rewards, one expects to get them over the long term. A trustful relationship also produces greater tolerance for divergent behavior and communication due to rationalization and cognitive consistency as noted above. So if the parties share values that help deescalate a (potential) conflict, then this increases the chances of ending the conflict. Since most business people seek to establish good relationships that essentially benefit both parties, this premise provides an opportunity to deescalate a (pseudo) conflict with effective communication.

In order to successfully deescalate conflicts, it is necessary to be empathetic and put oneself in the position of the other which also requires mutual tolerance, a positive attitude, and alternative coping mechanisms (Roloff & Ifert, 2000). Roloff and Wright (2013) point out that people wish to understand their social environment. That is why it is important for people to think about what is going on in a conflict, i.e. applying cognition. Another important aspect in resolving conflicts is awareness so that the conflict parties can practice self-monitoring and apply self-regulatory behavior to adjust their communication to the conflict situation and the other party. Other researchers come to similar conclusions (Canary & Lakey, 2006; Canary & Spitzberg, 1987, 1989; Roloff & Wright, 2013; Sillars et al., 2000; Sillars, 2010). This is usually described as social cognition. But social metacognition might actually be a better term as will be explained below.

Communication Competence and Conflict Resolution

Although there is some disagreement as to how communication competence is to be conceptualized and measured, there is increasing agreement about its fundamental characteristics (Lustig & Koester, 2013). According to Chen and Starosta (1998), intercultural communication competence is the ability to effectively and appropriately execute communication behaviors to obtain a desired response in a specific environment. This means that competent communicators not only know how to interact effectively and appropriately with other people in specific contexts, but also know how to fulfill their own communication goals while using this ability, i.e. adroitness (Chen & Starosta, 1998). In other words, one needs to properly perceive the intentions and behavior/communication of others, i.e. monitor one's own behavior and communication and that of others, be able to behave/communicate in a manner that is appropriate and is perceived as being appropriate by the others for this particular context, be aware of how one's own subsequent behavior/communication is being perceived by others so that one can react/communicate appropriately if the situation calls for such corrective behavior/

communication which, in turn, requires knowledge of whether one ought to act/ react/communicate or not in this specific situation; and if one ought to act/ react/communicate, then one needs to know how to appropriately act/react/ communicate in this particular situation (i.e. adroitness). This is a challenging task even for interlocutors coming from the same culture. The addition of culture complicates the matter further because different cultures generate different value systems and perceived meanings (Chen & Starosta, 1998; Lustig & Koester, 2013; Oetzel, 2009) which have a considerable impact on the preferred behavior, communication style, and norms and how they are perceived by others as noted above.

Gudykunst's Anxiety/Uncertainty Management Theory is based on the Uncertainty Reduction Theory; but it postulates that people express anxiety, i.e. stress, when confronted with unfamiliar intercultural encounters which motivates people to seek cultural adaptation and not just a reduction of uncertainty. According to Gudykunst (2005), people generally have a certain degree of anxiety and uncertainty in any encounter with strangers. And when the encounter is of an intercultural nature, people tend to be very aware of the cultural differences. In fact, they tend to overemphasize the relevance of culture and ignore individual differences. But when people are mindful, they will have better conscious control of their own communication (Gudykunst, 2005). According to Gudykunst, mindfulness refers to cognition, monitoring, and controlling one's own behavior and communication so that it is effective in specific situations and with specific individuals because the communicator does not apply general, stereotypical categories (i.e. schemata, scripts, and frames) when communicating with strangers. Instead, the effective communicator individualizes the categories so that these categories provide a better fit for communicating with one's counterpart at an individual and not a stereotypical level (Gudykunst, 2005).

From the above discussion, it has become apparent that knowledge and awareness of differences are important in understanding differences in meaning, i.e. cognition. Cognition refers to knowledge. The more one knows of the other person and his/her culture as well as the preferred style of behavior and communication, the better one can decode the behavior and communication of the other person (Chen & Starosta, 1998; Klopf, 1998; Lustig & Koester, 2013, Oetzel, 2009; Samovar et al., 2017). Furthermore, self-awareness, including self-monitoring, is important in discovering how one communicates, i.e. metacognition. Metacognition refers to the monitoring and controlling of one's own cognitive processes so as to improve its effectiveness (Brown, 1978, 1987; Flavel, 1979, 1987; Frith, 2012; Veeman, Van Hout-Wolters, & Afflerbach, 2006). Veeman et al. (2006) point out that metacognition relies on cognition. So specific knowledge of another person and another culture along with the preferred verbal and nonverbal communication is necessary in order to properly develop and apply metacognition. By also monitoring how the others react to one's own behavior and communication, one might be able to adjust one's behavior and communication on the basis of proper knowledge and awareness, i.e. cognition, so that one's behavior and communication correspond to the observed behavior and communication of one's counterpart and their expectations of how one is to behave and communicate with them in this specific context, i.e. social metacognition. Social metacognition can help manage conflicts effectively because it permits conflicting parties to see the conflict from the perspective of the other party and seeks to understand the motivation for the other party's behavior. This also requires sufficient knowledge of the other party and culture along with their preferences to better isolate and predict the possible behavior and communication of the other party and adjust one's own behavior and communication accordingly (Frith, 2012; Jost, Kruglanski, & Nelson, 1998).

In order to reach some convergence in meaning, it is, thus, necessary to essentially put oneself in the position of one's counterpart and attempt to perceive one's own behavior and communication as one's counterpart might perceive it. However, this requires considerable familiarity, i.e. cognition, of one's counterpart because familiarity fosters mutual self-disclosure and trust which creates better predictability. And it also requires monitoring, both self and other monitoring, as well as properly controlling one's behavior and communication so that it fits the specific context and is adjusted to the particular counterpart as Gudykunst (2005) pointed out above. In fact, people can learn metacognition and social metacognition. Metacognition (and social metacognition) is most effective if it is learned in the context in which it is to be applied (Veeman et al., 2006). Frith (2012) comes to a similar conclusion, noting that metacognition can be developed through interaction and a willingness to communicate with others about the reasons for one's own actions and perceptions as well as listening to the reasons one's counterpart presents to explain his/her actions and perceptions. This allows people to overcome their lack of direct access to the underlying cognitive processes in themselves and in others, hence, permitting the possibility of creating a more accurate image of the world and people, including of oneself and others (Frith, 2012).

Interestingly, the research of Keysar et al. (2012) indicates that the framing effect is typically not encountered when people communicate in a language that is not their mother tongue. It will be recalled that framing can have a negative impact on perception and interaction because frames contain preferred, biased styles of behavior, communication, and perception. Keysar et al. speculate that a second language provides greater cognitive and emotional distance, allowing people to interpret and evaluate a perceived message in a less biased manner. This is probably due to the fact that most people tend to process a second language less automatically than they do their native language. Consequently, people are more deliberate in their cognition which affects the decision making process; thus, creating decisions that are more systematic and involve more intense monitoring/self-awareness and control to see how one's messages are being perceived by others.

When communicating in one's native language, one is less likely to be actively monitoring the precise meaning of one's own words and the words of one's counterpart since much communication is often relegated to the unconscious level due to schemata, scripts, and frames because they help improve the communication flow. If one were to monitor everything, it would make for fairly ponderous communication and hinder its effectiveness. But that is exactly why communication in a second language is slower and more deliberate, because one is less familiar with the requisite scripts and frames of that language. However, this deliberateness facilitates and fosters metacognition. That is probably why native speakers of English do not deliberately apply metacognition if the business discourse is in English, their native tongue. They may actually be more focused on the business matter at hand than the communication. They may, thus, be less aware of how their behavior and communication is being perceived by their interlocutor. On the other hand, non-native speakers of English would probably be monitoring their own communication and that of their counterpart closer because they might be worried that they could be making mistakes and/or might be misunderstood (Keysar et al., 2012); unless they are very confident of their abilities and have a large blind area.

People should, therefore, enter an international business encounter with as few preconceived attitudes and frames as possible because existing attitudes and frames are often the basis for future attitudes which explains why people are unlikely to change existing attitudes and frames. New information can be negated if the prior attitude is held with a high degree of confidence. A mismatch of a person's implicit and explicit attitudes seems to encourage people to use more elaborate information processing (Song & Ewoldson, 2015) which supports (social) metacognition. That is why it is important for people to monitor the interaction and communicate their perceptions and meanings to their counterpart because if there is divergent meaning, it might be possible to identify it and to positively influence one's own evaluation and that of one's counterpart. Song and Ewoldson (2015) note that divergent information which is transmitted by trusted people "has a stronger influence on a person's perception of the validity or certainty of attitudinally relevant beliefs than that same information presented by the media" (p. 35) or society at large. This is another reason why it is important to build and maintain a trustful relationship since it encourages such constructive interaction.

The interrelationship of the elements discussed above may be depicted as follows:

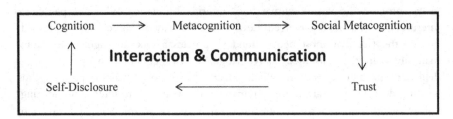

FIGURE 16.1 The relationship between cognition, metacognition, social metacognition, trust, and self-disclosure

Conclusion

From the above discussion, it is apparent that awareness and monitoring one's own behavior and communication as well as that of one's counterpart are important elements which can help reduce misunderstandings and misperceptions because they take into account knowledge that is required for effective communication; thus, permitting greater convergence in meaning. They also hone perception in that they expand the range and awareness of schemata, scripts, and frames. They also permit more accurate self-monitoring and other-monitoring. This is, however, only improved through constructive interaction with others because with the help of cognition and metacognition the interaction allows one to see if and how one's own behavior and communication are being perceived by one's counterpart. This interaction also involves self-monitoring and readjusting one's behavior and communication to correct misunderstandings and misperceptions, both in oneself and in one's counterpart. But here as well, it is necessary to interact and communicate with one's counterpart to ascertain whether one's own communication and self-evaluation are being perceived and interpreted as intended by him/her as Frith (2012) points out. This should then increase predictability which is also an important component of trust. On the one hand, trust requires a tolerance of vulnerability because one does not know what one's counterpart will do with the disclosed information. But without self-disclosure, trust cannot be built. And, on the other hand, trust creates a tolerance for greater divergence because with trust, one tends to give one's counterpart the benefit of the doubt through rationalization and cognitive consistency. Trust helps build stronger relationships because trust reduces uncertainty and anxiety and increases predictability. Predictability permits one to attune one's messages to one's counterpart because one knows how one's counterpart will react to a given message. Trust also increases the likelihood of both interlocutors practicing more self-disclosure. This increased mutual self-disclosure increases cognition, i.e. one gains more knowledge of one's counterpart's behavior and communication; thus, increasing shared meaning and resulting in greater convergence of meaning while also reducing uncertainty and anxiety. With more knowledge, it is possible to improve self-monitoring and controlling one's own behavior and communication, i.e. metacognition, as Veeman et al. (2006) note. And with more knowledge of one's counterpart, one will be able to improve one's ability to predict the behavior and reaction of him/her, i.e. social metacognition. This, in turn, will improve the overall communication and provide a more harmonious relationship with fewer misunderstandings and misperceptions; hence, deescalating or even preventing (pseudo) conflicts. And in the world of business, this creates mutually beneficial and profitable business relationships. That is why social metacognition is so important for successful business relationships and in avoiding or deescalating (potential) conflicts.

Notes

1.   Doise (1986), actually refers to four levels: Individual, interpersonal, intergroup, and cultural. For the purposes of this chapter, the focus is on the

individual, the interpersonal, and the cultural levels because these provide important insights into how these levels influence misunderstandings and misperceptions at the interpersonal level in international business encounters.

2. Collectivistic cultures tend to favor conformity while individualistic cultures tend to tolerate, to a certain degree, individual deviations from the cultural norm.

3. That explains, in part, why some people feel more attracted to people from their own culture than people from other cultures because they share the same cultural beliefs, values, norms, etc. with other members of their own culture (Klopf, 1998; Lustig & Koester, 2013; Oetzel, 2009; Samovar et al., 2017).

4. What is considered right and proper to be revealed to others about oneself is often influenced by culture. Americans, for example, reveal more about their private lives at work than Germans do. For Germans, such revelations would be considered unprofessional and, hence, unacceptable at work.

5. What are considered benefits in one culture may not be considered a benefit in another culture. Hofstede (1991) notes that individual bonuses at work are more important in individualistic cultures than group rewards which are preferred in collectivistic cultures.

References

Abelson, R. P. (1981). Psychological status of the script concept. *American Psychologist*, 36(7), 715–729.

Adler, R. B., Rodman, G., & du Pré, A. (2020). *Understanding human communication* (14th ed.). New York, NY: Oxford University Press.

Berger, C. R. & Calabrese, R. (1975). Some explorations in initial interactions and beyond: Toward a developmental theory of interpersonal communication. *Human Communication Research*, 1, 99–112.

Brekhus, W. H. (2015). *Culture and cognition: Patterns in the social construction of reality*. Cambridge, UK: Polity.

Brown, A. L. (1978). Knowing when, where, and how to remember: A problem of metacognition. In R. Glaser (Ed.), *Advances in instructional psychology* (Vol. 1, pp. 77–165). Hillsdale, NJ: Erlbaum.

Brown, A. L. (1987). Metacognition, executive control, self-regulation, and other more mysterious mechanisms. In F. E. Weinert & R. H. Kluwe (Eds.), *Metacognition, motivation, and understanding* (pp. 65–116). Hillsdale, NJ: Erlbaum.

Bruner, J. S. & Tagiuri, R. (1954). The perception of people. In G. Lindzey (Ed.), *Handbook of social psychology* (Vol. 1, pp. 634–654). Cambridge, MA: Addison Wesley.

Canary, D. J. & Lakey, S. G. (2006). Managing conflict in a competent manner: A mindful look at events that matter. In J. G. Oetzel & S. Ting-Toomey (Eds.), *The Sage handbook of conflict communication: Integrating theory, research, and practice* (pp. 185–210). Thousand Oaks, CA: Sage.

Canary, D. J. & Spitzberg, B. H. (1987). Appropriateness and effectiveness perceptions of conflict strategies. *Human Communication Research*, 14, 93–118.

Canary, D. J. & Spitzberg, B. H. (1989). A model of the perceived competence of conflict strategies. *Human Communication Research*, 15, 630–649.

Caughlin, J. P., & Vangelisti, A. L. (2006). Conflict in dating and romantic relationships. In J. G. Oetzel & S. Ting-Toomey (Eds.), *The Sage handbook of conflict communication: Integrating theory, research, and practice* (pp. 129–157). Thousand Oaks, CA: Sage.

Chen, G. M. & Starosta, W. J. (1998). *Foundations of intercultural communication*. Needham Heights, MA: Allyn & Bacon.

Cole, M. & Scribner, S. (1974). *Culture and thought: A psychological introduction*. Oxford, UK: John Wiley & Sons.

Collier, M. J. & Thomas, M. (1988). Cultural identities: An interpretive perspective. In Y. Y. Kim & W. B. Gudykunst (Eds.), *Theories of intercultural communication* (pp. 94–120). Newbury Park, CA: Sage.

Combs, A. W. & Snygg, D. (1959). *Individual behavior* (rev. ed.). New York, NY: Harper & Row.

Cook, M. (1973). *Interpersonal perception*. Harmondsworth, UK: Penguin Books.

Darley, J. M. & Oleson, K. C. (1993). Introduction to research on interpersonal expectations. In P. D. Blanck (Ed.), *Interpersonal expectations: Theory, research, and applications* (pp. 45–63). New York, NY: Cambridge University Press.

DeVito, J. A. (2015). *The interpersonal communication book* (14th ed.). Boston, MA: Pearson.

Doise, W. (1986). *Levels of explanation in social psychology*. Cambridge, UK: Cambridge University Press.

Dougherty, D. S., Mobley, S. K., & Smith, S. E. (2010). Language convergence and meaning divergence: A theory of intercultural communication. *Journal of International and Intercultural Communication*, (3)2, 164–186. doi:10.1080/17513051003611628.

Drake, L. E. & Donohue, W. A. (1996). Communicative framing theory in conflict resolution. *Communication Research*, 23(3), 297–322. doi:10.1177/009365096023003003.

Duval, S. & Wicklund, R. A. (1972). *A theory of objective self-awareness*. New York, NY: Academic Books.

Entman, R. M. (1993). Framing: Toward clarification of a fractured paradigm. *Journal of Communication*, 43(4), 51–58. doi:10.1111/j.1460-2466.1993.tb01304.x.

Fisher, G. (1997). *Mindsets: The role of culture and perception in international relations*. Yarmouth, ME: Intercultural Press.

Flavel, J. H. (1979). Metacognition and cognitive monitoring: A new era of cognitive-developmental inquiry. *American Psychologist*, 34, 906–911.

Flavel, J. H. (1987). Speculations about the nature and development of metacognition. In F. E. Weinert & R. H. Kluwe (Eds.), *Metacognition, motivation, and understanding* (pp. 21–29). Hillsdale, NJ: Erlbaum.

Friman, M., Gärling, T., Mattsson, J., & Johnston, R. (2002). An analysis of international business-to-business relationships based on the Commitment-Trust theory. *Industrial Marketing Management*, 31(5), 403–409.

Frith, C. (2012). The role of metacognition in human social interactions. *Philosophical Transactions of the Royal Society B*, 367, 2213–2223. doi:10.1098/rstb.2012.0123.

Gamble, T. K. & Gamble, M. W. (2012). *Communication works* (11th ed.). New York, NY: McGraw-Hill.

Giles, H., Coupland J., & Coupland, N. (1991). Accommodation theory: Communication, context, and consequences. In H. Giles, J. Coupland, & N. Coupland (Eds.), *Context of accommodation: Developments in applied sociolinguistics* (pp. 1–68). Cambridge, UK: Cambridge University Press.

Goffman, E. (1974). *Frame analysis: An essay on the organization of experience*. Cambridge, MA: Harvard University Press.

Gudykunst, W. B. (2005). *Theorizing about intercultural communication*. Thousand Oaks, CA: Sage.

Hall, E. T. (1976). *Beyond culture*. New York, NY: Doubleday.

Hamacheck, D. (1992). *Encounters with the self* (3rd ed.). Fort Worth, TX: Holt, Rhinehart and Winston.

Hartley, R. E. (1965). Perceptual accentuation as a problem in the psychology of judgment. *The Journal of Social Psychology*, 67(1), 149–162. doi:10.1080/00224545.1965.9922265.

Hofstede, G. (1991). *Culture and organizations: Software of the mind*. London, UK: McGraw-Hill.

Imahori, T. T. (2010). The great cultural divide in international business communication: High and low-context communication. In M. B. Hinner (Ed.), *The interface of business and culture* (pp. 249–265). Frankfurt am Main, Germany: Peter Lang.

Jost, J. T., Kruglanski, A. W., & Nelson, T. O. (1998). Social metacognition: An expansionist review. *Personality and Social Psychology Review*, 2(2), 137–154. doi:10.1207/s/15327957pspr0202_6.

Keysar, B., Hayakawa, S., & An, S. G. (2012). The foreign-language effect: Thinking in a foreign tongue reduces decision biases. *Psychological Science*, 23(6), 661–668. doi:10.1177/0956797611432178.

Klopf, D. W. (1998). *Intercultural encounters: The fundamentals of intercultural communication* (4th ed.). Englewood, CO: Morton Publishing Company.

Krippendorff, K. & Bermejo, F. (2009). *On communicating*. New York, NY: Routledge.

Kruger, J. & Dunning, D. (1999). Unskilled and unaware of it: How difficulties in recognizing one's own incompetence lead to inflated self-assessments. *Journal of Personality and Social Psychology*, 77(6), 1121–1134. doi:10.1037/0022-3514.77.6.1121

Kuypers, J. A. (2009). Framing analysis. In J. A. Kuypers (Ed.), *Rhetorical criticism: Perspectives in action* (pp. 181–204). Lanham, MD: Lexington Books.

Lee, P. S. N. (2014). A study on Chinese-American cultural differences in interpersonal conflict management. In M. B. Hinner (Ed.), *Chinese culture in a cross-cultural comparison* (pp. 441–461). Frankfurt am Main, Germany: Peter Lang.

Luft, J. & Ingham, H. (1955). The Johari Window, a graphic model of interpersonal awareness. *Proceedings of the Western training laboratory in group development*. Los Angeles, CA: UCLA.

Lustig, M. W. & Koester, J. (2013). *Intercultural competence* (7th ed.). Boston, MA: Pearson Education.

Markus, H. R. & Kitayama, S. (1991). Culture and the self: Implications for cognition, emotion, and motivation. *Psychological Review*, 98(2), 224–253. doi:10.1037/0033-295X.98.2.224.

Nisbett, R. E. & Miyamoto, Y. (2005). The influence of culture: Holistic vs. analytic perception. *Trends in Cognitive Science*, 9, 467–473.

Oetzel, J. G. (2009). *Intercultural communication: A layered approach*. New York, NY: Vango Books.

Piaget, J. (1954). *The construction of reality in the child*. New York, NY: Basic Books.

Pick, A. D., & Pick, H. L. (1978). Culture and perception. In E. C. Carterette & M. P. Friedman (Eds.), *Handbook of perception* (Vol. 10, pp. 19–39). New York, NY: Academic Press.

Plous, S. (1993). *The psychology of judgement and decision making*. New York, NY: McGraw-Hill.

Rahim, M.A. (2002). Toward a theory of managing organizational conflict. *The International Journal of Conflict Management*, 13(3), 206–235.

Rochat, P. (2003). Five levels of self-awareness as they unfold early in life. *Consciousness and Cognition*, 12(4), 717–731. doi:10.1016/s1053-8100(03)00081-3.

Roloff, M. E. & Ifert, D. E. (2000). Conflict management through avoidance: Withholding complaints, suppressing arguments, and declaring topics taboo. In S. Petronio (Ed.), *Balancing the secrets of private disclosures* (pp. 151–163). Mahwah, NJ: Erlbaum.

Roloff, M. E. & Wright, C. N. (2013). Social cognition and conflict. In J. G. Oetzel & S. Ting-Toomey (Eds.), *The Sage handbook of conflict communication: Integrating theory, research, and practice* (2nd ed.) (pp. 133–160). Thousand Oaks, CA: Sage.

Ruhly, S. (1982). *Intercultural communication* (2nd ed.). Chicago, IL: Science Research Associates.

Samovar, L. A., Porter, R. E., McDaniel, E. R., & Roy, C. S. (2017). *Communication between cultures* (9th ed.). Boston, MA: Cengage.

Seidelhofer, B. (2005). Key concepts: English as a lingua franca. *ELT Journal,* 59(4), 339–341. doi:10.1093/elt/ccio64.

Servaes, J. (1989). Cultural identity and modes of communication. In J. A. Anderson (Ed.), *Communication yearbook* 12 (pp. 383–416). Newbury Park, CA: Sage.

Sillars, A. L. (2010). Interpersonal conflict. In C. R. Berger, M. E. Roloff, & D. R. Roskos-Ewoldsen (Eds.), *The handbook of communication science* (2nd ed.) (pp. 273–290). Thousand Oaks, CA: Sage.

Sillars, A. L., Roberts, L. J., Leonard, K. E., & Dun, T. (2000). Cognition during marital conflict: The relationship of thought and talk. *Journal of Social and Personal Relationships,* 17, 479–502.

Sillars, A. L. & Weisberg, J. (1987). Conflict as a social skill. In M. E. Roloff & G. R. Miller (Eds.), *Interpersonal processes: New directions in communication research* (pp. 140–171). Newbury Park, CA: Sage.

Song, H. & Ewoldson, D. R. (2015). Metacognitive model of ambivalence: The role of multiple beliefs and metacognitions in creating attitude ambivalence. *Communication Theory,* 25(1), 23–45.

Swann, W. B., Jetten, J., Gomez, A., Whitehouse, H., & Bastian, B. (2012). When group membership gets personal: A theory of identity fusion. *Psychological Review,* 119(3), 441–456. doi:10.1037/a0028589.

Thibaut, J. W. & Kelley, H. H. (1959). *The social psychology of groups.* New York, NY: Wiley.

Ting-Toomey, S. & Oetzel, J. G. (2007). Intercultural conflict: A culture-based situational model. In P. J. Cooper, C. Calloway-Thomas, & C. J. Simonds, *Intercultural communication: A text with readings* (pp. 121–130). Boston, MA: Pearson.

Veeman, M. V. J., Van Hout-Wolters, B. H. A. M., & Afflerbach, P. (2006). Metacognition and learning: Conceptual and methodological considerations. *Metacognition and Learning,* 1, 3–14. doi:10.1007/s11409-006-6893-0.

Walter, A., Ritter, T., & Gemünden, H. G. (2001). Value creation in buyer-seller relationships: Theoretical considerations and empirical results from a supplier's perspective. *Industrial Marketing Management,* 30(4), 365–377.

West, R. L. & Turner, L. H. (2007). *Introducing communication theory: Analysis and application.* Boston, MA: McGraw-Hill.

Yep, G. A. (1998). My three cultures: Navigating the multicultural identity landscape. In J. N. Martin, T. K. Nakayama, & L. A. Flores (Eds.), *Readings in cultural contexts* (pp. 79–85). Mountain View, CA: Mayfield.

Yeung, I. Y. M. & Tung, R. L. (1996). Achieving business success in Confucian societies: The importance of *guanxi* (connections). *Organizational Dynamics,* 25(2), 54–65.

17

INTERCULTURAL CONFLICTS IN TRANSNATIONAL MERGERS AND ACQUISITIONS

The Case of a Failed Deal

Juana Du and Ling Chen

Introduction

Transnational merger and acquisition (M&A) is an important driver of corporate and economic growth and has been receiving increasing attention from both professionals in practice and academia in recent decades. However, a large proportion of mergers have failed to produce value for the shareholders of the acquiring firms (e.g., Bruner, 2002). Cultural issues have been identified as the most important cause of transnational M&A failure, according to Firstbrook (2007) who pointed to a few high profile cases as examples: The merger between German-based Daimler-Benz and U.S.-based Chrysler Corporation in 1998 failed largely because of the differences in business culture between the two corporations. That of Sprint and Nextel was to create a $70 billion firm with a stronger customer base, however, the notable cultural differences between the two corporations led to mistrust and conflict. The company took the name Sprint Nextel Corporation when it merged with Nextel Communications in 2005, then returned to using simply Sprint Corporation following the shutdown of the Nextel network in 2013. Citibank Corp (Citicorp), one of the largest commercial banks in the world, faced a troubled situation after the merger with Travelers Group, reportedly due to the corporate cultural clash between the two partners. In 2001, HP and Compaq merged and created a global technology leader with sales of $87 billion. Again, disagreement and dispute arose, as many considered the deal to be bad for HP, the stock market reacted negatively, and the expected synergies did not materialize. In line with popular perceptions in the market, a survey of 123 firms conducted by Avon Hewitt (2011) shows that 58 percent of the firms responded that they had no specific approach to assessing and integrating culture in a deal, and no firm (0 percent) reported that their cultural integration practices were effective. The top three reasons cited for unsuccessful cultural integration included: a lack of top

DOI: 10.4324/9781003252955-20

management agreement on the desired culture (48 percent), culture-related risks not recognized during the due diligence phase (48 percent) before the actual deal takes place, and a lack of top management support (44 percent). Corporate culture is the focus of attention in firm performance after M&A, but culture, both corporate culture and larger cultural difference, may similarly be cited as a contributing factor to a deal failure. This reasoning is based on the fact that national culture is reflected in corporate culture to a large extent and should undergo close scrutiny to better understand the intercultural aspect of transnational business deals.

In response to the call for research addressing practical needs, there appears to be a growing interest in the importance of culture in M&A performance, in particular, how the cultural differences between corporations lead to intercultural conflict during an acquisition and what the intercultural dynamics are at the individual, organizational, and national levels. However, little work is done by way of either theory or empirical investigation in this area. This study aims to extend the discussions about intercultural conflicts in the global workplace to the organizational level, by exploring the role of cultural differences in conflicts in an M&A that involved an Indian firm, a U.S. firm, and a Chinese joint-venture partner of the U.S. firm. Specifically, the objective is to explain how cultural differences among organizations, at the individual, organizational, and national levels, may interplay and lead to cultural conflict during acquisition. The findings may contribute to current theoretical discussion in this area and also have practical and managerial implications for corporations.

Past Studies

For decades, scholars have studied intercultural conflicts in the global workplace, particularly how conflicts take place in workplaces between employees from diverse cultural backgrounds (Ting-Toomey, 2005). Although the traditional approach emphasizes cultural differences between religions, social values, norms, and behavior of the employees in an organization, the new era of globalization and corresponding increases in M&A have multiplied the number of occurrences and heightened the importance of studies of cultural conflicts between/among organizations. While some have examined the cultural differences at the individual level, discussing how the differences in individual cultural backgrounds leads to intercultural conflicts because of the divergence in communication styles, cultural perceptions, expectations, etc., others have studied this phenomenon primarily at the level of organizational culture, by examining the clashes between the corporate value and culture of the combining organizations in M&As (e.g., Ashkanasy & Holmes, 1995; Weber & Pliskin, 1996; Weber, Shenkar, & Raveh, 1996).

The literature on culture clashes in M&A cases to date has several limitations. First, most of it is based on observations by practitioners and consultants, with little theoretical guidance or sufficient empirical support (e.g., Pritchett, 1985; Pritchett, Robinson, & Clarkson, 1997). Second, although M&A cases differ with respect to such factors as relatedness and types of industry, many studies have been conducted on the assumption that M&A cases are homogeneous and so have failed to consider the possibility that the impact of culture clashes on organizational effectiveness might differ from one case to another. Third, the extant literature does not look into why and how cultural differences may cause intercultural conflicts and give rise to integration problems in M&A situations, and if or how any possible relationships between cultural differences and other situational factors affect the process and results of acquisition.

Our interest is specifically focused on the intercultural dynamics and interplay of factors of cultural differences that may lead to intercultural conflicts between organizations, and on examining cultural variances at the individual, organizational, and society levels. Following the existing framework of intercultural conflict studies, which mainly emphasize the individual level, we extend the work to the organizational level, and integrate cultural variables with discussions about situational factors.

Cultural Variability and Communicative Strategies

Using culture-based conflict lenses, cultural dimensions such as individualism and collectivism, etc. often color conflict attitudes, expectations, and behavior when people are involved in emotionally frustrating episodes (Cohen, 1987, 1991). People from an individualistic culture are found to more likely to focus on factual details, rely on linear reasoning, and use personal equity norms to achieve conflict effectiveness, while people from a collectivistic culture tend to focus on process and the holistic picture, rely on spiral and metaphorical reasoning, and use communal or status-based norms to achieve conflict appropriateness (Ting-Toomey, 2005). Similarly the cultural dimension that is relevant in consideration of intercultural conflict is small-large power distance (Ting-Toomey, 2005). People from a large power distance culture would be more likely to respect people at higher power status and to use avoiding behavior in a conflict situation, whereas people from a small power distance culture are likely to be more willing to use competitive behavior and confront people at higher power status. Additionally, Hall (1959) made a distinction between high-context culture and low-context culture, and used this concept to explain the fact that when people communicate how much they take for granted about what the listener knows about the subject under discussion varies across cultures. In low-context communication, the listener is assumed to know very little and must be told practically everything; while in high-context communication, the listener is assumed to be already "contexted" and does not need to be given much background information. In a conflict situation where information is not shared transparently and appropriately, people might experience greater uncertainty and anxiety. Based on their cultural values and cultural background, people would use different communicative strategies to get more information and attempt to resolve the conflict.

Applying a Situational Perspective to Choice of Communicative Strategy

Most existing studies have concentrated on cross-cultural differences, but in an increasingly connected world, particularly in the context of an M&A with time pressure to make decisions, research needs to address the extent these cultural differences still manifest and what role situational factors play and interact with cultural factors.

Putnam and Wilson (1982) argued early on that the type of across-the-board application of conflict management inventories favored by many researchers is underwritten on the assumption that people will respond in the same characteristic way to all conflict situations. They suggested following contingency theory to understand conflict strategies. The theory highlights research showing that the choice of style can vary a great deal according to the situation, as well as, we may add, the cultural background. Lee and Rogan (1991) and Chiu and Kosinski (1994), for example, found Americans measuring higher on both assertive and non-assertive styles than Koreans and Chinese, respectively. This indicates that Americans possibly perceived themselves as using a variety of styles when dealing with conflict depending on the situation. Studying the intercultural negotiations between Americans and Taiwanese, Drake (1995) also found that the role of culture was reduced by personality factors and situational concerns for the individuals involved: Neither the Americans nor the Taiwanese adhered to the styles predicted by cultural norms and cultural differences alone, but they managed negotiations locally. Chan and Goto (2003) found that the cultural/ethnic identity of the other affects the choices of conflict resolution styles, by studying the conflicts that happened between Hong Kong Chinese, mainland Chinese, and Americans. It is reported that Hong Kong Chinese only adhere to expected norms when dealing with other Hong Kong Chinese, not with mainland Chinese or Americans.

One of the situational factors likely to affect the choices of communicative strategies during an intercultural conflict episode is time urgency. Brislin and Kim (2003) discussed the role of time urgency as one of the most salient stressors in the increasingly connected business world. How people value, perceive, and use time impacts the communicative strategies and conflict rhythms in intercultural conflict contexts. Regarding time, Hall's (1959) work on monochronic and polychronic time also provides a useful reference point about cultures. Western cultures are said to often have a synchronous approach to time, which results in emphasis on agenda setting, objective criteria, precise schedules, deadlines, and sequential, efficient task performance. By contrast, Eastern cultures are more polychromous in their approach to time, with less emphasis on prioritizing tasks and an approximate attitude to time frames. Polychronic individuals tend to work in a relational atmosphere and a contextual setting; calendar time holds little meaning if the relational rhythms between people are out of sync. When it comes to conflict management, monochronic time individuals tend to reach and implement tangible conflict outcomes and move faster to address substantive problem and conflict resolution issues, while polychronic individuals would prefer to spend more time building up trust and commitment between the conflict parties and are willing to deal with the deadline in a more flexible and patient manner. As meeting a deadline and tight schedule has become a source of continual stress in the modern workplace, Brislin and Kim (2003) suggested that stress in the modern workplace will increase individualists' directness and terseness in communication acts, whereas collectivists are more likely to be able to retain their composure, for the reason that collectivists are more able to draw on social support from other team members than Western individualists who tend to be achievement-oriented and goal-driven.

Building on the studies of intercultural conflict and negotiation, and incorporating a situational perspective to communicative strategies, we present a detailed analysis of the intercultural dynamics of conflicts among organizations during transnational acquisition and seek to answer two research questions:

RQ1: How are intercultural dynamics playing out among organizations in a transnational acquisition at the individual and organizational levels?
RQ2: How may situational factors influence communication strategies at the different stages of acquisition?

Methodology

Case studies can be used to explain, describe, or explore events or phenomena in the everyday contexts in which they occur (Yin, 2009). It is particularly useful to employ when there is a need to obtain an in-depth appreciation of an issue, event, or phenomenon of interest in its natural real-life context. The case of the M&A between Apollo Tyres (Apollo from hereon) and Cooper Tire & Rubber Company (Cooper from hereon) was selected. Cooper has a joint-venture with Chengshan Group, Chinese Chengshan Tire (CCT), and the latter becomes much more involved in the matter than expected. By closely examining the narratives and perspectives of the three parties respectively, this study provides a comparative analysis of intercultural conflicts happening during the acquisition and negotiation. In particular, it attends to those cultural factors that lead to conflicts between the three parties at the individual, organizational, and national levels, and how those situational factors influence and interact with cultural factors at various stages of the acquisition, including initial communication, intensive negotiation, court battle, and cessation of the negotiation.

We selected this particular case of an M&A between Apollo and Cooper, for three main reasons: Firstly, it is one of the then emerging cases of transnational M&A, which was widely reported with relatively accessible information about its process and dynamics. It has many implications for advancing the development of theories in the arena of intercultural conflicts. Secondly, the scope of this M&A case (which would have resulted in a 2.5 billion deal) likely has a significant impact on the industry and transnational M&As, which drew attention to the practices in management of multinational enterprises and, particularly, transnational M&As. Third, the cultural complexity (companies from three national cultural backgrounds are involved: India, the U.S., and China) and intensity of this unsuccessful merger means that it is a case that provides insight and has implications for both academic research and professional practices.

For this case study, we gathered information and news reports from the corporate websites of the three parties, as well as reports from media, in the period from May 1, 2013 to Jan 31, 2014. In total, 76 news reports were collected, some from the three corporate websites: 11 from the corporate website of Cooper (http://coopertire.com/News.aspx), 11 from the corporate website of CCT's Chinese partner Chinese Chengshan Group (www.chengshantire.com/news.aspx), and 1 from the corporate website of Apollo www.apollotyres.com/india/media/news.aspx). The remaining 53 news articles were gathered from the internet by searching the key words "Apollo," "Cooper," and "acquire" using search engines, such as Google.

The Case

Cooper, headquartered in Findlay, Ohio, U.S., announced in late December 2013 that it was terminating a proposed $2.5 billion merger agreement with Apollo Tyres, Gurgaon, India. This unilateral announcement of the deal's termination came just 48 hours before the deadline for completing transactions. It ended a bitter month-long standoff. Cooper said that the decision to terminate the deal was taken after it was notified by Apollo that it had failed to find the funds for the proposed acquisition.

This merger was announced by the companies in June 2013 after months of initial discussion. According to the agreement of the deal, Apollo was to acquire Cooper in an all-cash deal worth $35-a-share, which would transform this Indian company into the world's seventh-largest tire manufacturer.

Cooper's joint-venture partner (minority holder of 35 percent interest) in China was Chengshan Group, a state-owned enterprise. Chengshan was opposed to the merger plan with Apollo, expressing concerns over Indian management of Chinese employees, and brought a lawsuit against its American partner seeking to dissolve their partnership. Cooper tried and failed to gain arbitration of the dispute in courts in Hong Kong. There was a CCT worker strike (June–July, 2013) resulting in reduced production at this location (25 percent of Cooper's annual revenue); Cooper managers were then locked out of this subsidiary (Aug–Sept) and had no access to its current (changed) finance information that was needed for the merger.

In the meantime, Cooper's unit in the U.S. failed to reach a contractual agreement with the labor unions. The ensuing arbitration resulted in favor of the latter and found that it was entitled to a labor negotiation with the new owner, which went nowhere (June–Sept). The need for renegotiation with U.S. workers was then cited as a reason for Apollo to seek a (approximately 25 percent) price discount. Apollo blamed the U.S. partner for not submitting a complete picture of the working of Cooper's joint venture in China, and a lack of cooperation from Cooper on its CCT matters, which was a major obstacle for Apollo in its efforts to raise the capital needed for the acquisition. Cooper sued Apollo shortly afterward in a Delaware court trying to force it to complete the deal on the agreed terms, in reaction to its request for a discount on the purchase price (October). The

Delaware court ruled, in favor of Apollo Tyres, that Apollo had not breached its obligations.

Analysis

We first examined a common intercultural problem, possible miscommunication between the parties involved, and noted its occurrence between U.S. Cooper and Indian Apollo executives at the initial negotiation stage. This probably furthered misunderstandings and the intercultural conflicts between the three business partners later and could be explained in light of the differences between high-context/low-context culture and different communication styles. The differences in cultural values (at both the individual and society levels), the different organizational communicative strategies, and different approaches to conflict are all relevant to the subsequent disputes between the business partners and the final court battle. We examined these cultural differences and conflicts from the cultural lenses of individualism-collectivism and power distance, and discuss how situational factors interplayed with value differences and led to various communicative and conflict approaches at different stages during an international acquisition.

Miscommunication at the Initial Stage of Negotiation (Apollo and Chengshan Group)

The misunderstandings and miscommunication that occurred at the initial stage of negotiation between the executives of Chengshan Group, U.S. Cooper's Chinese partner, and Indian Apollo point to the cultural differences between high-context culture/low-context culture, and different communication styles. Very early in the process, while carrying out due diligence prior to reaching merger agreement, Neeraj Kanwar, the managing director of Apollo, visited China to ensure that the partners had a mutual understanding about the move and that Cooper's joint venture partner in China was comfortable with working with Apollo, the new partner. He had a meeting in Beijing, China, with Cooper's Chinese unit (and the minority owner) on May 13, 2013, visiting Hongzhong Che, the chairman of Chengshan Group. At the meeting Kanwar had a hard time grasping what Che was trying to convey. According to a news report, Hongzhong Che kept saying one thing over and over again, it went as follows: "I have been a good son and the father is good. Now the father is divorcing me and the stepfather is coming in." Neeraj Kanwar was confused and later shared this, "He was trying to say something to us that we really didn't understand." (News report 1.) Kanwar had made a point of outlining the benefits of the merger, but Che kept on repeating his issue with the "stepfather" and, in the end, asked what was in it for him. It appears that Che expressed a wish for compensation should they agree to have the merger go through. This expressed wish went unheeded at the time and was only recalled after the event. Ultimately, the actual purpose of the visit was not achieved as conceived. Also lost were matters that would seem to be important for the process.

These never really came up, in the meeting or later in Apollo's internal discussion, according to Forbes India's report (Mishra, 2014), including such questions as: Did Che feel comfortable with working with Apollo? If not, what were the issues and could they be resolved? If, on the other hand, Che wanted out, how much was he expecting for his share? If Che were to exit, could Apollo run the subsidiary in China on its own? All the above involves an understanding of intercultural matters. For a more careful look, we focus on the crucial statement from Che that particularly confused Kanwar.

Hongzhong Che used the metaphor of "father-son" to describe the relationship between the parent company, Cooper, and the joint-venture, CCT. According to his descriptions, both "the father" and "the son" are good, which refers to the mutually successful effort to build a relationship between them. He used the metaphor of "stepfather" to describe Apollo, the Indian company, and likened the acquisition as a "divorce" between Cooper and CCT. Metaphors developed and used in a specific cultural context require culturally specific understandings and explanations. Using metaphor in complex intercultural communication situations can lead to possible misunderstandings and complicate the matters to be communicated. Widely held and incorporated in the Confucian school of thought, a fundamental philosophy of Chinese society, family is regarded as the prototype of all social organizations. At the center are five cardinal human relationships: ruler-subject, father-son, husband-wife, older-younger brother, and friends, three of which are about family and act as the model for the rest. It helps explain the reason Hongzhong Che used the metaphor of family and the father-son relationship to describe the relationship between Cooper, the parent company, and CCT the joint-venture, where Chengshan Group is the minority partner. Che was complaining about the parent in an implicit way for not keeping its word in this important relationship by wanting to sell the subsidiary, its own child, which can be taken as a grave injustice in this light. Without shared cultural knowledge and understanding, Neeraj Kanwar found it puzzling and could not understand what Hongzhong Che really meant by this comment. Yet he did not attach much significance to it at that time despite his perplexity, and just continued as planned, continuing with his view of the matter, and thus laid the ground for a problematic beginning.

It should be noted that Hongzhong Che came from a high-context culture. As the Chinese chairman of CCT, by using metaphor, he expressed the dissatisfaction and hesitation regarding the acquisition in an indirect way, without indicating his misgivings and resentful thoughts explicitly. He might have expected people to interpret and understand the implicit meaning by sharing the same communicative context, yet was unaware of the need for sharing cultural context: the metaphor implied that CCT/the Chinese partner had not been treated properly in this partnership and deserved better treatment before giving their consent to the merger. Neeraj Kanwar, the Indian director came from a culture that is comparatively lower-context in communication (e.g., Nishimura, Nevgi, & Tella, 2008) with a different tradition. In such cultures, meanings are stated more explicitly through language and the main information is expected to be in the transmitted message needed to cover any information that is missing or unclear in the context (both internal and external). A person from a low-context culture would expect further explanations and would probably request as much if something remained unclear, particularly in an intercultural communication situation, which tends to be high in uncertainty with mutual unfamiliarity between the communication partners. When none is forthcoming, we could expect (communication) problems out of likely ignorance. India being in the middle of the high-low context continuum, Indian communicators such as Kanwar might welcome or expect an explanation when confused though not actually seeking it. These different expectations caused confusion and misunderstanding when Kanwar was talking to Hongzhong Che in their meeting. The conflict was apparently perceived by Chengshan Group without Apollo being aware of it, setting the stage for its intensification.

What happened subsequently demonstrates the development of this misunderstanding and miscommunication: in June, Mr. Kanwar announced this complex, international $ 2.5 billion takeover of Cooper Tire which later turned out to have "depended heavily on the goodwill" of Hongzhong Che (News report 4). Neeraj Kanwar's assumed understanding of Hongzhong Che's meaning or overlooking of the confusion illustrates how differences between higher-context and lower-context culture communication styles can lead to intercultural conflicts and create obstacles in a M&A case.

Subsequent Manifest Dispute (CCT & Cooper)

Using the lenses of cultural dimensions to examine the intensive negotiations between U.S. Cooper, Indian Apollo, and Chinese partner of CCT, we get a more comprehensive picture of cultural conflicts that happened between the three parties. In terms of Hoftsede's cultural value dimensions, Indian culture, scoring 48, is a society with both collectivistic and individualistic tendencies, China scores 20 and features a high collectivistic tendency, and the U.S. scores 91, which is a high individualistic culture. For the dimension of power distance, both Chinese and Indian cultures feature large power distance with scores of 80 and 77 respectively, while the U.S. scores 40, featuring small power distance. These differences in individualism-collectivism and power distance dimensions appear to have manifested in the communicative strategies and practices of the three business partners in the subsequent disputes.

As a result of miscommunication and misunderstandings between the top executives of Apollo and CCT at their initial contact, this conflict was first felt by the CCT/Chengshan Group and, apparently, internal mobilization ensued as a way of dealing with it. Workers quickly went on strike shortly after the acquisition announcement and, in letters to the public, expressed grievance as neglected stakeholders and concerns over uncertainty, potentially high risks, and new management from another culture (i.e., India)—conflict was now out in the open. By late July, factory executives had revoked Cooper's access to the joint venture's financial records and stopped producing Cooper-branded tires. This collective action clearly voiced the strong opposition to the Cooper decision on M&A by CCT the Chinese partner, which was implicitly expressed at their Beijing meeting with Mr. Kumwar, yet was not picked up, less still understood. The CCT workers' protest manifests the collectivism culture prevalent where the company is situated. This unexpected action surprised both U.S. Cooper and Indian Apollo, as expressed by Robert Cepelick, a partner in Deloitte financial advisory services who commented on Cooper's loss of control over a consolidated subsidiary: "It is a highly unusual situation, I have never seen anything like it" (News Report 6), speaking from the perspective of a legally based corporate world (in the West) —Chengshan Group as the minority holder of the subsidiary had no legal say in the parent company's M&A decision.

However, the CCT reaction makes sense in a collectivistic, hierarchically conscious culture. Group actions represent collective opinions and a unified stand about what is expected by workers of CCT, affiliated to Chengshan Group, a state-owned firm. We can see workers deploy a collective narrative voiced by the labor union, connecting personal feelings and dissatisfactions to collective memories and collective rights, as is seen in several examples from news reports from the corporate website of CCT citing the Union:

> *The Labor Union of CCT, object to the Apollo's acquisition of Cooper. We strongly protest this transaction, which disregard the living rights of employee. We require the termination of this transaction. We keep our rights to take further actions. My dear fellow members, let us unite and protect our rights and interests together.*
>
> *(from Executive Committee of Labor Union, June 18, 2013)*

The background to this strong wording of protest by the CCT union is the collective experience of the previous seven years of great efforts to integrate the corporate culture between Cooper and CCT. It is reported that five managers had been replaced in the first four years after Cooper and Chengshan Group set up the joint venture that is CCT. These previous experiences probably led CCT workers to have doubts about and be wary of new movements of a similar nature with yet another party, since CCT had only recently started to make a profit and be in good shape after seven years of integration. The employees expected their efforts to be repaid with stability, steady growth, and continuing prosperity. All this now was under the dark cloud of ominous uncertainty. In addition, lack of direct communication and consultation before the merger announcement possibly also made CCT (its workers and Chinese partner) feel they weren't trusted and had been neglected. Rather than being motivated by the new blueprint described by both Apollo and Cooper, CCT workers considered it as "disregard [for] the living rights of employee" and demanded termination of the deal.

Moreover, uncertainty and potential high risks are always associated with acquisition, which underscores the need for trust in business relationships. In this case, the strong collectivistic value which regarded the group interests as prevailing is also demonstrated by the emphasis on trust relationships between joint-venture partners Cooper and CCT. As expressed in a letter to the public from the CCT Labor Union:

> To our further astonishment, till now we, as the representative of our Labor Union members, haven't received any letters of inquiry regarding the proposed merger.

Absence of communication, perceptions of no transparency, and being neglected as stakeholders in this matter directly point to the issue of trust and, by implication, of control, with CCT getting the short end of the wedge. As a result, CCT workers raised many questions regarding the uncertain future:

> We can't resist asking these questions: is such a high leverage affordable for our company with such annual profit? Will the employee benefit continued to be guaranteed? Will the maintenance of facilities and ordinary business operations not be exposed to any risk? Will the cash flow meet our daily business?
>
> (from Executive Committee of Labor Union, June 18, 2013)

This is supplemented by an advertisement CCT placed in The Wall Street Journal, which asked, "Who can guarantee the success of integration between Chinese culture and Indian culture?" A CCT union leader was cited explaining their opposition, particularly because "Apollo is an Indian company ... if it was Michelin; we might have agreed" (Indian deal for Cooper Tire riles Chinese workers, 2013). Such was the mistrust/belief that it could hardly be allayed by an assurance of continuing prosperity given at the first meeting with Mr. Kumwar, whom CCT hardly knew and for whom it had little faith or respect.

This collective expression of opposition to the acquisition is situated in the CCT corporate and cultural context. The CCT Chinese partner had probably felt they were on the same wavelength as Cooper where business was concerned and were on an equal footing as a partner. On both accounts the expectation was that they should have a say in what would happen, regardless of their legal rights as a minority holder with no participation in share-price sensitive decisions. After all, Chengshan Group is state-owned, and all its workers are owners in a sense, and ought not to be out-ranked, which is revealed to be a perceived power matter. Possible different understandings of what is meant by joint venture and where the partner's respective place is gave rise to indignant feelings of being slighted on the part of CCT, the Chinese partner. More open communication and information sharing to the extent that was possible, even though limited, could possibly have helped reduce the great uncertainty and risks perceived by CCT workers, especially in such an acquisition scenario. It might also have communicated the respect CCT considered was its due. However, that didn't happen, which led to more severe disputes between the three business partners and a court battle. The collective expression of the opposition to the acquisition was also strongly influenced by the

CCT's cultural context, which features high collectivistic and high power distance, in comparison to the culture of Cooper with an emphasis on fairness upheld in legality and personal freedom. These cultural differences were manifested in various communicative and conflict strategies and approaches used by the three companies involved in this case once the intensive negotiation turned into a court battle.

Negotiation with USW and Court Battle

On the other side, Cooper and Apollo approached the conflict with various communicative strategies and practices associated with a number of corporate values, which turned things into a court battle at a late stage in the process. In the U.S., United Steelworkers (USW), the industrial union, had won a block on the sale of two of Cooper's factories in the U.S. to Apollo. USW (representing about 2,900 workers at Cooper plants in Ohio and Texas) had argued that the takeover entitled the union to a new collective-bargaining agreement. The block imposed by an arbitrator on Cooper's labor agreements would be lifted only when the USW reached agreement with Apollo on pensions, job security, and a range of other issues.

Apollo executives along with Cooper managers negotiated with Cooper workers represented by the USW union. Two management parties used very different communicative and conflict strategies, and the negotiation has been perceived in very different ways. As the union had laid out specific demands, moving from there Cooper wanted to get things settled. Apollo representatives, on the other hand, used the talks to test the waters and get to know the others first, which was perceived by Cooper representatives as Apollo being unprepared to make proposals while attending a meeting with the USW. From Cooper's perspective, Apollo was making no serious effort to resolve the dispute. However, from Apollo's perspective, Mr. Kanwar had explained that they wanted to know more and to understand Cooper better so that they would have a better understanding of how to deal with this issue. From his standpoint, the meeting agenda was about relationship building (with future employees) and getting to know one's business partners is a necessary step to finding the best way forward. These different approaches and the various corporate values between U.S. Cooper and Indian Apollo could be explained by different values of the cultures from which the two companies came. Coming from a culture that features individualism and low power distance, Cooper expected to solve the conflict in an effective manner with a focus on outcome and effective management of conflict. The speed and protection of shareholder value is prioritized, which is consistent with the value of personal freedom and equal treatment. However, the corporate culture of Apollo represents the Indian cultural values, which are a combination of large power distance and moderate individualism/collectivism. Indian executives place more emphasis on relationship building and are keen to work out the most appropriate procedure to solve the conflict, rather than resolve the conflict with immediate effect. This stronger focus on process, relationship, and conflict appropriateness represents the underlying value of obligation to the other party and the value of asymmetrical interaction. The differences between the content goal oriented approach and the relational goal oriented approach was also manifested by the communicative strategies used by Cooper and Apollo respectively. As a result of the value differences and communicative strategies, U.S. Cooper displayed more competitive behavior with a self-face concern in the conflict negotiation situation, whereas Indian Apollo was more concerned about other-face and relationship building, and took the approach of avoiding confrontation and conflict.

The situational elements, e.g. time urgency and business goals, also played a crucial role in the late stage of negotiation and court battle between the three business parties. Cooper is from a culture of monochronic time, which is demonstrated in their executives' tendency to reach and implement tangible conflict outcomes with a clearly established timetable. While this time orientation also explains why they felt Indian Apollo was not negotiating with any serious intention of solving the conflict; the urgency of making a deal was a situational factor and the need to take time to put a good deal together was another. On the other hand, being from a polychronic time culture, Apollo tended to work on the relational atmosphere, in order to build rapport and trust, probably at the expense of the deadline consideration. Their efforts to spend more time building trust and commitment were not appreciated by their U.S. partners, who interpreted it in a negative way without cross-cultural awareness and understanding. Cooper's U.S. unit failed to reach a contractual agreement with labor unions, although negotiations with USW in the later stages went on with no Cooper involvement as requested by Apollo. When the two parties met again, Apollo put forward a request for a price reduction. In October Cooper launched legal action to force Apollo to complete the merger quickly, the situational factor of urgency was probably made more acute given the new request from Apollo. The following month saw a Delaware judge dismissing Cooper's appeal. Late December, Cooper announced that it was terminating a proposed $2.5 billion merger agreement with Apollo Tyres. Apollo blamed the U.S. partner for not submitting a complete picture and a lack of cooperation from Cooper on its Chinese partner CCT, which was a key obstacle for Apollo in its efforts to raise the capital needed for the acquisition.

The miscommunication and misunderstanding at the initial stage of the business conversation, the value differences and various communicative and conflict approaches at the intensive negotiation stage and the court battle stage, and the effect of the situational factors all contributed to a situation where the acquisition turned into a failed deal.

Discussion and Conclusion

This case study analyzes the intercultural conflict that happened between three companies from various cultural backgrounds in an M&A and extends previous studies on intercultural conflicts by exploring the interplay of cultural variability at different levels of organization and situational factors. We attend to differences at the individual, organizational, and society levels, which may lead to intercultural conflict in a business context. In particular, we look into the intercultural mechanism of conflict at different stages of negotiation, and how cultural and situational factors influence communicative and conflict strategies. It contributes to the literature on intercultural conflicts in transnational M&A and extends the discussion of intercultural conflict, which mainly emphasizes individuals, to intercultural conflicts between organizations at the cultural level.

We note that at the individual level, reflected in various communication styles, differences between high-context and low-context culture and usage of metaphors between key players of organizations (e.g., executives of companies in this case) in a negotiation context can cause misunderstandings and miscommunications, which then lead to intercultural conflicts between companies at the organizational level. The cultural differences at the individual level play out in various organizational contexts and interact with situational factors, e.g. time urgency and business interest, which would need different organizational communicative strategies and complicate matters in a conflict scenario. It will be fruitful to further examine specifically how cultural differences at the individual level are demonstrated in an organizational context, and how these cultural differences at the individual level interplay with the corporate culture and value which might have an impact on conflict resolution.

Examining the interplay of cultural variability and situational factors at the organizational level and the society level provides a more comprehensive picture of intercultural conflict in an organizational context. Individualism/collectivism and power distance—two cultural dimensions of work-related values—help explain how these value variety patterns fundamentally influence communicative strategies of the individuals representing the corporation as well as corporate practices in an intercultural conflict situation. Future research could further explore other cultural variety dimensions (e.g., uncertainty avoidance, masculinity/femininity, long-term/short-term orientation) and apply these cultural dimensions to explain how different values can lead to intercultural conflict in international business contexts.

The analysis also reveals three common intercultural issues. First, cross-cultural ignorance or unawareness is seen in Apollo and Cooper managers with respect to the Chinese partner/workers and their culture, and in Cooper managers with respect to the Indian counterpart reflected in Apollo negotiation representatives. All this is associated with the miscommunication and misunderstanding described above. This is a difficult issue and calls for a mindful approach particularly of ignorance about other cultures. A second issue is preconceptions and uncertainty/anxiety avoidance. The case illustrates this with CCT union's unflattering pre-perception of Indian culture, balking at the prospect of an Indian management and probably that of Chengshan Group management and their bias against an Indian joint-venture partner, since Chinese unions of state-owned companies are structurally associated with the management. The tendency to avoid or resist engaging in a situation with an unknown partner may give rise to more intercultural problems. The third issue is possible strategic maneuvers by business, taking advantage of the mutual confusion due to cultural difference and ignorance, as may be deduced from Apollo's request for a price reduction. CCT Chinese partner's maneuver for compensation or payoff on their part has a similar flavor—all this could very well be business strategy, at least in part, where parties engage in foul-crying as a persuasion strategy.

This case study discusses intercultural conflict in the context of transnational M&A with an empirical analysis of a multinational acquisition case. For further studies, it would be meaningful to discuss intercultural conflict in other organizational contexts, e.g. conflicts that arose in international collaborations in business settings, conflicts between different types of organizations, as well as different business units within an organization with local cultures. This research does not make comparisons between corporate value and cultural differences, which might also have an impact on conflict strategy and resolution. Future studies could further explore how corporate culture and value differences, as well as a variety of corporate sub-cultures could impact communicative strategies and conflict.

The managerial implications for managers of corporations are as follows. The case study demonstrates the importance of cultural value differences at the individual, organizational, and society levels and how they might impact communicative strategies and lead to cultural conflict within/between organizations. Managers need to pay particular attention to the culturally diverse background of employees and understand how this may impact communication within organizations or between organizations. Also it pays to be mindful of non-understanding or confusion in intercultural communication, in order to seek clarification, facilitate communication, and reduce possible conflicts. For international M&As, corporations have to develop culturally appropriate communicative strategies and plans at an early stage, and maintain transparent and two-way communication, which could help all the parties involved to understand the meaning of various actions and facilitate the progress of the acquisition. Corporations should also consider the variation in corporate values and the possibility of integrating corporate cultural differences in an M&A. In relation to intercultural issues, there is a need for better training on ignorance and awareness, not just cultural literacy but cultural intelligence. Cultural intelligence will also help with issues related to preconception and possible strategic manoeuvre issues.

Despite these insights and implications, this study suffers from a number of limitations that should be addressed in future work. Firstly, we only chose news reports written in English and a few in Chinese (from the corporate website of CCT), and didn't include news reports written in other languages, e.g. Hindi, which might have contributed a different insight to analysis and research findings. Secondly, we studied the three companies involved in this case which came from the U.S., India, and China, future research needs to examine companies with other cultural backgrounds, to provide more empirical data to examine the dynamics of intercultural conflict in M&As. Thirdly, we examined corporate values mainly emphasizing the cultural background of those corporations, and didn't look closely at the espoused corporate values of each company. Future study could further examine the espoused corporate value and how it would interplay with other cultural factors and impact corporate conflict resolutions.

References

Ashkanasy, N. M. & Holmes, S. (1995). Perceptions of organizational ideology following merger: A longitudinal study of merging accounting firms. *Accounting, Organizations, and Society*, 20, 19–34.

Brislin, R.W. & Kim, E. S. (2003). Cultural diversity in people's understanding and uses of time. *Applied Psychology: An International Review*, 52, 262–382.

Bruner, J. (2002). *Making stories: Law, literature, life*. Cambridge, MA: Harvard University Press.

Chan, D. K-S. & Goto, S. G. (2003). Conflict resolution in the culturally diverse workplace: Some data from Hong Kong employees. *Applied Psychology: An International Review*, 52, 441–460.

Chiu, R. K. & Kosinski, F. A. (1994). Is Chinese conflict-handing behavior influenced by Chinese values? *Social Behavior and Personality*, 22, 81–90.

Cohen, R. (1987). Problems of intercultural communication in Egyptian-American diplomatic relations. *International Journal of Intercultural Relations*, 11, 29–47.

Cohen, R. (1991) *Negotiating across cultures: Communication obstacles in international diplomacy*. Washington, DC: U.S. Institute of Peace.

Connor, P. E. & Becker, B. W. (1994). Personal values and management: What do we know and why don't we know more? *Journal of Management Inquiry*, 3, 67–73.

Drake, L. E. (1995). Negotiation styles in intercultural communication, *International Journal of Conflict Management*, 6, 72–90.

Firstbrook, C. (2007). Transnational mergers and acquisitions: How to beat the odds of disaster. *Journal of Business Strategy*, 28(1), 53–56.

Hall, E. (1959). *The silent language*. New York, NY: Faweell.

Hewitt, A. (2011). *Trends in global employee engagement, consulting: Talent and organization*. Retrieved from: www.aon.com/attachments/thought-leadership/Trends_Global_Employee_Engagement_Final.pdf.

Hofstede, G. (1980). *Culture's consequences: International differences in work-related values*. Beverly Hills, CA: Sage.

Hofstede, G. & Hofstede, G. J. (2001). *Cultures and organizations: Software of the mind*. New York, NY: McGraw-Hill.

Lee, H. O. & Rogan, R. G. (1991). A cross-cultural comparison of organizational conflict behaviors. *International Journal of Conflict Management*, 2, 181–199.

Mishra, A. K. (2014, Jan 31). How the Apollo, Cooper deal was botched, *Forbes India*. Retrieved from http://forbesindia.com/article/boardroom/how-the-apollo-cooper-deal-was-botched/37019/1.

Nishimura, S., Nevgi, A., & Tella, S. (2008). Communication style and cultural features in high/low context communication cultures: A case study of Finland, Japan and India. *Proceedings of a subject-didactic symposium, Helsinki* (Feb. 2, 2008), Part 2, pp. 783–796.

Pritchett, P. (1985). *After the merger: Managing the shockwaves*. Homewood, IL: Dow Jones-Irwin.

Pritchett, P., Robinson, D., & Clarkson, R. 1997. *After the merger*. New York, NY: McGraw-Hill.

Putnam, L. L. & Wilson, C. E. (1982). Communicative strategies in organizational conflicts: Reliability and validity of a measurement scale. In B. M. Doran (Ed.), *Communication yearbook* 6 (pp. 629–652). Beverly Hills, CA: Sage.

Ting-Toomey, S. (2005). The matrix of face: An updated face-negotiation theory. In W. B. Gudykunst (Ed.), *Theorizing about intercultural communication* (pp. 71–92). Thousand Oaks, CA: Sage.

The Wall Street Journal. (2013, July 31). Indian deal for Cooper Tire riles Chinese workers. Retrieved from www.wsj.com/articles/SB10001424127887323997004578639810333722862.

Weber, Y. & Pliskin, N. (1996). Effects of information systems integration and organizational culture on a firm's effectiveness. *Information & Management*, 30(2), 81–90.

Weber, Y., Shenkar, O., & Raveh, A. (1996). National and corporate cultural fit in merger/acquisitions: An exploratory study. *Management Science*, 42, 1215–1227.

Yin, R. K. (2009). *Case study research: Design and methods*. Thousand Oaks, CA: Sage.

18

LEVERAGING DIFFERENCES

Perceived Complementarity as a Synergy Potential in Sino-German Cooperation

Marcella Hoedl and Peter Franklin

Introduction

Since its opening in 1979, China has rapidly developed from a low-cost into a high-tech economy. Both the Chinese government and Chinese companies have realized that in view of increasing human resource costs they have to cooperate with foreign partners in order to stay competitive on the international market (Huang & Bond, 2012). Especially since the conception of China's *New Silk Road Initiative* and the pursuit of the *Made in China 2025* goals, Germany has attracted more Chinese investment than any other European country, due to its core competence in innovative key technologies (Welfens, 2017; Wübbeke, Meissner, Zenglein, Ives & Conrad, 2016; Xia & Liu, 2021). At the same time, German companies are interested in establishing themselves in the Chinese market as a result of China's large number of potential customers and their ever-increasing affluence and appetite for high-quality products. As a consequence, the number of Sino-German cooperations is increasing.

Thanks to its cultural diversity, which may manifest itself in diverging attitudes, perceptions, values, practices and behaviours, this kind of bi-national cooperation presents challenges as well as opportunities. The German and Chinese cultures are often said to be diametrically opposed and therefore potentially especially problematic. These differences, such as individualism vs. collectivism, high vs. low uncertainty avoidance, high vs. low power distance, task- vs. relationship-orientation, monochronic vs. polychronic orientation, some of which emerge in the discussion of our results, and the resulting difficulties are very well documented in the research (Hofstede, 2001; Hofstede & Minkov, 2010; Hampden-Turner & Trompenaars, 1997; Schroll-Machl, 2003) and do not require further elaboration here.

This view of the contrasting nature of country-level values, behaviours and practices is common, because since its inception intercultural management research has relied heavily on the classical etically generated concept of culture, in which

DOI: 10.4324/9781003252955-21

country cultures are assumed to be rather stable constructs of values and behaviours which can be depicted on a linear continuum and broken down into measurable and comparable parts in order to predict and explain the outcome of intercultural encounters. This etic view sees cultures as static constructs which, when they collide spin off each other like billiard balls without changing (Wolf, 1982). Cultural differences, therefore, have often been treated as a source of difficulties in international encounters.

This chapter, however, adopts a more constructive and constructivist view focusing on the dynamic and positive aspects of culture and cultural differences in Sino-German cooperation, investigating perceived complementarity and, therefore, potentially synergistic aspects of Sino-German cultural differences.

The Constructivist Paradigm of Culture

More recent research has revealed that individuals can integrate different cultural orientations which are activated by the social context in which they interact. It has, for example, been observed that Chinese employees (Leung, 2012) and leaders (Lin et al., 2018) in multinational companies display organizational behaviours which are untypical of their national cultures; Western expatriates working in China have also been found to adopt and integrate new practices (Lynton & Thøgersen, 2006).

The contextual stimuli of the environment seem not only to prompt a different way of thinking (Leung, 2012; Liu & Almor, 2016), but, in line with the constructivist view of culture as dynamic patterns of thinking, feeling and acting which are constantly constructed and re-constructed through interactions with others, it has also been assumed recently that "organizations and individuals can adapt their value portfolios according to specific situations, context requirements, and changes over time, thus making sense of paradoxes and cultural dilemmas" (Pauluzzo Guarda, De Pretto, & Fang, 2018, p. 258).

Cultural complementarity describes a state in which these seemingly contradictory, but equally important, value-based characteristics of individuals belonging to different groups complement each other in order to form a whole. Such characteristics are, for example, shared attitudes, norms, patterns of thinking, feeling and acting (practices) (Barmeyer & Franklin, 2016). When this new cultural whole is more than the sum of its parts, meaning that it creates an added value for the organization and its actors, it is called cultural synergy. In this respect cultural complementarity can be regarded as the potential for generating cultural synergy.

The latter can be created through constructive intercultural management, which is defined as the conscious handling of cultural characteristics and cultural diversity in organizational contexts, whereby individuals succeed in constructively using these characteristics as enriching and complementary resources through the application of mutual adaptation and development processes (Barmeyer, 2018). According to Adler (2008), culturally synergistic organizations would manage to create new management structures and practices which transcend the cultures of their employees. The resulting cultural whole, however, should not be confused with cultural sameness, as it does not describe a state of being but a process by which, as in a piece of music, the interplay of various cultural aspects leads to a unique and ever-changing composition. In this respect, instead of ignoring or reducing diversity, it can be used as a resource to develop the organization in a continuous process (Adler, 2008; Verghese, 2016).

This transformation of cultural differences via complementarities into synergies implies a move from comparative studies mainly following a functionalist paradigm to new qualitative studies examining how cultural differences are perceived and what is learned from them. The challenge lies in recognizing different cultures' strengths and integrating them without extinguishing their individuality.

The Constructivist Paradigm of Culture in Chinese Thinking

While this harmonious interplay of contradictions is a relatively new concept to Western minds (Nisbett, 2003), it is deeply rooted in the Chinese philosophy of Daoism, in which the opposing forces of Yin and Yang (Chinese: 阴阳 yīn yáng) complement and balance each other in a constant process of change (Chen & Lee, 2008; Fang, 2012; Ji, Lee, & Guo, 2010; Ng, Lee, & Cardona, 2012).

Verghese (2016) states that as in the Chinese conception of the Middle Way (Chinese: 中庸 Zhōngyōng), a synergy effect would not imply a compromise, as nobody would have to abandon their particularities, but everyone could gain or integrate something new. This would be an ongoing dynamic process of adapting, re-evaluating, learning and integrating (Verghese, 2016). In this sense, the ideal cultural reality in a bi-cultural context could be epitomized as harmony within opposites, unified and balanced through a dynamic, ongoing process.

Constructivist Interculturality in General

The research landscape on positive qualitative intercultural research remains under-developed. As Stahl and Tung's (2015) content analysis of a total of 644 journal articles published in two leading intercultural management journals (namely, the *Journal of International Business Studies* (JIBS) and *Cross Cultural Management: An International Journal* (CCM)) shows, it is the negative aspects of cultural differences and interculturality which have been the major focus in intercultural management research for the past quarter of a century. The potential benefit which intercultural differences can bring about is overlooked in international management research because synergy is seen as the homogenization of two cultures, whereby one culture adapts to the other, instead of mutually learning from and complementing each other to form a new whole (Lian, 2014). From an intercultural perspective it is precisely the differences which have the potential to release synergies.

This is why in the past few years more and more scholars, for example, Barmeyer and Davoine (2014, 2015, 2016, 2019), Barmeyer (2018), Cameron (2017), Primecz, Romani, & Sackmann (2011), Stahl, Miska, Lee, & De Luque (2017, Stahl, Tung, Kostova, & Zellmer-Bruhn (2017)) and Stahl and Tung (2015) have called for a more solution-oriented, constructivist approach which examines the positive side of interculturality.

Constructivist Interculturality Related to China

Although research related to China has focused on the problems and challenges resulting from bi-national cooperation with Western organizations (e.g., Jin et al., 2013; Zhang, 2004), some researchers, for example, Chen, Chao, Xie and Tjosvold (2018), Chia and Holt (2007), Du, Ai and Brugha (2011), Gallo (2011), Li (2014, 2016), Pauluzzo et al. (2018) and Weick and Putnam (2006), have also pointed out how Western and Chinese philosophical concepts and theories, reflected in different attitudes and ways of thinking, complement each other. However, these mostly theoretical and conceptual attempts to reveal complementarities and thereby potential synergies view the West as one cultural complex, neglecting the differences between Western cultures. Little attention appears to have been paid so far to the specifics of the Sino-German context.

This study therefore attempts to rectify this situation in the empirical investigation of the positive aspects of Sino-German cooperation from a cultural perspective by identifying mutually perceived complementarities as potentials for cultural synergy as well as the influencing factors that might either facilitate or inhibit the virtuous learning circle leading to cultural synergy. We address the following two questions:

1.   Which differences are perceived as complementary by individuals on both sides in Sino-German cooperation?
2.   Which factors facilitate or inhibit a positive attitude towards these differences?

Methodology

In order to identify complementarities and potential synergies, a semi-structured interview guide intended to shed light on perceived and experienced differences and interviewees' attitudes towards them was developed. This interview guide was translated from German into Chinese and although no formal back-translation took place, the use of specific terms was discussed and adjusted with the help of a native-speaker of Chinese.

Semi-structured interviews with a total of 28 German and Chinese skilled employees, senior managers and experts were conducted regarding their experiences, perceptions and attitudes towards Sino-German workplace interaction, with special regard to the fostering of joint innovation. The interviews were either conducted in person in the interviewees' offices or on the phone in either German or Chinese. The quotations that follow are our own translations from German or Chinese into English. All the interviews were recorded and saved in an audio-file, transcribed and analysed regarding the reported perceived differences.

Sample

Twenty-eight interviews were conducted with 18 German nationals and 10 Chinese nationals from 23 different companies. In order to protect data privacy, the names of the interviewees are anonymized by using designations such as *Chinese employee Z* and *German senior manager Y*.

Table 18.1 gives an overview of the interviewees' profiles:

TABLE 18.1 Overview of sample

Nationality & position	Gender	Industry	Interview language	Foreign language competence (Chinese or German)
German senior manager P	male	Logistics	German	–
German senior manager L	male	Logistics	German	–
German senior manager K	male	Logistics	German	–
German senior manager M	male	Logistics	German	–
German senior manager U	male	Logistics Appliances	German	–
German senior manager Z	male	Logistics	German	–
German employee F	male	Logistics	German	–
German senior manager R	male	Consulting	German	✓ Chinese intermediate
German senior manager J	male	Consulting	German	✓ Chinese intermediate
German employee K	male	Consulting	German	–
German employee M	male	Consulting	German	–
German senior manager H	male	Pyro Technology	German	–
German senior manager D	male	Green Technology	German	–
German senior manager G	male	Automobile/ Machinery	German	–
German employee W	male	Glass Processing	German	–
German expert S	male	Research	German	–
German expert T	male	Research	German	–
German expert W	male	European Chamber of Commerce + Pharma	German	✓ Chinese intermediate
Chinese senior manager B	male	Automobile/ Machinery	Chinese	–
Chinese employee A	female	Automobile	Chinese	✓ German intermediate

Nationality & position	Gender	Industry	Interview language	Foreign language competence (Chinese or German)
Chinese employee M	female	Automobile	Chinese/ English	✓ German intermediate
Chinese employee L	male	IT, Automobile	Chinese	–
Chinese employee S	female	IT	Chinese	✓ German intermediate
Chinese senior manager Y	male	Consulting	Chinese	–
Chinese employee Z	male	Consulting	Chinese/ German	✓ German advanced
Chinese employee H	female	Consulting	Chinese	–
Chinese senior manager X	female	Media	Chinese	–
Taiwanese employee C	female	Electronics/R&D	German	✓ German advanced

Selection criteria for the German interviewees were their German nationality, the German origin of the organizations in which they worked and a clear connection of the organization with China in the form of existing collaboration projects, joint ventures or subsidiaries in China. Three of the German interviewees were classified as experts on Sino-German cooperation because they headed research and/or not-for-profit organizations with a focus on China and thus possessed expert knowledge and experience in Sino-German cooperation. Selection criteria for the Chinese interviewees were either their Chinese or Taiwanese nationality and work experience in both the Chinese and the German cultural contexts.

Results

The Chinese and the Germans are not only mutually perceived as holders of different types of competence and knowledge and related different talents and skills, but are also aware of these differences and their synergy potential.

Chinese Relationship Management and German Task Management

In the study, evidence emerged of the German emphasis on task as opposed to the Chinese emphasis on relationships and the emotional means to handle relationships. The Chinese are regarded as very good at managing people-related issues such as relationship development (Guānxi) that require interpersonal skills such as emotional intelligence: "In Germany working ability is more important than emotional ability and in China it's the other way round" (Chinese employee M, 26.09.2015).

This also equips the Chinese with the potential for a high sensitivity to contexts. Taiwanese employee C, 29.03.2015 reported that the Chinese possess a deeper understanding of the complex, dynamic local Chinese markets and their specific local cultures and customer psychology and are therefore better at designing appropriate sales strategies and marketing campaigns which require detailed, culture-specific knowledge as well as a sensitivity to intra-cultural differences, which is difficult for foreigners to develop.

This potential is explained by Chinese senior manager X (29.09.2015), who described the early relationship between the Shanghai office and German headquarters and its development:

> They all listened quite a bit to the German office, that's why their performance in the first ten years faced neither losses nor increases. (…) I thought I should have the last say in everything, because I understand the local circumstances here.

This opinion of the Chinese side, which regards itself as the holder of local market and customer-related knowledge, is in line with the perception of the German interviewees, the majority of whom believed that it is "impossible to understand the Chinese market without an understanding of the local culture" (e.g., German employee M, 30.09.2015) and therefore stress the importance of both sides working together.

As German senior manager J, 30.09.2015 reported, this is especially true of interpersonal relations, for example, "dealing with local government authorities, institutes, customers and landlords", which "is left to the Chinese employees, because in a Chinese context they can express themselves and solve problems in a different manner".

This German self-perception in the sample coincides with how they are perceived by Chinese senior manager Y (30.09.2015), who experienced the Germans as "relatively serious", which was also reflected in their very "factual language", which is different from the "rather blurred" Chinese way of conveying meaning (Chinese senior manager Y, 30.09.2015).

This "blurred" way of expressing meaning relates to the different Chinese working style, which involves a blurred distinction between subject (the people involved/their relationships) and object (the matter/task/a certain problem). This leads to a greater "distinction between insiders and outsiders" (Hall, 1989, p. 113), and also to the Germans not being able to make any progress in Sino-German negotiations without the help of their Chinese counterparts, who hold this tacit knowledge on how things are done in China.

In summary, the Chinese particularistic, context-dependent and relationship-oriented working culture is perceived by both sides as having a positive effect on operating in the Chinese market whereas the German distinction between subject and object, person and matter, could be beneficial in constructive conflicts which can stimulate creativity.

German Risk and Uncertainty Avoidance and Chinese Experimentation with Diversification

The Germans perceive themselves as "always trying to plan every detail in advance and having five alternative plans in case one plan cannot be followed" (German senior manager L, 01.04.2015) and as being better at formally documenting and then "striking things off the list" (German senior manager L, 01.04.2015), a typically monochronic (Hall, 1990; Schroll-Machl, 2003) and uncertainty avoidant (Brodbeck, Frese, & Javidan, 2002; Hofstede, 2001; Sorge, 2018) working style, where one does one thing after the other in order to avoid mistakes and not simultaneously, intuitively and experimentally as in the more polychronic (Hall, 1990) and less uncertainty avoidant (Hofstede, 2001) Chinese culture. The resulting working styles are a rather slower "systematic [German] approach versus [Chinese] speed, flexibility, experimenting, but both together can set free beautiful forces making efforts successful" (German senior manager J, 30.03.2015).

The Chinese thus achieve their goals with comparatively more spontaneous improvisation and flexibility and the Germans with comparatively more careful planning and organizing in advance. Speed in Chinese action is perceived by the German side as "often compromising completeness". One German senior manager explained, "In Germany you would first intensively observe a thing and think it through before you voice your opinion. In China ideas are first shot out and afterwards they will look in how far it can be realized" (German senior manager K, 11.04.2015). To critically question something would not be the first priority of the Chinese (German employee K, 30.09.2015). Consequently, the Chinese would often say "没关系，不会有事" [méi guān xì, bù huì yǒu shì], meaning "No problem, nothing will happen" and the answer of the Germans in this case would often be "But what if something does happen?" (Taiwanese employee C, 29.03.2015), which shows their different capacity to accept risk, a feature related to the difference in the need to avoid uncertainty (Hofstede 2001).

This is also reflected, as, for example, German expert S (31.03.2015) reported, in the Chinese employees' relatively greater "willingness to quickly launch and quickly withdraw products from the market" and their diversification strategy of "develop[ing] and launch[ing] a lot of products simultaneously" in contrast to the Germans' concentration on their core competence, "where a product is prepared longer in order to achieve a higher possibility that it will be a success".

On the Chinese side, there seems to be "no reluctance" (German employee F, 17.04.2015) to implement ideas. "They are very flexible in their way of working, can implement things exceedingly fast, don't stick to certain businesses or opinions, but manage to think speedily into another direction and can adapt themselves very quickly" (German senior manager L, 01.04.2015).

The Chinese also perceive the advantages and disadvantages of both working styles and their potential for complementarity. Implying both the benefit it brings for greater innovation but also the existence of a certain risk, Chinese senior manager X (29.09.2015) explained, "the Chinese mentality is comparatively more courageous, willing to try out new things, try out the possibilities of everything".

Chinese employee M (26.09.2015) pointed out, while "the Germans follow the rules" and have a "working flow", which "keeps the work function[ing]", "it kills innovation, because no accident" is allowed to happen. Moreover, "when the process is too slow, the resulting inspiration might already be old-fashioned and not usable anymore" (Chinese employee L, 03.04.2015).

However, the Chinese sample also acknowledged that,

> sometimes they are rather weak at controlling risks. At this time, Germans can just activate their advantage and balance it. When the Chinese are courageous and integrate their courage into the German input, the success of innovation will be guaranteed.
>
> *(Chinese senior manager X, 29.09.2015)*

German Love of Detail and Chinese Big Picture

While the Germans, according to German senior manager J (30.03.2015), have "a love of details" and are "organized, structured and the like", the Chinese would "suddenly start to sing on the street for unimaginable reasons, drive their cars somehow in this chaos, it's the spontaneous and the not planned".

"The Chinese point of view is rather more holistic" (Chinese employee L, 03.04.2015), implying that their thinking is more intuitive and anticipative and they are able to make sense of and manoeuvre through what appears to Germans to be chaos, because they manage to view everything holistically as a whole, seeing the big picture and how everything connects to everything else: "What they still have is this holistic leadership" (German senior manager H, 02.04.2015).

The Chinese do not get held up by details. This makes them very efficient in managing large scale projects, which is also acknowledged by the German side: "There is no project and no change too big [for the Chinese]" (German employee F, 17.04.2015).

On the other hand, as Nisbett (2003) notes, this focus is generally less suited to scientific research, where small parts of a whole may be observed separately and where details matter. Both sides are aware that the Chinese strength lies in development, such as "innovations mostly revolv[ing] *around* the products" (Chinese senior manager B, 24.09.2015, emphasis added) and marketing and product design development due to their "sense for aesthetics" (German senior manager D, 29.09.2015). The Chinese are also commonly known for their cost innovation and ability to combine existing technologies with something new or to combine existing technologies to create something new. According to German senior manager H (01.04.2015) the Germans "admire the Chinese … ability to create more out of less".

The perceived German strength lies in science and technological innovation with a focus on precision and quality. "If you bring this together and try to leverage the good aspects of both, for example, German technology and knowl-edge and Chinese greatness [thinking in huge dimensions] ... this, I think, brings both sides a lot" (German senior manager J, 30.03.2015).

The Germans' perceptions of the Chinese are in line with the Chinese self-per-ception and it is acknowledged that "this advantage [precise, systematic approach] is exactly the disadvantage of the Chinese" (Taiwanese employee C, 29.03.2015).

German Pursuit of Perfection and Chinese Pragmatic Solution-Orientation

However, in line with the Chinese tradition of holistically viewing things as nei-ther solely bad nor only good, this pursuit of perfection, seen as an advantage of the Germans, is also seen as a weakness by four of the Chinese interviewees. Metaphorically speaking "whereas the Germans use a different hammer for each nail, the Chinese [would] use the same hammer for all nails" (Chinese employee L, 03.04.2015). This reflects the Germans' universalistic belief in a correct way or solution and only one truth. The Chinese belief that there is not a single correct way and that rules will change according to context makes their actions comparatively fast and flexible in the perception of the Germans: "In Germany you have a lot of rules, you plan a lot, but here people just start to run and simply do it" (German senior manager J, 30.09.2015). This pragmatic "can-do-mentality" (German employee F, 17.04.2015) and "willingness to always walk new ways" (German expert S, 31.03.2015) of the Chinese, which recalls Deng Xiaoping's saying "Crossing the river by feeling the stones", is admired by the Germans in the sample.

The potential for mutual learning is identified in the advice of German expert T (09.04.2015): "The Germans could learn to be less perfectionist and the Chinese could learn to become more perfectionist". While reducing complementarity, this mutual learning could lead to synergistic results.

Influencing Factors Facilitating and Inhibiting Synergy Realization

While analyzing the interviews, it was possible to identify factors facilitating and inhibiting the potential synergy realization on the individual and team level.

Individual-Level Influence: Positive Attitude to the Cooperation due to Perceived Similarity

The attitude in the samples towards the Sino-German cooperation was both on the Chinese side (eight out of 10 positive and optimistic, one rather neutral, one rather unsatisfied) and on the German side (15 out of 18 positive and optimistic, three rather neutral) quite positive and there was a clearly perceived mutual influence: "The influence does not only come from the German side; our influence on the Germans is also very clear, and it is a very huge influence" (Chinese senior man-ager X, 29.09.2015).

According to the perception of the Chinese employees, cooperation between the Chinese and the Japanese and between the Chinese and Germans involves fewer obstacles and difficulties than cooperation between the Chinese and Americans or the French. The Chinese particularly like working with Germans. This was exemplified by Chinese senior manager X (29.09.2015), who also works with other European partners: "I think the cooperation with Germans feels comparatively very joyful, because a few very clear advantages of the Germans like their perseverance and precision are very helpful for the innovation as a whole".

German employee F (17.04.2015), for example, stated that he is full of admiration for the Chinese belief in the future and Chinese employee Z (13.04.2015) also pointed out a similarity when he said "I think the Chinese are also hard-working". Even though Germans have the reputation of being more structured in their work and the Chinese enjoy the reputation of being more hard-working, in the perception of German employee M (30.09.2015) they both contribute equally to the company's success. This perception is also held by the German senior managers and is also reflected in the Chinese interviewees' perception: "A similarity ... I think the objectives are the same" (Chinese employee Z, 13.04.2015).

The data shows that the positive attitudes of both sides could be related to a certain degree of cultural similarity, especially in values connected with long-term orientation such as high aspirations and ideals, discipline, hard work, learning, assiduousness, enduring hardships in the pursuit of future rewards, long-term objectives, perseverance and planning for the future (Hofstede, 2001, pp. 354–356).

Chinese Pragmatism and Garmony-Orientation

The realization of cultural synergies also implies a certain degree of change and the acceptance of different ways of doing something. The Chinese side is perceived by a small majority of the Chinese (six out of 10) and German (nine out of 18) interviewees as more willing to learn from and adapt to the German side. "The willingness to adapt is far higher over there [in China] than here" (German senior manager R, 02.04.2015). This can be related to the fact that Chinese pragmatism and harmony orientation have a positive influence on adaptation and learning. Less than half of the Chinese (four out of 10) and German (five out of 18) interviewees perceived the willingness to adapt as equal and only a minority, one Chinese and three German interviewees, perceived no necessity for adaptation at all. "The Germans must learn to learn" (German expert S, 31.03.2015).

Foreign-Country Experience

The results revealed that those individuals able to critically reflect on their own thinking and practices also tended to be more able to perceive and appreciate the particularities of the other side's culture. "This energy you can feel in their companies and this willingness to always walk new ways is not only impressive, but again and again also very inspiring" (German expert S, 31.03.2015).

This high degree of meta-cognition related to culture and the mutual apprecia-tion of cultural characteristics was especially high in individuals that had already had extensive contact with the other culture by having worked in the respective country for some time and speaking the language. Those individuals with only a sporadic contact with the other culture and a lack of language skills tended to take a rather ethnocentric stance, overrating their own culture and practices.

Those individuals who had already engaged more intensively with the other culture were able to identify areas where both cultures and their respective prac-tices could complement each other and even reported how over time they could realize cultural synergies in their teams: "We have known each other for a long time now and are used to working with each other and with the other culture. Therefore, we are able to positively transform it or mutually support and enhance each other" (German senior manager J, 30.09.2015).

Those individuals also perceived themselves to be different from others in their home country and reported that over time they started to integrate the other side's culture into their own thinking and acting:

> I have been in China for 25 years now and I definitely think rather holistically, let's say in different structures than a German who has never been abroad.
> *(German expert W, 30.09.2015)*

> We are different from the Taiwanese that never worked abroad.
> *(Taiwanese employee C, 29.03.2015)*

In line with the constructivist view of culture, Celik and Lubart (2016) explain this phenomenon with the argument that conflictual and incompatible demands of others that challenge individuals' established belief system are the key to integrating complexity and multicultural experiences, as they would exhibit a subjectively felt pressure on them to explain, negotiate and reconsider or adjust these previously held beliefs.

Language in particular seems to play an important role in that it gives the employees better access to the other side. Expatriates refraining from learning the language and the local culture, perhaps overrating their own culture and practices, are disliked and "perceived as arrogant" (Taiwanese employee C, 29.03.2015) by their Chinese counterparts.

However, the Chinese, especially those without foreign-country experience, who prefer to remain in their in-group and tend to be rather indirect and reserved towards Europeans with whom they have not yet established a good relationship, are also often perceived as "arrogant" (German senior manager M, 14.04.2015) by the German expatriate out-group. As a result of their ethnocentric attitude this group, in turn, does not manage to develop a relationship and establish an in-group with the Chinese. The Chinese and German interviewees with foreign-country experience are aware of this problem and seem to be able to overcome these obstacles.

Team-Level Influencing Factor: Trust Development as Key to Synergy Realization

The German interviewees underlined the importance in China of establishing good relationships before starting to work together in a team. A Chinese interviewee supported this insight, reporting "first you get to know each other a little bit privately and then you start to work together" (Chinese employee Z, 13.04.2015). We can attribute this need to a relationship-orientation fostered by the collectivist (Hofstede, 2001; House et al., 2004) and diffuse nature of Chinese country culture (Hampden-Turner & Trompenaars, 1997; Parsons & Shils, 1951), where very good relationships are a prerequisite for working together. In Germany, which is regarded as more task-oriented (Brodbeck et al., 2002; Schroll-Machl, 2003; Stewart et al., 1994) and individualist (Brodbeck et al., 2002; Hofstede, 2001), this is often the other way around and private activities are not necessary for working effectively in a team.

Therefore, not all Germans understand the importance of this relationship for the functioning of a team. The Chinese interviewees found that their German colleagues often do not have spare time to meet colleagues and feel that "they do not really like to go to their homes to do something together" (Chinese employee S, 01.04.2015). This preference can be attributed to the major German culture standard referred to as *differentiation of personality and living spheres* (Schroll-Machl, 2003), as a consequence of which Germans tend to keep the private and professional realms strictly separated. They often fail to notice the crucial role this building of an in-group plays in the openness of their Chinese counterparts in discussions and in releasing creative potential.

Discussion

The results highlight the importance attached to intensive engagement with individuals from other cultures for the development of intercultural awareness and self-reflection, which seems to be a starting point and facilitating factor in a process of cultural change which might eventually lead to synergy through the identification of complementarities and their appreciation.

Due to their positive attitude towards learning and adapting, the Chinese seem to be supported by their particularistic world view (Hampden-Turner & Trompenaars, 1997) that there is not just one right and good way of doing something and are very open to learning from the Germans. As Confucius observes, "The superior man, in the world, does not set his mind either for anything, or against anything; what is right he will follow" (Legge, 2013, p. 168).

Hampden-Turner and Trompenaars (1997) also relate the tiger economies' tendency to quickly adjust new Western initiatives and technologies to their circular learning, which enables them to constantly "borrow Western skills and add their own to create an unbeatable infinite composite" (pp. 149–150). As this attitude towards learning and constant development is said to be common in all long-term-oriented Asian economies, such as China, Hong Kong, Taiwan, Singapore, Japan and South Korea, but not in other short-term-oriented Asian cultures, such as Thailand, the Philippines and Malaysia, which do not show these high development rates (Hofstede et al., 2010), this attitude seems to be related to the influence of cultures with different values and preferences and is not simply an expression of opportunism.

As Cameron (2017) discovered, a focus on the positive aspects instead of the negative aspects of cultural differences leads to higher performance. Our research results show that this positive attitude is greater in individuals with a high degree of self-reflection. Self-reflection also seems to trigger a positive view of interculturality. People tend to see the positive aspects of differences by acknowledging that their own ways of thinking and acting have their flaws and are not a perfect fit in any given context.

This meta-cognitive process of self-reflection might be further promoted by the use of the other side's language, as those interviewees with foreign language competence reported. Such respondents were reported by others to have integrated over time some of the other side's cultural elements into their thinking and acting. Language is assumed to define experience and therefore results in different world views and different thinking (Hall, 1989). Many particularities of Chinese thinking, such as their context-dependence, dialectic thinking and distinction between in- and out-groups, are also reflected in the composition of their language, its words and proverbs (e.g., Chen, 2002; Cheng, Lo, & Chio, 2010).

Even though both sides were hard-working, optimistic about their cooperation and contributed their utmost to achieving their shared objectives, differences also existed in the way they are achieved and what kind of skills and types of knowledge are applied. The respondents in this sample revealed the complementary strengths of both sides, which in their extreme forms could turn into weaknesses. Spontaneity, improvisation and flexibility might lead to errors in processes; for example, such attributes could lead to quality-assurance issues in production due to a lack of planning, data visualization, product simulation and prevention of all possible problems in advance.

Too much planning and bureaucracy, on the other hand, inhibit rapid adaptation to unforeseen obstacles and fast-changing market realities. Apart from ensuring high quality it is also important to make sure that the products meet local customer demands and are continually adapted to customers' changing needs and tastes.

Even though the Germans' systematic, structured, formalized approach might be beneficial to managing quality and risks, if too many resources are bound up in routine, detailed documentation in order to be able to justify one's actions and possible errors (cf. Power, 2007), developments and opportunities outside the organization might not be detected, as there is too much focus on the companies' internal procedures. An excess of paperwork also slows down communication.

The Germans' competence in research and technological innovation, on the one hand, paired, on the other, with Chinese competence in developing existing technology according to local market needs and their creativity in non-technological innovations is a very strong combination that can enhance each other's value. German explicit knowledge can be paired with Chinese implicit knowledge, intuition and wisdom, thereby fostering systems thinking (i.e., the integration of reason and intuition) in Sino-German collaboration. To take the bird's eye view, the Chinese can provide imagination and vision, while the Germans can transform and integrate these inputs into detailed analysis and new technologies.

The Germans' focus on tasks and individual achievement need not hinder the development of the whole team and company. Individual achievements, like individually generated information and creative insights, can also be shared and used to contribute to the collective effort, which could be described as what Hampden-Turner & Trompenaars (1997) refer to as "individual groupism" (p. 117). In this sense, creativity and innovation result from social and cultural relationships between people thinking individually (Glăveanu, 2016).

Both sides' ability to reflect on these advantages and disadvantages holds huge potential for mutual learning and the proactive combination and balancing of these seemingly contradictory differences. Negative perceptions only resulted from communication problems related to a lack of language skills and intercultural competence. Despite the Chinese side's openness and eagerness to learn together and develop, Chinese relationship-orientation and in- and out-groupism require the ice to be broken before they actively start to exchange ideas and openly engage in constructive conflict in teams.

Managerial Implications

The results imply that it is essential for senior managers and employees to overcome negative perceptions inhibiting effective and appropriate communication by developing employees' intercultural competence. An interest in the other side's culture and language can serve as an ice-breaker and language courses as well as cultural information and intercultural training should therefore be provided by the leaders of Sino-German teams and organizations. The importance of the meta-cognitive process of self-reflection revealed in the study can be taken account of by providing intercultural coaching.

The findings also have implications for human resource management. Language skills and foreign country experience are very important aspects to be considered in the employee selection process, as individuals with this experience and language competence proved to be more able to reflect and perceive as well as appreciate differences and were also more able to overcome obstacles posed by these differences and establish good relationships with the other side.

The younger Chinese generation has become more innovative, dares to challenge authority and wants to be challenged and appreciates the freedom to be creative and take on more responsibility. It is the strength of a good leader of Sino-German teams to allow "chaos corners", in which the employees are allowed to be creative and conduct their own projects to generate new products or services.

In view of the fact that a positive attitude fosters high performance in bi-national cooperation, German companies and employees collaborating with Chinese companies and employees should try to overcome the stereotype of the Chinese stealing their knowledge and instead join in the endless process of mutual improvement in order to achieve more together, which is what is at the heart of cultural synergy.

To really make a Sino-German cooperation successful and innovative, developing a mutual in-group through good personal relationships and thereby creating trust is key. It is essential to attach great importance to initial team-building activities before starting to work in a Sino-German context and also organize regular out-of-work and off-site activities. Only then can a leader leverage the maximum potential out of Sino-German cultural differences.

Limitations and Implications for Future Research

The relatively small size and heterogeneous sectoral and corporate composition of the sample need to be borne in mind when reviewing the results. As most of the senior managers and employees interviewed did not work for the same company, there may be differences in their perception of what is relevant in their particular working context.

However, what is perhaps even more surprising is how the perceptions of the individuals of this diversified sample coincided and how many complementary aspects for mutual learning were identified. Future research should therefore conduct case studies examining the process of cultural synergy creation within one company, department or team.

Furthermore, future research could also consider differences within Chinese culture. The Chinese interviewees in this study originally came from different regions of mainland China and one even came from insular China, namely Taiwan, which all have their own particular cultural features. Three of the Chinese employees were also relatively young - compared to the other four. Different socialization due to regional differences and time of education could have led to different cultural orientations, especially in view of the rapid changes in the Chinese education system and the different speed of development in different regions. These aspects of the expression of intra-cultural differences in Chinese thinking and organizational behaviour could also be a focus of future research.

As only six of the 28 interviewees were female and only one of these six female interviewees was German, future research needs to integrate more female views to prevent a male bias in perceptions.

Furthermore, the organizational cultures in big state-owned companies differ from those in small- and medium-sized, privately owned Chinese companies and therefore in the socialization of employees who have had prior work experience in either of these types of company. This aspect could be further examined in comparative cases of Sino-German joint ventures and mergers and acquisitions of privately owned and state-owned enterprises.

Conclusion

This study revealed the bright side of Sino-German collaboration and the potential thereof that waits to be leveraged. A high degree of self-reflection, congruence of perceptions and mutual appreciation by the sample of perceived complementarities in Sino-German cooperation indicated a high potential for cultural synergy.

While the Germans are perceived to be more analytic, systematic, structured, focused on their work and tasks and to pay greater attention to detail in order to prevent bad outcomes, which is considered to be beneficial for quality and risk management as well as technological innovation, the Chinese are perceived to be more relationship-oriented, pragmatic, flexible and open to changes and experimentation, which is considered to be beneficial in human relations management as well as the development of non-technological innovations and creativity in design, marketing, sourcing and new business models. It was felt that the strengths of the respective other side complement and balance each other and therefore had potential for joint innovation.

Consequently, Sino-German teams and organizations should be able to accommodate and combine both sides' cultures, whilst acknowledging and respecting their unique characteristics and competencies, and form a new, harmonious cultural whole, which is more than the sum of its parts.

Language competence and foreign country experience were identified as facilitating this potential synergy-creation as they increase the individual's ability to reflect on, appreciate and integrate cultural differences. A certain degree of perceived cultural similarity in terms of values such as perseverance and the pursuit of long-term objectives seems to serve as common ground between both sides which fosters a positive attitude towards cooperation.

However, a lack of understanding of the importance of and the necessity for trust development through personal relationships and therefore the building of an in-group prior to working together seems to hinder the identified potential positive effects of cultural differences in Sino-German collaboration. This is because the interaction between the two sides is inhibited and consequently leads to negative perceptions of the respective other side as being arrogant or reserved. Trust development is thus the key to synergistic Sino-German cooperation.

References

Adler, N. J. (2008). *International dimensions of organizational.* Mason, OH: Thomson SouthWestern.

Barmeyer, C. (2018). *Konstruktives Interkulturelles Management* [Constructive intercultural management]. Göttingen: Vandenhoeck & Ruprecht.

Barmeyer, C. & Davoine, E. (2014). Interkulturelle Synergie als "ausgehandelte" Interkulturalität: Der deutsch-französische Fernsehsender ARTE [Intercultural synergy as 'negotiated interculturality']. In A. Moosmüller & J. Möller-Kiero (Eds.), *Interkulturalität und kulturelle Diversität* [Interculturality and cultural diversity] (pp. 155–181). Münster: Waxmann.

Barmeyer, C. & Davoine, E. (2015). Konstruktive Interkulturalität. Impulse für die Zusammenarbeit in internationalen Organisationen am Fallbeispiel Alleo [Constructive interculturality. Impulses for co-operation in international organisations from the example of Alleo]. *ZfO – Zeitschrift für Führung und Organisation*, 6(84), 430–437.

Barmeyer, C. & Davoine, E. (2016). Konstruktives interkulturelles Management – Von der Aushandlung zur Synergie [Constructive intercultural management – from negotiation to synergy]. *Interculture Journal*, 15(26), 97–115.

Barmeyer, C. & Davoine, E. (2019). Facilitating intercultural negotiated practices in joint ventures: The case of a French–German railway organization. *International Business Review*, 28(1), 1–11. https://doi.org/10.1016/j.ibusrev.2018.06.001.

Barmeyer, C. & Franklin, P. (Eds.). (2016). *Intercultural management. Case studies in otherness and synergy*. London: Palgrave Macmillan.

Brodbeck, F. C., Frese, M., & Javidan, M. (2002). Leadership made in Germany: Low on compassion, high on performance. *Academy of Management Executive*, 16(1), 16–30. https://doi.org/10.5465/ame.2002.6640111.

Cameron, K. (2017). Cross-cultural research and positive organizational scholarship. *Cross Cultural & Strategic Management*, 24(1), 13–32. https://doi.org/10.1108/CCSM-02-2016-0021.

Celik, P. & Lubart, T. (2016). When East meets West. In V. P. Glăveanu (Ed.), *The Palgrave handbook of creativity and culture research* (pp. 37–55). London: Palgrave Macmillan. https://doi.org/10.1057/978-1-137-46344-9_3.

Chen, C.-C. & Lee, Y.-T. (Eds.). (2008). *Leadership and management in China: Philosophies, theories and practices*. Cambridge: Cambridge University Press.

Chen, C.-C. & Lee, Y.-T. (2008). The diversity and dynamism of Chinese philosophies on leadership. In C.-C. Chen & Y.-T. Lee (Eds.), *Leadership and management in China. Philosophies, theories and practices* (pp. 1–27). Cambridge: Cambridge University Press.

Chen, M. J. (2002). Transcending paradox: The Chinese "middle way" perspective. *Asia Pacific Journal of Management*, 19(2–3), 179–199. https://doi.org/10.1023/a:1016235517735.

Chen, N., Chao, M. C. H., Xie, H., & Tjosvold, D. (2018). Transforming cross-cultural conflict into collaboration: The integration of Western and Eastern values. *Cross Cultural & Strategic Management*, 25(1), 70–95. https://doi.org/10.1108/CCSM-10-2016-0187.

Cheng, C., Lo, B. C. Y., & Chio, J. H. M. (2010). The Tao (way) of Chinese coping. In M. H. Bond (Ed.), *The Oxford handbook of Chinese psychology* (pp. 399–419). New York, NY: Oxford University Press.

Chia, R. & Holt, R. (2007). Wisdom as learned ignorance. Integrating East–West perspectives. In E. H. Kessler & J. R. Bailey (Eds.), *Handbook of organizational and managerial wisdom* (pp. 505–526). Thousand Oaks, CA: SAGE Publications.

Du, R., Ai, S., & Brugha, C. M. (2011). Integrating Taoist Yin-Yang thinking with Western nomology: A moderating model of trust in conflict management. *Chinese Management Studies*, 5(1), 55–67. https://doi.org/10.1108/17506141111118453.

Fang, T. (2012). Yin Yang: A new perspective on culture. *Management and Organization Review*, 8(1), 25–50. https://doi.org/10.1111/j.1740-8784.2011.00221.x.

Gallo, F. T. (2011). *Business leadership in China: How to blend best Western practices with Chinese wisdom*. Singapore: John Wiley & Sons (Asia).

Glăveanu, V. P. (Ed.). (2016). *The Palgrave handbook of creativity and culture research*. Palgrave Macmillan. https://doi.org/10.1057/978-1-137-46344-9.

Hall, E. T. (1989). *Beyond culture*. New York, NY: Anchor Books.

Hall, E. T. (1990). *The hidden dimension*. New York, NY: Anchor Books.

Hampden-Turner, C., & Trompenaars, F. (1997). *Mastering the infinite game: How East Asian values are transforming business practices*. Oxford: Capstone Publishing.

Hofstede, G. (2001). *Culture's consequences: Comparing values, behaviors, institutions, and organizations across nations* (2nd ed.). Thousand Oaks, CA: SAGE Publications.

Hofstede, G., Hofstede, G. J., & Minkov, M. (2010). *Cultures and organizations: Software of the mind* (3rd ed.). New York, NY: McGraw-Hill.

House, R. J., Hanges, P. J., Javidan, M., Dorfman, P. W., & Gupta, V. (Eds.). (2004). *Culture, leadership, and organizations: The GLOBE study of 62 societies*. Thousand Oaks, CA: SAGE Publications.

Huang, X. & Bond, M. H. (Eds.). (2012). *Handbook of Chinese organizational behavior: Integrating research, theory and practice*. Cheltenham, UK: Edward Elgar. https://doi.org/10.4337/9780857933409.

Ji, L.-J., Lee, A., & Guo, T. (2010). The thinking styles of Chinese people. In M. H. Bond (Ed.), *The Oxford handbook of Chinese psychology* (pp. 155–167). Oxford: Oxford University Press. https://doi.org/10.1093/oxfordhb/9780199541850.013.0012.

Jin, B., Yu, H., & Kang, J. H. (2013). Challenges in Western-Chinese business relationships: The Chinese perspective. *Marketing Intelligence and Planning*, 31(2), 179–192. https://doi.org/10.1108/02634501311312062.

Legge, J. (2013). *Confucian analects, the great learning & the doctrine of the mean*. Mineola, NY: Dover Publications.

Leung, K. (2012). Theorizing about Chinese organizational behavior: The role of cultural and social forces. In X. Huang & M. H. Bond (Eds.), *Handbook of Chinese organizational behavior: Integrating research, theory and practice* (pp. 13–28). Cheltenham: Edward Elgar Publishing. https://doi.org/10.4337/9780857933409.00008.

Li, P. P. (2014). Toward the geocentric framework of intuition: The Yin-Yang balancing between the Eastern and Western perspectives on intuition. In M. Sinclair (Ed.), *Handbook of research methods on intuition* (pp. 28–41). Cheltenham: Edward Elgar Publishing.

Li, P. P. (2016). Global implications of the indigenous epistemological system from the East: How to apply Yin-Yang balancing to paradox management. *Cross Cultural & Strategic Management*, 23(1), 42–77. https://doi.org/10.1108/CCSM-10-2015-0137.

Lian, X. [连晓雾] (2014, August 27). 文化协同效应 [Cultural synergy effect]. MBAlib. http://wiki.mbalib.com/wiki/文化协同效应#_note-0.

Lin, L., Li, P. P., & Roelfsema, H. (2018). The traditional Chinese philosophies in intercultural leadership: The case of Chinese expatriate managers in the Dutch context. *Cross Cultural & Strategic Management Strategic Management*, 25(2), 299–336. https://doi.org/10.1108/CCSM-01-2017-0001.

Liu, Y. & Almor, T. (2016). How culture influences the way entrepreneurs deal with uncertainty in inter-organizational relationships: The case of returnee versus local entrepreneurs in China. *International Business Review*, 25(1), 4–14. https://doi.org/10.1016/j.ibusrev.2014.11.002.

Lynton, N. & Thøgersen, K. H. (2006). How China transforms an executive's mind. *Organizational Dynamics*, 35(2), 170–181. https://doi.org/10.1016/j.orgdyn.2006.03.003.

Ng, I., Lee, Y., & Cardona, P. (2012). Building teams in Chinese organizations. In X. Huang & M. H. Bond (Eds.), *Handbook of Chinese organizational behavior: Integrating theory, research and practice* (pp. 236–257). Cheltenham: Edgar Elgar. https://doi.org/10.4337/9780857933409.00020.

Nisbett, R. (2003). *The geography of thought. How Asians and Westerners think differently... and why*. London: Nicholas Brealey Publishing.

Parsons, T. & Shils, E. A. (Eds.). (1951). *Toward a general theory of action*. Cambridge: Harvard University Press. https://doi.org/10.4159/harvard.9780674863507.

Pauluzzo, R., Guarda, M., De Pretto, L., & Fang, T. (2018). Managing paradoxes, dilemmas, and change: A case study to apply the Yin Yang wisdom in Western organizational settings. *Cross Cultural and Strategic Management*, 25(2), 257–275. https://doi.org/10.1108/CCSM-08-2017-0094.

Power, M. (2007). *Organized uncertainty. Designing a world of risk management*. Oxford: Oxford University Press.

Primecz, H., Romani, L., & Sackmann, S. (Eds.). (2011). *Cross-cultural management in practice: Culture and negotiated meanings*. Cheltenham: Edward Elgar Publishing.

Schroll-Machl, S. (2003). *Doing business with Germans: Their perception, our perception*. Göttingen: Vandenhoeck & Ruprecht.

Sorge, A. (2018). Management in Germany, the dynamo of Europe. In R. A. Crane (Ed.), *The influence of business cultures in Europe* (pp. 69–113). London: Palgrave Macmillan UK. https://doi.org/10.1057/978-1-137-50929-1_3.

Stahl, G. K., Miska, C., Lee, H. J., & De Luque, M. S. (2017). The upside of cultural differences: Towards a more balanced treatment of culture in cross-cultural management research. *Cross Cultural and Strategic Management*, 24(1), 2–12. https://doi.org/10.1108/CCSM-11-2016-0191.

Stahl, G. K. & Tung, R. L. (2015). Towards a more balanced treatment of culture in international business studies: The need for positive cross-cultural scholarship. *Journal of International Business Studies*, 46, 391–414. https://doi.org/10.1057/jibs.2014.68.

Stahl, G. K., Tung, R. L., Kostova, T., & Zellmer-Bruhn, M. (2016). Widening the lens: Rethinking distance, diversity, and foreignness in international business research through positive organizational scholarship. *Journal of International Business Studies*, 47, 621–630. https://doi.org/10.1057/jibs.2016.28.

Stewart, R., Barsoux, J.-L., Kieser, A., Ganter, H.-D., & Walgenbach, P. (1994). *Managing in Britain and Germany*. London: St. Martin's Press.

Verghese, T. [湯姆・韋爾蓋塞] (2016). 探索文化认知 [An exploration into cultural cognition]. Hong Kong: Red Publish.

Weick, K. E. & Putnam, T. (2006). Organizing for mindfulness: Eastern wisdom and Western knowledge. *Journal of Management Inquiry*, 15(3), 275–287. https://doi.org/10.1177/1056492606291202.

Welfens, P. J. J. (2017). Chinas Direktinvestitionen in Deutschland und Europa [China's direct investment in Germany and Europe]. *Hans Böckler Stiftung*, 1–36. https://www.boeckler.de/pdf/p_mbf_report_2017_36_ci_welfens.pdf.

Wolf, E. R. (1982). *Europe and the people without history*. Oakland, CA: University of California Press.

Wübbeke, J., Meissner, M., Zenglein, M. J., Ives, J., & Conrad, B. (2016). MADE IN CHINA 2025. The making of a high-tech superpower and consequences for industrial countries. *MERICS Papers on China*, 1 (2). https://merics.org/sites/default/files/2020-04/Made%20in%20China%202025.pdf.

Xia, X. & Liu, W.-H. (2021). China's investments in Germany and the role of COVID-19 pandemic. *Intereconomics*, 56(2), 113–119. https://doi.org/10.1007/s10272-021-0962-0.

Zhang, Z. (2004). Cross-cultural challenges when doing business in China. *Singapore Management Review*, 38(3), 61–73.

19

INTERCULTURAL CHALLENGES IN MULTINATIONAL CORPORATIONS

Alois Moosmueller

Multinational corporations (MNCs) are considered the main driving force of globalization. The economic power of these hierarchically and centralistically structured organizations exceeds that of many nations. Having subsidiaries in various countries they can circumvent the limitations and hindrances generated by local politics, laws and fiscal demands and make use of location-specific advantages such as subsidies, low taxation, qualified and cheap personnel, etc. Indeed MNCs act opportunistically, which they cleverly conceal using elaborate rhetoric propagating corporate social and environmental responsibility (Hitt and Cheng, 2004). However, critical and concerned voices have grown much stronger recently, not only those of environmentalists and anti-globalization activists, but also of mainstream economists. They question whether the hierarchical and centralist MNCs are still able to sustain such a favourable position in a global economy in which knowledge has become the most valuable asset. IBM's former CEO Samuel Palmisano (2006) pointed out that the traditional setup and ethnocentric mindset of MNCs make it hard to really benefit from the potential and opportunities that an integrated global market offers. In view of the fact that power is still concentrated in company headquarters, which renders the globally distributed subsidiaries submissively dependent, MNCs are unable to exploit the creative and innovative potential of the subsidiaries. The employees in the subsidiaries still do not have the same career opportunities as their peers at the headquarters and therefore do not receive enough incentives to make use of their talents. Companies' policies and strategies still require a centralist hierarchical structure and an ethnocentric mindset, i.e. the belief that everything important has to be done and decided by the headquarters and that at the end only the headquarters' perspectives count. This mindset, according to Palmisano, hinders the headquarters from learning from the subsidiaries and exploiting global knowledge resources. Instead it keeps alive the counterproductive monodirectional information flow. Even worse, since MNCs

DOI: 10.4324/9781003252955-22

opportunistically exploit the differences in legal conditions and levels of income in the different countries in which the subsidiaries are located, they not only create serious social and economic problems but also frustration among their employees worldwide, who, as a consequence, are unwilling to give their best and hold back their knowledge and creativity.

Palmisano therefore calls for a "structural appreciation of cultural diversity" which is much more than just rhetorically valuing cultural diversity, as currently practised by MNCs. He maintains that MNCs need to be radically remodelled in order to become "globally integrated enterprises" and to be really successful on the global market. Only in a globally integrated enterprise would cultural diversity be fully recognized and dealt with at eye level and only then would there be a realistic chance of employees being able to develop the skills and competencies needed to cope with intercultural challenges and to successfully manage cultural diversity. In order to profit from cultural diversity, MNCs would have to deal with cultural diversity realistically and not just on a superficial level as is often now the case, as many MNCs seem to view cultural diversity as a cornucopia filled with all sorts of potential advantages. But they overlook the fact that cultural diversity cannot be diverted from intercultural problems and those problems have to be resolved if one wants to exploit the advantages. Indeed, in order to be recognized as competent and successful players on the global market, MNCs try hard to create an image of being open-minded culturally heterogeneous cosmopolitan organizations. But behind the shiny facades the reality is somewhat different: intercultural challenges are dealt with less than appropriately.

In this chapter, I shall focus on some of these shortcomings. After some theoretical reasoning I shall discuss examples that give a glimpse of real everyday life in cultural diverse MNCs. My approach is ethnographic in the sense that I describe and interpret intercultural situations "from the native's point of view" to use Malinowski's phrase, i.e. from the intercultural actor's point of view (Cefkin, 2009). The intercultural situations are taken from three ethnographic research projects I conducted in MNCs with their employees.

Culture and Economy

In modern economic theory, culture has never been considered as an important factor in explaining man's actions. Understandably, in a calculable world of rational action the fuzzy concept of "culture" has not been one that economists have found particularly attractive. Even during the early talk about globalization, there was a tendency to play down the role of culture: globalization was considered by many to be a vehicle to fulfil the dreams of modern economic theory, notably, the creation of one unified global market in which cultural differences cease to exist (Levitt, 1983). This changed rather abruptly in the 1970s and 80s, when Japanese products conquered global markets. Culture began to be recognized as a major influence on business behaviour. In the wake of Japanese companies' success, Japanese management concepts became very popular among business leaders worldwide. Western corporations tried hard to adopt Japanese business methods, in particular, creating a strong corporate culture, resolving conflicts, developing collective responsibility and establishing a strong feeling of belonging to the company. Nurturing a strong sense of togetherness and a feeling of belonging to a big family was quite challenging since it meant that employees had to learn to lower their self-interests in favour of collective goals and needs. In management it was widely believed that only those companies that were able to live up to this homogeneous work philosophy would be successful. Irrespective of where they were in the world employees had to adapt their behaviour, feelings and attitudes. Inspite of the importance that was increasingly attached to the cultural concept, employees were still seen as basically resembling the model of a *homo economicus*, i.e. acting rationally and being able to adapt to situational and contextual requirements. If the situation and business environment happened to demand more collective mindedness, employees were expected to behave accordingly. Culture was not conceptualized as something deeply rooted in personality but as an aspect of the business environment that could be dealt with by simply adapting individual behaviour. Some American management theorists even went a step further. They claimed that many aspects of "Japanese management" were actually originally American values and advised American MNCs to rediscover these "traditional American values" which could be understood as being more Japanese than the Japanese (Thurow, 1992; Hassard, McCann, & Morris, 2009).

When Japan's economic miracle abruptly ended in 1992 as the asset price bubble burst, the glory of Japanese management ideas was over and American management ideas regained popularity. So MNCs were quick to change course and follow a different line of management wisdom. Corporate familialism and homogeneity—which were now viewed as "typical Japanese" values—were no longer considered to be the road to success, quite the opposite: diversity, especially cultural diversity, was now seen as being "typically American". And indeed, MNCs headquartered in America took advantage of the idea that cultural diversity had always been constitutive to the nation (Thurow, 1992). Now that America had won the competition for economic world leadership, cultural diversity, which was praised as the nation's founding idea, was seen as an all-American value, therefore, American MNCs and MNCs with American management style were considered to have a competitive edge in the global battle for economic supremacy.

Just as Japan had done 20 years earlier, America now defined the rules that the global players had to follow. And instead of homogeneity heterogeneity was favoured. The idea that cultural diversity is an important asset, an invaluable resource, a prerequisite for success in the global economy spread from America to the world and soon became a central concept in management teaching. A demonstration of what can happen when these rules are not adhered to is when in 2010 Toyota had to recall eight million vehicles. It was widely claimed that the crisis had been handled very poorly due to a lack of internal diversity, as critics saw it. On 11 Feb, 2020, it was reported in *The Economist* that "If Toyota's board had included, say, a female German boss, a former American senator and a high-flying

Hong Kong lawyer, its response to the crisis might have been different." It has become very clear that the success of MNCs on the global market depends on cultural diversity and how it is managed. This, in turn, depends on how culture is conceptualized.

Cultural Diversity and Interculturality

As human beings we live in socially constructed and culturally framed environments. Our brain architecture, as recent findings in neuroscience indicate, is shaped by the environment we grew up in. Culture seems to have a deep impact on our personality, the way each of us perceives the world, how we feel, act, think, how we assume others feel, act and think. The fact is that we are culturally shaped, thus inescapably limited in the way we perceive, understand and behave (Vogeley & Roepstorff, 2009; Wexler, 2006). Irrespective of this central argument, we believe in our limitless opportunities, our ability to comprehend everything, etc. This hubris makes life in this global multicultural world complicated, because too many people don't realize how narrow their outlook is and see themselves as open-minded cosmopolitans.

The tendency to ignore culturally imposed limitations is widespread in multi-national corporations. One reason for this problem may well be due to the fact that the term "culture" does not denote a real empirical thing, but a construct, a heuristic instrument to describe and analyse the hidden dimensions of everyday behaviour, processes and structures. The construct culture helps us to understand that people are influenced by some hidden rules, i.e. routines, customs, habits, traditions, values, the "normal order" of things, etc., which they themselves have inadvertently created. Clifford Geertz (1973) maintains in his much-quoted definition of culture: "Man is an animal suspended in webs of significance he himself has spun. I take culture to be those webs" (p. 5). First, this means that it is easy to discern the culture of others, but as one is suspended in it, it is very hard to discern one's own culture. And secondly, that it is necessary to interpret culture, which is only possible when situational and contextual conditions are taken into consideration. Generalizations, if they can be construed at all, are speculative and must be handled with care.

I will focus on the concrete situational context-bound aspects of culture and give examples of everyday behaviour in MNCs. Examining these concrete examples, I will show that on the level of individual actors, cultural diversity not only brings about many intercultural challenges but that MNCs basically leave it to the individual actors to manage those challenges. And quite often it is even worse, since many MNCs do not acknowledge that there are intercultural problems. Instead they just praise the advantages of cultural diversity and in this way increase the pressure on the individual actors to successfully deal with intercultural problems and with the stress and irritations that accompany them. This somewhat two-faced approach to cultural diversity is one of the biggest problems facing MNCs.

Cultural diversity has two sides. One comprises potential benefits such as increased creativity, better adaptability to global markets, improved productivity and profitability, creation of a bigger pool of talent, etc. The other side comprises the potential drawbacks, because different cultural standards, habits, ways of doing things are being upheld, it makes it difficult to coordinate and control technical processes and routines, to find ways to exchange information and generate knowledge, to adequately manage the culturally diverse personnel and exert adequate leadership, etc. I will call this side "interculturality". It increases transaction costs, complicates communication and slows down processes. As research in intercultural communication shows in extenso, interculturality plays a crucial role, especially on the micro-level of human interaction, where it causes misunderstandings, discord and the deterioration of relations (Gudykunst and Kim, 1997; Matsumoto, 2010). How to cope with interculturality and the irritations and dissonances it causes is left to the individual actors. These irritations and dissonances compel the individual actor to find an immediate solution, to resolve the source of irritation and dissonance (Butcher, 2011). The prevalent way of accomplishing this is to explain the reasons for the irritations and dissonant feelings, thus to use hands-on explanations, such as common stereotypes and prejudices about other cultures. As individual actors try to resolve their problems and regain their psychological balance, they actually generate additional intercultural problems. Instead of decreasing, intercultural problems increase with the very endeavour of trying to diminish them.

Why is it that MNCs tend to only see the positive side of cultural diversity and ignore the negative side? One reason lies in the historical development of the discourse of cultural diversity. In MNCs, the discourse began in the early1990s when corporations where confronted with the challenges of a growing external and internal diversity in the wake of globalization and multiculturalization. However, it was actually initiated by the emancipatory movements of gender equality, human rights and, above all, civil rights. In the 1950s and 60s, the civil rights movement achieved major breakthroughs in the equal rights legislation for African Americans and confronted the long-standing cultural, political and economic consequences of past racial repression (Prasad, Pringle, & Konrad, 2006; Schwabenland, 2012). This tradition is still very important, although at first glance the discourse about cultural diversity in MNCs seems to be seen only from a utilitarian perspective. But it is impossible to rid cultural diversity of its emancipatory implications. The conflation of utilitarian and emancipatory motives is probably the very reason why cultural diversity is seen in such a positive light and why the problems that are related to it are ignored. The problems that the emancipatory movements seemed to solve were thought to be due to power imbalance and the denial of equal rights to minorities. The same was considered to apply to cultural minorities in societies, i.e. giving them the opportunity to live life according to their culture and treating them as fully accepted members of civil society would solve many of the problems experienced in society hitherto. As a consequence, cultural diversity was viewed in MNCs in a similar fashion: acknowledged and respected cultural otherness would turn into a cornucopia of knowledge, skills, creativity, efficiency and ultimately success.

The declaration of cultural diversity as a prerequisite for success in the global market has since become standard rhetoric, first in the USA., then in Europe in the new millennium. The preamble of the European Diversity Charter reads as follows:

> By committing to encourage diversity, a company needs to clearly identify its stakes in promoting diversity and choose the key topics it will address that apply to its context. In an effort to assert and facilitate the incorporation of the diversity policy into the company's general strategy, the commitment will be made at the highest level by the company's chief officer. This commitment shall also be visible and known to all who come in contact with the company.
>
> *(Diversity Charter, 2014)*

This is aptly demonstrated by the way companies present themselves on the World Wide Web. For instance on the homepage of the Hongkong and Shanghai Banking Corporation (HSBC), one of the world's biggest banks, one can read: "We believe that diversity brings only benefits for our customers, our business and our people. The more different perspectives we have, the better equipped we'll be to meet the demands of our hugely diverse global customer base" (HSBC, 2022). On the homepage of the German chemical firm Bayer, one can read:

> Fostering equal opportunities in a workforce characterized by diversity means acknowledging the know-how, experience and potential of individual employees. This approach is fixed in our Shared Values and Leadership Principles: respecting and valuing the national and cultural diversity of the people in our company is the basis for our daily work.
>
> *(Bayer, 2022)*

Similarly on the Homepage of the engineering firm Siemens:

> Our diversity is an invaluable source of talents and fosters creativity. The diverse mix of skills, experience and points of view creates a wealth of ideas forming the basis of our innovative strength. This is a competitive advantage for Siemens that we want to convert into value added for our customers and employees alike. That is why we are pursuing a holistic approach to promoting diversity at our Company.
>
> *(Siemens, 2022)*

This manner of promoting diversity in general and cultural diversity in particular made it difficult for MNCs to realize that it is of utmost importance to deal with the problems that accompany cultural diversity. Although big companies take managing diversity seriously—it usually concerns various kinds of diversity, i.e. gender, age, etc., in addition to cultural diversity (Konrad et al., 2006)—there continuous to be a tendency to ignore interculturality. Cultural diversity must indeed be acknowledged as an ambiguous phenomenon with positive as well as negative aspects. Managing diversity must come to terms with the potential and the challenges of cultural diversity; otherwise, the potential of cultural diversity cannot be exploited (Vallaster, 2005). Many MNCs still think it is sufficient to simply declare that diversity is the cornerstone of the company's policy and to communicate this policy internally and, above all, externally. Whether or not it is true, companies strive to show how they excel in managing cultural diversity. The rhetoric that cultural diversity is an invaluable resource has come to dominate the discourse about cultural diversity in MNCs and has made it hard to deal with intercultural problems appropriately. But this reluctance to face the challenge of interculturality might also be due to structural problems within MNCs.

Research has developed various concepts regarding the effective functioning of an employee in the multicultural global business environment. This ideal employee would have a "global mindset" (Jeannet, 2000), would be "diversity loving" and would be able to think and act in a relativist manner (Bennett 1998), would be a "rooted cosmopolitan" and feel at home in local as well as in global contexts (Appiah, 2006), would possess a "protean personality" and would therefore be able to flexibly change his/her mind and adapt to any social and cultural environment (Lifton, 1993), would feel comfortable being a "global nomad" (Pollock 1999) and would be capable of becoming an "intercultural competent person" (Deardorff, 2009). Research also stresses that it takes a great deal of effort to develop this type of personality and that at present far too few people possess these characteristics. The quintessence is that it takes time and dedication for MNCs to develop such staff. Unfortunately, MNCs do not have enough of either. This has grave consequences because MNCs expect their employees to perform effectively and to be able to make the best use of cultural diversity. Obviously employees try to comply, and this puts them in a difficult position. Many employees pretend to be as global-minded, cosmopolitan, diversity loving, interculturally competent, etc., as is expected of them and are reluctant to admit otherwise. MNCs should encourage their employees to admit when they are struggling with the challenges of cultural diversity and to openly discuss such issues. This would create an opportunity for everyone to learn to be open and to be realistic about their capabilities. As most humans have a natural tendency to avoid problems and conflict in the first place, when they do experience problems and conflict, they do not like to talk about it openly and honestly. Companies therefore need to create an atmosphere that allows everyone to be honest and open about their struggles with intercultural issues, which is a prerequisite for intercultural learning. Failing to do so, according to Palmisano (2006), makes it almost impossible for an MNC to change and become a "globally integrated enterprise".

Intercultural problems will remain an ongoing issue for some time to come. MNCs must therefore develop "intercultural knowledge", i.e. viable ways to contend with interculturality. It may be helpful to assume the following: First, interculturality is not just a problem it also offers ways of coping with intercultural issues, in other words, intercultural knowledge is implicitly contained within it. Secondly, intercultural knowledge generated within the company is far more useful to the company than any knowledge coming from outside, for instance from intercultural consultants and trainers, could ever be. That is to say the company actually possesses the knowledge of how to contend with intercultural issues. The challenge is how to access and disseminate this knowledge within the company. Let us imagine there are intercultural problems at the headquarters that must be dealt with. Somebody in one of the subsidiaries may know how to cope with it, as may one of the many "business nomads" working in the company, who has worked and lived all over the world, as may one of the many employees who are experienced in intensive long-lasting international teamwork. Indeed all these employees know a lot, but they "don't know what they know", they possess, to use Michael Polanyi's (1966) term, "tacit knowledge". In other words, intercultural knowledge, i.e. the knowledge of how to cope with interculturality, has to be extracted from the tacit knowledge immersed in the intercultural interactions and situations within the globally dispersed company—quite a challenging task.

Experts in the field of intercultural and international management have been trying to initiate and support intercultural learning for some time. As Condon and Yousef (1975) pointed out in their seminal work, intercultural learning should not be abstract and general but practical and specific and as close as possible to real-life situations. In other words, it is time that MNCs started to acknowledge and respect how employees experience and encounter intercultural situations in everyday business life.

Examples

Although a lot of research has been done on intercultural communication in business settings, it is nonetheless difficult for MNCs to realistically assess the intercultural experiences of their employees. Moreover, the expectation of MNCs that they will acquire "objective" intercultural knowledge is destined to be disappointed, as intercultural knowledge always depends on perspective, allowing different "truths" for the same phenomenon. Therefore, the key to intercultural learning is to accept otherness and the fact that not everything can be explained to everyone.

In the following, I will present and explain some examples of intercultural interaction as encountered and described by interculturally experienced employees in various situations. The first example relates to Japanese assignees in German companies located in Germany. The data come from a research project on "Inpatriation and Informal Transnational Networks" which I supervised from 2005 to 2008. The second relates to the collaboration of expatriate Japanese managers and European managers and staff in a Japanese company in Germany. The data come from applied research, which I conducted in 2001. The third example relates to tri-cultural teamwork in a Japanese-American-German joint venture in the USA. The data come from applied research, which I conducted in collaboration with fellow researchers in 1994 and 1995 in the USA.

The first example consists of three excerpts from interviews with Japanese "inpatriates" in the German headquarters, who describe their experiences in

Germany. (The term "inpatriate" denotes an employee of a MNC who is transferred from a foreign subsidiary to the corporation's headquarters.) The first excerpt
is from an interview with a Japanese inpatriate conducted upon his return to Japan
after a sojourn of two years in Germany:

> While I worked in Japan, being Assistant General Manager, I was always in the
> group of the final decision-making committee. But in Germany, I was kind of
> out of it. Out of the decision-making process in a sense. Sometimes they asked
> me to join. And sometimes they didn't even send me a notice about it. I do
> understand this, because when the things get complicated, they like to com-
> municate in their mother language, so that they could express in detail, freely
> and faster. This, I kind of understand. And also this is the case for Japanese
> companies as well. In this respect, the German and the Japanese corporate
> governors are pretty similar. The head is always German or Japanese ...

The second is from an interview with a Japanese inpatriate conducted after he had
been living in Germany for one and a half years:

> But then I decided myself that maybe I should go with my colleagues, by
> showing my abilities and capabilities and maybe some result, some success.
> Otherwise people do not believe me. I felt, like I was sort of in the field sur-
> rounded by, not enemies, but not friends. Just in some society, I had no clue
> how to work with them. So, my [German] boss [in Japan, who sent him to
> Germany] had just put me in the cold water. But it is getting warmer and
> warmer. So it is ok now, but at the beginning I was a little bit surprised. But
> from the eyes of German people, maybe what they expect me to ..., actually I
> actively figured out what I could contribute to the company. But in most of
> the cases, Japanese are passive; they look and wait for the orders or concrete
> tasks. But people described me as "you are not Japanese". Half Japanese, half
> Western. But still, in my heart I am still Japanese, pure Japanese. But anyway, I
> actually learned how to swim.

The two excerpts give insight into how Japanese transferees in Germany experience, conceptualize and cope with interculturality. The first Japanese inpatriate
"explains" his frustration by saying that the very same thing could happen back
home in a Japanese business environment. In his opinion, it makes no difference
whether one is in Germany or in Japan. To him it is human nature that people
simply tend to exclude foreigners. There is not much one can do about this but to
bear the burden of being an outsider. This "explanation" supposedly makes it easier
to bear the burden. The second inpatriate seems to think that there is a problem
that is common for Japanese working in Germany. Notably Japanese employees are
too passive and do not behave as expected. Therefore he tried to behave differently, to be proactive and to strive to be accepted by his German colleagues. This is
a quite stressful way of coping with interculturality. However, in a way his

endeavours were in vain as he began to have identity problems. He could not share this with his German colleagues because they accepted him for his "un-Japanese-ness," but, deep down, being Japanese was still the most important thing to him. It is as if he tried to "explain" the problem by referring to particular characteristics of Japanese people and their culture. Although he changed his behaviour as a consequence of his "explanation", he was again frustrated because he was neither willing nor able to completely give up his Japanese identity.

The third excerpt is from an interview with a Japanese inpatriate conducted on his return to Japan after a sojourn of three years in Germany:

> The whole organization has three to four Japanese people. Once a week I met them in the canteen, "kind of Japanese Mafia," we called that, shared some videos and ideas. And in the end, sometimes on the weekend, we had some barbecuing with the families. Because they were living in Germany already longer, they could tell me how to live in Germany as Japanese. And which doctor is good or something, real tips! Most of the cases, the people they talk to all day are Japanese. They don't talk to German people. For them they are foreigners. Although they are foreigners in Germany they think that Germans are foreigners. So, they don't have to speak to foreigners.
>
> My wife had a network with Japanese people living in Germany. I introduced some Japanese colleagues to my wife, and I also knew one Japanese woman who married a German. I contacted her and asked her to give us any support. We couldn't build relations with the local German people. If we had had a child, of a certain age, then it would have been easier, but we were without child. So, it was not so easy. We knew some German people with Japanese wives, so we have contact with such people.

This clearly describes a situation where social contacts and building social networks to satisfy basic social needs are a necessity. Obviously the Japanese inpatriate could not satisfy his and his partner's social needs with German colleagues or Germans outside the company and therefore he had to resort to other compatriots living in Germany. The tendency for migrants to adhere to their own ethnic or national social groups is very common. This also applies to elite migrants such as the Japanese inpatriates, even if the standard of living abroad is higher than at home. Both elite and ordinary migrants share the feeling that they don't really belong to the society and culture of residency and of not really being accepted by the local people. Living and working in a social and cultural environment which in many ways is strange, puzzling or even rejecting can be extremely stressful. Thus, migrants try to find situations and surroundings where people and things are familiar and where they feel at ease and comfortable. They consciously or unconsciously look for anything that makes them feel somehow "at home", be it familiar smells and tastes, like the food from home served in ethnic restaurants, be it a familiar language or a familiar way of talking, looking, gesturing, making jokes or showing emotions, such as an easy and relaxed conversation in one's native language. This inner drive to seek the familiar, which Avtar Brah (1996) calls "homing desire", brings together like-minded people with similar cultural, ethnic or national backgrounds. As a rich body of research shows, the tendency of migrants to form diaspora communities is very strong (Lavie and Swedenburg, 1996; Sheffer, 2003). Although comparatively little research has been done on transient elite-migrants, such as international transferees in big companies, we know that the psychological dynamics of acculturation is more or less the same with permanent non-elite migrants. They too must develop strategies to cope with transition stress and intercultural problems and to organize life in a strange cultural environment (Berry, 2003). Diaspora networks are very helpful in this respect because they can provide a basis for retaining old habits and ways of doing things. But at the same time, diaspora networks also help to adapt to local standards and get used to the new culture. Living in a diaspora community is simultaneously living in the home culture and the residence culture, which some researches would call living in a "third space" (Bhabha, 1994).

MNCs regard this with scepticism. They expect their transferees to immerse themselves in the local culture in order to become interculturally competent. Living between cultures, they might reason, is a waste of time because the transferee doesn't really get to know the local culture. Furthermore, inpatriates are sent from different locations in the world to the headquarters so that they can absorb the knowledge and culture of the headquarters and convey it to the subsidiaries. On returning to their home organization, they are expected to act as mediators between headquarters and the subsidiary, and to build up or strengthen transnational communication networks in order to reduce cultural differences and foster standardization. Indeed, inpatriates play a central role in an MNC's global strategy. In order to be able to do so, inpatriates are expected to adopt the culture of the company's headquarters, or the culture of the country in which the headquarters are located. However, as the examples indicated, real life tells a different story. MNCs must come to terms with the actual needs and necessities as they arise in intercultural situations.

The next example deals with a problematic situation that arouse in the German subsidiary of a Japanese MNC. The Japanese expatriate managers and their European colleagues including their subordinates complained about numerous "communication problems". I was asked to investigate and find a solution. I decided to conduct narrative interviews with the Japanese and European (British, Dutch and German) managers. At that time the Japanese subsidiary employed more than 500 people. About 30 Japanese managers had been sent there from the headquarters in Japan. In this dynamic, newly founded Japanese subsidiary, the Europeans expected the Japanese to adapt to what they referred to as "the European style of management", whereas the Japanese managers expected the Europeans to adopt what they called "the style of the company". The Japanese managers criticized the European staff for not working hard enough, taking too long vacations, not foregoing holidays when there where critical situations in the company, being inflexible and unwilling to work longer hours in the evening or at weekends, not helping and supporting each other proactively, etc. The European managers accused the Japanese managers of withholding information and being secretive about strategic issues, acting indecisively and uncandidly, not communicating forthrightly and comprehensibly, lacking fundamental managerial skills, being unable to lead and motivate employees and not understanding that incentives are an essential management instrument. In contrast, Japanese managers assumed that "working for such an excellent company" must be enough motivation to be a dedicated worker. They were "really shocked" when they learned that acting in what was for them an opportunistic and selfish manner was considered by the European managers to be something that was completely normal. Even after having worked in Germany for several years, the Japanese managers were still unwilling to accept this attitude and were therefore unable to trust their European staff.

The Japanese and European managers who were interviewed seemed to be quite aware of these fundamental differences in the way "the Japanese" and "the Europeans" view and conduct everyday business life. But nobody really bothered to try to understand the differences, less still to try to accept cultural differences. Rather, they were convinced that their own view of what was happening in the company was "the objective view", and, with this ethnocentric attitude, they would accuse the other side of not being willing or able to change and adapt due to the lack of a professional attitude and proper managerial skills. In other words, the challenges of cultural diversity were not perceived and conceptualized as cultural issues, but as professional or personal shortcomings. Apparently this company, one of the world's leading MNCs, still has to find a way of benefitting from cultural diversity. However, the narrated experiences could be seen as containing implicit intercultural knowledge which—with the help of intercultural communication professionals—could be transferred into explicit intercultural knowledge.

The last example relates to the so-called "Triad Project", a tri-cultural joint venture in the 1990s operated by three MNCs from the USA, Japan and Germany for almost four years. The Triad Project team consisted of about a hundred R&D people from the three companies. All the functions in the team were organized trilaterally: Top management positions were shared equally by Americans, Japanese and Germans; everyone was assigned to work in trilateral sub teams; trilateral staff distribution was also applied in the offices. The objective was to ensure that intercultural cooperation also worked on the informal level in order to generate cultural synergy. After a euphoric start and a rather successful first half year, the Triad Project encountered serious problems that management made every effort to solve. They asked an international team of researchers and intercultural specialists (in which I participated) to investigate the problems and to find a solution. We interviewed several key players in the Triad Project, designed and conducted training measures (Moosmüller et al., 2001).

Research on multinational work groups reveals that consensus is necessary in order to deal productively with diversity. Therefore, it is important that team members are able to change perspective, tolerate ambiguity and deal with varying actions adequately. According to the team-building theory, there are four phases.

In phase 1, the members try to adapt to each other with national stereotypes and national status playing an important role. In phase 2, the actual influence of cultural diversity on routine team actions is foregrounded, e.g., how time is dealt with or which leadership style predominates, how problems are solved and decisions are reached, etc. In phase 3, subgroup alliances are built with cultural similarity playing an important role. There is a great danger of polarization into national subgroups and of intensifying ethnocentric attitudes. In phase 4, the team has learned to cope with these difficulties and diversity is no longer a handicap but is viewed as an opportunity (Smith & Noakes, 1996).

When we started to work with the Triad Project team it seemed to be in phase 3. The team members complained that the formal exchange of information in meetings, presentations or discussions was ineffective, and that the informal exchange of information did not come about as expected. The initial willingness to help each other with mutual cultural understanding had waned markedly after a few months. The three national groups began to stick together and team members increasingly complained about the lack of mutual trust. Many staff members were disappointed because the excitement of the first few months had subsided and management's proclaimed "open, innovative and synergy generating climate" had not set in.

Team members had difficulty coming to terms with the challenges of cultural diversity. For instance when Americans, Japanese and Germans exchanged information, gave presentations and discussed matters in meetings in order to try to reach a common decision, they were unaware that the behaviour and respective expectations of the different national team members varied considerably. For example, when giving a presentation, the Japanese team members started their presentation with detailed facts and did not get to the results until the end. The American team members, on the other hand, started with the results, subsequently backing them up with arguments and facts in the course of the presentation. Whereas the German team members briefly outlined the problem or even presented a historical survey of it and then proceeded like the Americans. Such different "culturally programmed" behaviour usually remains concealed from the interactants. One's own ethnocentric expectations and practices continue to be the unquestioned standard according to which others' actions are considered "not normal"; thus the Japanese were seen as "not logical", the Americans as "not credible" and the Germans as "meticulous". This erroneous assessment of each other impedes the desired quick uncomplicated trustworthy exchange of information but instead favours turning to one's own cultural group. But still, as we experienced in the training sessions, when difficult situations arouse, there was usually someone who intuitively understood the actor's different expectations and different ways of doing things. However, this person was not really able to keep track of what was going on or was unable to explain the situation to others. Thus, intercultural knowledge was already there, but dispersed, bound to specific situations and people and therefore not palpable. Our job as intercultural specialists was simply to find ways to explicate the implicit intercultural knowledge and make it usable for the Triad Project.

Conclusion

Cultural diversity is considered an important asset in international business. Unfortunately, interculturality, which in one way or other is an integral part of cultural diversity, is still ignored or seen as something that employees have to cope with on their own in everyday business life. Empirical research reveals that this is rather difficult since employees are often not as flexible, global-minded and interculturally competent as the company thinks. Nevertheless, these examples show that the individual actors not only experienced difficult situations but that they managed to survive and in this way somehow gained implicit intercultural knowledge. For instance, the Japanese inpatriates "knew" what it meant to live and work abroad, how to mediate between conflicting identities, etc. In the second example the conflicts European and Japanese managers experienced made them aware of what they thought was or was not "professional" and how "effective business" ought to be conducted. Of course, this was done ethnocentrically, but it still included "knowledge" concerning cultural differences and maybe even concerning ways of coping with it—of course only implicitly. The same applies to the trilateral teams, where everyday intercultural interactions offered ample opportunities to learn how to cope with intercultural diversity. Obviously, it is a big problem that many MNCs do not really acknowledge interculturality and instead of dealing with interculturality on the organizational level, they leave it to the individual actor. However, they could do a lot more to improve the situation, for instance they could listen to their employees' narrations about their intercultural experiences, learn from the intercultural insights these narrations offer and find ways to transform implicit intercultural knowledge into explicit knowledge.

References

Appiah, K. A. (2006). *Cosmopolitanism: Ethics in a world of strangers*. London, UK: Allen Lane.

Bayer. (2022). www.sustainability2011.bayer.com/en/diversity-declaration.pdfx.

Bennett, M. J. (Eds.). (1998). *Basic concepts of intercultural communication*. Yarmouth, ME: Intercultural Press.

Berry, J. W. (2003). Conceptual approaches to acculturation. In K. Chun, P. Organista, & G. Marine (Eds.), *Acculturation: Advances in theory, measurement, and applied research* (pp. 17–37). Washington, DC: American Psychological Association

Bhabha, H. K. (1994). *The location of culture*. London, UK: Routledge.

Brah, A. (1996). *Cartographies of diaspora: Contesting identities*. London, UK: Routledge.

Butcher, M. (2011). *Managing cultural change: Reclaiming synchronicity in a mobile world*. Farnham, UK; Ashgate

Cefkin, M. (Ed.). (2009). *Ethnography and the corporate encounter: Reflections on research in and of corporations*. New York, NY and Oxford: Berghahn.

Condon, J. & Yousef, F. (1975). *An introduction to intercultural communication*. Indianapolis, IN: Bobbs-Merrill.

Deardorff, D. K. (Ed.). (2009). *The Sage handbook of intercultural competence*. Thousand Oakes, CA: Sage.

Diversity Charter (2014). www.diversity-charter.com/diversity-charter-actions.php.

Geertz, C. (1973). *The interpretation of cultures.* New York, NY: Basic Books.

Gudykunst, W. B. & Kim, Y.Y. (1997). *Communicating with strangers: An approach to intercultural communication.* New York, NY: McGraw Hill.

Hassard, J., McCann, L. & Morris, J. (2009). *Managing in the modern corporation: The intensification of managerial work in the USA, UK and Japan.* Cambridge, UK: Cambridge University Press.

Hitt, M. A. & Cheng, J. (Eds.). (2004). *Theories of the multinational enterprise: Diversity, complexity and relevance.* Oxford, UK: Elsevier.

Hongkong and Shanghai Banking Corporation (HSBC). (2022).:http://www.hsbc.com/citizenship/diversity-and-inclusion.

Jeannet, J.-P. (2000). *Managing with a global mindset.* London, UK: Financial Times/ Prentice Hall.

Konrad, A. M., Prasad, P., & Pringle, J. (Eds.). (2006). *Handbook of workplace diversity.* London, UK: Sage.

Lavie, S. & Swedenburg, T. (Eds.). (1996). *Displacement, diaspora, and geographies of identity.* Durham, NC and London: Duke University Press.

Levitt, T. (1983). The globalization of markets. *Harvard Business Review,* May–June, 92–102.

Lifton, R. J. (1993). *The protean self.* New York, NY: Basic Books.

Matsumoto, D. (2010). Introduction. In D. Matsumoto (Ed.), *APA handbook of intercultural communication* (pp. ix–xv). Washington DC: American Psychological Association.

Moosmüller, A., Spieß, E., & Podsiadlowski, A. (2001). International team building: Issues in developing multinational work groups. In M. Mendenhall, J. S. Black, T. Kühlmann, & G. Stahl (Eds.), *Developing global leadership skills* (pp. 211–224). Westport, CT: Quorum Books.

Palmisano, S. J. (2006). The globally integrated enterprise. *Foreign Affairs,* 85, 127–136.

Polanyi, M. (1966). *Tacit dimension.* Chicago, IL: University of Chicago Press.

Pollock, D. C. (Ed.). (1999). *The third culture kid experience: Growing up among worlds.* Yarmouth, ME: Intercultural Press.

Prasad, P., Pringle, J. K., & Konrad, A. M. 2006. Examining the contours of workplace diversity: Concepts, contexts and challenges (pp. 1–22). In A. M. Konrad, P. Prasad, & J. Pringle (Eds.), *Handbook of workplace diversity.* London, UK: Sage.

Schwabenland, C. (2012). *Metaphor and dialectic in managing diversity.* New York, NY: Palgrave Macmillan.

Sheffer, G. (2003). *Diaspora politics. At home abroad.* Cambridge, UK: Cambridge University Press.

Siemens. (2022). https://de.scribed/document/165739946/Siemens-Sustainability-Report-2012.

Smith, P. B. & Noakes, J. (1996). Cultural differences in group processes. In M. A. West (Ed.), *Handbook of work group psychology* (pp. 477–501). Chichester, UK: John Wiley & Sons.

The Economist (2010, 11 Feb.)

Thurow, L. 1992. *Head to head: The coming economic battle among Japan, Europe, and America.* New York, NY: Warner Books.

Vallaster, C. (2005). Cultural diversity and its impact on social interactive processes. *International Journal of Cross-Cultural Management,* 5(2), 139–163.

Vogeley, K. & Roepstorff, A. (2009). Contextualising culture and social cognition. *Trends in Cognitive Science,* 13(12), 511–516.

Wexler, B. (2006). *Brain and culture: Neurobiology, ideology, and social change.* Boston, MA: MIT Press.

20

UNDERSTANDING INTERCULTURAL CONFLICT IN VIRTUAL SPACE

Characteristics, Approaches, and Management Styles

Ping Yang

Introduction

Since McLuhan (1962) coined the term "global village," the world has been more and more closely interconnected via communication technologies. The frequent occurrence of communication across cultures becomes inevitable against the backdrop of growing internationalization and interdependence of people from every part of the world. Intercultural communication in virtual space is a fascinating research area for scholars of communication and many other disciplines to investigate.

New media are ubiquitous, changing the landscape of culture and communication practices. It creates a new context for understanding the characteristics of conflict and intercultural conflict management strategies. Previous studies have contributed to the study of intercultural conflict by emphasizing the dialogical approach in bringing harmony to situations involving conflict (Broome, 2013; Buber, 1958), managing intercultural conflict in the space of interculturality (Dai, 2010; Dai & Chen, 2017), a Yin-Yang theory of human communication (Chen, 2018; Dai & Chen, 2017), the conflict face negotiation theory (Ting-Toomey, 2015), and a reflexive multi-dimensional contextual framework (Broome & Collier, 2012) in building peace and arriving at harmonious situations. These existing studies have examined conflict management through diverse theoretical frameworks and contextual situations.

Advanced communication technologies have established a unique cultural context for studying intercultural conflict. Many scholars have highlighted the relationship between media and communication (Hepp, Hjarvard, & Lundby, 2015; Hjarvard, 2013; Leader-Elliott, 2005; Shuter, Cheong, & Chen, 2016). They argue that contemporary culture and society cannot be conceived of as being separate from media technologies because of the ubiquity and power of the media. The

DOI: 10.4324/9781003252955-23

process of mediatization and changing cultural landscape are subject to perpetual conflict and compromise between what is established and what is preferred. This research focuses on conflict experiences, characteristics, and management strategies of people during online interactions. Understanding conflict situations and various approaches to conflict plays a significant role in increasing cultural sensitivity and communication effectiveness in dealing with intercultural conflict situations.

Changing Cultural Landscape on New Media

Starting in the 1950s, the Internet has become a mass medium and created a new dimension for global communication (Barnes, 2003; McPhail, 2006). Statistics indicate a rapid increase in international online access. The number of Internet users had reached approximately 5.17 billion worldwide by March 2021 (Internet World Stats: Usage and Population Statistics. n.d.). The most recent statistics indicate that the United States has 89.9 percent of its population online, a total of 297 million (Internet World Stats: Usage and Population Statistics. n.d.). There is a huge impact of modern technologies on human life and communication. The worldwide online environment has influenced people's communication experiences in all kinds of fields. In the fast developing and highly competitive world, studies on intercultural communication in cyberspace have great potential to help people to interact more effectively with others.

The cultural landscape is viewed as a place of cultural exchange, a site at which practices and processes of cultural exchange become forms of cultural heritage. It defines the sense of a place, its meanings, cultural practices, cultural values, and enables understandings of the focus of communication (Leader-Elliott, 2005; Rapoport, 1992). Leader-Elliott, Maltby, and Burke (2004) compare landscape to a language, with obscure and indecipherable origins. Like a language, the landscape is the slow creation of all elements in society. It grows according to its own laws, rejecting or accepting neologisms as it sees fit, clinging to obsolescent forms, and inventing new ones. It is the subject of perpetual conflict and compromise between what is established by authority and what the vernacular insists on preferring. The cultural landscape refers to the material–cultural complexes that result from the interaction over time of the cultural characteristics of certain populations and groups with the physiographic and ecological specifics of a place (Rapoport, 1992).

Culture is mediatized in virtual space. Previous research has explored the relationship between intercultural communication and new media, illustrating how culture affects the social uses of new media, and how new media influences culture (Hepp et al., 2015; Shuter, 2012). The increasing use of modern communication technologies across the globe, including social networking sites, smart phones, video conferencing devices, and multi-player online games are revolutionizing the ways people interact with one another in the digital age. The characteristics of online communication such as lack of nonverbal cues, anonymity, pseudo-anonymity, and identity experimentation present scholarly challenges (St. Amant, 2002; Shim, Kim, & Martin, 2008). In order to give a thorough description of the complex realities of online interactions, especially in conflict situations, this chapter explores the dynamic and dialectical nature of conflict approaches and management styles as they are experienced online. The dialectical approach advocated by Martin and Nakayama (1999, 2022) suggests six intercultural dialectics in examining cultural phenomena, including privilege-disadvantage, personal-contextual, individual-cultural, differences-similarities, static-dynamic, and history/past-present/future. The employment of the dialectical perspective in this chapter provides a unique lens through which to examine conflict management in virtual space by avoiding essentializing cultural differences while enabling the author to explore cultural differences from multiple perspectives and provide an in-depth understanding of lived online experiences as they exist in social, cultural, and historical time and space.

Conflict Perceptions and Approaches

Conflict is defined as involving a perceived or real incompatibility of goals, values, expectations, processes, or outcomes between two or more interdependent individuals or groups (Wilmot & Hocking, 2010). According to Floyd (2021), in addition to incompatibility and interdependence, conflict is an expressed struggle that often arises when two or more people perceive incompatible goals, scarce resources, and interference from the other party in achieving their goals. Intercultural conflict occurs between or among people of different cultural groups due to opposing viewpoints (Mafela & Ntuli, 2018). As noted by Dai and Chen (2017), intercultural conflict may arise as a result of inappropriate behavior or contradictory expectations.

Intercultural conflict differs from other kinds of conflict because it is more ambiguous than intracultural conflict (Martin & Nakayama, 2022). People from diverse cultural backgrounds may see conflict from different perspectives, sometimes they may not even think there is a conflict, thus resulting in different perceptions of the situation and relationship. A lot of ambiguity is involved in intercultural conflict. As pointed out by scholars, language is a significant issue in studying online conflict (Fischer, 2013; Lü, 2018). Language may result in conflict but is also an important tool in solving intercultural conflict. Furthermore, intercultural conflict is characterized by contradictory conflict styles (Martin & Nakayama, 2022). People from different cultures have different levels and understandings of directness, formality, and politeness when dealing with intercultural conflict. This sometimes causes more problems and leads to more conflicts.

The management of intercultural conflict distinguishes between two approaches toward conflict: productive versus destructive, and competitive versus cooperative (Deutsch, 1987). In a productive conflict, individuals or groups try to identify the specific problems, focus on the original issue, direct the discussion toward cooperative problem solving, and value leadership that is centered around achieving a mutually satisfactory outcome. However, in a destructive conflict, people make sweeping generalizations and have negative attitudes, escalate the conflict from the original issue, try to seize power, and polarize behind single-minded and militant leadership (Martin & Nakayama, 2022). According to Deutsch (1987), people in competitive conflict are likely to use coercion, deception, suspicion, rigidity, and power communication, whereas in a cooperative atmosphere, people tend to use perceived similarity, trust, flexibility, and open communication to resolve conflict.

Conflict Management Styles

Conflict style refers to the patterned responses or characteristic mode of managing conflict across a variety of communication episodes (Mao & Hale, 2015; Oommen, 2017). Scholars have approached intercultural conflict with different style models (Cai & Fink, 2002). The dual concern model (Blake & Mouton, 1964; Cai & Fink, 2002; Pruitt & Rubin, 1986; Rahim, 1986) proposes five styles for handling conflict situations, namely, integrating, obliging, dominating, avoiding, and compromising. This model predicts that when an individual has great concern for both his/her own interests and those of the other person, that individual is most likely to engage in problem solving and use an integrating style. If concern for one's own interests is low and concern for the other person's interests is high, the model predicts that the person will use an obliging conflict style. The most confrontational style is dominating which is predicted to result from a high concern for one's own interests and a low concern for those of the other party. Avoiding is a non-confrontational style that is a consequence of having little concern for either one's own or the other's interests. The fifth style is compromising, which reflects a moderate concern for both one's own interests and those of the other party. The compromising style demonstrates a modest effort to pursue an outcome that is mutually acceptable.

The second model of conflict styles this research project is based on is the four dimensions model (Hammer, 2005). The four dimensions model involves the direct/indirect approach and the emotional expressive/restraint approach to conflict (Hammer, 2005; Martin & Nakayama, 2021; Ramayan, Bakar, Kutty, & Rosa, 2020). The former approach explains how some cultural groups prefer to use the direct method to approach conflict while others seek indirect ways. The latter approach explains the role of emotions in conflict—some groups think it is better to express emotions during conflict while others communicate in a calm manner. Based on these two approaches, four conflict styles are proposed: discussion, engagement, accommodating, and dynamic (Hammer, 2005). The discussion style emphasizes both the direct and the emotionally restrained dimensions in handling conflict. The engagement style emphasizes a direct and emotionally expressive manner. The accommodating style values an indirect and emotional restrained method, while the dynamic style prefers an indirect style along with emotional expressiveness.

Research Method

This research project aims to provide an in-depth understanding of the characteristics of intercultural conflict and management styles in virtual space. It explores both stability and changes reflected in new media contexts as social network sites have become everyday tools of transmission of messages for young people in the digital age. Cyberspace creates opportunities for increasing intercultural interactions to occur with a changing cultural landscape and communication practice. This chapter examines the complexity of culture in new media contexts in the hope of showing an understanding of conflict and conflict management in the digital age which may inspire us to push boundaries, explore possibilities, and think imaginatively about what new media and new media technologies can and should be.

An interpretive approach provides a detailed understanding of the conflict and conflict management strategies used in online social networks. This research took place at a public university on the east coast of America. Research participation was completely voluntary and there was no reward or punitive measures associated with the students' choice to participate in the study. The research procedure was approved by the internal review board. Online discussions and personal descriptions were the primary strategies for data collection. The researcher set up an online discussion forum in intercultural communication classes in the Spring and Fall of 2021 by providing discussion questions on the instructional device D2L—Desire to Learn—an online course management system. This forum invited students to share their intercultural conflict experiences on the Internet and how they approached and managed the intercultural conflict. A total of 119 postings were collected from the forum in Spring 2021 (65 posts) and Fall 2021 (54 posts). Additionally, 15 personal descriptions were collected from students regarding the conflict experiences they or someone they knew had had online. Data were collected after students had completed the discussion posts and descriptions. Student consent was obtained, and absolute anonymity and confidentiality were guaranteed.

Since the objective of this research is to explore how people experience conflict in online social networks, grounded theory is used for data analysis. Grounded theory looks at ideas and themes that emerge from texts and notes and assigns each idea to a category. It constantly applies the comparative method as the data analysis proceeds (Treadwell & Davis, 2019). Grounded theory provides the opportunity to do coding and data collection at the same time. The new experiences in the field continuously alter the scope of analysis (Lindlof & Taylor, 2002). Therefore, the researcher collected data and read it many times to come up with different levels of themes and categories. During the analysis and writing processes, pseudonyms have been used to ensure anonymity of the research participants. The following section presents the research findings and analysis. The esearch results have revealed the complicated roles that culture plays in managing conflict in the digital age and how these roles provide opportunities that may empower young people to make positive contributions to their communities/societies and to change their lives.

Characteristics of Intercultural Conflict Online

Many students' online intercultural conflict experiences have shown similar factors that characterize intercultural conflict in general, such as language barriers and ambiguity. At the same time, students' online experiences have also revealed unique characteristics of online intercultural conflict, related to complexity, non-verbal communication, quicker escalation, more violence, and issues of power and control.

A few students have shared their intercultural conflict experiences online by pointing out that they arose due to lack of nonverbal cues; online conflict has more complexity, challenges, and difficulties. When someone makes a written response to conflict, their replies can be misinterpreted, and as a result, lead to even more conflicts. One student's narrative illustrated her intercultural online experiences and the challenges that she was faced with.

> In high school I took a French class, and as a requirement we were to communicate with a pen pal. It was definitely difficult to communicate with her, especially because we were speaking each other's languages. Some characteristics that differ from face-to-face conflict could be the language barrier. Most of the time it is easier to understand someone when we are face-to-face than through a screen. Another difference is that face-to-face you can read better body language and see if you can understand the conversation better that way. I think that the characteristics of online intercultural conflict as different from face-to-face is that online intercultural conflict is much more complex and complicated.

Students' posts have repeatedly shown how online communication makes it harder to tell people's mood, emotions, attitudes, and opinions, thus resulting in ambiguity and misunderstandings.

> My sister is a teacher and I know she had some situations where there was conflict. From when she started her teaching career, she taught a full year online and recently started teaching in person at the beginning of this year. When it came to dealing with these situations online, from what I understand, it was a lot harder for her to understand their mood. When people communicate online, it is hard to tell their tone of the situation. Whatever they type in an email, it may seem like they are mad or upset, but that may not be the case every single time.

One of the characteristics of online intercultural conflict is that people frequently use online tools. They are able to look up what they are struggling with before responding in a few minutes or hours, while in face-to-face conflict, communicators are unable to do this. While the Internet provides useful tools to deal with language barriers by translating and assisting in understanding and responding, these tools bring both benefits and disadvantages, as noted in the following student's experience:

> Regarding translation, programs like Google Translate are not always 100% accurate because they tend to not care about sentence structure and different uses of the same word. They just translate word by word exactly as it is

written. For example, in Spanish, adjectives go after the noun and for words like 'there,' there is a different word for the different distances the object is from you. Spanish has different words for the same English word based on the situation. Google Translate doesn't take that into account which causes confusion. This is like when Jimmy Fallon does Google Translate Songs where songs are translated into another language and then translated back into English, and they end up being completely different lyrics but still being a little similar.

Other unique characteristics of online communication are related to time differences, such as time zone differences, when a person is expected to reply, and how frequent the replies will be. A few students have shared their experiences of when conflict occurred because they had to wait for a long time or a few days for a response, and in some cases there wasn't one.

I have communicated interculturally with former classmates online when I studied abroad during the spring semester of 2020. Since my classmates and I were sent home early due to the pandemic, we had to use WhatsApp to communicate … Whenever faced with cultural conflict, especially when we would hold our 3-hour French class over Zoom, where we could only communicate in French, we would try to speak as many words in French that we knew to ask or describe something. A big intercultural conflict we ran into in the beginning of transitioning to an all-online class was the time differences. Since my teacher was still in Paris, but most of my classmates were either in Asia or in the U.S., there was a major time difference. At first, our teacher was still holding class at the same time it would have been for him in France, which for us was at 5 in the morning. We eventually used the cooperating style to resolve this conflict, and my teacher asked us all what time would work for everyone.

In online conflict situations, the fact that both sides are sitting behind a computer may contribute to a quicker escalation and more violence. People feel that they have more confidence to fully express their feelings, emotions, and say something that they would not say if others were sitting in front of them. Online communicators are bolder, more direct, and less reserved in making hurtful remarks. One of the students shared the following experience:

Online intercultural conflicts are harder to deal with because people tend to be less specific online and less detailed than if you were to ask them in person. Conflict online also can escalate quicker and more violently than it would in person. Online if someone is saying things you don't understand, you can just log off and forget about your interaction, but in person you are less likely to walk away, and thus solve your conflict with the person. Part of this is because you aren't talking physically to a person but to a screen, which also allows you to forget that there is a human on the other end.

Students' experiences have revealed the privilege-disadvantage dialect as discussed by Martin and Nakayama (1999, 2022). According to Martin and Nakayama (1999, 2022), the privilege-disadvantage dialect recognizes that people may be simultaneously privileged and disadvantaged or privileged in some contexts and disadvantaged in others. This dialectic is significant in critical scholarship because the intersection of privilege and disadvantage applies to many intercultural encounters which involve the issue of power. This is especially so during online interactions, because of the fluid, flexible, and dynamic nature of virtual space. Participants in online interactions may sometimes feel privileged in having the power to use translation apps and online devices, hide or experiment with cultural identities, and become more confident and bolder. However, at the same time, they are also experiencing disadvantages because of the ambiguity, lack of nonverbal cues, deception, insecurity, verbal aggressiveness, and even violence during online intercultural conflict situations.

Approaches to Intercultural Conflict and Conflict Styles in Virtual Space

The participants' experiences of their online intercultural conflicts have shown the variety of approaches to intercultural conflict and use of different communication styles. The approaches, namely productive vs. destructive conflict and competitive vs. cooperative conflict have all been used in students' online interactions. The majority of the students have emphasized that the approaches they used were mainly productive and cooperative as these were the most effective ones to solve conflict rather than escalating the issue.

> Most online interactions can be very hostile and mean since the person is hiding behind a screen and feel they have more power over the other person. When it comes to face-to-face, we can see some hostility, but it can generally lead to having a more productive outcome since you are physical with the person. A conflict I have been a part happened when a friend of mine got into a discussion about the COVID vaccine online. We did have a fight, but it was more civil in the sense it wasn't an all-out brawl. The interesting part is, we decided to follow a similar approach to the argument. We were more productive because we both heard out each other's side of the story. The dialogue helped us understand each other but we both did not want to cave to the other side.

It is easy to see that the participants in situations involving conflict feel that their approaches are more productive and cooperative, but the other party has been using more competitive and destructive approaches. The messages from the other side are defensive, have a lack of respect, and sometimes even reach the point of being offensive. The problematic attitudes and approaches toward conflict online sometimes cause more conflicts to occur.

> [Online] we get to use texts, messages, pictures, videos, or even emojis to communicate which can make communicating fun but also cause conflict as well when everyone has a different experience that impacts how we analyze and interpret circumstances. We approach the conflict differently because their approaches are different than mine. I have a productive and cooperative approach whereas they have a destructive and competitive approach. I seek win-win solutions while they want to be right. This can in part be because of their cultures and how they were raised.

In addition to viewing the other side's approaches as more competitive and destructive, the research findings also show that online conflict styles are dynamic, changing, and flexible. Participants in online conflict situations may switch their approaches to conflict depending on the situation, communicators, and goals to achieve. No matter which approach a person chooses initially, in order to resolve the conflict and achieve desired results, a productive and cooperative approach is necessary.

> Online you can't read social cues, body language, or tone. Many also say things online that they wouldn't have the guts to say face-to-face to someone because they may cause an online bullying community. I have had online conflict because of not being able to know what one really means. I approached the conflict at first as destructive, as humans we naturally react, but ended up being productive. It was also competitive as first until we described what we really meant, and then it became cooperative.

Regarding conflict styles, almost all of the conflict styles have been mentioned by research participants during their conflict situations. The unique contexts of online interactions have contributed to a few students' observation of the other parties' frequent use of the dominating style. Their mind is set to compete and win the conflict no matter which conflict styles the other parties use.

> In my intercultural conflict situation, which took place online, I would say that I approached the conflict from a productive and cooperative standpoint while the other person was more destructive and competitive ... I started out using the collaborating style and then had to switch to the compromising style as the collaborating was clearly not going to work because the other person was not being receptive at all. They definitely used the competing style of conflict and were not willing to give in any way. I am not sure exactly how culture would have impacted their conflict style choice, but my family definitely influenced mine. My mother raised me to always try to find the best possible solution to problems that would not cause harm to anyone involved as much as possible.

Because online conflict can easily escalate and result in verbal abuse, one conflict style that is applied repeatedly is the avoiding style. No matter which cultural background the student is from, many of them indicate their preference for using the avoiding style to walk away from the conflict situations. The students said that avoiding conflict was an important tactic in their lives, especially with the increasing number of online encounters with others. In online conflict situations, they have the freedom to walk away from their computer without having to resolve the issue.

> The online interaction that my friend had recently involved someone of a different nationality/political belief in a comment thread … The interaction was about the political nature of the U.S. (my friend is a political science major) compared to that of other countries. While my friend approached the conversation productively, the other party approached the conversation competitively and destructively, using insults and other methods to try and prove their point. They were not able to resolve the conflict between them, as is the case with many online interactions. To give a conflict style for where the story ends, my friend decided to stop replying to the conversation, using the avoiding style, and the other party tried to prove their point through no real evidence, using the competing style.

Another method that was repeatedly mentioned was the "agree to disagree" style demonstrated in students' online intercultural interactions. Many of the participants have concurred that due to the complex nature of online interactions, "agree to disagree" is how a conflict frequently ends. Sprague (2009) analyzes the relationship between "agree to disagree" and power. It resolves conflict by all parties tolerating but not accepting the opposing positions. When both sides agree that further conflict is pointless, unnecessary, and undesirable, they will rely on the "agree to disagree" style in handling online conflict.

> Online conflicts are very different from a conflict that occur face-to-face. First, you may not even know the person. Being online, anyone can talk to you or see what you are posting, from around the world. Oftentimes people feel more confident saying something over the internet, while they hide behind their screen in the comfort of their own home. With that being said, in person you do not have time to think of a response, while online you can sit and think of what is to come next. Typically, I see many conflicts resulting in a dialogue consisting of yelling and most times it just ends in the "agree to disagree" method, with no party wanting to change their opinion.

The variety of approaches discussed above to intercultural conflict online and conflict styles being used in virtual space has been related to the personal-contextual dialectic proposed by Martin and Nakayama (1999, 2022). There are some aspects of communication that remain relatively constant over many contexts. The personal-contextual dialectic states that people communicate in particular ways in particular contexts (Martin & Nakayama, 1999, 2022). As revealed in the current study, in online conflict situations, the participants' choices of approaches and conflict styles are related to the specific contexts, relationships between the communicators, goals they want to achieve, as well as the power issues embedded within the specific situation.

Conclusion

In this fast developing and highly connected world, studies on intercultural conflict in cyberspace have great potential to help people interact more effectively in this tightly-knit global village. It is very important to investigate conflict management and intercultural communication in order to arrive at harmony in relationships. This chapter explores the complexity of online conflict, its characteristics, approaches, and management styles by focusing on the lived experiences of students' online intercultural interactions.

Research findings have shown that participants' conflict experiences confirm some factors that characterize intercultural conflict in general, but at the same time reveal some unique characteristics in online contexts. Their personal narratives have demonstrated the complexity and ambiguity of conflict environments in virtual space, with opposing views toward use of Internet apps, expression and nonverbal cues, as well as issues of power and control during virtual interactions. The privilege-disadvantage dialectic has been applied in analyzing how the communicators may feel privileged and disadvantaged simultaneously during conflict situations in cyberspace.

The experiences of participants' online interactions have demonstrated their use of various approaches to intercultural conflict and different communication styles, depending on the contexts, topics, relationships, and desired outcomes. The productive versus destructive and competitive versus cooperative approaches have been used in students' online interactions, resulting in the preferred styles such as integrating, compromising, discussion, engagement, avoiding, and "agree to disagree." The personal-contextual dialectic is of importance in examining the ways online communicators view conflict and select conflict styles in particular communication contexts.

We encounter intercultural conflict more frequently than ever. Effective management of conflict and a better understanding of its characteristics will assist us in developing healthy relationships in the future. In the shrinking time and space relations of a virtual community, being aware of the unique contexts helps us understand and manage intercultural conflict more effectively and efficiently.

References

Barnes, S. B. (2003). *Computer-mediated communication: Human-to-human communication across the internet.* Boston, MA: Allyn and Bacon.

Blake, R. R. & Mouton, J. S. (1964). *The managerial grid.* Houston, TX: Gulf.

Broome, B. J. (2013). Building cultures of peace: The role of intergroup dialogue. In J. G. Oetzel & S. Ting-Toomey (Eds.), *The Sage handbook of conflict communication* (2nd ed., pp. 737–762). Thousand Oaks, CA: Sage.

Broome, B. J. & Collier, M. J. (2012). Culture, communication, and peacebuilding: A reflexive multi-dimensional contextual framework. *Journal of International and Intercultural Communication*, 5(4), 245–269.

Buber, M. (1958). *I and thou* (2nd ed., R. G. Smith, Trans.). New York, NY: Scribner.

Cai, D. A. & Fink, E. L. (2002). Conflict style differences between individualists and collectivists. *Communication Monographs*, 69(1), 67–87.

Chen, G. M. (2018). A Yin-Yang theory of human communication. *China Media Research*, 14(4), 1–15.

Dai, X. D. (2010). Intersubjectivity and interculturality: A conceptual link. *China Media Research*, 6(1), 12–19.

Dai, X. D. & Chen, G. M. (Eds.). (2017). *Conflict management and intercultural communication: The art of intercultural harmony.* New York, NY: Routledge.

Deutsch, M. (1987). A theoretical perspective on conflict and conflict resolution. In D. Sandole & I. Sandole-Staroste (Eds.), *Conflict management and problem solving: Interpersonal to international applications* (pp. 38–49). New York, NY: New York University Press.

Fischer, M. (2013). Language choice as a potential source of intercultural discord in English-Mandarin business encounters. *China Media Research*, 9(4), 45–52.

Floyd, K. (2021). *Interpersonal communication* (4th ed.). New York, NY: McGraw-Hill.

Hammer, M. R. (2005). The intercultural conflict style inventory: A conceptual framework and measure of intercultural conflict approaches. *International Journal of Intercultural Relations*, 29, 675–695.

Hepp, A., Hjarvard, S., & Lundby, K. (2015). Mediatization: Theorizing the interplay between media, culture and society. *Media, Culture & Society*, 37(2), 314–324.

Hjarvard, S. (2013). *The mediatization of culture and society.* London: Routledge.

Internet World Stats: Usage and Population Statistics. (n.d.). Retrieved from: www.internetworldstats.com (accessed October 12, 2021).

Leader-Elliott, L. (2005). Cultural landscapes of a tourism destination: South Australia's Barossa Valley. *Understanding cultural landscapes symposium* (pp. 11–15). Adelaide, Australia: Flinders University.

Leader-Elliott, L. Maltby, R., & Burke, H. (2004). Understanding cultural landscape. Retrieved from: http://fhrc.flinders.edu.au/research_groups/cult_landscapes/definition.html.

Lindlof, T. R. & Taylor, B. C. (2002). *Qualitative communication research methods* (2nd ed.). Thousand Oaks, CA: Sage.

Lü, P. H. (2018). When different "codes" meet: Communication styles and conflict in intercultural academic meetings. *Language & Communication*, 61, 1–14.

Mafela, M. J. & Ntuli, C. D. (2018). South African experience on media and intercultural conflict and adaptation. *China Media Research*, 14(3), 82–87.

Mao, Y. & Hale, C. L. (2015). Relating intercultural communication sensitivity to conflict management styles, technology use, and organizational communication satisfaction in multinational organizations in China. *Journal of Intercultural Communication Research*, 44(2), 132–150.

Martin, J. N. & Nakayama, T. K. (1999). Thinking dialectically about culture and communication. *Communication Theory*, 9, 1–25.

Martin, J. N. & Nakayama, T. K. (2021). *Experiencing intercultural communication: An introduction* (7th ed.). Boston, MA: McGraw Hill.

Martin, J. N. & Nakayama, T. K. (2022). *Intercultural communication in contexts* (8th ed.). Boston, MA: McGraw Hill.

McLuhan, M. (1962). *The Gutenberg galaxy.* Toronto, Canada: University of Toronto Press.

McPhail, T. (2006). *Global communication: Theories, stakeholders and trends* (2nd ed.). Malden, MA: Wiley-Blackwell.

Oommen, D. (2017). A test of the relationships between host and home national involvements and the preferences for intercultural conflict management styles. *Journal of Intercultural Communication Research*, 46(4), 314–329.

Pruitt, D. G. & Rubin, J. Z. (1986). *Social conflict*. New York, NY: McGraw-Hill.

Rahim, M. A. (1986). *Managing conflict in organizations*. New York, NY: Praeger.

Ramayan, S. K., Bakar, I. A. A., Kutty, V. S. S., & Rosa, K. K. (2020). Causes of intercultural conflict and its management styles among students in Sunway University. *Ideology Journal*, 5(2), 197–212.

Rapoport, A. (1992). On cultural landscapes. *Traditional Dwellings and Settlements Review*, 3 (2), 33–47.

Shim, T. Y., Kim, M. S., & Martin, J. N. (Eds.). (2008). *Changing Korea: Understanding culture and communication*. New York, NY: Peter Lang.

Shuter, R. (2012). Research and pedagogy in intercultural new media studies. *China Media Research*, 8(4), 1–5.

Shuter, R., Cheong, P., & Chen, Y. (2016). The influence of cultural values on U.S. and Danish students' digital behavior: Exploring culture, new media, and social context. *Journal of International and Intercultural Communication*, 9(2), 161–178.

Sprague, J. (2009). Ontology, politics, and instructional communication research: Why we can't just "agree to disagree" about power. *Communication Education*, 43(4), 273–290.

St. Amant, K. (2002). When cultures and computers collide: Rethinking computer-mediated communication according to international and intercultural communication expectations. *Journal of Business and Technical Communication*, 16(2), 196–214.

Ting-Toomey, S. (2015). Facework/facework negotiation theory. In J. Bennett (Ed.), *The Sage encyclopedia of intercultural competence* (Vol. 1, pp. 325–330). Thousand Oaks, CA: Sage.

Treadwell, D. & Davis, A. M. (2019). *Introducing communication research: Paths of inquiry* (4th ed.). Los Angeles, CA: Sage Publications.

Wilmot, W. & Hocking, J. (2010). *Interpersonal conflict* (8th ed.). New York, NY: McGraw-Hill.

INDEX

Please note that page references to Figures will be in **bold**, while references to Tables are in *italics*.

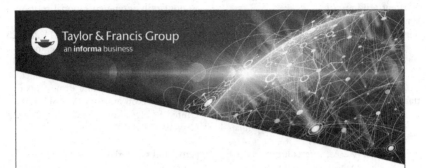

Printed in the United States
by Baker & Taylor Publisher Services